Building Security: Strategies & Costs

David D. Owen and
RSMeans Engineering Staff

RSMeans

Building Security:
Strategies
& Costs

- Risk Assessment
- Security Planning
- Cost Data for Construction
  & Security Systems

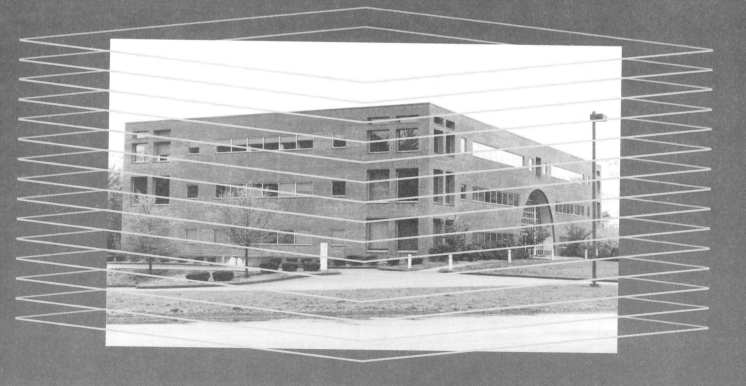

David D. Owen and RSMeans Engineering Staff

 Reed Construction Data

Copyright © 2003
Construction Publishers & Consultants
63 Smiths Lane
Kingston, MA 02364-0800
781-422-5000

The editor of this book was Andrea St. Ours. The managing editor was Mary Greene. The production manager was Michael Kokernak. The production coordinator was Marion Schofield. The electronic publishing specialist was Paula Reale-Camelio. The proofreader was Robin Richardson. The book and cover were designed by Norman R. Forgit.

Printed in the United States of America

10 9 8 7 6 5 4 3 2 1

Library of Congress Catalog Number Pending

ISBN 0-87629-698-3

Table of Contents

Acknowledgments

In preparing this book, it became evident that I would need the counsel of many people highly experienced in the expanding field of security. Good fortune brought me into contact with some extremely capable and experienced individuals.

James E. Beadel, Chief Security Officer for PG&E's National Energy Group in Bethesda, Maryland, was responsible for security improvements at over 50 off-site power plants and numerous national and regional offices. Jim's background—as a former Washington, DC Metropolitan Police Department Detective Sergeant, Task Force Leader, Internal Affairs Agent, and Narcotics Investigator—as well as his years of direct responsibility as Security Coordinator and Manager for Baylor College of Medicine, Compaq Computers, and Exel Logistics of Houston, Texas—kept my focus on the practical aspects of security.

Sandy and Neal Garelik, father and son principals of Excel Security Corporation in New York City, were extremely generous with their time, conferring with me on the complexities of operating a large security company in a major metropolitan area. Sanford D. (Sandy) Garelik, as former Chief of Department for both the New York Police and Transit Police Departments and President of the New York City Council, was able to provide me with invaluable insights into security issues I would never have known existed. Neal C. Garelik's experience with Excel Security Corporation, as well other related companies engaged in all facets of the security industry (including licensed security personnel and installation of a wide variety of electronic equipment in commercial and residential environments, confidential investigations, and alarm response), permitted me to view the inner workings of a fully integrated security company.

George Radwan of Chapel Hill, North Carolina, founder of GAR Associates—a custom architectural furniture design, drafting, detailing, and design firm; a good friend; and a creative and superb designer—provided invaluable assistance in the development of some of our graphics.

Mary Greene, editor of this book, as in the past, provided me with *stick and carrot* motivation and guidance, especially when I began to feel overwhelmed trying to define portions of the multi-faceted and rapidly evolving world of security. This book would not exist if it were not for Mary Greene. Mary, thank you.

—*David D. Owen*

About the Authors and Contributors

David D. Owen, the author of this book, is the founder of David D. Owen Associates, a facilities management and real estate consulting firm engaged in development consulting for corporate clients and personal investment. Mr. Owen's projects include serving as the owner's representative for the Continental Corporation in the programming, design, and construction of its 1,100,000 S.F. world headquarters building in New York, and as Project Manager for PG&E Corporation's National Energy Group in Bethesda, Maryland, where he oversaw the programming design, construction, furnishing, and relocation of its corporate headquarters, and designed and implemented a total building security system. Mr. Owen is the author of *Facilities Planning & Relocation*, also published by RSMeans, which won the International Facility Management Association's 1995 Distinguished Author Award. He is also a seminar presenter on facilities planning in the United States and overseas.

Ted K. Gaughan, co-author of Chapter 9, is Principal of Technical, Engineering & Development Services Company, LLC (TEDSCO). He is an Information Technology Project Management (IT PM) consultant with over 30 years of IT engineering and operations management experience, including satellite, microwave, tropospheric scatter, telephony, local and wide area networking (LAN/WAN), systems integration, and facilities IT infrastructure design and implementation (Technology Construction Management). Mr. Gaughan is also a Project Management Institute (PMI®) Certified Project Management Professional (PMP) and a Computing Technology Industry Association (CompTIA®) Certified IT Project Professional.

Robert Bastoni, editor of the Security Cost Data section (Part Two) of this publication, is a Contributing Editor and Cost Researcher at RSMeans, where his responsibilities include updating and enhancing material prices for the Means cost database and quarterly construction cost indexes, as well as research for consulting projects. He has more than 15 years of experience in the construction trades, including his tenure as a housing inspector in Massachusetts.

John Chiang, PE, also contributed to the research and compilation of the cost data section of this book. He is an Electrical Engineer at RSMeans and Senior Editor of the publications, Means *Electrical Cost Data, Electrical Change Order Cost Data*, and *Building Construction Cost Data, Metric Version*. Mr. Chiang has worked on many consulting projects, including the Xerox plant expansion and Maine Medical Center, as well as court facilities and nursing homes. He regularly assists with the provision of custom cost estimates at different construction stages for owners, engineers, and contractors, and has also contributed to several Means reference publications on cost estimating topics.

Phillip R. Waier, PE, who reviewed this publication and contributed to the cost data development, is a Principal Engineer at RSMeans and Senior Editor of the annually updated publications, Means *Facilities Maintenance & Repair Cost Data* and *Building Construction Cost Data*. Mr. Waier manages the activities of editors, cost researchers, and consultants for private and public agencies throughout the United States. He has spent 30 years in the construction industry, serving as President and Chief Engineer for a mechanical contracting firm, Project Manager for numerous industrial construction projects, and Structural Engineer for major foreign and domestic construction projects. Mr. Waier is a registered professional engineer and a member of the Association for Facilities Engineering (AFE), Associated Builders and Contractors (ABC), and Associated General Contractors (AGC).

Dr. Michael T. Chipley, PhD, reviewer of this publication, has over 26 years of experience in the areas of threat, vulnerability, and risk assessments; information technology hardware and software development and implementation; and emergency operations/disaster recovery. He is currently employed at UTD Inc., an engineering firm that supports clients in technical analysis and field support, and equipment and instrumentation research and development. Dr. Chipley has served in numerous positions, including Chief of Engineering at a major command and for the Secretary of the Air Force Executive Issues team. His experience in war planning, engineering, construction, and information technology infrastructure has given him a broad understanding of engineering systems, facility design, emergency response procedures, recovery plans, and implementing and managing information technology systems.

Mark D. Hester, also with UTD Inc., reviewed this publication. He has over 20 years of experience conducting threat, vulnerability, and risk assessments; managing programs; and performing engineering design. He has served in numerous positions culminating in executive program management of the Air Force's installation management programs. This position includes responsibility for infrastructure systems operations and management, recovery, and survivability. Previous assignments include airbase infrastructure systems operations; maintenance and repair; and large, high-security facility projects supporting national capabilities. Mr. Hester has served as a government COTR (Contracting Officer's Technical Representative), Program Manager, and Design and Construction Engineer and as an Assistant Professor of Civil Engineering at the United States Air Force Academy.

Michael J. W. Kaminskas, PE, also with UTD Inc. and reviewer of this publication, has over 28 years of experience in real property facilities and utilities systems covering planning, programming, design, construction, operations, and maintenance—including vulnerability and risk assessments, and emergency operations/disaster recovery. He has served in numerous engineering positions, including facility electrical design engineer, facility corrosion control engineer, and assistant professor, as well as Civil Engineer Chief of Operations at a large northern tier base, and Chief, Electrical Division, Technical Support Directorate (AFCESA), providing facility electrical guidance to the 65,000 Air Force civil engineers worldwide. Mr. Kaminskas has hands-on experience with facilities assessments as a structural engineer with the Joint Staff Integrated Vulnerability Assessment (JSIVA) Team.

Brian Healey, reviewer of this publication, is Director of Business-Security at VFA, Inc., a leading provider of capital planning and asset management solutions based in Boston, Massachusetts. He has over 20 years of environmental health, safety, and security experience, and has consulted for various organizations, including the Department of Energy, W.R. Grace, Harvard University, the Bermuda Government, Raytheon, Verizon, Yanase Trading, Alcoa, the State of Massachusetts, Mitsubishi, and the Pentagon. Mr. Healey also has extensive experience in product development, including Kontrol Kube, a pressure differential control chamber for airborne hazards, which is used in hundreds of locations around the world.

Introduction

The purpose of this book is to consider real or potential threats to
our safety and security, and to assist facilities and plant managers,
building owners, and transportation and service providers in
assessing their facilities, preparing an emergency response plan,
and contemplating and pricing security-conscious design practices
and equipment. Since the measures we take—in the form of
installing security programs, equipment, and building systems,
have a distinct cost for materials and installation—the book also
includes cost data for devices and construction approaches.

Danger and risk of potential damage or injury seem to dominate
the news. For those who are charged with establishing and
maintaining levels of safety and security for our facilities,
property, and personnel, life has become complex, often confusing,
and full of questions. What to do? When to do it? How much to
do? How to figure it all out? Knowing that the measures we take
must be funded, and also that those we choose not to take have a
potential cost in terms of an organization's liability, profit, and
even human life, the process of developing the "right" level of
building security is not an easy one. We will attempt in Chapters
1–3, to review the appropriate considerations in identifying the
type, size, and likelihood of risks to a particular facility, and how
damaging a loss would be in the event of a given disaster. What
might be done to ensure security and what is feasible are not
always the same. It is at this point where some tough judgment
calls will have to be made and accepted.

Chapter 4 focuses on the personnel who will contribute to an
organization's security program and response plans—from senior
management who must instigate and approve security directives,
to in-house department members and consultants. Chapter 5
follows, with guidance on security-conscious space planning and

design. If given a construction opportunity, a different approach to design plans can provide substantial protection from various types of loss, whether physical damage or espionage. These design techniques can be incorporated into remodeling projects and tenant fit-outs, as well as new building construction.

Chapter 6 offers some basic information on chemical, biological, and radiological agents, with guidance on steps that can be taken to minimize the damage in the event of potential exposure. Chapter 7 addresses evacuation and emergency response considerations based on possible threats and available equipment. Chapter 8 reviews many security-enhancing devices and construction systems and their applications in facilities. Costs for these items and materials can be found in Part Two of this book. Chapter 9 continues with more security systems, in this case focused on IT security, monitoring, and integration and enterprise safety. Since intrusive, destructive, or hostile elements are a concern regardless of the personnel, facility, or site to be protected, responses to those elements tend to employ the same fundamental practices, designs, personnel, and equipment (devices), on varying scales depending on the location, size, and character of the facility.

Part Two of this book contains cost data, organized according to the CSI MasterFormat and the UNIFORMAT II classification systems, for security devices and equipment, as well as building construction systems that enhance security. The introduction to Part Two identifies some special costing considerations for estimating security items. Location Factors are included to provide for cost adjustments for various regions in the U.S. and Canada.

Part Three of this book includes several tools, including a facilities audit checklist to assist in security assessments, a glossary of terms used in this book (and a separate glossary of security terminology used by the Federal Government), and an extensive Resources section that includes contact information and Web sites for security publications, organizations, and products and services.

The final element of this book is the Web site (**http://www.rsmeans.com/supplement/bldgsecurity.asp**), which provides downloadable, interactive forms to assist with the assessment and reporting of a facility's security needs.

Part One
Risk Assessment & Security Planning

Chapter One

People and Property

Before developing a security program, it is necessary to assess the people and property to be protected. We will begin with our most important concern, people — employees and tenants, contractors, and visitors — even the unwelcome or uninvited ones.

People

Providing safety and security for the official work force (including full- and part-time contract workers and temporary workers) is the highest priority and a primary responsibility. Solely from an asset perspective (despite attempts to reduce reliance on particular individuals), an organization's work force remains one of its most valuable commodities. The loss or incapacity of key personnel could result in temporary or permanent loss of vital information and resources.

Public Image

To assess personal risk, it is helpful to examine the organization's public image — with an objective and even cynical point of view. This assessment may produce a few surprises and a list of possible targets within a facility or organization.

During the year 2000, there were over 23,000 violent acts committed on various employees in all areas of employment in the United States, and these are just the ones that were reported.

Targets for assault include:

- **Within the general business community:**
    - Executives, officers, or other key personnel — vulnerable by virtue of their positions and actual or perceived responsibilities, which some employees, customers, or others could find sufficiently offensive to wish to injure or kill them. (The Unabomber killed and maimed out of a misguided sense of outrage at individuals he did not even know, but whom he believed represented industries injurious to society.)
    - Human Resources Personnel — susceptible because of their role in terminations of employment.
    - Employees at any level — as potential victims of violence connected with personal relationships.
    - Men — according to the Justice Department, are the victims of 80% of all workplace violence. Most are executives, managers, or other key personnel. Women share an increasing vulnerability in these same roles.

- **In specific industries or fields:**
    - Operators of facilities that generate (or are perceived to generate) pollution — electrical utilities, nuclear plants, petroleum refineries and chemical plants, and large-scale farming operations.
    - Other entities perceived as threats to the environment — lumbering companies involved in clear-cutting or lumbering old-growth forests, or electric utilities whose hydroelectric dams result in backwaters or drain wetlands.
    - Researchers whose work involves animals or breeders of fur-bearing animals — potential targets of animal rights activists.
    - Abortion clinic workers — vulnerable to violence from extreme "right-to-life" groups or individuals.
    - Healthcare workers who may be victims of a distraught relative or friend of a patient — and patients who may be accidental victims of an event.
    - According to the Bureau of Justice National Crime Victimization Survey, 69,500 nurses were assaulted at work from 1992-1996.
    - The National Institute for Occupational Safety and Health reports that 9,000 healthcare providers are attacked on the job every day.
    - Bureau of Labor Statistics figures for 1999 show that 43% of all non-fatal assaults and violent acts resulting in lost workdays across all industries occurred in health services.

- Government facilities and public buildings.
- Large facilities used for sports or entertainment venues.
- Transportation facilities, such as rail lines and railroad and bus depots and marshalling yards, airports, hangars, fuel bunkering facilities, ship docks, container facilities, warehouses, and storage facilities.
- Police, firefighters, and other security workers.
- Students and faculty — either as direct targets of disturbed individuals or as accidental victims of a collateral event.

It is nearly impossible to define all of the facilities and/or individuals who may find themselves at risk or in danger. Consequently, a security assessment committee or group must try to think in terms of protecting their facility and its users from completely undefined or unanticipated sources, as well as from the more commonly considered sources. The above list simply highlights some of the people and facilities that may be at increased risk.

Invited Guests

At any given time, there are likely to be other people, in addition to regular personnel, within a facility. Not only should the presence of these visitors be recorded from a security standpoint, but the host entity should recognize that it has assumed a responsibility for their safety and security. One method of helping both visitors and normal building users to avoid risks is by prominently labeling high-risk and/or restricted areas. Invited guests may include:

- Business guests: local or out-of-town associates and colleagues.
- Professional guests/consultants, such as attorneys, accountants, engineers, interior designers, and architects.
- Customers/clients.
- Outside contractors.
- Repair, maintenance, and construction personnel.
- Cleaning personnel.

Uninvited Guests and Others

The fact that people are not directly invited, but may be within a facility does not preclude or limit responsibility for their safety and security. Visiting family members, sightseers, sales persons, solicitors, and even potential "bad guys" are due a level of safety and security. Knowing who is in the facility and where they are should be a primary goal of a security program. The days of the "open" building or facility are over.

Property

Although the safety and security of people is the highest priority of a security program, property is, by far, at the greatest risk and likely to sustain the most frequent loss or damage. There are essentially two forms of property for which a security program should provide protection: physical and intellectual property.

Physical

Physical property is the most visible, vulnerable, and accessible to theft, sabotage, vandalism, or just plain loss. The loss of physical property may be a double- or triple-edged sword. There is not only the monetary value of the property, but the additional costs associated with replacement or repair, plus the time lost by personnel in securing a replacement or repair. In the case of a laptop computer, the loss extends to the value of stored data and software, as well as the possible misuse of stored information — both personal and business.

The security team should begin a program of review and assessment of all of the physical property within its scope of responsibility to determine:

- What is at risk.
- How critical it is to current and future operations.
- Whether to provide special protection for it.
- How to protect it.

Following is a short list of property types, which may stimulate further consideration.

- Buildings and structures — from storage sheds to aircraft hangars, compounds, campuses, docks, and vessels — together with their infrastructure components, such as roads; mechanical and electrical systems, including boilers, transformers, power transmission, distribution, and switchgear; water, sewer, or gas lines; fire and ejector pumps; and storage tanks.

- Within a structure or building there are various spaces, equipment, and components to which special attention should be paid. These include elevators and elevator hoist rooms and escalators, both of which require very heavy power loads; cooling towers, central chillers and circulating pumps of differing functions, incremental and/or fan coil units, Local Area Network and Wide Area Network Facilities (LAN and WAN), Main Distribution Frame (MDF) Rooms, Intermediate Distribution Frame (IDF) rooms, telephone demark rooms, Telephone Systems Entry Rooms (TSERs), Private Branch Exchange (PBX) equipment, telephone recording rooms, laboratories, clean rooms, refrigerated or critically cooled storage rooms, emergency response rooms, public affairs or information centers and communication centers, and outside (fresh) air supplies for either or both the buildings' main and/or ancillary supplies.

- Furniture and furnishings; devices; production, service, and educational equipment; and support and ancillary equipment. This category includes everything from works of art to lawn mowers.
- Specialty equipment and machinery such as trucks and trailers, bulldozers, busses and automobiles, aircraft, and boats.
- Hospital, medical, and other critical electronic equipment that can become vulnerable to spiking electromagnetic impulses transmitted, possibly amplified through the use of a Transient Electromagnetic Device (TED). These devices are inexpensive to acquire or make and are readily available.
- Telephone and teleconferencing equipment such as PBX switches, cellular phones, satellite communication links, fax machines, television cameras, and monitors.
- Computer and related communications equipment such as receivers, repeaters, recorders, hubs, turrets, processors (such as mainframes, servers, routers, desktop computers and monitors), printers, plotters and laptops, and public address systems.
- Support equipment and systems such as Power Distribution Units (PDU), Uninterruptible Power Sources units (UPS), Emergency Power Systems (EPS), and generators and generator fuel tanks.
- Wire and cable materials such as copper and fiber cables.
- Miscellaneous equipment for repair, measuring, calibration, testing and installation, and tools.
- Employees' and guests' personal belongings, such as purses and wallets, clothing, laptops, Personal Digital Assistants (PDAs), books, tools, photographs, artwork, and other decorative items.

An entity's self-assessment will determine what sort of defensive actions are required to protect its people and property. At the very least, protection of people from ordinary personal injury risks is a must. Protection of property from theft, sabotage, and vandalism is just good business sense.

Intellectual Property (IP)
Intellectual property or assets include information on how the organization:

- Conducts its business, and with whom.
- Keeps confidential information out of the hands of people or entities that could profit by that knowledge.
- Accesses its intellectual assets and stores its information.

- Transmits its information.
- Retrieves or recovers information assets.

All of these points should be reviewed and assessed from a standpoint of security. Protection of some intellectual property is often the purview of the Information Technology groups. However, these departments frequently focus on information loss as a result of hardware or software failure or interruption, rather than other security risks. It is important to work with the IT groups to coordinate and ultimately document a universal plan that identifies the intellectual property that merits protection, and the appropriate level of security.

One of the world's major oil-producing companies decided that neither a UPS nor an EPS was needed to back up its database of mammoth geological information on the theory that being unable to access that information for a short period of time or until basic power was restored was an acceptable risk. On the other hand, the organization did require UPS/EPS backup of its accounting, customer, and vendor systems — not merely the databases, but the entire system. Entertainment recording and computer software companies are highly vulnerable to intellectual piracy, knock-offs, counterfeiting, and other forms of industrial and military espionage. Each entity must assess its own particular threats, hazards, assets, and vulnerabilities and plan security measures accordingly. (See Chapter 9 for more on IT security.)

Communications Security

This is one of the most overlooked areas in need of protection. Communications have progressed from a quick walk to an associate's desk for a few words on "what to do" or "how to do it," to a simple telephone call through a Private Branch Exchange (PBX), to a typewritten memorandum, to voice mail and e-mail. Suddenly we have the benefits and risks of Internet communications and are moving toward Voice Over Protocol (VOP) and Voice Over Network (VON) systems. The more technically advanced communication systems become, the more vulnerable they can be to eavesdropping and sabotage. Given the ready availability of long-range, portable listening devices, conference rooms located along the exterior walls may also become vulnerable.

Emergency Response

In the past, the greatest concern has been protecting people from fire and smoke, and evacuating them from facilities in an emergency. It has now become equally important to protect personnel from the dangers of unwanted people and hazards getting into the building. The question is, how?

Are there official, structured security and emergency response teams in the facility that are familiar with the various emergency response plans? Have their members been drilled on the different responses required for different emergencies through tabletop and walk-through exercises? Some of their responses can be tested and evaluated by a designated monitor without their having to even leave their meeting room. Desktop, or tabletop-level exercises may include initiating alarms, announcing that it is a drill, but not going through evacuation and shut-down. Exercising the full plan, complete with systems shut-down, is costly and usually reserved for critical facilities. In such cases, one unit might be shut down, and personnel evacuated. For multi-story buildings, evacuation exercises can be conducted by level, with each floor reporting to a central security station. (Chapter 4 addresses Emergency Response Teams, how they are assembled, and how they work. Chapter 7 has more on evacuation.)

- Have fire and/or floor wardens (and possibly bomb wardens) been appointed, and have they been trained? Has there been a recent fire, bomb threat, tornado, or hurricane drill? In the case of bomb threats, in-house personnel who are familiar with the area should perform a local search before the professionals arrive. They might be able to identify anything that appears out of place. They should report such observations to the command center. In an actual event, explosive ordnance professionals would inspect the area and confirm or deny the threat.
- Is there a plan for locating personnel and directing EMS personnel to them in an emergency?
- Are there well-developed emergency response plans in place to address differing types of emergencies, designed to mitigate panic and disruption to the greatest extent possible, yet adequately address the situation?

The above plans and measures should be checked, reviewed, and possibly updated annually to ensure that they will continue to function properly. Most, if not all, of these questions relate to safety and security events. The safety of all personnel and guests, and the safety of various forms of property are closely tied to established security measures. Monitoring the presence of visitors and knowing how to protect property has become a necessity for many. Safe and secure environments are conditions that an organization or facility is obligated to provide.

Conflicts Between Security and Safety

There are conflicts between safety (particularly life safety) and security. In focusing on security, it is important not to lose sight of the need for safety. Most life safety codes are based on National Fire Protection Association (NFPA) codes and standards (www.nfpa.org). The NFPA *Fire Prevention Code-1* has been in existence for many years and has become the hallmark document for all United States jurisdictions and for over 300 jurisdictions around the world. In 2003, it will be superceded by the *Comprehensive Consensus Codes™ (C3) set.*

The American Society of Industrial Security (ASIS), a premier organization for security professionals, was organized in 1937. In recent years, ASIS's primary focus has been changing from physical asset protection to protection of individuals, and from protection from thieves and an occasional disturbed assailant to protection from terrorist sources.

The security professional may be charged with protecting hundreds of individuals from such threats. In an effort to provide this protection, security professionals may find themselves in the position of attempting to install protective materials, barriers, or systems that are in direct conflict with existing codes or standards, developed over more than a hundred years and focused on life safety and fire prevention.

NFPA has been issuing codes and standards since 1896. The great fire in October 1871 in Chicago and the Station nightclub fire in West Warwick, Rhode Island in February 2003 underscore the critical need for stringent life safety codes and their enforcement. Preservation of physical assets is secondary. It is generally acknowledged that there are safety and security conflicts built into the Life Safety Codes. The essential value of the Life Safety Codes continues to be its protection of the greatest number of lives from the most frequent and dangerous hazards. At the same time, however, a terrorist attack can injure or kill hundreds or thousands of people in one event—a factor that can lead security professionals to conflict with the Life Safety Codes. The fact is, the likelihood of loss by fire far exceeds the likelihood of loss by terrorist attack. In 2001, NFPA reported that there were 1,734,500 fire calls in the United States with 6,196 civilian deaths — 3,745 deaths excluding those resulting from the September 11, 2001 event.

In spite of the loss of life involved with the World Trade Center disaster, it is likely that the then existing Life Safety Codes saved more lives than they may have been responsible for taking. Whether or not one or more fire tower stairways were blocked (because fire tower doors may not be opened from the tower side, thereby trapping and preventing people from escaping from one fire stairway tower onto a floor to seek another fire stairway) may never be known for certain. Still, it is recognized that preventing too many fire tower doors from being opened at the same time helps to prevent depletion of tower pressurization. The negative is that it prevents people from leaving a tower during a fire to seek refuge on a lower floor. Overall, this code requirement is more likely to save lives than not.

Interior designers and security personnel are frustrated by having code limitations to installing glass as side lights at entry doors between public corridors and office suites. Security personnel plead for the safety of receptionists who feel the need to know *who is requesting entry*, yet are unable to see through solid walls or doors. Fire codes require fire-rated walls between office suites and public corridors that lead to fire stairways. Conventional tempered glass does not meet the fire code. In the event of a locked entry door, so-called bulletproof materials or laminated glass are too resistant to firefighting personnel trying to get into the office suite to extinguish a fire.

Security professionals must learn how to work within the many life safety and building codes and standards. By working in collaboration with the code writers, solutions may be found that will provide greater security for both people and property—from fire as well as other hazards.

Conclusion

A security plan begins with the desire and need to protect people and property from potential threats. This chapter reviewed categories of businesses and personnel, as well as types of facilities to consider. It also included a short list of facility infrastructure, equipment, and property items to stimulate consideration of what may need protection. Communications security, emergency response plans, and potential conflicts between security and traditional safety approaches, all introduced in this chapter, are addressed in greater detail in subsequent chapters.

Once an organization has identified what it needs to protect, the next step is determining its own particular vulnerabilities. Chapter 2 begins that process by addressing the types of threats that need to be considered. These include criminal acts such as theft (physical and intellectual property), assault, vandalism, and sabotage; as well as accidents and acts of nature.

Chapter Two
Identifying Security Threats

This chapter explores the kinds of threats that today's organizations must consider when planning for security. The dangers include theft, assault, vandalism, and sabotage. The individuals and motivations behind these actions can vary widely. Consideration of these factors may help to plan for security equipment and construction approaches, and may also influence facility and business operational procedures.

What Can Happen

What are the current major security and safety concerns in public and private sector office buildings? Since 9/11, terrorism seems to have become a major focus. More people in all endeavors have become truly security-conscious, rather than merely security-aware. This consciousness has caused safety and security personnel to re-assess the programs they have in place. A survey by *Security Magazine* indicated the following re-prioritizing.

Top Ten Security Concerns by Priority for 2002

	2001	2002	Up/Down
Terrorism	Not Listed	1	NA
Employee Theft	1	2	Dn 1
Computer Security	5	3	Up 2
Property Crime	2	4	Dn 2
Access/Egress	3	5	Dn 2
Violent Crime	4	6	Dn 2
Vandalism	9	7	Up 2
Burglary	8	8	Same
Parking Lots, Garages	6	9	Dn 3
Liability Insurance	7	10	Dn 3
White-collar crime	10	11	Dn 1

Statistics from Security Magazine, *Business Publishing, January 2002 (Comparison column added by author)*

The clearest shift from the year 2001 to 2002 was the addition of terrorism. Among the other concerns, the largest swing downward involved parking lots and garages and a non-physical issue — liability insurance, while property crime, access/egress, and violent crime went down marginally. Upward shifts include a 20% increase in concern for vandalism and a similar rise for computer security, with a marginal shift upward for property crime. The increased concern regarding vandalism could possibly be linked to terrorism. The rise in computer security may indicate a deepening concern on the part of IT personnel for the vulnerability of their systems, especially after what happened or could have happened to data and communication systems after 9/11.

Top Ten Safety Concerns by Priority for 2002

	2001	2002	Up/Down
State and Federal OSHA Requirements	4	1	Up 3
Worker's Comp.	1	2	Dn 1
Natural Disasters	5	3	Up 2
Fire	3	4	Dn 1
Workplace Violence	2	5	Dn 3
Liability Insurance	6	6	Same
Emergency Comm.	9	7	Up 2
Machinery Accidents	7	8	Dn 1
Vehicle Accidents	10	9	Up 1
Building Codes	8	10	Dn 2

Statistics from Security Magazine, *Business Publishing, January 2002 (Comparison column added by author)*

Safety and security personnel view the continued tightening of federal and state OSHA requirements as their greatest concern, having moved this issue up by 30% on the list. Even though 2001 was a relatively benign year in terms of natural disasters with few major storms or earthquakes, and most forest fires limited to non-urban, non-security-sensitive areas, the concern for natural disasters moved from 5th place in 2001 to 3rd place in 2002.

Threats to Personnel Safety

Stress is increasing in all portions of society due to the pace and structure of life. People are exposed to an onslaught of information on worldwide tragedies and injustices, violence and hatred, along with conflict in the media and politics. In addition, there are economic and time pressures, with longer work hours, fatiguing commutes, family issues, illness, and weather-related inconveniences. Stress can result in frustration and distrust, sometimes leading to anger and violence against a perceived enemy. It is not the purpose of this book to assess the sociology of the workplace. However, security professionals recognize the fact that employees bring their personal stresses to work with them. Since they may spend as many, if not more, waking hours at work as outside of work in their active work lifetimes, the odds are increased that an event could occur during work hours, in the workplace.

The threat of violence in the workplace is enormous. There are about 2,000,000 assault incidents every year, and the rate is increasing. According to the FBI, general assaults account for 42% of all crimes in the U.S. Every day an estimated 16,400 threats are made against someone in the workplace or against the workplace itself. Every day over 700, or in excess of 200,000 per year, workers are attacked on the job. Assuming that there are roughly 13 working hours during the average American, coast-to-coast, workday (8:00 AM on the East Coast to 6:00 PM on the West), there is nearly one worker assaulted every minute. Every day nearly 44,000 workers are harassed, and every year about 1,000 workers are victims of a workplace homicide. These statistics do not consider injury from major catastrophic events such as terrorist attacks, nor acts of violence against physical or intellectual property.

In-House: Employees
Terminations

Anger or rage is one the most common sources of workplace violence. Festering anger may be the most common, but rage, or the explosive manifestation of anger, is usually more violent. Many of the more common causes of workplace anger can be anticipated and dealt with through informed management. "Roller coaster" employment and lay-offs can leave discharged employees feeling disrespected and unfairly treated. The combined fear of being unable to support themselves or their families, insult to their capabilities, embarrassment of termination, a question of "Why me, not him or her?" and where their next job will come from (and when) can fester into a strong resentment and a desire for retribution.

A discharge "for cause" can be even more likely to cause resentment, which may result in a violent act against the employer or company representative. The target can be anyone from the CEO to a co-worker. Termination or separation interviews conducted by people trained in dealing sympathetically with both downsizing and for-cause terminations can prevent a large portion of retaliatory assaults against physical or intellectual property or systems. The "Clean out your desk, while I wait" approach could ignite a firestorm of resentment.

Insult and Emotional Trauma

Another potential source of latent anger in employees can result from perceived insult or hurt feelings. Incidents such as being passed-over for promotion or having requests for a transfer to a new position denied can cause deep-seated resentments. More common is the persistent demeaning of an individual by a superior. These conditions can be difficult to discern, frequently continuing for years out of the victim's fear of retaliation or discharge. Skilled interviewers can often unearth these conditions through annual reviews or recognition of frequent requests for transfer. Not only can these conditions become dangerous, but also persistent harassment of one employee by another (and especially a superior) is illegal. In these days of frequently impersonal relations between management and workers, Human Resources, Health and Safety, and Security departments need to work together to prevent not only legal action, but the potential for violent incidents.

Threats from Outside: Criminals, Including Gangs and Fanatics

Gangs

In nearly any major city and a number of smaller ones, gangs are a major source of theft and personal violence. It is estimated that there are over 25,000 gangs in the United States. Gangs are no longer just rowdies confined to particular neighborhoods, but are more often well-organized, armed, and in possession of high-tech communications equipment. They survive on extortion, theft, and trafficking of drugs and other contraband, as well as murder for hire and sometimes kidnapping. These crimes are conducted at an organized level for profit. Gangs exist not only on the streets, but also in factories and in the military, as well as in colleges, universities, and schools, public and private. They have their own society and their own law. Contrary to popular perception, most gang members also have some form of legitimate employment — which means that a work associate could potentially be a member of a violent or criminally active gang.

Fanatics

So far, this section has addressed sources of violence in the categories of local crime or from within the organization itself, and those that may be work-related. Fanaticism, defined by *The American Heritage Dictionary* as "extreme, unreasoning" behavior in support of a cause, can also occur from within the workplace, but it is more often triggered by outside conditions or causes.

Social Causes Industries that pollute (or are thought to pollute) the air, water, and soil — or that waste resources — have critics and opponents. Potential targets include chemical plants, military facilities, sewage treatment plants, paper and wood pulp mills, foundries and steel mills, nuclear and fossil-fueled energy generating plants, large-scale farming operations, and others. Research laboratories are also vulnerable to threats and violence and have experienced strong opposition from extremists in the animal rights movement. Often these critics take on the role of "protector" of nature or humanity. Companies or agencies that operate in these and related industries are obvious targets for opposition, ranging from passive public demonstrations to violent acts of sabotage.

Religious and Political Groups It is difficult for anyone living in a society of religious and political freedom to raise a flag of caution regarding zealots or extremists who represent religious, nationalistic, or political causes. It is important, however, to recognize that there are many people whose beliefs are fundamentally adverse to democratic tolerance. Some may choose acts of violence as a means of demonstrating their rejection of an entity or activity that offends their principles. Their views on a particular political cause or religious belief, whether emanating from personal or doctrinal conviction, often result in a mindset that can result in overt acts of violence aimed at almost anything or anybody whose destruction or injury can point out the deep-set rejection of that which they feel offends their principals or is a wrong.

Whether faced with peaceful demonstrators or possible acts of lethal violence, security planners and personnel should recognize that threats from these sources do exist and may have to be dealt with. Because fanatical behavior is fundamentally irrational, it is unpredictable. Developing a strategy to deal with fanatical acts requires careful planning, documentation, and review by law enforcement and legal counsel.

Pathological Behavior

Pathological behavior is abnormal and dysfunctional and is often self-destructive, as well as outwardly destructive. A related act of violence may be more difficult to predict because the motivation behind it may not follow accepted social guidelines.

Consequently, such an act may occur with little, if any, warning. A security plan should recognize the possibility of a pathologically evoked incident and be prepared, to the extent possible, to address it. One of the best ways to prevent serious injury from pathological behavior is to prevent the availability of means that might be used to inflict injury (guns being the most obvious example). A clearly posted notification that guns are prohibited, backed up by a metal detector, is one approach.

Note: Metal detection devices require an operator or a least someone monitoring the device's output. Walk–through type detectors range in cost from $3,000–$7,000, while hand-held devices range from $80–$400. Walk-through detectors can be set up to send an alarm signal to a remote station, such as a security or nurse's station, where appropriate defensive actions may be activated. Hand-held units are sufficiently simple to operate that after a short period of training, a teacher, custodian, or nurse would be capable of detecting large or even small amounts of metal and then employ a silent signal to security personnel of a possible threat.[1]

Terrorism

Terrorism is defined as "the unlawful use or threatened use of force or violence by a person or an organized group against people or property with the intention of intimidating or coercing societies or governments, often for ideological or political reasons," by *The American Heritage Dictionary*. As is the case with religious and political extremists, terrorist groups tend to possess absolute convictions that their beliefs are the only correct ones and therefore superior to those of non-believers.

In the United States, a country founded on the bedrock of religious tolerance, it is difficult to bring ourselves to indict some members of one particular religion as "terrorists." However, it is critical in creating a security plan to acknowledge that there are extremist elements within nearly all religions and some political groups, some of whom firmly maintain that the West (Europe and America) are non-believers, barbarians, and infidels. Some fanatical elements view Western "infidels" as the cause of their lack of similar cultural, technological, military, and economic success. They see themselves as having been deprived of their rightful place in the world.

Cells of fanatical or extremist groups are known to exist inside the United States. There are at least three known terrorist networks operating in the Europe and the United States, as well as the Mid-East and Southeast Asia, other than Al Qaeda, Osama Bin Laden's terrorist network. These groups are large, with members who are highly trained in terrorist activities, well financed, and represented by well-paid legal counsel, all dedicated to the destruction of "the Infidel."

Accidents and Acts of Nature

Earthquakes, hurricanes, tornadoes, floods, and lightning strikes are all acts of nature that can have devastating effects on a facility and its inhabitants. Flying glass and debris from windows broken by sheared-off treetops and other debris can cause massive injuries and unquestionably cause the greatest physical damage during hurricanes. No matter how well-engineered a building's structural system, its glazing system is not likely to be a laminated glass type that will stop hurricane- or tornado-force debris from penetrating windows. The resulting glass shards become as lethal as bomb shrapnel.

Shoreline tidal surges and wind-blown waves flood out entire communities and structures. Tornados, with enormous power and unpredictability, can destroy whole towns and rip forests into matchsticks. Falling ice from high-rise building ledges and roofs can and do kill and injure people every year. Safety and security personnel need to consider the possibilities and have fully-defined safety, multiple evacuation, and response plans in place, yet most do not.

Accidental Explosions

Building, fire, and electrical codes have done much to produce facilities that are among the safest in the world, yet accidents can still happen. Major fire incidents can occur. A diesel engine may catch on fire, causing a tank to explode, spreading flaming fuel over a wide area. Or a boiler may explode, projecting iron and steel debris, along with live steam or boiling water, throughout a wide area. Are there safety/security plans and response mechanisms in place to address these kinds of disasters?

Theft of Property

Theft may occur from one of two sources: those within the organization and outsiders — and usually for the same reason — money. There are exceptions to both of these statements. Theft can occur when there is a conspiracy between an insider and someone on the outside. It can be motivated by a desire for retaliation, or as a means of gathering information on a competitive entity, such as a business, nation, or sports team. Theft can be as simple as putting a laptop computer in a brief case, or a PDA or wallet into a shirt pocket. These thefts usually are committed by one person and are thefts of opportunity — almost always brought about by the victim's own negligence. ("I was only gone for a second. I was sure I locked that door, I always do.")

Transmitting a business plan, operating statement, battle plan, or high-tech design or formula to an outside location or source is usually a planned, premeditated theft, although it, too, may be spontaneous. Planned thefts often occur in the early morning hours before other workers arrive, or in the evening when all others have left.

Stockroom and Inventory Theft

Stockroom and inventory theft is often on a grander scale, frequently involving more than one individual. Collusion between someone on the inside and someone on the outside is the most common method and may involve partnerships such as between a cashier and a customer, a receiving clerk and a truck driver, or an employee and someone on a cleaning crew. The types of property at hand will frequently determine the type of thief and the type of crime. Readily disposed of materials such as televisions, computer equipment, weapons, drugs, tires, or cigarettes that can be sold on the street, are most often burglarized by gangs who have ready outlets for their stolen goods. Weapons, chemicals, or other dangerous substances can also be targets of terrorists or extremists, as well as of common thieves stealing for pure profit.

Competitors and Espionage

Espionage is "the act or practice of spying or of using spies to obtain secret information, as about another government or a business competitor."[2] Espionage can range from newspaper clipping to wire-tapping. Practiced internally, nationally, and internationally, it may involve hiring away a key employee or planting a spy within a company or organization; poring through 10-K forms filed with the Securities and Exchange Commission (SEC); and pirating trade secrets, advertising programs, football play books, music, videos, computer software or hardware, or weapon designs. It is practiced on a huge scale.

Nearly every business, team, or command does whatever it can to learn all it can about its competitors. In many ways it is seemingly a benign activity — a practice taught in today's business schools. "Know your competition." However, from the point of view of security, loss of inside information to a competitor is a real loss and one to be prevented. Most significant losses of this type occur as a result of someone on the inside either selling information for money or for personal reasons. Today, given the ubiquitous use of e-mail and the Internet, fax machines and scanners, the transfer to anyone, anywhere, of internal written information can occur in seconds, and often with little trace.

Vandalism and Sabotage

The American Heritage Dictionary defines vandalism as "willful or malicious destruction of public or private property," and sabotage as "destruction of property or obstruction of normal operations, as by civilians or enemy agents in time of war or a treacherous action to defeat or hinder a cause or an endeavor, a deliberate subversion." Security people are just now beginning to address the tip of the iceberg. Physically booby-trapping computers with explosives or other harmful devices is a frequent strategy of terrorists. Stealing, selling, or tipping trade secrets or insider information is a rampant form of sabotage.

While vandalism and sabotage may derive from different intentions, the end results are the same. Property or operations are destroyed or damaged either way. Strategies to prevent these activities will differ mainly in the type of property requiring protection and in the security efforts employed to prevent the damage. Again, this is a matter of assessing the organization's or individual's image and potential opponents. Saboteurs have a desire or motive to cause injury. They may not necessarily select a target that would cause the greatest harm, but rather the one that appears to afford the greatest chance for success. Vandalism is more often an act of opportunity and may be performed by someone who is merely angry at society. This person may be a thrill- or power-seeker, whether wielding a can of spray paint or a hacker's computer. The target may be important only as an opportunity or a challenge.

Conclusion

This chapter examines some of the risks to organizations and facilities, the potential sources, and some of motivations behind these actions. Some of the risks include theft, assault, vandalism, and sabotage. Sources include disturbed present or former employees, criminals, extremists, and fanatics — whether driven by money, social causes, religious or political beliefs, or pathological behavior. The chapter briefly touches on the possibility of accidental damage to facilities and injury to personnel through acts of nature such as tornados, hurricanes, earthquakes, floods, and forest fires, and the need for an emergency response plan (covered in Chapter 4).

The following chapter offers some guidelines for assessing risks in terms of both the probabilities of various destructive events and the potential loss associated with them. A spreadsheet method is used to demonstrate one way to determine the relative risk based on the potential hazards and the criticality of particular assets. This process is a step toward prioritizing in order to determine where to invest in security measures.

[1] www.securitydetectors.com, www.protagesystems.com, www.andersondetectors.com

[2] *The American Heritage Dictionary of English Language*, 4th edition Houghton Mifflin, 2000.

Chapter Three

Assessing the Risks

Before assessing a facility's or organization's own particular risks, it is important to review the potential threats. The ultimate goal, as outlined in the following chapters, is to define the risks to the organization/facility and its components and to develop a plan or a series of plans that can provide safeguards against those risks. These assessments and plans should include:

- Steps that should be taken to formulate a security plan.
- Segments of a facility or operation and assets that are most valued and at the greatest risk.
- Events or incidents that may take place.
- Plans that need to be made to safeguard these operations and assets.

Assigning the Assessment and Response Team

One of the first considerations is who will prepare the safety, security, and response plans, and the risk assessment evaluation. These projects are ideally suited for a key internal work group. If the project is large enough, it may be best to secure the services of a qualified consultation firm to lead the group. Consultants should have experience in the fields of safety, security, and especially emergency response planning. *(A sample Request for Proposal for selecting a security consultant is provided at the end of this chapter.)* The group leader or guide should be familiar with the various physical and electronic devices available, as well as with suppliers and contractors, and should not be captive to any one manufacturer or concept of security. It will be the consultant's function to aid in the preparation, or to actually prepare, the final report or security and response plan, but only in close conjunction with the internal work teams.

If an outside consultant is not a consideration, the group leader or facilitator should be an individual with a high level of leadership, motivational, and communication skills. This person should be able to clearly envision the organization or entity's image, its core functions, its physical facilities, and its internal functional processes, including communications and IT functions. Importantly, the facilitator should have the time to devote to preparing for and conducting the necessary meetings, documenting the group's work product, and then instituting (and/or obtaining approval from senior executives to institute) the directives that result from the group's conclusions. If an internal member of the organization serves as the group leader, then this person will prepare, working with key members of the group, the final security and response plan.

If a consultant is to be used, the consulting agreement should call for their assistance in:

- Defining the composition of the group.
- Briefing group members on their duties and responsibilities, and providing them with the various kinds of information they will need.
- Assessing their abilities and willingness to attend meetings.
- Explaining what they are to do and when to do it.

It is not recommended that the consultant be the sole producer of documentation, reports, and plans. It is the consultant's duty to establish the process by which the internal team will develop the safety, security, and contingency or emergency response plans. In the event of a disaster, major or minor, it will be the disaster recovery teams, not the consultant, who must be able to assess the problem and put into effect the appropriate contingency solutions. Documentation of the group's work is extremely important from standpoints such as:

- Forming a consensus on the purpose of the security plan.
- Establishing the policies, cost, and recovery plans.
- Defining the recovery teams and outlining their roles, authorities, and responsibilities.

This documentation can be reviewed and then periodically re-reviewed for approval by management. However, if the end result of these efforts is just a manual or computer program that resides untouched on a shelf, then only the first half of the work has been done — possibly identifying how to keep the "bad guys" out. The other key aspect is developing the emergency response plans and preparing the response teams (including their knowledge of their own roles and objectives) in the event that a disaster calls them into action. If the recovery team members' knowledge is contained primarily on paper or electronic media and only remotely in their minds, this effort has not succeeded. (Chapter 4 addresses the recovery teams — how they are assembled and prepared, and their actions immediately following an event.)

Periodic Review of Documentation

Regardless of the form the security and response plans take, or whether they are prepared as in-house, proprietary plans or with the assistance of an outside consultant, the complete documents should be reviewed whenever there is a substantive change in the organization's structure or core objectives, but no less often than annually. Aspects of the plan, such as telephone trees, supply sources, floor wardens, departmental supervisors, and facility layouts, additions or deletions, may have to be reviewed and perhaps updated as frequently as monthly. An outdated plan may be better than no plan at all, but only as a "bare-bones" guideline. Missing or outdated information can be the cause of serious loss of time and increase crisis stress. This periodic review is conducted by the individuals who prepared the original plan. It is performed separately from the review by management described in the previous section.

Assembling a Risk Assessment Group

Input from the individuals listed below will be needed to identify threats, hazards, and critical assets (personnel, equipment, and processes). Not everyone is needed for every step in the process, however. The whole group might get together at the beginning to try to anticipate what management might do under varying circumstances. They might all reconvene in the middle of the process for a focus group to brainstorm on threats, hazards, and critical assets. At the end, they are likely to assemble once again to finalize the plan and make sure all agree that it will work.

Risk assessment group members should be drawn from a number of internal disciplines, such as:

- Internal security and safety department(s)
- Facilities management, real estate, or other physical space-related groups
- Internal or corporate physical services, such as supplies, provisioning
- Accounting, finance, and/or internal operations
- Production, or the core business or services
- Human resources
- Employee or union representation
- Internal communications and telecom

- IT or Datacom services
- Risk management and legal
- Senior management liaison

The group should have a designated senior management liaison, someone who can report progress to senior management and secure direction. This individual can also approve and present the group's risk assessments and proposed emergency response plans. Future plan reviews or revisions should be based on changes in the entity's:

- Size
- Location
- Business purpose
- Critical assets
- Critical processes
- Threat and vulnerability assessment
- Response capacity

In addition to possible changes in physical risks, organizations constantly face and address daily risks of major market shifts, new or declining business competition, the economy, and other financial influences. Any one of these forces may alter their view of critical assets. Only senior management is likely to know of as-yet undisclosed plans that may have a direct influence on the assessments and response plans.

Deciding Where to Focus Security Measures

Chapters 1 and 2 raised the issues of who or what needs protection. Not all of the individuals within an organization require unusually high levels of security, nor are all of an organization's or facility's physical or intellectual assets likely to require special security attention. When an organization has reviewed both the potential risks to personnel and assets (based on its image, physical location, and other factors) and the criticality of its various assets, it can begin to determine the scope of a potential loss. This is the organization or facility's true vulnerability, and where its security investment should be focused.

This book is about security, not enterprise management. Therefore, a risk assessment begins with a policy statement that encompasses the organization/enterprise, but is limited to managing operational and asset risks. This type of assessment requires an in-depth understanding of how products or services are delivered to customers, where the vulnerabilities exist in that operational chain, and how these areas can be protected and readily re-established. The policy statement will be, in essence, a business continuity plan.

Computerized Risk Assessment Software Packages

Several risk assessment programs are available as software packages. Most were developed a few years ago in conjunction with the U.S. Department of Defense. These programs are complete, form useful guidelines, and produce excellent results, providing the information fed into them is reliable and complete. However, they contain many fields and cells and some potentially confusing terminology and may be burdensome for the needs of some organizations. They are all algorithmic-oriented, fundamentally designed for government or very large institutional users, and primarily concerned with criminal or terrorist threats. They are priced from $600 to $20,000. Some of the better known systems that meet various regulations and guidelines include ISO-1779, BSA 7799, NIST 800-14, Risk Watch® www.riskwatch.com, Buddy Systems® www.buddysystem.net, Risk Access® www.ppm2999.com, and SaSSy® www.akelainc.com.

Such programs can be helpful as a format or guideline for developing a risk assessment. However, a small group of internal, knowledgeable people with a clear understanding of the organization's operations and assets, and a recognition of the various threats and vulnerabilities is likely be more effective than a computer-oriented package.

Computer-aided assessment plans are statistically based and are particularly valuable in dealing with physical assets, but are not as valuable in addressing more mundane and frequent interruptions, such as computer failures, software bugs, hackers, or communication outages. The best defense against IT risks emanating from hackers, cyber-terrorists, or a malcontent employee is an aggressive monitoring program to stop breaches and misuse. The response should be swift and aimed at removing or prosecuting offenders when possible and developing firewall protections against future breaches or offenses.

Assessing the Facility

The following lists are intended to challenge the team to review the type and location of the facility and the significance of its features. We may be so accustomed to seeing the trees, that we become oblivious of the forest.

Type of Structure

What kind of facility or facilities is being assessed? For example:

- Aircraft/Airport
- College or University Campus
- Factory/Manufacturing
- Free-standing retail facility
  — High-rise
  — Mid- or low-rise
  — Loft

- Multi-family residential units
- Office building
- Office complex or campus
- Parking structures and basements
- Port
- Residential community
- School
- Ship
- Suburban shopping center or downtown retail shopping area
- Warehouse
- Other

The next step is defining the facility location and its significance. Again, the team is urged to refine the list with their own additions and to eliminate qualifications that do not apply.

Location Assessment
- Where is the organization/entity physically located?
  — Locally
  — Nationally
  — Internationally
- What is the nature of the physical location(s)? For example:
  — A target (high-profile, such as a major high-rise; or a building or facility that houses other potential target organizations/entities), e.g.,
    – the largest cruise ship afloat
    – a location in midtown Manhattan
  — An unlikely target, e.g.,
    – the outskirts of a small town in Iowa
- Who are the neighbors? For example:
  — A ballet school
  — A local CIA office
  — A sports stadium or arena
  — A nuclear or other electrical generating plant

Image Assessment
- Who is the owner organization?
- What is its mission?
- What does the outside world think is its mission, its responsibilities as a community citizen, or think of the entity as a whole?
  — Competitively
  — Locally/community relations (involved or anonymous)
  — Nationally

— Internationally
— Politically
— Socially (a desirable neighbor, undesirable, or anonymous)
- What image does the owner organization project?
  — To peers
  — To competitors
  — Locally
  — Nationally
  — Internationally

General Assessment

Is or could the facility be a potential site-specific target?

- Because of the occupying organization — the sole or primary user of this facility.

- Because of another user or occupant or user.

- Because it is located in an attractive target.

- Because it is located near or adjacent to an attractive target.

In developing a Risk Assessment, each of the above questions should be reviewed and answered precisely and with candor. Most organizations prefer to think of themselves as friendly, innocuous entities. Serious consideration of these questions may reveal individuals or groups who do not share that view. For example, an insurance company representative points to explicit language in the policy that would deny a claim. The policyholder disagrees and feels cheated out of a justifiable settlement. A talk show host or news reporter may offend some individuals or groups, despite the fact that the television station or network considers itself a guardian of the First Amendment. A public utility may consider itself a faithful and indispensable provider of water or energy to a dependent public, while others may view it as an environmental polluter or an attractive terrorist target.

A review of the above questions is not only a key part of risk assessment, but also begins to set the stage for the next step in the preparation of a security and contingency response plan, which is evaluating or assessing potential hazards and overall risk.

Assessment of Specific Risks

- What is the likelihood of unauthorized people entering the facility who may wish to cause physical or intellectual property damage?

- How likely is it that the organization's own personnel will gain access to information about its operations to which they are not authorized?

- How great is the likelihood of consultants, contractors, delivery personnel, and couriers gaining access to unauthorized areas of the facility?

- What is the likelihood of unauthorized vehicles gaining access to the restricted areas of the grounds or facility?
- What is the likelihood or probability of wandering or lost visitors gaining access to confidential, proprietary information and other assets?
- How should one assess the likelihood of too much information made available through Web pages, government agencies, etc., and how should it be controlled?
- How should the government's and the public's right to know be balanced against the organization's right to privacy?
- How does one assess the likelihood of designs, maps, plans, and layouts of facilities and internal critical areas being released without a security review and without first verifying a requestor's need and usage of material?
- What is the probability of an accidental release of facility-owned toxic or highly combustible substances?
- What is the likelihood of an accidental or hazardous biological and/or chemical exposure from an external source?
- What is the probability of occurrence of an internal fire?
- What is the likelihood of water damage resulting from an activated fire sprinkler head or some other source?
- What is the likelihood of a radiation event?
- What is the probability of a bomb-threat or an actual bomb attack?
- What is the likelihood of an accidental explosion?
- What is the likelihood of an earthquake, hurricane, tornado, or flood?
- What is the probability of occurrence of flying glass or other debris as result of wind- or explosion-driven materials smashing through the windows?
- What is the likelihood of a mandatory evacuation, and for how long?
- Others (which should be specifically defined).

The above list suggests some of the possible threats. Clearly, many will never become serious or even real risks for a given facility. Others may be possible or even likely. Individual lists should be prepared for each facility. Even if some of the questions seem a bit far-fetched, it is better to consider a question and eventually discard it than to make an early, ill-considered judgment that may overlook a real threat or hazard.

Probability of Occurrence

When a Risk Assessment list has been prepared for each facility, values can be assigned based on an estimate of the probability and degree of risk associated with a particular threat. Factors can be assigned to specific threats. The evaluations of the facility's location and the organization's image are useful in helping to determine the probabilities of an occurrence.

The following are five suggested probability factors that can be helpful in assessing the likelihood of a particular threat.

Not at all	0
Possible but not likely	0.5
Possible	1.5
Somewhat likely	4.5
Likely	13.5

Because probabilities of events range from not at all likely to highly likely, it is recommended that the assessment be kept as simple as possible. A structured and visually organized assessment, such as the example in Figure 3.1, can be a very useful tool. Note that in some of the matrices in Figure 3.1, the factor has been modified, or skewed, in order to tailor the assessment to the particular conditions, based on the preparers' judgments. This skewing is an organizational preference, not a standard. It is important to consider what sort of arithmetic progression is appropriate in preparing such a matrix. The key is to keep it reasonable and a true progression.

The potential risks should now be evaluated from three viewpoints.

- **First, what is the probability of a real occurrence?** The likelihood of a tsunami in Kansas is not very great, but a tornado is a real possibility. On the other hand, the potential that someone might walk off with an expensive laptop computer could be quite high, no matter where the facility is located. If many people in a facility have laptops or other compact equipment at their workspaces, the probability of such a loss would be substantially higher than in a building where there are few, if any, laptops.

- **Second, what is the anticipated value of the damage or loss and disruption, given the entity's vulnerability?** A tsunami in Hawaii is a real possibility, even if unusual. If the facility is located low enough and close enough to the ocean, the degree of damage could be quite extensive and costly. This threat may receive a higher rating than the theft of a facility's single laptop computer, which, with new software, may have a

	Physical Loss Assessments	Probability of Occurrence		Value of Initial Loss		Value of Future Loss		Overall Risk
1	Unauthorized people entry	10	×	2	+	0	=	20
2	Unauthorized personnel accessing information	5	×	2	+	5	=	15
3	Consultants contractors, delivery personnel accessing unauthorized areas	1.5	×	2	+	2	=	5
4	Wandering visitor accessing information	2	×	2	+	1	=	5
5	Too much information available via government, etc.	1	×	3	+	2	=	5
6	Uncontrolled release of plans, maps, etc.	1	×	1	+	1	=	2

	Business Interruption Assessments from Physical Events	Probability of Occurrence		Value of Initial Loss		Value of Future Loss		Overall Risk
7	Accidental release of toxic or explosive substance	0.5	×	4	+	4	=	6
8	Invasion of toxic or biological substance	0.2	×	4	+	4	=	4.8
9	Internal fire	10	×	3	+	1	=	31
10	Water damage	7.5	×	2	+	0	=	15
11	Radiation event	0.5	×	3	+	3	=	4.5
12	Bomb attack	0.5	×	4	+	5	=	7
13	Explosion	4	×	3	+	2	=	14
14	Hurricane or other storm	5	×	4	+	1	=	21
15	Flying glass	5	×	2	+	1	=	11
16	Major evacuation	3	×	3	+	0	=	9

Ed. Note: This matrix is available to purchasers of this book for downloading at the following dedicated Web site, http://www.rsmeans.com/supplement/bldgsecurity.asp

Figure 3.1: **Probability of Risk**

replacement value of $2,000–$3,000. If no intellectual property is lost with the computer, this would not be a major financial loss.

- **Third, what is the potential monetary loss of production and/or operating capacity?** The loss of an individual's laptop might be a major annoyance, especially if belongs to the CEO. Depending on what files are maintained on it, the intellectual property loss could range from zero to catastrophic.

As mentioned previously, Figure 3.1 is a sample of a simple matrix that can be used to provide indications of "Probability of Risk" for various types of loss, and how they rank. It is important to segregate the risk of physical asset loss from that of business interruption loss. It is easier to calculate and insure against the monetary cost associated with physical damage or loss. Business interruption losses are more difficult to evaluate, and actual recovery can be even more difficult. It is generally acknowledged that businesses that experience an interruption as brief as ten days are at significant risk of failure within the following two years.

Some items, such as fire and water damage, can be classified both as physical loss items and business interruption items. Such items can be included twice, once in each category.

Assessing Facilities by Type

The next step is developing a basic list of the organization's various facilities that are subject to threats of one type or another. It is essential that a separate assessment be prepared for each facility within the scope of the organization's concerns, as no two are precisely alike. Each facility will have its unique set of attendant risks. Each should be evaluated from three viewpoints:

- Probability of occurrence
- Immediate or initial physical loss and disruption
- Extent of future loss

Different degrees and/or probabilities of loss will provide different patterns of concern. The objectives are three-fold:

- Prevent undesirable people, forces, or damaging agents from accessing the facility.
- Prevent acts of injury, damage, or theft from occurring within the facility.
- Develop emergency response contingency plans or strategies for recovering from damage.

Once the assessment has identified the threats or hazards and the facility's critical assets, and has considered the likelihood of these hazards occurring, the initial risk analysis is done. The next step is to consider the organization or facility's specific vulnerabilities and determine the risk based on that vulnerability.

If the vulnerability is high, risk is increased because consequences are more likely to occur and to be damaging. If a perpetrator is contemplating an attack of some sort on a facility, what is the possibility that he will in fact target it because it is more vulnerable? Following are some examples of vulnerabilities and ways to reduce the threat, thereby changing the assessment of threat and risk, and what might need to be done to protect the facility and its users.

- A propane gas tank on the traffic side of a building versus on the less accessible back of the building.

- Distribution of site maps: The frequency of occurrence may be only one time per year, but this sort of sensitive information getting into the wrong hands, even once a year, can make a facility, personnel, or equipment extremely vulnerable.

- Parking areas too close to a school classroom. This arrangement could result in a high level of vulnerability. Shifting use of space so that a storage room occupies the front, or traffic-side of the building would reduce vulnerability.

- Office space in a conspicuous, potential target building. Selecting a less obtrusive suburban area may reduce apparent vulnerability.

To achieve the objective of assessing and addressing the organization or facility's risks, it will be necessary to quantify both the degrees of risk and the probabilities of occurrence. Developing the appropriate lists and assessments establishes guidelines that will help put into place the appropriate measures to protect the facility or organization from hostile or damaging outside forces. These measures include control of the movement of strangers, as well as the organization's own personnel and guests, within the facility.

Following, in Figure 3.2, is a sample of an assessment prepared for a hypothetical high-rise office building.

Building Security Assessment
The XYZ Company Building Headquarters
1000 Main Street
Chicago, Illinois

January 14, 2003

Beginning in September 2002, a security assessment group was assembled to review the XYZ Company building headquarters, here in Chicago. Work group members included our Chief of Security and representatives from Data Communications and Telecommunications, Facilities Management, and our architectural firm.

XYZ Company is in the pipeline gas distribution business, nationwide. As such, its pipeline assets are moderately vulnerable to sabotage, accidental damage, and vandalism. However, its corporate headquarters facility and personnel do not appear to be at a high degree of vulnerability, or at least no more than any other downtown office building or personnel.

XYZ Company has a relatively low-key public image. It is neither the producer of natural gas, nor the end distributor. It does not buy gas for its own account, nor does it sell gas to end customers. Therefore, its functions attract little public attention. Its greatest operating vulnerability would be the result of a pipeline explosion, resulting in collateral damage and accidental loss of life or injury.

The XYZ building is 11 stories, with 6 levels of underground parking, residing on a large plaza on a downtown corner in Chicago, Illinois. Its immediate neighbors are buildings of similar height and, except for one, are all multi-tenanted. The neighborhood is considered desirable and stable. Police reports indicate some after-hours assaults, but no more than in any other area of downtown Chicago. Thefts include a high number of laptop computers from offices. The fire department reports very little fire activity in the area and has an active fire inspection routine involving all area buildings at least once a year, including storage of combustible or hazardous materials. EMS services are available from a local EMS station, which is located 6 blocks away. A fire station is located 14 blocks away. Good Samaritan Hospital, a general hospital with emergency room service, is located 8 blocks away. The local electrical utility reports only moderate power interruptions or surges, mostly caused by underground distribution line maintenance.

Heating and cooling of the building is by electricity only. The XYZ building does possess a 1.25-megawatt diesel generator, which must be inspected and test-run every 6 months using a load bank. The generator is fueled by a 1,000 gallon fuel tank, housed in a room separate from the generator with a containment wall capable of holding any fuel spill resulting from overfill or a fuel tank leak.

XYZ Company has no computerized facilities management system, and therefore no updated mapping of egress paths to fire exits and stairs, nor assigned location of individual employees, other than the original move-location drawings produced by the architects at the time of move-in.

Security Issues
Perimeter Security

A very basic form of access control using prox cards limits or controls ingress, but not egress to the building and parking structure, whether through the main lobby front doors, rear plaza doors, truck dock, fire exits, or parking facility.

Internal Security

The company's security department is concerned with the movement of XYZ personnel and non-XYZ persons (guests, casual visitors, service, and construction individuals) from authorized areas to unauthorized areas. The Security Department realizes that no perimeter security is unassailable, but is nonetheless concerned with preventing those who might have breached the perimeter security from achieving access to critical areas of the facility such as LAN rooms, IDF rooms, and personnel file areas. Other concerns include theft prevention of physical assets and property, as well as industrial espionage of intellectual property. The Security Department is also concerned with maintaining the normal life-safety practices, as well as active and prompt responses to illness or trauma.

XYZ Company Building Perimeter Security

XYZ Company building is reasonably well designed for the creation of a perimeter security system. Normal access to all floors (2-11) above the first or main floor is through the main floor building lobby and elevators.

There are four means of accessing the main building lobby from the outside.

1. The main building or front entrance off of Main Street.

2. The main building lobby of the plaza entrance.

3. The two elevators, which service the parking facility only and terminate in the main building lobby.

Figure 3.2: **Building Security Assessment** (cont.)

4. One of the main building passenger elevators, which also serves as a freight elevator and provides service from the P1 (first) parking level is at the same level as the truck dock.

Of the two fire tower exits, one terminates on the P1 level and exits from that level through a man-door adjacent to the truck dock entrance. The second terminates in an area of refuge and exits into a rear portion of the building lobby, then through the rear lobby door onto the plaza. Both of these doors may be secured, alarmed, and enunciated to prevent ingress into the fire stair towers.

Access and use of any main or first floor spaces and restrooms will likely use the same exiting patterns as those from the fire towers. If a high occupancy space should be developed on the main floor, special fire exiting may have to be created.

It is anticipated that the main floor elevator lobby will be accessed through visual guard screening of pre-issued ID/prox card badges or fobs and uniquely issued self-expiring temporary badges to guests and other authorized visitors or service personnel. The Security Department has considered the use of so-called "turnstiles" to augment lobby security personnel. Alternately, the entire the lobby can be secured with e-card (smart cards) access devices controlling anti-piggy-backing revolving doors, in combination with voice or doorbell door releases for guests without smart cards.

Conclusion Regarding Perimeter Security

A higher quality perimeter security system can be installed using off-the-shelf devices incorporating existing technology. Combined with a limited number of trained security personnel, such a system should achieve a high degree of controlled access and accountability.

The XYZ Company building is not well designed from the standpoint of an efficient internal security system. This condition is due to the placement of the building cores in the center of the floors, and placement of fire stairways outside of the areas of the upper floor elevator lobbies. This condition makes the securing of floors off of the elevator lobbies on floors 2-11 extremely difficult. Current Life Safety and Building Codes prohibit the creation of lock-off areas that do not contain a fire exit. The exception is the so-called "15 second type doors," which may be secured with an electronic-accessible lock. However, these doors must be able to be opened from the secured side within 15 seconds of receiving no more than 15 pounds of pressure for one second, plus other life safety conditions, such as loss of building power, fire alarm, etc. In addition, a sign printed in block lettering no less than 1" high must be placed within 12" of the door, stating "Push Until Alarm Sounds. Door will open in 15 seconds."

Given a primary circulation geometry, which encircles the building core's access, controlled elevator lobbies should not present major impediments to XYZ Company personnel movements.

High-security areas such as LAN rooms, fire stairway access to floors, IDF rooms, telephone equipment rooms, security device rooms, CCTV and other monitoring rooms, executive suites, and boardrooms, can and should be secured through the use of access control devices, some limited exiting doors, and CCTV.

Conclusion Regarding Internal Security

It appears that the creation of an internal security system through the use of electronic monitoring devices and/or electronic access devices would:

1. Be moderately costly, but highly desirable in some areas.
2. Provide an extra level of security, whether from internal or external unauthorized persons.
3. Cause only limited impediment to personnel movement.

Security Philosophies: Employees

1. All employees would be issued a unique smart card or fob. This card should bear a photograph of the employee and his/her name. It should be uniquely encoded to permit an employee to enter the building during certain hours or at all hours, through specific doors, or all doors, the garage, and such other areas or rooms where he or she might have authorization to access, such as LAN rooms, IDF rooms telecom rooms, etc. (Most prox, or proximity, cards carry only limited amounts of information. It is the main control system that is programmed to permit individuals to enter specific areas or to use certain facilities or devices.)

2. Upon entering the building or garage control gate, an employee would present his or her card to a card reader, if necessary, at an access reader at an entrance door, or to a card reader at a turnstile. The system would record the employees entering the building, the time and date of entry, and that he or she should be in proximity to or at his or her workstation or office.

Figure 3.2: **Building Security Assessment** (cont.)

3. If deemed desirable, an employee leaving the building or garage could be logged out by presenting the card to an exit reader. Security and Health and Safety or other interested parties would then be able to know whether or not the individual is on the premises.

4. As a basic security philosophy, it is suggested that all employees leave the building through the main lobby, and record their departures at card readers, whether they are planning to leave through the front or plaza pedestrian doors or through the two elevators to the various parking levels.

Guests:

1. Guests, service, and construction personnel should also be instructed to depart through the main building lobby, turning in their temporary badges and temporary e-cards at the lobby security guard station before departing through the truck dock or parking structure.

   Often it will be necessary to issue temporary e-cards to visiting guests, service personnel, or contractors, in addition to the temporary badges. Unless the contractor is working on a long-term contract basis, such as a consultant, his or her e-card should be turned in at the end of each day at the main lobby security station.

   To the extent possible, prior notification of an expected visit by a guest should be transmitted to the security office either in person, by telephone, or by e-mail. This will enable security personnel to log the guest into the system and to prepare or print a temporary badge in advance of the guest's arrival. Exception routines should be devised to permit admission of unexpected or as-yet unidentified persons, such as service personnel who have been called to deal with an urgent matter.

2. Once a guest is logged into the system and directed to the appropriate floor, the sponsoring XYZ Company employee should meet the guest(s) in the upper floor elevator lobby and personally conduct them to wherever their meeting is to take place. Once in the building, the guest becomes the responsibility of the sponsoring employee. When the guest is ready to leave, the sponsoring employee should accompany the guest into the elevator lobby.

   It is suggested that the guest's temporary ID badge contain not only the name of the individual, but also his or company affiliation, the sponsoring employee's name, and a number identifying the floor or floors to which the guest is authorized. Contract consultants should be issued regular ID/e-cards similar to regular employees, but with a differentiating background color identifying them as an authorized non-employee.

3. XYZ Company employees should be aware of and prepared to question guests wearing an inappropriate badge number or color for the floor on which they are found. The employee might inquire whether he or she might be of assistance in locating a certain individual, office, or conference room for guests. Assisting guests to the restroom and then leaving them alone is not good security. Strangers without badges might be "assisted" in a similar manner and conducted to the floor's elevator lobby. This type of responsibility for guests should become a part of XYZ Company's Corporate Security Policy and understood by all employees. All personnel should be given some instruction on how to handle these kinds of situations, firmly but without offense. These instructions should be repeated periodically so that "real-life" experiences can be reviewed and used as learning experiences.

Guest Garage Security Garage security procedures would be similar to those in the building lobby, except that identification and logging would be for a vehicle only. The driver and passengers would be directed to the garage elevators and instructed to go to the reception/security desk in the main lobby for identification, authorization, and logging. Upon leaving the garage, only the vehicle need be logged out, as the guest should have been logged out before leaving the building lobby.

Physical security for all individuals utilizing the garage could be provided through the installation of Emergency Phone Stations at locations throughout each parking floor level and in particular at the elevator lobbies for the parking floors. These Emergency Phone Stations should be of a hands-free type and directly connected to the main security office. They should be equipped with enunciators so that security personnel could automatically identify the exact location of each station.

These stations should have a high visibility, identifiable by special lighting so they can be quickly located by anyone on any parking level. All stations should have a two-level call button, one for extreme emergencies requiring immediate help, and a send call button for more mundane problems, such as a driver with a blocked car, dead battery, or a flat tire.

The stations would be equipped with automatically triggered strobe lights and possibly audible alarms such as a claxon or horn, to be triggered in the event of an urgent event.

Some consideration has been given to the installation of CCTV cameras at parking level elevator lobbies. It is also suggested that CCTV cameras be installed at the inside and outside of the parking grilles and on the outside of the truck dock man-door into the P1 building level.

Figure 3.2: **Building Security Assessment**

Conclusion

The first three chapters have provided some guidelines for assessing the people and property to be protected, identifying hazards or threats and their likelihood, and determining a facility's particular vulnerabilities. This assessment will assist security planners in prioritizing and formulating a plan for the investment of the organization's available resources in the most effective security measures.

The next chapter outlines an approach that can be used to prepare for and manage a crisis following a destructive event. The challenge of developing a pre-defined, specific plan or solution to a crisis resulting from an as-yet unknown actual event means that crisis management plans must be highly flexible. Those responsible for executing recovery plans must have an intimate knowledge of their fields of responsibility and must know their team members. They also need to practice their solutions until they are comfortable with the duties they must carry out.

Request for Proposal

Dear Security Consultant,

We are a (small, moderate, or large) organization engaged in producing (type of product or service). We are located in (facility location) with (number of) employees and with (no other facilities, branches with ____ employees, subsidiaries with ___ employees, divisions with ____ employees, or offices with ___ employees) in (none, many other parts of this city, other cities, or other countries). Our annual published sales (or unpublished—if privately owned) are (dollar amount).

Because of (where we are located in what we perceive as a highly vulnerable area, or the characteristics inherent in the products we produce, or the local community and/or worldwide perception of our industry or specific business), our (insurance carriers, bankers, board of directors, or other entities) believe we should have a security assessment performed possible leading to a security and contingency response plan.

We would like you to provide us with a Proposal outlining your present qualifications in preparing security assessments and contingency response plans for organizations of our type and size and image together with an estimate of the amount of time required for the preparation of the assessments and plans (broken down into phases and/or time lines). All estimates should be inclusive of all costs for all phases.

You are asked to identify the personnel presently in your employment, who would be assigned to this project throughout your commitment to the project, including their areas of expertise and years of experience with your organization.

Please identify at least three references, listing the organizations' location and contact individual(s) (after confirming their continued association with the organization), as well as telephone numbers and e-mail addresses. Please detail the services you performed, and when you began and completed work for them.

You may visit our site(s) at a mutually convenient time for the purpose of surveying the scope of work to be incorporated into your proposal. Kindly contact the undersigned should you wish to make such a visit.

We reserve the right to accept or reject any one or all proposals submitted to us.

Sincerely,

_____

Figure 3.3: **Sample Request for Proposal for Security Consulting Services**

Chapter Four
Crisis Management

This chapter begins with three key terms in crisis planning:

Contingency: A contingent event or condition, as, **a:** an event (as an emergency) that may, but is not certain to occur; trying to provide for every *contingency*, **b:** something liable to happen as an adjunct to or result of something else.

Catastrophe: A momentous, tragic event ranging from extreme misfortune to utter overthrow or ruin; an utter failure; fiasco.

Disaster: A sudden, calamitous event bringing great damage, loss, or destruction; *broadly*: a sudden or great misfortune or failure.[1]

Making Crisis Management Plans

Creating a contingency or emergency response plan is not high on anyone's list of desirable tasks, but it is a major part of an overall security effort or plan. It is the part of the plan that addresses post-event conditions after serious damage has been sustained. Such possibilities and concerns are distressing to contemplate, and may include losing control of business operations, money, and perhaps even lives. A Crisis Management Plan requires an examination of hypothetical events and ways of coping with them. If the particular losses or problems are not yet known, how it is possible to develop answers? Given the possibilities of an event serious enough to disrupt a business or mission, an organization had better be prepared to respond promptly and efficiently. To quote Abraham Lincoln, "You cannot escape the responsibility of tomorrow by evading it today."

The first three chapters of this book dealt with the analysis of an organization's vulnerability based on its image, location, and the forces, groups, or individuals that might affect it. That evaluation process, and the measurement of risks through processes such as shown in the Chapter 3 matrix (Figure 3.1), represent a significant amount of planning and preparation. The next step is figuring out how to respond to a damaging event. Because it is impossible to know in advance what type of disaster could occur, when, or how extensive the damage will be, the plan must be flexible. Maximum flexibility is achieved when those developing the ad hoc Crisis Management Plans are the people who must put them into effect.

Crisis Management Planning is, in part, a training exercise. Its purpose is to prepare individuals within an organization to respond to a calamitous event. An effective response requires:

- Knowledge of how to assess conditions after the event, and
- The ability to put into effect actions designed to return the organization or facility to its defined business.

Recovery Teams must respond immediately and calmly. Mac Burdette (Colonel, United States First Army, Emergency Preparedness Liaison Officer for the State of South Carolina, and Town Manager of Mount Pleasant, South Carolina) had this to say about Hurricane Hugo in 1989: "No one can ever be fully prepared for a worst-case scenario. A major disaster's aftermath compares to a combat zone. Your leadership will be in shock; your staff will be in shock."

Just as in a combat zone, people must be trained to respond to a plan. The plan must aid in defining mitigation and cleanup, and, ultimately, in both the short- and long-term recovery plans. As with any military campaign, a strategic plan should be prepared, documented, and agreed on in advance.

Who Prepares the Plan?

Planning and recovery will take place at three levels, plus a review and approval by senior management, who must not only approve, but also select and empower their own representative to the Recovery Teams. Although senior management must approve the plans, it is the department heads and managers who will create and execute them. These are the people who have the day-to-day knowledge of how things get done, and what tools they must have to perform the job. Senior management is charged with establishing direction and setting policy within the scope of the organization's capabilities and assets. It would be impractical and inefficient for personnel at the senior management level to possess detailed knowledge of every aspect of every operation sufficient to be able to provide an immediate, temporary, and ultimately permanent recovery. This is why they must rely on those who process the work daily and keep the basic business going.

The three planning and response levels are:

- The Crisis Management Team
- The Departmental Recovery Planning Groups
- The Infrastructure and Departmental Recovery Teams

Throughout the balance of this chapter, the terms "work groups" (or "planning groups") and "work teams" (or "management" or "recovery teams") will be used. Groups are not the same as teams. Groups provide consultation, but are not held accountable for a specifically defined product, as are teams. Because the teams' and groups' involvement is so central to the organization's recovery plan, the topic of how teams and groups are assembled and work together is addressed in its own section, later in this chapter.

The Crisis Management Team

This team, composed of permanent personnel, is defined as:

- A permanent or standing team.
- A command and control team.
- A coordinating team.

Departmental Recovery Planning Groups

These groups:

- Are composed of personnel from each of the organization's departments.
- Anticipate or foresee any externally caused disruptions that could impair their operations. They must ask the question, "What can happen to us?"
- Develop contingency plans to deal with the anticipated disruptions, from a minor event to a near total loss of personnel, systems, and facilities.
- Select an individual or individuals, with backups, to represent them on a Departmental Recovery Team, which would be formed in the event of a crisis.
- Hold regularly scheduled meetings to review their plans and to rehearse recovery efforts.

The Infrastructure and Departmental Recovery Teams

Depending on the nature of a disruption, particularly a physical disruption, the Crisis Management Team (CMT) will likely activate various Recovery Teams. Among these will be:

- The Infrastructure Recovery Team.
- One or more Departmental Recovery Teams, as may be needed depending on the nature of the disaster and which departments have been damaged.

A Departmental Recovery Team can be formed from each department whose functions would have been defined by the Departmental Recovery Planning Groups. These teams must continuously coordinate their efforts with the Crisis Management Team.

Departmental Recovery Team members are selected by their respective Departmental Recovery Planning Groups. The representatives and their backups must be empowered to act on behalf of their departments. Their job is to put their department back into full or sustaining operation as quickly as possible.

Note: Later in this chapter, a fictional case study is used to illustrate the possible effects of a disaster event on an organization's ability to continue its operations. The Crisis Management Teams' members and functions are demonstrated, along with the teams' anticipated solutions and recoveries.

The Crisis Management Team

In developing Crisis Management Plans, the first task is to establish a Crisis Management Team — a permanent, small core group. As noted in Figure 4.1, this team will include representatives from senior management, human resources, corporate services, real estate and/or facilities services, as well as Datacom and Telecom and a public relations advisor. The team may also include a contingency planning person, who may be the organization or facility's Chief Security Officer.

The Team's Initial Functions

The team will have at least five initial functions:

1. Anticipate the types of disaster events that could occur.

2. List and inventory the facilities and portions of facilities that could be critically affected by a disaster event.

3. Anticipate and list the divisions, departments, and functions that might be crippled or destroyed by the possible events.

4. Develop and maintain Departmental Recovery Groups and contingency plans based on the groups' assessment of the nature and severity of a given event.

5. Catalog a set of Emergency Notification names and telephone or contact numbers in the form of a telephone tree, which must be updated monthly.

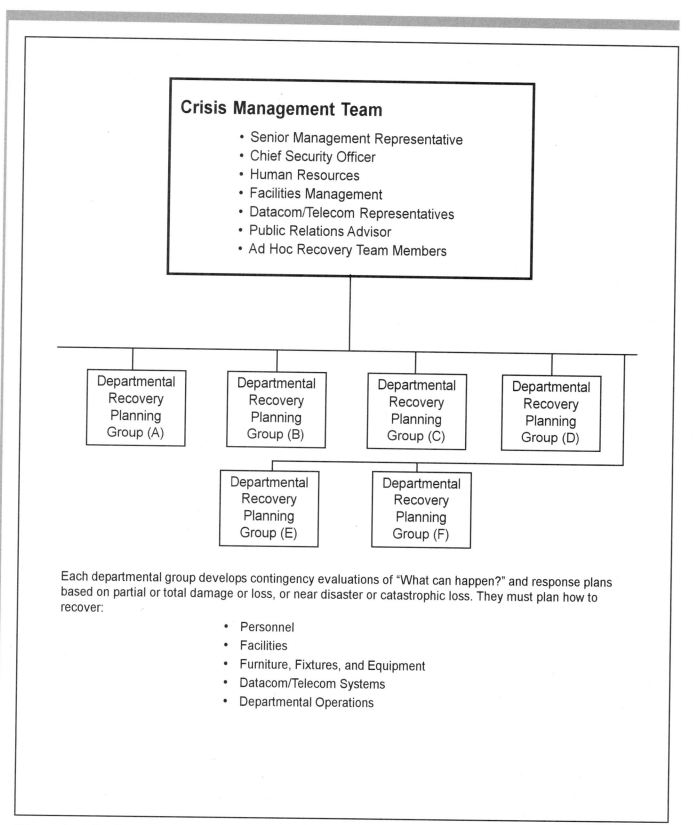

Crisis Management Team

- Senior Management Representative
- Chief Security Officer
- Human Resources
- Facilities Management
- Datacom/Telecom Representatives
- Public Relations Advisor
- Ad Hoc Recovery Team Members

Departmental Recovery Planning Group (A)

Departmental Recovery Planning Group (B)

Departmental Recovery Planning Group (C)

Departmental Recovery Planning Group (D)

Departmental Recovery Planning Group (E)

Departmental Recovery Planning Group (F)

Each departmental group develops contingency evaluations of "What can happen?" and response plans based on partial or total damage or loss, or near disaster or catastrophic loss. They must plan how to recover:

- Personnel
- Facilities
- Furniture, Fixtures, and Equipment
- Datacom/Telecom Systems
- Departmental Operations

Figure 4.1: **Sample Crisis Management Team Composition**

```
┌─────────────────────────────────────────────────────────────┐
│              Infrastructure Recovery Team                    │
├─────────────────────────────────────────────────────────────┤
│ This team has hands-on responsibility for all infrastructure │
│ recovery planning and execution.                             │
│        • The team coordinates with the Crisis Management     │
│          Team.                                               │
│        • Members may be the same as the members of the Crisis│
│          Management Team.                                    │
│        • Members are selected and activated in response to a │
│          disaster event.                                     │
├─────────────────────────────────────────────────────────────┤
│ Members should include:                                      │
│        — Senior Management representative or liaison with     │
│          spending and contracting authority                  │
│        — Facilities Management and/or Real Estate            │
│        — Corporate Services                                  │
│        — Security                                            │
│        — Public Relations                                    │
│        — Human Services                                      │
│        — Datacom and Telecom                                 │
└─────────────────────────────────────────────────────────────┘
```

Figure 4.2: **Infrastructure Recovery Team**

```
┌─────────────────────────────────────────────────────────────┐
│               Departmental Recovery Team                     │
├─────────────────────────────────────────────────────────────┤
│ This team has hands-on responsibility for all departmental   │
│ recovery planning and execution.                             │
│        • The Departmental Recovery Team is assembled to deal │
│          with an event.                                      │
│        • Members will be pre-selected from qualified         │
│          departmental personnel, or are selected and         │
│          activated for a particular disaster event.          │
├─────────────────────────────────────────────────────────────┤
│ The team is comprised of:                                    │
│        • Team Leader, selected by the team                   │
│        • Departmental Recovery member or members             │
│        • Liaison member(s) to:                               │
│          — Crisis Management Team                            │
│          — Infrastructure Recovery Team                      │
│                                                              │
│ Note:  Team members may by assigned to work with particular  │
│ elements of the Infrastructure Recovery Team and with the    │
│ Crisis Management Team.                                       │
└─────────────────────────────────────────────────────────────┘
```

Figure 4.3: **Departmental Recovery Team**

The Crisis Management Team's Functions in a Disaster Event (Act of Nature or Man-Made)

Initial Phase

(Note: The Chief Security Officer should be the first person notified of any type of destructive event.)

1. Meet immediately to assemble information and assess the event: What has happened, and what are the effects on the facility/organization?
2. Determine whether the event may be handled using ordinary procedures, such as working through the Infrastructure Recovery Team and calling in the facility's usual local contractors — or whether it is necessary to declare an emergency and make such a recommendation to senior management.

Second Phase

1. If the event is deemed a disaster, begin contacting the affected departments, thereby setting in motion the necessary Departmental Recovery Plans through the Departmental Recovery Teams.
2. Working in conjunction with the organization's public relations advisor, prepare (or have prepared) a corporate media statement to include:
   - The type of event that has occurred.
   - How the organization is responding to it.
   - How the organization intends to go about restoring operations.
   - When it expects to resume normal operations.
3. Coordinate the Recovery Teams, assign responsibilities, define limits to their areas of involvement, and arbitrate any territorial conflicts.

What Are the Critical Objectives?

Assigning an Organizational Structure

In preparing the Crisis Management Plan, it is important to consider what portions of the business or facility could be disabled or completely destroyed. To more effectively address damage and recovery, it may be necessary to break the organization down into operational segments or departmental groups. These can be used to form an organizational chart for developing the recovery plan. These segments, or groupings, when put into operation, may cut across the normal departmental lines or combine functions that would not be combined under normal business operations.

For example, a particular office may have had its local payroll process damaged or lost, but the organization's main office payroll system is still in perfect order. Three or four team members may be representatives from the main office payroll department.

47

Another may be a representative of IT or Datacom (assuming the break in the payroll process is Datacom-related or can even be quickly repaired by Datacom). The immediate solution may be a hand-calculated and produced payroll, or possibly retaining an outside payroll service company. A third team member, a representative from Security, may be able to ensure payroll privacy, as well as providing normal security to prevent theft.

The point is that an organization's recovery plan should incorporate the ability to rearrange operational segments. With the data networking that exists in most businesses, the old vertical organizational structure has been flattened into a horizontal one, with many, if not most departments operating almost autonomously. In preparing the Crisis Management Plan, it is important to always keep in mind that it is not possible to predict what portions of the business will be negatively affected or lost, when, how severely, or for how long. Once the plan is defined, senior management should review and endorse it before proceeding to the next step, which is how to establish the Recovery Teams.

Establishing Recovery Teams

At this point, the Departmental Recovery Groups should have:

- Anticipated various externally caused disruptions and outlined contingency plans to deal with them.
- Selected the Recovery Team members (and backup members).
- Initiated desktop or walk-through rehearsals or practices. The teams will conduct the actual desktop or walk-through rehearsals of the recovery plan. The recovery groups will observe these rehearsals, then address any problems that are identified, by making appropriate changes to the plan.

A Recovery Team must be, by its very nature, an ad hoc team whose members are selected from those appointed by the Departmental Recovery Planning Groups. Recovery Team members will likely include representatives from the various disciplines whose involvement is critical to the recovery of their respective departments' functions. All Departmental Recovery representatives should possess broad departmental knowledge and skills, as well as an understanding of the organization's core objectives. They should be able to call on departmental specialists and their backups. Departmental Recovery Team representatives should also have the ability to work effectively as team members. (Note: See "Teams and Teaming" later in this chapter for more on what defines a team versus a group, and the qualifications of each.)

Formulating a Crisis Recovery Plan

In order for the Departmental Recovery Planning Group to plan for what is not yet known, they need to create a series of "what if?" scenarios, from a mild interruption to a catastrophe, and to develop desktop responses to these scenarios. Departmental Recovery Planning Group members' focus should be on their particular contingency response functions.

Following is a list of elements that should be defined and documented as part of an overall Crisis Management Plan. Whether some or all of these items are put into effect will depend on when and where a disaster takes place, how severe it is, and what must be done for recovery.

Since it is not known what parts of the business operations will be damaged or disabled, each Departmental Recovery Planning Group must develop highly flexible responses to multiple types of damage events.

Elements of the Plan

Response plans should be supported by identification of:

- Existing in-house personnel
- Consultants
- Outside temporary personnel
- Suppliers
- Shipping sources
- Potential locations for relocation of:
  - Office space
  - Operating plants or facilities
  - Warehousing
  - Communications.

(Contact information for all of these individuals and organizations must be part of the plan: addresses, telephone numbers — and alternative numbers, and e-mail addresses.)

The Role of the Departmental Recovery Team and Desktop Practice

As the Departmental Recovery Work Groups prepare their plans, they must consider who the Departmental Recovery Team members will be. Department Recovery Team members may or may not be members of the Departmental Recovery Work Groups. Defining the roles and responsibilities of the Departmental Recovery Team members is one of the most critical tasks of the Departmental Recovery Planning Groups. Recovery Team members should be selected early on in the planning process and should begin desktop rehearsals during the Work Group planning process. Recovery Team feedback and responses are vital to the development of a viable plan.

The following elements should be defined and documented as part of an overall Crisis Management Plan. Whether some or all of these items are put into effect will depend on when and where the disaster takes place, how severe it is, and what must be done for recovery.

Evacuation and Safety Procedures and Materials

Evacuation Plans should include:

- Written evacuation procedures and checklist.
- Floor maps, including "People Locators," showing offices, rooms, workstations, furniture, and exiting paths.
- A current list of personnel who may be within the premises.
- The names of "First Responders," such as a Floor Warden or Bomb Warden.

Evacuation Plans

These are one of the first sets of documents to be prepared by the Crisis Management Team. These documents should include evacuation procedures and checklists.

Types of Evacuations

There are two types of evacuations. The most common type (and the one controlled by building codes) is for fire, including bomb threats, explosions, or similar events. In these situations, everyone must be evacuated from the facility via fire exits and stair towers. A second type of evacuation may be necessitated by an act of nature, such as an earthquake or tornado. In this case, the Crisis Management Team must use their judgment. An earthquake evacuation will likely be similar to a fire evacuation. For example, elevators may be so racked that they will not function, and fire exits and stairs will be used. Falling debris and a weakened structure may dictate a full building evacuation. On the other hand, the safest course of action in a hurricane or tornado event may, in some cases, be to go to a part of the building that is protected from high water, as well as flying glass shards and other wind-blown debris.

Floor or Area Wardens "First Responders"

The floor or area warden's function is to inspect all parts of the area of his or her responsibility to locate damage or fire, or to identify anything unusual that may require further investigation or action.

The First Responder should immediately report all findings to the Chief Security Officer or his deputy, who, in turn, should report to the responding police or fire department. It will be up to the police or fire department to select the next appropriate course of action.

Floor or area wardens should be appointed, along with backup personnel who can be called into action through a PA system, telephone tree, and e-mail. These wardens should have authority to require evacuation, even in the event of drill. (The person who feels that his or her time is too valuable for them to leave may cause others to lose their lives.) All wardens should be well acquainted with their floors or areas and with the floors or areas below or around them. Evacuation routes may be difficult to navigate in darkness or semi-darkness, especially when personnel and the wardens themselves are suffering from shock brought about by an event. Sometimes fire stair towers are blocked or so damaged at floors below that an alternate exit or tower may be the only possible evacuation route. Knowing the evacuation routes for floors below the wardens' designated floors may save lives.

Floor Maps

Floor maps showing offices, rooms, workstations, furniture, and exit paths should be prepared, together with a "people locater," a map with room or space identification that identifies the location of specific individuals. An additional map should be provided that locates physically impaired people who may need special assistance in evacuating. This drawing or map should be prepared even if there are no other existing maps showing the location of all personnel or workstations.

If the facility's security systems have the capability to provide a real-time list of all personnel within the premises, then the Security Department might have sufficient time or Internet capabilities to send this information to their floor wardens so that visitors or guests within the premises can be accounted for. Floor or area wardens should perform a final inspection check before they leave the area in order to ensure that no one has been overlooked or left behind.

After the Event: Preliminary Assessment, Mitigation, and Security Actions

The Crisis Management Team defines the crisis level of an event, and then requests that management empower them to organize a special Recovery Team or Teams to assess the scope of the event and to recommend courses of action. As a matter of practicality, the Crisis Management Team may have already notified the appropriate Recovery Teams when they submitted their initial report and recommendations to management. (Keep in mind that at least one management representative is already a member of the Crisis Management Team and will have contributed his/her observations and recommendations to the plan.)

The first order of business for the Crisis Management Team is to:

- Assess and document what (and/or who) is damaged or destroyed (or injured or lost).
- Determine how to prevent further damage or loss.
- Establish safety conditions for surviving personnel.
- Determine how to establish legal liability safeguards or firewalls.
- Establish a secure environment for surviving assets:
  — Production
  — Services
  — Products

Initial Assessment and Documentation of Damage

The Crisis Management Team must have a plan in place for documenting losses, using video or still photos. If additional damage occurs following the initial event, it, too, should be documented, so it can be readily acknowledged as part of this particular loss. This form of documentation will assist insurance adjusters in assessing and inventorying damaged items. Other aspects of assessment are covered after the next section.

Prevention of Further Damage or Loss

Not all of the damage may have been sustained at the time of the initial event. The contingency crisis plan should provide for prevention of continuing losses, ranging from theft or damage to unprotected intellectual property and hard assets, such as inventories, computers, machinery, or other equipment. Preventive measures could be as straightforward as providing shelter from inclement weather.

Failure to mitigate future losses — including personnel, information, inventories, materials, facilities, and the organization's credibility, stability, and image — can be extremely costly. The Crisis Management Team should consider the need to obtain extra security forces to protect assets. Protection may be needed to prevent collateral damage and injury to members of the organization and to outsiders, especially after the official fire and police services have left the site. At this point, everything is vulnerable. It is also at this point that the Crisis Management Team will be permitted on the site to make an in-depth assessment of the degree of damage sustained, and responses that need to be made. In this initial assessment, the team will identify which departments have been affected, which will determine the Recovery Teams that need to be assembled.

The Overall Assessment Following the initial assessment, a series of further assessments will need to be made. The Recovery Teams should consider:

- Who is qualified and available to assess (and who determines the response to):
  - Present damage?
  - Potential continuing damage?
- Who is missing or unavailable?
  - Who is the immediate replacement or substitute?
  - Who will be the permanent replacement?
- Who is temporarily out-of-action?
  - Who is the immediate replacement or substitute?
  - Who replaces the replacement?
- What equipment or facilities have been destroyed?
  - What equipment is available to be used as the immediate replacement or substitute?
  - If from in-house, what replaces the substituted replacement?
  - What is damaged and temporarily unavailable?
  - What is the immediate replacement or substitute?
  - If from in-house, what replaces this "borrowed" equipment?

These are neither easy nor pleasant questions to answer, but they must be asked to begin the assessment process. Once the Crisis Management Team has completed its review, it will be in a position to provide a fairly accurate and comprehensive report as to the post-event status, and what may be required to maintain and recover the business or operations.

The above list repeatedly suggests replacement of personnel, facilities, and equipment from in-house sources. The presumption that such replacements will be available in-house, especially with the proper skill sets, is only partially valid. Specialists in real estate are probably not available in-house. Facility planners and designers may or may not be available in-house. Substitute shipping and receiving personnel might well be available, or at least brought up to speed quickly. (All department managers should have backup personnel capable of operating their departments at a fair level of competence for at least six weeks.) Basic accounting functions, such as billing and funds receipts, should be defined, personnel delegated, and their duties clarified. In other words, the plan should encompass all functions required to maintain basic business cash flow. There should be lists of substitute workers who are at least informed of their potential responsibilities. Basic "how to" procedures should be pre-defined for them. Some functions, such as real estate, furniture, equipment, and supply searches, probably should be outsourced to capable firms. For example, the organization might contract:

- Real estate brokers who are familiar with the locations that the plan might consider as acceptable.
- Architects, engineers, and interior design teams familiar with the non-functioning facilities.
- Furniture and equipment vendors or suppliers with whom the organization is currently doing business.

These firms' functions, names, addresses, telephone numbers (multiple, with alternates), and e-mail addresses should be completely documented in advance as part of the recovery plan.

Communications

The recovery plan should address the establishment of communications after an event, including:

- Recovery Teams
- Internal Personnel and Operations

They must provide for communication among the organization's personnel, and with its customers and the public.

The Crisis Management Plan or contingency plan has recognized that the two most probable areas of loss from a physical event are likely to be personnel and hard assets, including normal loss of communication. Operations may have to be sustained for a period of time without computerized data systems by reverting to hard copy documents and processes. Since many telephone Private Branch Exchange (PBX) systems today are run by computer systems through a data interface, the crisis management plan must also consider the loss of both telephone and e-mail. If the facility is located in a major metropolitan area, Personal Communication Service (PCS) wireless telephones can probably be secured for the short term. While digital service is fundamentally secure and reliable compared to the older analog systems (which are not at all secure), their broadcast range is considerably shorter than analog. Digital service is becoming the standard for so-called cellular service, and as more transmission towers are built, it is becoming the system of preference. A public address system might be another appropriate solution for temporary communications.

Telecom and Datacom The first order of business must be to provide communications systems for the Recovery Team. Along with a physical space in which the teams can meet and function, they must also have communication systems in the form of wireless phones and computer connections. Other personnel will also require as much of a communication system as possible. As previously mentioned, many current phone systems are run through a data interface with the computer systems, which may have been destroyed or disabled in an event. In addition, infrastructure cable systems for both Telecom and Datacom may have be destroyed or damaged. These conditions may require temporary restoration of business phone communication via various wireless PCS systems and highly powerful remote access, which once installed, can function as effectively and more cost-efficiently than most land line systems, such as evolving wireless broadband Internet platforms like Motorola's© Canopy system (http://motorola.com./canopy).

The organization's Information Technology (IT) group has most likely put in place backup systems for its data, along with a backup-processing site. The challenge for the Recovery Team and IT will be providing the desktop or user level of service. IT will likely be capable of acquiring new desktop hardware and bringing it up to operating status (together with cabling for both Telecom and Datacom). However, they may have to rely on the Infrastructure Recovery Team for electrical power — hopefully with backup uninterruptible power supply (UPS) and emergency power supply (EPS) systems, and the necessary mechanical systems to prevent the local data and telephone systems from overheating.

Cleanup and Salvage

This phase follows documentation of damage and involves several different types of specialists and activities, including:

- Insurance review, damage inspection, and claims adjustments.
- Recovery and preservation of valuable materials and documents.
- Reconstruction of the facility.
- Disposal of rubble.
  — Contaminated materials:
    – Who must assess and determine requirements?
    – What permits must be obtained?
    – Where must the materials be transported?
  — Non-contaminated debris:
    – What permits must be obtained?
    – Where can it be disposed?

Cleaning up the mess is not as simple as getting a contractor in to provide dumpsters or trucks and hauling the debris away. There is a strong probability of insurance claims, and insurance companies may be slow to review the damage. The team may have to bring in some fairly high-powered members of senior management to encourage insurance adjusters to take a quick look at the damage. The organization's own risk management department should become involved early to make sure no actions are taken that could negatively impact insurance claims. The risk management experts will have the first-hand relationships with the organization's insurance carriers and can probably ensure quicker action.

The organization's health and safety personnel should be involved with the actual cleanup process, which includes checking all debris, by area and type, for contaminated or toxic materials. If they are not directly equipped for this task, they should employ professional, licensed inspectors who can perform the necessary survey and provide reports and cleanup, and/or supervision or direction for the cleanup. These professionals should also be able to provide guidance on any dump-required sorting of debris. There are disposal contractors who can provide this guidance, perform the sorting work, and secure the necessary dumping permits.

If there are real contamination issues, professional, licensed remediation specialists should be engaged. Many remediation companies employ extremely knowledgeable staffs and may be able to respond much faster and at lower cost than others. During the cleanup process, it is important to be aware of airborne dust and materials that are off-gassed as a result of either combustion or material fracture. Dust (readily visible during and after the 9/11 disaster, for example) poses a potential health hazard and requires the use of dust masks and/or appropriate breathing apparatus. (We are beginning to learn that most ancient Egyptians died of one of two diseases, one of which was the result of windborne dust.)

Keeping the Business or Objective Alive and Maintaining Cash Flow

Customer Service The objective of the recovery plans is safeguarding employees or occupants and keeping the business, mission, or endeavor running. The single most important objective, in terms of maintaining the business, is to continue to maintain customer service. It is the people who deal with inventories, raw materials, parts, components, finished goods, and or services who must assess the disruption and determine how best to continue customer service. In developing a business resumption and recovery plan, it makes little difference how the disruption was created — natural disaster, fire, or building collapse — the plan should anticipate various degrees of disruption at different points in the production or delivery system, and how to cope with them. The plan should also anticipate the possibility that regular personnel might not be available, and what to do about backup personnel or substitutes.

Customer service may involve multiple-department activity. Account executives and managers should begin contacting customers as soon as possible, providing reassurance that the customers' needs will be taken care of as soon as physically possible. Honesty is critical in dealing with customers, as it is in addressing the media. If it will not be possible to provide product or service to customers, they should be so informed, so that they might find an alternate, interim source. Assistance might even be offered in finding a source. After all, who knows the competition better? Customers may, in the future, remember that act of assistance and the company's concern for their interests.

Keeping the business alive involves maintaining these functions:

- Shipping, receiving, and/or service
- Cash flow, billing, and cash receipts
- Inventory control or supply chain management
  - Finished goods inventory—customer service
  - Work in process
  - Assembled product components
  - On-hand product parts
  - Raw materials
  - Customer service replacement parts

Cash Flow The next most critical concern after customer service may be maintaining cash flow, especially if the computer systems are out of service. Fortunately, invoicing or billing is near the end of the business-operational sequence and can be readily adapted to a manual system with good controls, even if it is a bit more cumbersome and comparatively slow. If necessary, new forms can be purchased from office supply sources or designed and printed at a commercial copy center. Bank lock box systems can be established in a matter of hours as a substitute for in-house payment receipts. Most importantly, cash flow is needed to continue operations. The plan should anticipate a disruption at any point or points in the service and delivery process. Backup measures should be planned to access customer names and address, prepare and deliver invoices, and collect receivables—without access to the normal Datacom systems.

Payroll and Accounts Receivable and Payable Payroll is likely to be a high priority. This requires determining who is working and who is not. Next in line would be accounts receivable and accounts payable. To feed accounts receivable, billings must be processed as soon as possible after products or service are in the delivery pipeline. These functions can all be performed manually. The controller can select which accounts to bill first, those to press for payment, and those that can wait. Financial personnel should be in touch with the organization's bankers and lenders to keep them up to date with the cash flow management methods being used, as well as any problems. The bank may be of help in collecting a slow receivable through its direct contacts.

Inventory Management Inventory, or Supply Chain, Management, should be made aware of its critical role in keeping the business operating. Stocking activities should be accelerated, and finished goods (bin) inventory level data should be maintained as current as possible. The organization's survival may depend on the extent to which customer needs can be met out of inventory stocks. Production, if still in working order, may have to move from EOQ (Economic Order Quantity) production to shorter lead times at the expense of higher production costs. Shipping and Receiving must be aware that delays related to use of a favorite carrier or a better rate may detract from customer service.

Media Relations

Post-event media relations functions include the following:

1. Work with Public Relations and Legal departments to prepare media news releases.
2. Be available as quickly as possible to the media.
3. Be candid.
4. Try to be helpful.
5. Try to establish specific times of availability for answering questions.
6. Try to establish a specific location for the media to congregate.
7. Do not lose control.

The recovery plan should include a process for conveying to whatever public may have an interest, the most up-to-date and complete information available. Individuals skilled in public presentation should be fully and truthfully briefed on the present status of the incident and what may be expected in the near future. These representatives should be available to respond to questions and make public statements. Public Relations expert Michael Strick, commenting on Arthur Andersen's initial handling of some of its actions related to the Enron disclosures, said, "The silence was deafening early on, and when you don't say anything, the media tends to fill the vacuum. You're letting other people define you."

Johnson & Johnson's handling of the 1982 Tylenol® tampering situation is a classic example of an immediate, clear, and candid public relations response to an extremely serious problem. Company spokespersons quickly went public with as much information as they apparently possessed. Their prompt and continued presence before the media and public brought reassurance and rapidly defused what might have been a public relations disaster. It may be possible to cloud an issue in front of one or two reporters, but sooner or later, enough questions will be asked to begin to expose the facts. If a company stonewalls too long and too hard so that the true facts are sufficiently obscured, the media will begin to invent "possible" facts, which will likely be far more damaging than the real ones. It is important to remember that shareholders, creditors, vendors, providers, employees, and their families may also rely on the media for their information. Provide up-to-date information quickly and clearly and most of all, truthfully.

Television and newspaper reporters are often generalists, usually with minimal knowledge of a particular business or organization. As a result, some of their questions may seem naïve, ill-considered, or even offensive. A patient, helpful approach is best, as reporters attempt to do their jobs. Again, a candid response is best, even when there is no answer because the information is not yet available. It is important not to lose control of the media situation. The organization does have control, since it is the source of most of information the media receives. If a reporter has uncovered information of which the organization spokesperson is not aware, it is best to admit that this was not known and ask for that person's help on the subject in exchange for provision of exclusive follow-up information on that particular item.

It is recommended that a specific location be established where the media can congregate for information updates at designated times. This conveys to them a sense of stature and respect. Most importantly, it helps keep them from wandering around the site and questioning people who are not equipped to respond, taking undesirable photographs, or putting themselves at risk. News stories often focus on conflict, loss, damage, or injury. Any sort of physical event is probably worth a picture or two. The organization's media representative might offer to conduct a tour through safe areas where photographs of sensitive materials are not likely to be taken.

A Word of Warning In making public statements or answering questions, the balance between candor and liability exposure can be difficult. Only authorized personnel should respond to questions from any source or issue statements. Public Relations and Legal departments should be involved in preparation of media news releases.

Customer Service, Vendor, and Financial Services Communications

1. Set up hotline communications with customers and vendors. Be candid about the situation.
2. Try to immediately determine:
   — What do the customers need?
   — What do the customers want?

— How can the organization continue to serve their needs and wants?

— How quickly can services or products be provided?

3. Advise vendors of production or service needs.

— When can they expect to be able to deliver to the organization?

— When can they expect payment on existing receivables?

— When might they expect payment on new orders?

— What are they to do with material or supplies in the supply chain, which the organization cannot use or even receive?

4. Advise lenders of circumstances, conditions, and recovery plans.

— Is the organization going to be able to meet its current debt service obligations?

— If not now, when?

— If a date cannot yet be determined, when will the organization have a plan to submit to its lenders?

Infrastructure

Determine whether temporary or replacement facilities are required for:

- Office Space
- Warehousing
- Shipping and Receiving
- Rail Sidings, Ship Docks, Roadways, etc.
- Production
- Equipment
- Supplies

Infrastructure Replacement Once the Crisis Management and Recovery Teams have competed their assessments, they should know whether the organization can continue business in the same location or site by doubling up during reconstruction, or whether it is necessary to find replacement space. The plan must consider that various portions of a facility or facilities may not be suitable for occupancy or may not exist at all. This leaves a few questions:

- How much space will be required to service the organization's needs?
- Will the new space be temporary, or will it become the organization's new home?
- Where can it be located to be able to continue to serve the organization's needs?

- Is such a space available in the locations required?
- Who will provide this information and conduct the search?

If there is a facilities manager on staff, and therefore on the Infrastructure Recovery Team, this person should be able to produce a needs analysis defining the organization's relocation space requirements. Whether this new space is temporary or permanent is one of the first recommendations that the Crisis Management Team must make—and make almost immediately. The organization should have an established relationship with a commercial real estate broker (either through prior business dealings or through a peer recommendation). The team will need to turn to this person to help locate suitable replacement space.

Once space has been located, a determination must be made of modifications required to render it suitable for the organization's requirements. Most organizations do not have designers, architects, and engineers in-house with the staffing hours necessary to produce such plans. As with the commercial real estate broker, it pays to have an existing relationship with a design group that possesses the necessary mechanical, electrical, and plumbing engineering staff to produce construction documents for the replacement space.

The next big question is whether the organization can afford the cost of the relocation space, and how they will pay for it. Insurance proceeds may be slow in coming for two reasons: one, insurance adjusters need to verify the degree of loss and determine whether the insurance company is indeed liable. All of this analysis takes time. Secondly, insurance companies tend to be slow to pay. In the meantime, the organization must attempt to get back into operation and commit to new space and design costs.

If the physical loss is substantial, the organization's bank may be reluctant to advance lines of credit while its very survival is unknown. The Crisis Management Plans should foresee this dilemma and attempt to work out lines of credit secured by insurance proceeds and through prior settlement discussions with insurance carriers. Lastly, a senior management member of the Crisis Management Team should be empowered to either make or secure financial commitment decisions with little or no delay.

Documentation of Infrastructure Design and Construction

Since the objective is getting the organization back into operation as quickly as possible, actions need to be taken promptly, and it is important to record as much information as possible as it is developed. During the mitigation and reconstruction process, the organization will be working within very close time lines. The process of programming, schematic design, design development, and construction documents will probably be severely curtailed or limited. The Infrastructure Recovery Team is likely to engage an architectural or engineering firm to prepare construction drawings as quickly as possible, and the usual thoughtful process of developing plans and documents will be abbreviated. A great deal of information will be conveyed orally. Architects and designers will be working from quick site reviews and possibly landlord's space plans, which are often out of date. The organization's usual furniture and fixtures sources may not be quickly available. Substitute furniture and other materials may have to be ordered from whatever sources are available. Mistakes may be made, and the end product may not be built or furnished to the preferred level of satisfaction.

Inasmuch as haste was required, all decisions made should be recorded—with as much information as possible—as they occur. All attendees to meetings, however brief or seemingly routine, should make notes of their interpretations of what was discussed, and particularly what decisions were made. Copies of all notes should be maintained in one binder, by date. Sketches detailing work should also be maintained in binders or files, by date. All drawings used for actual construction or furnishing should be carefully maintained. Drawings that have been superseded with revised versions should be marked as "Superseded,"or should be destroyed. Modifications, additions, or changes (MACs) must be tracked either through a Change Order Log or through the "Notes" binder. These documents will become the only link to work actually performed. Conversion to a Computer-Aided Facilities Management (CAFM) system, such as Aperture™, will depend on maintaining complete and accurate documents. Even if it is not possible to utilize a CAFM system, these documents are invaluable as archival information as to not only what was done, but why. They must not be lost, which means not loaning them out, or leaving them in the sun where they will fade (http://www.aperture.com).

Stabilization, Reorganization, Re-Growth, and the Apocalyptic (or Revelation) Syndrome

Whether planning for a minor interruption or a major catastrophe, contingency response planning is a matter of determining where the organization's efforts, and its surviving assets and personnel, can be best used or will be most needed. The next step in developing the Crisis Management Plan is determining how to stabilize business operations. In planning, it is not possible to know how severe the damage to operations may be or how long it may to take return to the pre-event activity level.

It is interesting to note that once a major disruptive event has occurred, most businesses never return to precisely the same organization they were just prior to the event. Once the business or operation is stabilized, senior management may react to an apocalyptic experience with a major revelation. The normal evolution of a business is more often a matter of adding more, and sometimes better, ways of providing products or services to customers. When existing resources are destroyed or severely damaged, senior management will frequently ask questions, such as "Why were we running our business this way?" and will be inclined to examine possible long-term changes. Sustaining operations in what was anticipated to be a short-term condition may turn out to be a transition to a substantially changed or even a totally new method of doing business. Stabilization of operations may not only begin the recovery process, but could be the beginning of a substantially modified endeavor.

Senior management's assessment will include these questions:

- How secure are we?
- How financially strong are we?
- Where do we go from here?
- How do we get there?
- What resources will we have to commit?
- Do we have the wherewithal to make the commitment?

What Now?

The Crisis Management Team's assessment report and recommendations to senior management will evoke serious and immediate questions, as they should. Senior management should have information about market forecasts (anticipated growth or shrinkage). They will possess sensitive knowledge of the organization's current financial condition. They should be aware of the organization's key personnel longevity, cost, and opportunities for replacement or elimination of positions. All of this information must be weighed and balanced prior to committing to a Recovery Plan, and it must be done quickly. Senior management must make the hard decisions, i.e., go ahead as planned, cancel the recovery plan, shrink back, or delay (including whether they can afford to delay and think it over).

Once management has approved a Recovery Plan and activated the Recovery Teams, to some extent they have committed substantial funds, time, and the efforts of many supportive individuals. Stopping in midstream to reverse course or even substantially change direction could result in significant loss of funds and a major decline in morale. Worse, such an action may suggest that management does not know what they are doing.

Teams and Teaming

Because the Work Teams, such as the Crisis Management Team and the Recovery Teams (Infrastructure and Departmental), will be critical to the organization's recovery and future, the following section offers some guidelines on expectations of groups and teams, and what makes them effective. Both groups and teams will be needed to create, document, and gain approval for the organization's Crisis and Recovery Plans. The Crisis Management Team will be a true team, as will the Infrastructure Recovery Team and Departmental Recovery Teams.

Work Groups Versus Teams

Work Groups lack the specific definition and accountability of teams, which are held accountable for their collective performance. Groups are frequently called upon to give advice, render opinions, or prepare contingency plans, or procedures, among the first objectives in creating a plan. Work Groups are more like councils, assembled to provide consultation or deliberation. Work Teams are more like committees with defined roles, such as investigating, considering, reporting, deciding, and then acting on a matter.

As outlined in the first part of this chapter, Departmental Work or Planning Groups (also called Recovery Planning Groups) are essential to the preparation and continued viability of the Crisis Management Plan. They possess detailed knowledge of their particular departments' responsibilities and functions and must generate and regularly update plans for its continued operation in the event of a major disruption. These groups must try to anticipate what sort of losses of facilities, equipment, operations, and personnel may occur. They must also select personnel to be members of the Departmental Recovery Team, and must select substitute, or backup members, in the event that the originally selected Recovery Team members are no longer available. The Departmental Planning Groups must also empower the Recovery Team members and assist the Teams during the recovery process.

Teamwork

Teamwork is critically important to any enterprise. It is an attitude and the practice of working together. While members of senior management may frequently refer to themselves as the "Management Team," more often than not, they are not really a team. What they are saying is that they try to get along well together and that they frequently communicate with one another on matters of strategy. However, their individual and assigned objectives are separate and too general to qualify them as a focused work team. All teams must employ teamwork. But merely practicing teamwork may not accomplish the end result.

The Work Team

The Work Team is a specific group that may consist of between 3–30 or more members, depending on the size of the organization, assembled to perform a specific function. They will have compatible, but not necessarily the same skills. Together, they will define their specific purpose. They will establish particular tasks and goals required to achieve their stated plan or purpose. They will elect a specific approach or approaches toward their purpose. Most significantly, they will establish a mutual respect for one another's skills, motives, and personal beliefs. They will become mutually accountable for the Team's performance. Because Work Teams are comprised of people with different skills, backgrounds, and personalities, their compositions and characteristics cannot be absolutely defined. There are, however, some fairly well agreed-upon criteria for a Work Team:

- A specific purpose or goal.
- Team disciplines: meeting rules, conduct, and often leadership.
- Skills needed to achieve their goal. (If they do not possess these skills, they must figure out how to secure them.)
- Knowledge (or sources to obtain needed information) required to achieve their goal.
- Their collective abilities to recognize ideas, which will result in Team wisdom.
- A "team" mentality of joint and individual support.

The Team will develop and implement a clearly defined "plan of attack." They will constantly be aware of what the plan is, how it is being performed, and whether it needs modification in order to continue on track. Because they can only guess what a potential disaster might be or how or where it will affect the organization, it is vital that the Recovery Teams be capable of developing their specific Recovery procedures (ad hoc) to match the specific damages. They must be capable of modifying the defined procedures or plans, "on the fly," to adapt to new or changing conditions.

Finally, a Work Team will develop a team mentality of joint and individual support and accountability. This mutual interaction will result in a feeling of personal satisfaction, in working together to get the job done.

Putting Together an Effective Work Team

Work Teams are not self-appointed. They do not just start up on their own. The Crisis Management Team will have identified Infrastructure and the appropriate Departmental Recovery Teams to address the recovery task. Selecting compatible people is critical to any Team's potential for success. Random appointments may lead to random results.

It is also important to define the Team's "reason for being." What does the team organizer expect the team to accomplish? What is its purpose? Is the anticipated result realistic, or merely "eyewash" to satisfy a request to do something? Only through desktop, or "tabletop," rehearsals or practice is it possible to know whether the Recovery Teams will be capable of accomplishing the defined objectives. When forming a team, always ask the hard question, "Is this a team for the sake of having a team, or is it truly empowered to do the job?"

Selecting Team Members Team members should possess relevant cross-functional backgrounds, have necessary and complementary skills—technical and communications—and have a demonstrated capacity to be mutually accountable to fellow team members.

Team Rules and Conduct: Defining the Purpose and Executing the Plan Teams must establish their own rules of team conduct, both structural (for example, when to meet and where) and cultural (e.g., how to deal with idea exchange, roadblocks, or lack of performance by a team member). They should come to an understanding of the need to undertake equal shares of the work. Although management may have provided the team with a mandate for its purpose, it will be up to the team to execute the plan, so they must fully recognize their purpose. As team members, they must come to feel accountability for each other and for the team as a whole.

The Team Environment

Team members are apt to be working at a greater than normal energy level to meet their task and should be provided with the best available physical environment in which to perform their work. The organization's attitude toward the team should be hospitable, despite the fact that the conclusions they reach might conflict with the opinions of many in management, as well as some employees. The team may produce a plan that requires changes in methods of doing business. They may find that it is necessary to completely restructure some procedures and production techniques in order to achieve their objectives.

Team Leadership and Facilitators

The person who articulates the plan or purpose may or may not remain as the organizer, team leader, or facilitator, and may not even remain a member of the team. The team members often select the team leader or facilitator. Or, the team leader or facilitator may rise to this role by virtue of superior skills or experience. The role may be handed off from one team member to another as the team's emphasis shifts, or as progress is made from one stage to another.

The team leader or facilitator should have knowledge of the organization's specific business recovery plan or purpose. This individual knows that he or she does not have all the answers and should be able and willing to function as an equal team member. Patience, leadership, motivational skills, dedication to the purpose and the team, and superior communications skills are all required for this position. The team leader should never point the finger of blame, but on the other hand, should not excuse a shortfall in performance.

Crisis Management Example

The Event

Plant 4, a cereal production and distribution facility operated by the Yum-Yum Food Company in Corntown, Iowa was totally destroyed by fire, possibly the result of a grain dust explosion in an adjacent grain silo. This plant produces 50% of the Yum-Yum Corporation's mini-package cereals, which contribute 30% of its gross income. Without this plant's contribution, the company could have a continuing operating loss, which could force it to shut down or face bankruptcy. Corporate headquarters are in Chicago, Illinois, where all accounting (including payroll and purchasing), Datacom, product research, sales and marketing, and long-term purchasing commitments are handled.

The Corntown plant was self-contained, to the extent that it performed its own:

- Grain, sugar, and other food component scheduling, and supply line and inventory control required for all cereal production.
- Packaging and miscellaneous materials purchasing, supply line, and inventory control.
- Production scheduling and staffing, and plant and machinery maintenance.
- Shipping and traffic control, based on orders and order scheduling received from Chicago.

Chicago calculated payrolls, based on daily time sheet data transmitted from Corntown via the company data network. However, actual payroll check-writing and related deposits were handled by Corntown.

Corntown has a small LAN facility and employs about 16 office employees, including the local general manager.

Accounts receivable and payable were handled by Chicago, based on purchase order and shipping and receiving document data received from Corntown via its Internet platform. Because Yum-Yum prepared and sold considerable foodstuffs in the form of individual packages of cereal to the U.S. government, it had a fairly active and involved security department, including a small security staff in Corntown.

Damage

The two-story, 200,000 S.F. production building containing 7,000 S.F. of office space was completely destroyed. The rail sidings and loading docks appear to be intact. Truck docks, ramps, and parking lots are intact, although primary and secondary electrical switchgear and lead circuits are damaged or destroyed. Site water and sewage are damaged at the surface, but may be intact underground. Primary electric service (lines, transformers, and disconnects) from the utility is a total loss. All telephone service has been lost or destroyed. Service loops from the power utility and telephone company are intact at their nearby manholes. Underground natural gas lines are intact, but all regulators and aboveground piping has been destroyed.

Sunday, August 6th

Shortly after the second shift, around 6:00 PM on Sunday, August 6th, there was a large explosion in one of five adjacent grain silos. It is presumed that the resulting fire spread across and through the roof of the adjacent old production building. The building was not equipped with a sprinkler system. Because the explosion acted as a warning, the only personnel still working in the building Sunday evening were able to evacuate. There were no deaths or injuries. The building was fully involved before the local fire department could reach the site. Local television, radio, and newspaper reporters were on the scene prior to the fire being brought under control. At this time, 11:30 PM, the fire is still smoldering in spots and is under the jurisdiction of the local fire department. No personnel other than fire and police are allowed on the site. The fire department states that it may be able to release the site by 12:00 PM on August 7th. Local and state fire inspectors are at the site trying to determine the cause of the explosion and resulting fire.

The Response in Corntown

Both Corntown and Chicago have well-defined and trained Crisis Management Teams. At 3:30 AM Monday, August 7th, the Corntown plant General Manager telephoned the Chief Security Officer in Chicago to inform him of the event and the current status. Because the Corntown plant has a limited security staff, the plant GM acts as the leader for the Corntown Crisis Management Team. The Corntown GM also began a process of notifying all Corntown plant employees through the use of a pre-established telephone tree, that only specific employees should report to the plant site, and then only when told to do so.

The Response in Chicago

The Chief Security Officer (CSO) immediately notified the Chicago Crisis Management Team, Senior Management Representative, that he, the CSO, was declaring that a major disaster had occurred at the Corntown facility. It was incumbent on the Senior Management Representative to notify all relevant senior management personnel. The CSO also called for all Crisis Management Team members to meet at 8:00 Monday morning, August 7th, at which time they began disaster assessment (as understood by the Chicago office), and began assembling the Chicago-based Infrastructure and Departmental Recovery Teams. (The Departmental Recovery Team members needed to address this particular event were selected from the representatives originally chosen by the Departmental Recovery Planning Groups in the planning phase.) These Team members had to address both Chicago-based departmental functions and the functions normally handled in Corntown that could not be performed there at this time. While Corntown had a plant and equipment maintenance staff, it did not possess personnel skilled in real estate or facilities planning and management. These skills had to be provided by the Chicago standing Infrastructure Recovery Team.

Monday, August 7th

On Monday morning, the Corntown GM had his Datacom/Telecom acquire 15 PCS phones with direct link capabilities and established a series of mobile phone numbers for him, other local personnel, and those individuals who might be arriving from Chicago. He called the manager of Chicago Telecom and advised him of the Corntown assigned numbers, names, and functions. On Monday evening, the Chicago office advised the Corntown GM that they would be sending an Infrastructure Recovery Team and a Departmental Recovery Team to Corntown on Tuesday, the 8th. They requested a block of rooms and a conference room at the local Corntown motel, beginning on Tuesday for an as-yet undetermined time.

Tuesday, August 8th

The Chicago facilities manager had called Des Moines and secured the services of a structural engineer who was to meet him in Corntown on Wednesday morning.

Wednesday, August 9th

By Wednesday morning, all four teams were in Corntown. The representative from Chicago Purchasing met with the Corntown representative to begin the process of shutting down the supply chain by stopping all shipments to Corntown of grain, sugar, and other foodstuffs, as well as packaging materials and other goods. The Chicago purchasing department also began a process of trying to assist vendors who were prepared to ship or had already shipped product to Corntown, to recall their products and to find alternate customers or temporary storage facilities for those already-committed goods. Chicago purchasing also arranged to transfer the existing grain in the remaining four silos to other Yum-Yum production facilities as soon as silo space became available.

Both the Chicago-based PR representative and the locally engaged PR company spokesperson called a press conference Wednesday for 1:00 PM. They told the reporters what the fire inspectors had told them — that it appeared that the fire started as a result of a grain dust explosion in the Number 2 grain silo and spread to the production plant. They relayed the fact that there were no injuries or deaths, that the explosion appeared to be spontaneous, and that there were no reasons to think that the explosion was the result of mischief or hostility.

At 11:00 AM, the structural engineer from Des Moines arrived and met with the facilities manager from Chicago. While touring the site, the structural engineer expressed concern over the probable condition of the old building's exterior and interior foundation walls. She took samples of the blackened concrete foundations to tested in Des Moines for integrity. The engineer and the facilities manager both noticed what appeared to be asbestos around the inside perimeter of the building, and surmised that it might have been from old steam-heating pipe insulation. Although not in the structural engineer's area of specialty, she took a sample back to Des Moines for testing at the same lab as the concrete sample.

A Chicago-based Risk Management representative engaged a local professional photographer to shoot video, and black and white and color still photographs of the entire site, copies of which were to be made available to the insurance adjusters on their arrival.

On Wednesday morning, the Corntown Security Officer contacted a local fencing company to install a chain-link fence around the entire destroyed plant and silo site, with three sets of truck gates and man-gates, secured with forged-link chains and padlocks. The fencing company arrived on site at 4:30 PM and installed all fencing, placing it 20' outside of the destroyed building perimeter.

Monday, August 13th

The Des Moines structural engineer called the Chicago facilities manager in Corntown to report that lab tests confirmed that damage to the foundation walls was such that they could not be reused. In addition, the suspected asbestos material proved to be asbestos.

A conference call that afternoon between the facilities management representative in Corntown and the remediation and demolition contractors in Des Moines indicated that little, if any, demolition work could begin until the asbestos had been removed under the jurisdiction of the federal and Iowa Environmental Protection Agencies and the local County Fire Marshall.

The remediation contractor indicated that, given the need for permitting and the contractor's present commitments, no remediation could begin for at least 30 days. He predicted that the remediation would take a minimum of 60, and more likely 90 days.

The risk management representative reported that discussions with the HELP Insurance Company's adjustment division indicated that adjusters could be on the site in one week, and that they should be able to complete their review within the 30-day demolition permitting period.

The demolition contractor indicated that their work could begin as soon as the remediation contractor is off the job, and that the demolition would take about 60 days, and possibly as long as 90 days.

The senior management representative reported to Chicago that it appeared that no rebuilding work could commence before six months, or about February or March of the following year. Chicago reported that it would respond to Corntown by Friday morning, August 17th.

Tuesday, August 14th

Chicago telephoned its facilities manager and production manager in Corntown and requested that they contact Plant Construction, Inc., a Cleveland, Ohio design/build construction company that specialized in processing plants. The Corntown General Manager and Production Manager, along with the Chicago Facilities Manager and the Chicago Production Manager, were asked to describe the type of plant that Yum-Yum wished to have built and where, and to find out how long it would take to produce construction drawings and to build the plant, once authorized. Plant Construction representatives agreed to send a team to Corntown that night to review the situation and to provide Yum-Yum with a tentative plan.

Wednesday, August 16th

At 7:30 AM, the Plant Construction team, including an architect, a structural engineer, a mechanical-electrical engineer, and a process engineer, met the two senior management representatives from Chicago and Corntown — the facilities manager and the production manager. The Plant Construction team felt that it could produce a similar plant, equipped with state-of the-art material handling, mixing, cooking, and baking and packaging equipment using a design/build, fast-track system in 14 months, once the pad site was cleared and ready for work. The new plant would be a bit smaller due to higher-speed production equipment and would be more flexible in what it could produce, package, and ship.

The difficulty seemd to be with the six months required for remediation and demolition of the existing site, which would extend the project out to 20 months. This would put the plant into production in about April or May two years off. That afternoon, the information was relayed to Chicago by the Chicago and Corntown management representatives.

Thursday, August 17th

Chicago Senior Management telephoned the management representatives in Corntown to convey the fact that April or May of the year after next would be too late to prevent a probable bankruptcy for the company. They asked if there was any way the new plant could be put into production earlier. Chicago management cancelled their Friday call.

Chicago Risk Management conferred with their casualty insurance carriers to get a reading on how long it would take to arrive at a settlement. The carrier suggested that it might take up to six months. The Chicago chief financial officer conferred with Yum-Yum's commercial and investment bankers. The commercial bank agreed to advance a line of credit to be used for rebuilding the Corntown plant, using an assignment of the insurance proceeds as collateral. These funds could be available within 45 days.

Friday, August 18th

The ad hoc team of the two senior management representatives, the production manager, and the plant construction team members met. The Plant Construction architect suggested that a great deal of time could be saved if the new plant could be built on a different site. The team reviewed the site drawings and concluded that if the new plant were built on the existing employee parking lot, together with two small residential properties on one side of the site, and the new plant designed in a more square rather than rectangular configuration, the total construction time might be reduced by six months or more. The team documented their plan with a written description and a copy of the site plan with the new plant sketched on it. The plan showed the two properties that would need to be acquired, a straightening of the rail spur, and relocation of the existing employee parking area to the cleaned-up old plant site. The Chicago senior management representative and the Chicago Facilities Manager conveyed the plan back to Chicago, where it was presented to senior management over the weekend.

The Period from Saturday August 19th to Friday the 25th

Chicago senior management reviewed the Corntown plan and approved it on condition that Yum-Yum's bankers likewise approve. However, senior management added a strong request that the new production equipment be capable of producing a new complete-breakfast bar, in development in the company test kitchens, in addition to the present cereal product line. During the normal business week, the Corntown team and the CFO met with the bankers and their consultants, reviewing the plan and the qualifications of Plant Construction, Inc. The bank approved the plan on their condition that the facility would be operating by the end of next year, and that Yum-Yum's Recovery Budget funds would cover the cost of a lender's representative to monitor all commitments and job progress.

Monday August 28th to Friday September 1st

The Corntown team returned to Corntown and contacted a local realtor, asking him to make "above-market" offers to both of the owners of the properties needed for the new plant construction. By the end of the week of September 1st, both properties were under contract. The local attorney representing Yum-Yum was expediting the closing, had met with the Corntown zoning board, and had received assurances that re-zoning the two properties would pose no difficulties. He had also traveled to Des Moines to ask the State Economic Development Board for assistance in expediting the various approval processes required for plant construction.

The Chicago Facilities Manager contacted Plant Construction in Cleveland and advised them to proceed with the preparation of both construction documents and a list of contractors and suppliers needed to construct and equip the new plant.

The Chicago public relations representative met with the local public relations individuals and prepared a news report to be released to local media first, and then to national media, as soon as the two small residential properties being acquired had been transferred.

The Chicago Crisis Emergency Recovery Structure

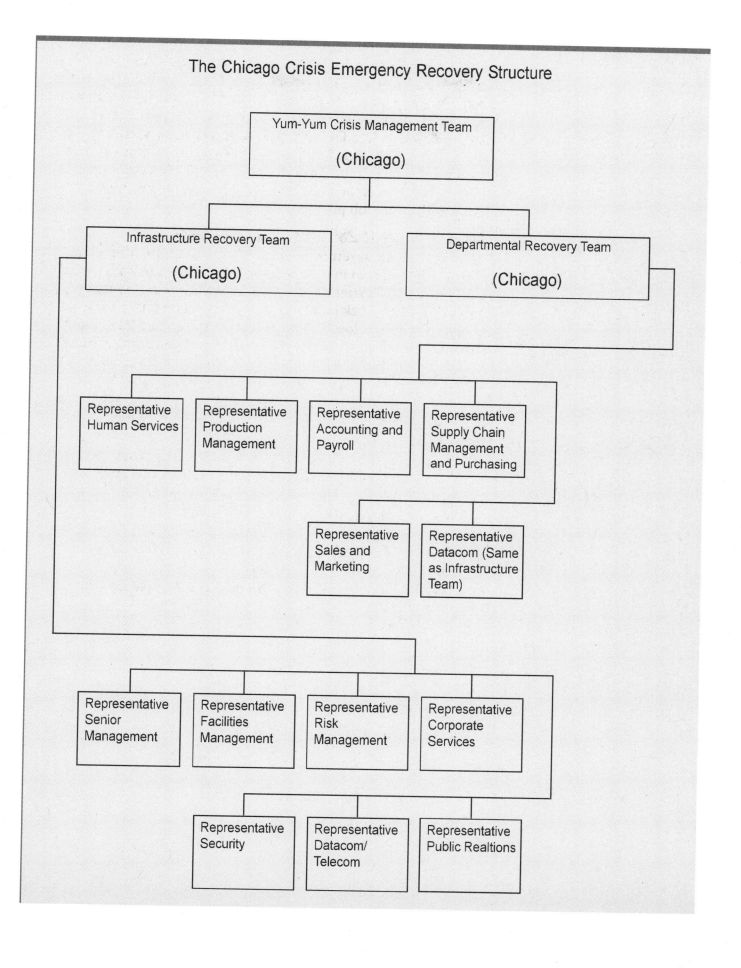

The Corntown Crisis Emergency Recovery Structure

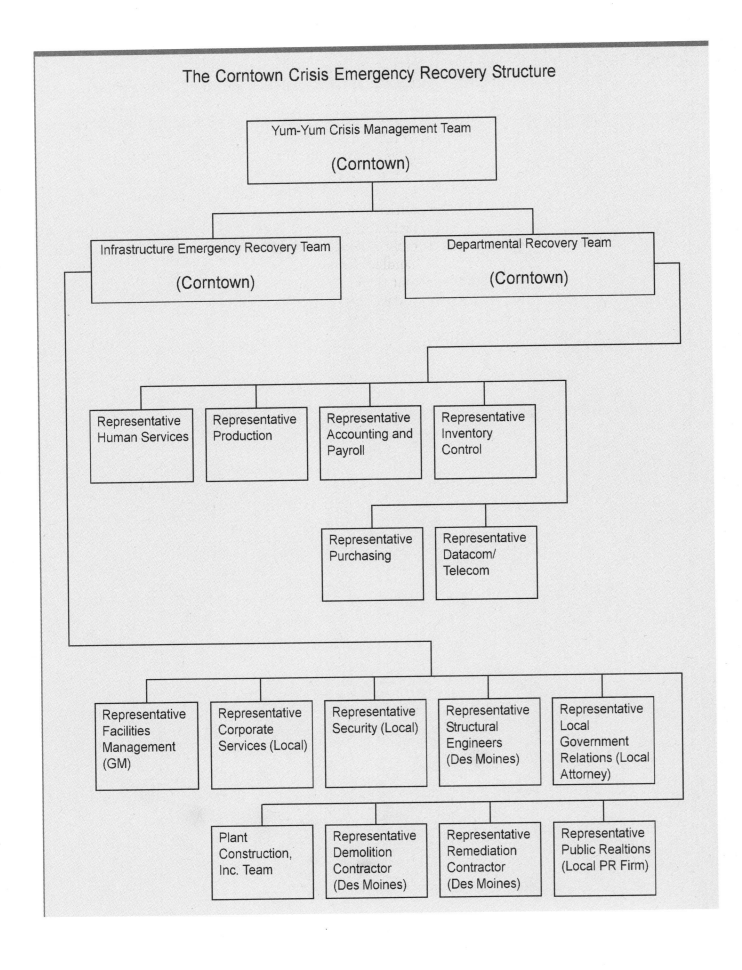

Conclusion

The preceding example has been prepared to demonstrate the ebb and flow of team events, participation, and leadership in a crisis. What started out as four separate teams from two different locations and functions (and quite possibly, different business cultures), quickly merged into what became one highly flexible team. Team members were added on an as-needed basis; others dropped out as their objectives were accomplished. Team leadership shifted from one team member to another as team assessments were developed, and new objectives were defined. The capabilities and special knowledge the Yum-Yum Team members lacked, they sought out. With their public relations announcement, the most urgent parts of the Crisis Management had been handled. Reconstruction would not be easy or without problems, but the crisis had been dealt with, and the balance of the Recovery was execution of the plan.

[1] *The American Heritage Dictionary*, 4th Edition. Houghton Mifflin, 2000.

Chapter Five

Security through Planning, Design, and Operations

Not all security requires the use of guards or detection devices. Security-conscious design and space planning can substantially protect both personnel and facilities. This concept applies to modifications to existing facilities, as well as new construction. This chapter addresses some design approaches that can assist in an overall security plan.

It may be helpful to first establish definitions that distinguish planning from design, since these terms are often used as synonyms. For the purposes of this chapter, planning will be considered the act of viewing or envisioning the physical arrangement of spaces. Design will be considered the physical documentation and embellishment of the plan. A number of plans or schemes may be developed for a facility, but only one design document is likely to be created that will serve as the basis for executing the plan. The plan can be thought of as a strategy, and design as the tactics.

One of the prime objectives of security-conscious design is to prevent unauthorized people and hazardous or toxic substances from entering the facility. One way to approach this goal is to establish an effective single point of entry, or as few points of entry as possible, while still maintaining code- and safety-proscribed egress requirements. At the same time as unauthorized access is to be prevented, authorized people must be able to enter the facility with the least amount of inconvenience. Another primary objective is to protect the facility from the effects of catastrophic accidents or acts of nature, such as explosions, earthquakes, tornados, hurricanes, and floods; and to the extent possible, from chemical or biological terrorist intrusions.

The Urban Setting

Any number of circumstances involving neighboring buildings may place a facility at increased risk. Some factors can be identified; others may not be identifiable. A facility located in an urban setting, i.e., on a normal downtown street, is faced with risks and limitations inherent in existing conditions, such as proximity to vehicular traffic and adjacent buildings, including neighboring buildings that may house unknown hazards or present other risk factors.

Three Approaches to Physical Protection

Three fundamental types of physical protection can be utilized to protect facilities:

- Obstruction
- Absorption
- Diversion/Deflection

Obstruction

One approach to protecting a particular building or site is obstruction, in various types and degrees. While absolute, hard, or impenetrable protection may not always be feasible or possible, alternate techniques can often be used to delay, lessen, or frustrate an intrusion. Distance, in the form of setbacks, may be an option. If it is not possible to increase the setback distance of an existing facility, the next best thing may be to impede or slow down a penetration to a point where it can be more readily managed. Bollards or bollard-type structures, such as natural boulders or concrete barriers, cast in aesthetically pleasing shapes, might be effective. If space permits, the use of structurally hardened fountains, ponds, or gardens, or even reinforced concrete benches, may be sufficient to prevent someone from crashing into the building with a vehicle. Planters, benches, and similar features can be set on a temporary or fixed basis. Bollards can be set permanently or in sleeves, where they can be padlocked in place and removed for relocation to provide vehicular access to the building. Planters and benches designed to be heavy or massive, can be set without anchoring, or they may be pinned with reinforcing rod pins into a hardened surface such as stone, brick, or concrete. If there is a high level of security risk, all obstacles should be set with concrete-filled pipes deep into a concrete footing.

Driveway or roadway barriers can either be permanently installed or provided by portable barriers for areas requiring temporary protection. This type of barrier can be towed into position behind a truck and quickly erected. Some are capable of stopping a 5-ton vehicle traveling at 40 mph. The more permanent types can be set into a roadway below-grade, so that when the barrier is down, there are no obstructions. These barriers can a stop a 7-1/2-ton vehicle traveling at 50 mph. With proper equipment, these barriers can be erected in as little as one second.[1]

Another option is to design or re-design the lower portions of a building to support the goal of obstruction. Structural columns can be protected with composite construction (e.g., protecting fireproofed steel columns with filled and reinforced concrete masonry units or, if low enough within the structure, with cast-in-place concrete). An existing building's lower level beams might be protected with multiple layers of drywall.

Elevator, stair, communication, electrical, and fire sprinkler riser shafts should be protected by the use of filled and reinforced concrete masonry units, or multiple layers of drywall. Often sprinkler system risers are in the corner of one or more fire stairways. Likewise, emergency communications risers should be protected with multiple layers of drywall.

Communication floor penetration sleeves should be sealed with high-quality firestop material. A few chunks of mineral wool or fiberglass are inadequate and most likely will not meet current fire codes.

In newer buildings, floor-load capacities might be increased, even if this is not a current code requirement. Connections between columns and beams can be strengthened and more heavily protected from fire. Use of these structural techniques may tend to prevent "progressive collapse," as was noted in the World Trade Center buildings, where the weight of one or more floors falling on floors below led to a progressive collapse of the entire building.

Older buildings whose fire stairways are few and of minimal width might be candidates for additional fire stairs. Although expensive, adding one or more fire stairways may double or triple the number of people who can be evacuated in a short period. (The ancient Coliseum of Rome held about 50,000 spectators and had 80 entrance/exits. It could be emptied in a few minutes.)

Absorption

Reinforcing or "beefing up" a building might be referred to as the "fortress solution." A collateral approach might be to protect a building's structural system as well as its vital vertical systems from fatal damage, while at the same time permitting violent impacts or explosions to expend themselves on more absorbent and flexible materials.

A building that has a considerable amount of glazing at the sidewalk level might (depending on the security goals) be a candidate for replacement of the existing glass (probably a heavyweight, tempered plate glass) with laminated safety glass. This type of glass is now being specified in some building codes in areas where hurricanes are prevalent. *Laminated safety glass* is similar to the glass in the windshields of automobiles, while *tempered glass* is the same sort as in storm doors or shower doors. Laminated safety glass is constructed of two layers of glass with a layer of plastic sandwiched in between. It is much stronger than tempered glass due to the behavior of the plastic (polycarbonate or polyvinylbutryl) internal layer, depending on its particular specification. It will withstand a substantial impact, as might be delivered by a sharp blow and, if thick enough, a bullet. The sheet of glass receiving the impact begins to shatter, absorbing a portion of the projectile's energy. The inner plastic sheet flexes, while at the same time gripping the glass shards. The glass system bends without shattering and collapsing, thus preventing potentially lethal flying glass shards. Because safety plate glass has increased rigidity, it is less likely to pop out of its frame during a high wind, such as might be experienced in a tornado or hurricane, and can be an effective deterrent against flying debris.

Window Coverings

A somewhat recent and effective solution to explosive blasts is the use of specially manufactured and fabricated window covering curtains or drapes. These drapes are effective in stopping ballistic glass shards that result from an explosive force or wind-borne objects, such as tree limbs or other debris. Some of these drapes have been proven effective against particular types of explosives, including ammonium nitrate, C4, and TNT. They function by yielding inward with the thrust of the explosion and catching the glass pieces in the web of the fabric. As the explosive force dissipates, the drape (firmly anchored at the head) relaxes, dropping the glass shards on the floor beneath it. The basic material is white and can be printed or colored in a variety of contemporary looks, with the appearance of a conventional sheer drape. Many, if not most of these products are fabricated out of an enhanced polyester (polyparaphenyllene terephthalamide) or fiberglass. Safetydrape™ is one such product (http://www.safetydrape.com).

Surface Coatings

So far, we have addressed protection from violent intrusion at the street level, essentially in an urban environment, by vehicles and explosions or high winds, and generally through windows. The non-window portions of exterior building surfaces present a different set of conditions.

Most exterior materials are selected for their aesthetic and weather-resistant values. Common commercial exterior materials include granite or marble, pre-cast concrete, brick, spandrel glass, stainless steel, and aluminum. If these exterior surfaces are older and could be improved by some form of coating, there are new coating products available that can render them somewhat explosion-resistant. Some of these coatings are fire-retardant, spray-on elastomerics capable of achieving elongations of rupture of 89%, and tensile strengths in excess of 2,000 psi. Applied to a thickness of 1/8", these coatings have been tested to withstand an explosion of 50 pounds of TNT at a distance of 35'.

If the existing surfaces are newer, and the aesthetic appearance of an added explosion-resistant exterior surface coating would be objectionable, an alternative approach is to coat the interior surfaces with a product such as Paxcon®, produced by Line-X Corporation, which could mitigate impact and blast events. This technology, which has been extensively tested by the United States Air Force Research Laboratory, could, if used judicially, prove to be a highly effective mechanism against explosive and impact damage. As is the case with the drapery systems cited above, structural engineers and security personnel could work together to create protective systems that do not rely completely on concrete and drywall.

Coating materials can also be used on interior, high-sensitivity conferencing areas; LAN (Local Area Network), WAN (Wide Area Network), and UPS (Uninterruptible Power Systems); EPS (Emergency Power System) — or the more current description, BPS (Backup Power Systems) rooms; IDF (Intermediate Distribution Frame) rooms; electrical switch rooms; mechanical rooms; and demising walls between truck docks or loading areas and occupied portions of a structure. When possible, these protective coatings should be used on surfaces closest to personnel and/or sensitive equipment to provide them with protection from dangerous projectile surface debris (http://www.paxcon.com, www.line-xicd.com).

Diversion/Deflection

Another design technique is to impede or deflect an explosion or impacting force to a new or different, less harmful direction. If space permits, a winding drive or roadway is often sufficient to slow a hostile vehicle to the point that it loses impact force and becomes a much-reduced or nonexistent threat. Ponds or structured pools can also be formidable vehicular barriers, in addition to being attractive features, although they require maintenance. Formal anticlines (terrain scaled with a concave area around the building — similar to a golf course bunker) can effectively impede vehicles and, properly designed, can deflect major explosive forces. Low, architecturally attractive and hardened walls, especially when provided with a soil backing to absorb wall debris resulting from an explosion, can serve as controlling elements for both pedestrians and vehicles.

These kinds of design devices can also be effective in channeling people into desired corridors or paths of ingress and egress, and in helping to distinguish public areas from private spaces. There is one caution in designing a physical barrier such as a wall, anticline, or hogback (a ridge with steeply sloped sides and a sharp summit). That is, it is important to avoid inadvertently creating spaces that would make good hiding places for assailants or others bent on espionage, sabotage, or other forms of harm.

Public Space Versus Private Space

Security personnel are always trying to separate more secure areas or zones from less secure areas or zones. This is especially true in major metropolitan areas where there are large numbers of people moving to and from or past facilities, either on foot or in vehicles. We define areas or zones inside a facility's grounds or structure as "private," and the areas outside of the structure or grounds as "public." Even though the property's legal boundaries may end at a sidewalk or curb line, the separation between public and private becomes blurred in areas such as plazas constructed around a building, which are juxtaposed with a public sidewalk. Another example is the pedestrian malls in a shopping centers, which have been declared *semi-public* areas by some courts. (Refer to the "Prune Yard" case in San Jose, California, in which the United States Supreme Court decided on certain rights of the public to use plaza spaces inside a privately owned shopping area.[2])

Attempting to establish psychological lines between public areas and private spaces can be a challenge because contradictions often present themselves. Creating a protective perimeter of some sort around a private space — with controlled access — contributes to developing an internal safety zone, such as inside a building's lobby. However, what can be done about the peripheries, public or private, surrounding the building's internal safety zone? There are at least two schools of thought in this regard. One favors attempting to provide as much separation between the private and public areas as possible through the use of walls, barriers, fences, barricades, and formal spaces that create an actual physical, as well as psychological, barrier. The other school suggests value in a concept that might be called "eyes on the street." It is well established that criminals or others bent on harm are made apprehensive by the presence of people they either do not know or do not control. The challenge for the security plan is first to be able to distinguish the "bad guys" from the "good guys," and second, to recognize that the very crowd that might intimidate an assailant can also serve as a screen for the perpetrator of an assault or other form of harm.

These two visions of a security deterrent need not be mutually exclusive. Rather they can be planned to be mutually supportive, providing the security plan firmly defines which areas or zones it perceives as the facility's private space versus public areas, and creates the desired controls. Public areas or zones may benefit from the "eyes on the street" values, which may intimidate a prospective assailant. The "eyes on the street" deterrent may also visually penetrate into the "privacy zone," where it is possible to establish actual control over who is visiting and who is in the area.

Formally separated spaces and anticlines may be used to provide areas of refuge in the event of the need to evacuate a facility. Separation of private and public space is addressed in more detail later in this chapter, under "Interior Planning and Design."

Creating and Updating a Security-Conscious Building Plan

An overall objective of a secure building plan is to establish an effective single point of entry, or as few points of entry as possible, while maintaining code and safety proscribed egress requirements. Whatever the elements of each unique security plan, it is important to note that nothing is forever. A facility is likely to remain in place for many years, while the areas around it and immediately adjacent to it can and probably will change. More often than not, the building and, in many cases, the surrounding area will degrade rather than improve. Changes may not necessarily be social or economic, but rather functional. These changes will mandate revisions to the security plan, which should be reviewed at least every three years. Changes in the security plan will determine if changes to the physical aspects of a building are necessary.

Because changes in building use or surroundings are usually subtle and progressive, it is highly recommended that an outside consultant reassess the building layout and use of space from a security point of view. He or she should be able view the facility's site without bias, identifying new risks to which the facility's users and manager may have become desensitized.

Whether creating or updating a security plan, it is important to keep in mind two potentially different forms of risk: the everyday risk of assault or theft, and the catastrophic event, such as an accidental or intentional explosion; a biological or chemical event; or a natural disaster such as an earthquake, tornado, or hurricane. The first has a high degree of probability, with more manageable results; the latter two have a lower degree of probability, but potentially catastrophic results.

Whenever a substantial building or interiors design modification is undertaken, the design team should work carefully with Security in order to ensure that all proposed modifications would be in accord with the security plan. Regardless of how carefully the design team and security work together on any modification, a thorough review of the security plan should be made.

Single-User Versus Multi-User Facilities

The single-user facility in an urban or suburban setting will be easier to secure than a multiple-user facility. Those in charge of a single-user facility have greater control of individuals and vehicles entering and exiting the facility. Separation between public areas and privates spaces is easier to accomplish. Even within existing facilities, it may be possible to design some form of barrier system, as well as personnel and visitor control. Certainly any new facility can have vehicle, personnel, and visitor control designed into its exterior. Existing drop-off driveways may be converted to pedestrian plazas. Parking areas might be moved farther from the facility, or adjacent to a less critical part of the building. Access gates can be added to parking structures.

Facilities that already have gates and attendants should consider the use of a personal identification system, such as identification key cards or "smart cards" (e-cards). Visitors entering through controlled parking systems should be handled on a pre-authorized basis. If no pre-authorization has been obtained, the visitor should be directed to pull into a specified staging or holding area until the appropriate authorization has been made. The parking attendant can call the security desk and obtain the necessary clearance, prepare a "hang-tag" indicating the vehicle's approved status, and direct the visitor to the security desk to complete the registration and to receive a personal identification tag or badge.

A Word of Caution

In trying to protect a facility from vehicular attack or unauthorized intrusion from people intent on doing harm, security planners must be careful not to create an imminent danger to the building's normal users through poor lighting, poor ingress and egress, or by placing parking in a remote, high-risk area. It does not make sense to design facilities capable of providing protection from explosions or impact events that may never occur, while at the same time creating areas of potential assault. Physical assaults on personnel are a much more likely form of danger than a catastrophic event.

Storage of Volatile Materials

Diesel or heating fuels should be contained in below-grade bunkers or hardened-type containment vessels or facilities. Tanks storing other flammable materials, such as jet-fuel or propane, should not only be stored in below-grade, outdoor, bunkered containment vessels, but also located as far as possible from other structures or valuable equipment. Outdoors, below-grade fuel tanks will require large concrete pads beneath the tanks, to which the tanks must be anchored. Most petroleum products are lighter than water. When the underground water table rises or surface water floods into the containment bunker, it may permit the storage tank to try to float, whether empty or full. Fuel storage facilities should be covered to prevent water from getting into the containment vessel, but the roof or top should not be hardened. In the event of a fuel fire or explosion, it is desirable to have the explosive force project up, through the area of the roof, rather than blowing out the sides of the fuel tank containment vessel.

Multiple tanks should be in multiple containment vessels. If one tank explodes or catches on fire, it may be possible to contain the explosion or fire to a single tank. Every attempt should be made to locate fuel storage tanks in areas where fire or explosion will have the least effect on personnel or other facilities. Fuel tank caps should always be of a locking type, and protocol for fueling operations should indicate that fill pipes remain closed and locked at all times except when product is being received.

Protecting Utilities

Another way to mitigate risk through design is the use of hardened utility trenches in which electric power feeds are placed. If a 24/7 environment or critical information technology systems are involved, the design team might consider attempting to secure power from separate power stations, or even different electrical utilities. Telephone services might also be supplied from separate loops and fed through hardened trenches, in addition to separate telephone service companies. Backup systems might be designed for securing potable water, critical to the operation of most air-conditioning systems, as well as for personnel occupancy. Water might be supplied from redundant sources, or from a loop that can be shut off from an in-line valve in the event of a water line break, and back-fed.

Sometimes a less costly solution for cooling tower condenser water backup might be an underground water storage tank supplied from a water utility or possibly a containment cistern with flow controls designed to maintain adequate rainwater supplies while providing a settling tank and, if necessary, utility-supplied makeup water. These types of systems have obvious time limitations based on the evaporation rates of the condenser-water cooling towers, plus an estimated number of toilet flushes over a specified period versus the amount of contained water. It is not recommended that rain or surface water storage be used as a potable (drinking) water source. If water from an emergency storage facility (not supplied from a purifying source, such as a utility, and not stored in a sanitary vessel) is used for make-up water or toilet flushes, the building's water system will have to be purged and decontaminated when the emergency has passed, and the water system is re-converted to a conventional potable water system.

Ingress Concerns

Design approaches to security must inevitably overlap with security procedures, personnel, and devices. The planner or designer must consider how all of these elements will work together to achieve the desired level of security for the facility and its users. Consequently, the following sections address not only the ingress and egress points of a building, but include references to operating procedures and security-specific equipment as they fit in with good security design.

Truck Docks

Truck docks, fuel delivery, and storage areas require special design considerations and have their own particular security problems. Unlike occupants and visitors who can be screened when passing through the main entrance of a facility, almost everyone and every vehicle arriving at a truck dock is initially a stranger. Truck docks are vital to the operation of any facility and are usually active throughout the day. New materials and service personnel flow into the facility, while trash flows out. Some facilities have a steady stream of delivery and service vehicles serving multiple occupants. Often service vehicles must be parked in or near the truck dock for hours at a time. These vehicles represent a potential threat, either directly or because they may provide an inadvertent screen for individuals or groups who wish to commit acts of theft or violence. Truck docks must meet stringent fire codes. Most are constructed with fire-retardant walls, usually of concrete blocks or masonry units (CMUs). A non-reinforced or enhanced CMU wall is good fire protection, but only a fair protection against an explosion. A truck dock fitting some or most of these criteria may be a candidate for a truck dock master. This individual, by controlling service calls, deliveries, and parking, can provide a front-line defense.

Courier and Delivery Services
Package Delivery

Courier and package delivery vehicles and personnel are under heavy pressures from their employers to maintain delivery schedules. Highly obstructive screening or registration systems will be met with strong resistance or actual avoidance for these types of visitors. Incoming parcel delivery rooms or drop-off rooms may satisfy the need for all but "obtain signature" requirements. If there is no dock master, a system comprised of CCTV and hands-free, speed-dial phones located in the dock receiving area can provide delivery personnel with the ability to quickly contact and be recognized by occupants who can either remotely release locked doors or meet delivery personnel at the building dock entrance.

Contractors and Heavy Deliveries

Contractors and heavy-delivery personnel, such as a furniture installer or copier repairperson, present a different set of requirements. Occupants of facilities expecting deliveries of heavy or bulky products or anticipating a contractor's work should make advance arrangements, specifying the contractor or delivery company, date, time of day, and the individuals' names. In any case, the man-door between the truck dock and the building should be locked until released by the dock master or authorized personnel. Know who your contractors are. Know who their personnel are.

Controlled and Monitored Ingress

Initial entry to a facility can be controlled by designing open-appearing passageways, which funnel all persons entering a facility:

- through automatic gate-type devices called turnstiles (even though they are not actually turnstiles in the traditional sense),
- through a magnetometer (metal detector),
- past a guard station where IDs are to be checked, or
- past a facial-recognition closed-circuited television camera (CCTV).

Identification/Access Cards

Until recently, most single- and multiple-occupant facilities were open to users, visitors, and service personnel. Today, building management companies are in the process of establishing security systems whereby all incoming personnel, tenants, visitors, and service providers are being screened for authorized occupancy or entry. Securing the cooperation of all occupants, whether in a single-occupant or multi-tenant facility, may not be as difficult as it may seem — certainly not as difficult as it might have been before 9/11.

If a security system is being newly created, facilities or building management should develop a clearly defined plan for building security. It should include one or a limited number of basic controlled ingress points, together with an identification card for all regular occupants. The card should include a color-coded, photo ID that can be laminated to the card or that is photo-embedded. Laminated ID cards are easy, quick, and relatively inexpensive to produce. On the other hand, they are not too difficult to alter or copy. Photo-embedded ID cards take longer and are more costly to produce. One type of these cards is the so-called *e-cards*, encoded to electronically release or unlock pre-specified doors or equipment.

Establishing a New Physical Security Plan

A system might include a method by which an occupant may pre-register a visitor, contractor, delivery, or service person. Special temporary, color-coded ID/e-cards should be available for issue to special or heavy-delivery, or maintenance and service personnel for truck dock, freight elevator, service rooms (such as mechanical, telephone, and electrical closets), and some vestibule or lobby access. These outside people often require access to spaces within the facility to deliver materials, repair devices, perform routine maintenance, and inspect equipment. The facility can either provide full-time escorts or carefully check with contractors' employers. They can require that those employers check their personnel and provide the results of the background checks. Contractors' cards are usually color- and electronically-coded for entry to specific areas, such as freight elevators, man-doors into truck docks, and specific interior vestibule doors. Mechanical rooms, electrical closets, and telephone closets are sometimes included.

Because these cards provide access to many spaces that are normally secured, they should be logged out only to known personnel and turned in to the Security office or desk at the end of each use and at the end of every day, then re-delivered or issued if necessary the next day, on a "as needed" basis. Requiring some sort of security deposit, such as a driver's license, will go a long way towards ensuring prompt and regular return of temporary ID/e-cards.

Consultants, attorneys, accountants, auditors, and others who may be on-site for fairly long periods should be issued specially prepared color-coded visitor cards of a similar type to those given to contractors, but that access only limited spaces needed to perform their functions. Depending on the period of time that these people will be on-site, they may or may not be required to turn in their cards each day. However, they should be required to return their cards at the end of their engagement.

Short-Term Visitors

Not all visitors will require ID/e-cards that provide electronic access to specified areas, nor do all of them need a photo ID. Security desk personnel can issue these guests self-expiring temporary badges. These badges are typically made of a material sometimes known as *visually changing paper*. The badges are made in two parts: one part (usually called an *imager*) is pre-prepared; the second is usually an activator or catalyst. The badge is prepared with the visitor's identification through a simple printing device and on demand at the security desk or, if desired, at a parking structure control booth. One of the parts is coated with a pressure-sensitive adhesive. The two parts are combined at the desk or booth and handed to the visitor. These badges can display the name and business affiliation of the individual, and can be color-coded. They might contain other types of information, such as the floor or area for which authorization has been granted.

Budgeting and Startup

In establishing a security system, it will be important to prepare a carefully defined budget specifying the building owner's and the tenant's first cost; the cost of new, lost, or additional ID/e-cards; and maintenance or operating costs. Since this program is one being proposed by building ownership or management, which will have a cost impact on all occupants, management should schedule a series of personal meetings with each of the facility's organizations, whether sister companies/organizations or other tenants, to explain the plan and to go over the budget items, and to secure their agreement.

Inherent in the above is planning for developing controlled ingress from as few entrances as possible, which includes controlling the truck dock and parking ingress and establishing a security or reception desk at the main entrance lobby. These stations should have an image of authority, yet be manned by polite, well-trained, uniformed individuals. Uniforms may have a police or military image or be as simple as a dress shirt, tie, and blazer. They should never be casual, but always have a look of authority.

The Security Station

It is important that the lobby security station, like security personnel, present an image of authority. Whatever its design or degree of sophistication, the security station should appear to authorized personnel and visitors alike as a clear boundary between public and private space.

The security station is the public "front" of a security system. There is a strong likelihood that there will be a security office and a CCTV viewing space somewhere else in the facility. Security desks or stations should be conspicuous and located so that the individuals manning the desk have a clear view of all entrances. At a minimum, a lobby-situated or high visibility security station should be equipped with the necessary personnel and equipment to recognize validly issued ID cards or tags. Security personnel at the lobby station should also be capable of issuing temporary ID cards, upon proper authority, for authorized visitors, service technicians, contractors and heavy delivery personnel, courier and small parcel delivery personnel, and consultants.

Security stations should be equipped with special communication systems to instantly contact a higher security authority or local law enforcement and have both landline and wireless (cellular) telephones and capabilities. Security stations might also be provided with other equipment, such as computerized systems capable of developing databases of all currently authorized personnel, as well as knowing whether or not they are on-site. The systems might also include databases of all visitors presently on the premises and of all visitors maintained over long periods. This latter database is particularly useful if it can quickly recognize a returning visitor, confirm his or her identity and perhaps the purpose of the visit, and issue him or her a new ID badge. The computerized system might also be capable of recognizing parking passes and ID cards/tags that may have been issued for visitors — either at the parking facility gate or at a remote security station. A station that is responsible for more than one point of ingress might be equipped with CCTV monitors, which can provide continuous, real-time viewing of all ingress points.

Points of Egress and Refuge

In an eagerness to establish controls over points of ingress and over vehicles and individuals entering a facility, security planners should keep in mind that getting people safely and quickly out of the facility may be of greater importance than trying to keep the "bad guys" from getting in. Following one of the prevailing local building or fire codes is a good start, but it may not provide as much safety for personnel as is desired. After all, an organization's personnel are the most important concern. Knowledge of various operations, personnel loads, space configurations, and risks may prompt some organizations to exceed code requirements in particular areas and under particular circumstances.

Pathways

Pathways to exits and fire stairways should be carefully planned in conjunction with a facility's interior design team, and with those whose mission is to ensure security, health, and safety for the facility and its users. Designers, security, and health and safety personnel, insurance advisors, and government inspectors all have their individual concerns and approaches regarding security and safety.

Pathways or aisles should not merely meet code standards, but should be planned and maintained with consideration for the number of people who may be attempting to reach a designated or alternate exit. It is also important to recognize the distances to be traveled and the possibility that there may be little or no lighting during a crisis event.

Department heads often want to minimize the square footage for which their departments may be charged. They will press for adding more workstations, storage cabinets, or files in their areas, which may result in fewer or narrower exiting pathways. One of the most common forms of congestion is added file cabinets and boxes, which just seem to materialize.

Lighting

Both exterior and interior lighting play a major role in security and safety. Exterior lighting may have three functions. Aesthetic or architectural lighting is intended to make the facility and grounds look attractive at night. It has the disadvantage of rendering a facility an easy and attractive target for anyone interested in doing harm. A second function of lighting is to provide safety and protection from injury, e.g., slipping and falling; bumping into trees, bushes, or other obstructions that may be very observable during daylight hours, but far less so at night; and lighting exit pathways to be used during an emergency, such as a fire. Finally, exterior lighting can and does provide security — protection of personnel from assault or injury while arriving and departing from a facility and making it difficult for an intruder to approach the facility without fear of being observed.

Exterior Security Lighting

- Some basic precepts: parking lot and sidewalk lights should avoid producing shadows cast by trees and tall shrubs. Lights fixed to buildings should be set at a roughly 45–60° angles from the building so as to project their light as far out from the building as possible — without becoming obtrusive to neighbors or creating a direct glare into the eyes of personnel or visitors who are approaching the building on foot or in a vehicle.

- High-pressure sodium lights, favored for their lighting efficiency, are not favored by CCTV systems. High-pressure sodium lights do not meet the quality lighting color rendering index (CRI — somewhere in the range of 22–65) to faithfully render clothing colors and facial features as do metal halides (whose range is 65–85) or fluorescents (52–92). Mercury vapor lights have a CRI of about 50. This could be a critical difference in an identification process. The objective is to achieve the highest CRI possible for the benefit of the CCTV system. However, there are trade-offs. Metal halide lighting is not very energy-efficient when compared to fluorescent lighting. On the other hand, fluorescents are not very light-efficient in cold weather due to a drop-off in lumens, in addition to which, the longer tubes of a fluorescent lamp require larger lighting fixtures.

- If heat-sensitive or infrared television cameras are employed, no lighting of any sort will be used. Infrared cameras view only in shades of a single color, usually gray or a soft green.

Interior Safety and Security Lighting

Interior safety and security lighting follows many of the same precepts as exterior lighting. Again it is important to avoid deep shadows or under-lighted areas where an intruder could find cover, especially in storage and stock rooms, long narrow corridors, and corridors with alcoves or recesses and 90° turns in them. Good security means increasing light intensity and cover in hallways, fire stairways, lobbies, and support work areas, such as copy centers, pantries, and storage and file rooms, particularly those where there is not a regular complement of personnel or in areas not regularly frequented.

Other Lighting Recommendations

Increasing the number and output of emergency lighting fixtures is often recommended. Since emergency lighting fixture circuits can be severed or disrupted in the event of an explosion or fire, it may be preferable to have each fixture on its own trickle-charged battery. Real panic may occur when there is a visible fire or after an actual explosion. People in a state of panic often avoid red exit signs, confusing them with a source of fire. Some states are already moving toward the use of green, rather than the traditional red emergency directional signs, especially the exit signs. Exit signs as well as evacuation directional lighting have been migrating towards the floor level. It is likely there will be less smoke at that level, and it will be much easier for someone crawling on their hands and knees to see the signage when at just above the floor. California has adopted green exit lights placed just above floor level for this reason.

Fire Suppression and Alarm

Many facilities are required by code to have automatic sprinkler and monitored fire alarm systems. However, many facilities are not, especially single-story buildings. A fire sprinkler and alarm system may be one of the cheapest forms of security that can be acquired. These are among the reasons why:

- A single-story building can burn as fast, or faster than a multi-story building.
- The first cost of a sprinkler system or alarm system may appear quite reasonable when applied to the life span of a building, especially one containing costly or sensitive materials.
- A substantial reduction can be achieved in insurance rates.

Interior Planning and Design

The following are some basic planning and design concepts, some of which have been alluded to previously.

It is highly important in designing for security to provide clear border or boundary definitions of private versus public spaces. A reasonable individual must be able to recognize when he or she is transitioning from public to private space. All individuals should be aware or made aware of the areas in which they are and are not permitted. This is a relatively simple matter for the facility's regular users or specially authorized personnel. It is a bit more difficult in the case of strangers, guests, visitors, or service personnel. As noted earlier in this chapter, clearly defined transitional zones are not always an easy solution.

Providing a visitor with clear directions as to how to find the restrooms or the beverage station is not only good security practice, but good manners. Much the same can be said for directing or actually conducting service personnel to the devices or equipment they have been called to service. They, too, should be given clear directions to restrooms or other spaces they might need to access, such as mechanical rooms, and electrical or telephone closets.

Inside the facility's so-called private areas, passageway doors can be installed that are always in the closed position, but never locked. Passageway doors can also be locked in only one direction, but always open in the other direction — always in the direction of the fire exit. Even the never-locked doors, solid with a sidelight or window, present a significant visual and psychological barrier to an accidental or even an intentional intruder.

It can be useful to display floor maps of department, conference room, and restroom locations, together with informational signs that direct visitors to specific spaces. Every attempt should be made to control the random movements of visitors without being officious about it. On the other hand, such signage might be *too* useful if it helps to direct undesirable individuals to areas where they should not be. This is a judgment call depending on the facility's level of risk and how the organization decides to deal with risk assessments. Whether through establishing doorway barriers or through providing careful directions, the objective is to never put a visitor in the position where they can say, "Gee, I got turned around looking for the restroom."

Areas of Assembly

If the facility is to have a space for larger, quasi-public assemblies for social, training, or media-related purposes, these areas should be planned with unique, non-obtrusive, but controlled, ingress and egress, hopefully to the outdoors or other public area. These facilities should be equipped with their own restrooms, pantries, copy, and telephone rooms. They should be planned and designed so that they can be under unobtrusive surveillance by both on-site security personnel and CCTV.

In some cases, it is desirable to increase the perception of surveillance. This can be accomplished in a couple of ways, one of which is to conspicuously display CCTV monitors showing live views of visitors and building users. Another is to create funneling passageways, which require all personnel and visitors to pass by or through some form of reception area or accessing or screening device. (See Figure 5.1.)

Planning for Visitors

Not all of the people entering a facility or space are intent on doing harm. On the other hand, some who appear quite innocuous may not be. Some may even appear to be allied with the organization in some manner or other, such as shareholders — who may also be shareholders of competitors. Some visitors may be bankers and investment bankers who have been invited to render investment advice or services — but who may also be preparing an underwriting for a competitor. Others may be accountants — who may also represent competitors, and not least of all, visiting attorneys who may turn out to be adversarial. Planning and floor designs should be such that these visitors can reach the offices and conference rooms they are to visit without passing through areas where they can observe critical documents or ask seemingly innocuous questions of friendly personnel. Again, most of these visitors do not intend to do any harm. However, if they are in areas of a facility where they might be able to observe critical documents, computer screens, or other forms of information in which there may be potential gain — temptation might rule.

Conference Centers

Many organizations continue to struggle with conference facilities that are neither efficient as major meeting spaces, nor secure for the conferees or hosts. Too often, the center of activity is a large conference room next to the CEO's or senior executives' suites or offices. Amenities such as breakout conference rooms and pantries often do not exist, or a nearby office is commandeered for the purpose.

One of an organization's most useful spaces is a well-planned and designed conferencing center — perhaps more than one depending on the level of anticipated or actual experienced activity. A well-planned conference center should consist of a large conference room with more than one entrance, at least two private breakout conference rooms where the negotiating teams can caucus in private, a VTC (video teleconference) room, and a copy/pantry room. Additional useful amenities might be worth considering at

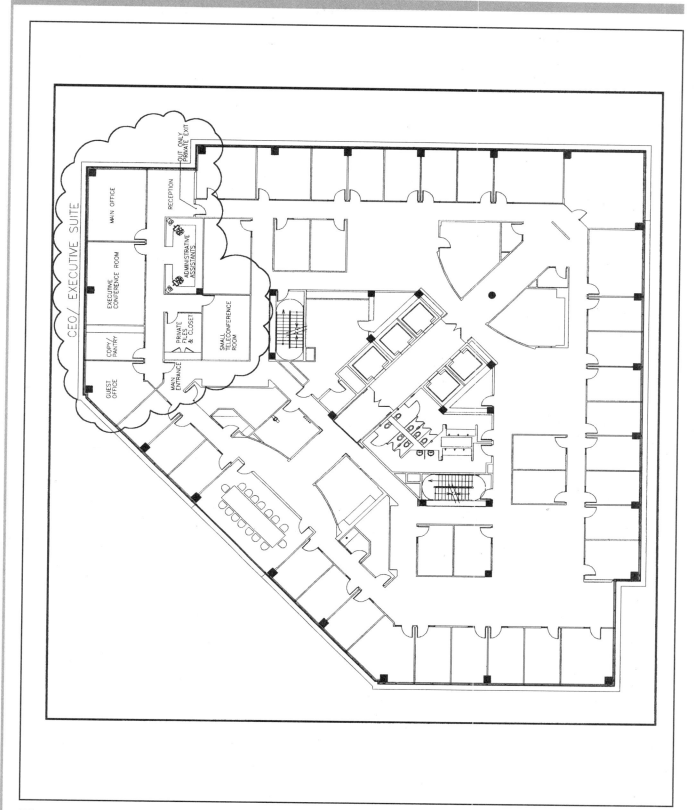

Figure 5.1: **Executive Conference Center**

the same time, such as a couple of telephone closets, coat closets, some lockable storage shelving for boxes of files and large rolls of drawings, and an anteroom or foyer large enough for food service.

The design team should be made aware of specific security concerns and concepts. If more than one conference center is under consideration, they should not be on the same floors, or if they must, they should be as far apart as is physically possible, given the other design criteria. Designers should consider placing multiple conference centers on non-contiguous floors, as shown in Figure 5.2. The objective is to prevent different negotiating teams from accidentally running into one another as they enter or leave the facility or take breaks from their meetings.

It is best to place conference centers at the ends of elevator lobbies or corridors, as close to the point of ingress to the floor or space as possible, and on a direct line. This may prevent visitors from passing through areas occupied by people engaged in potentially sensitive work. This approach also gives visitors easy access to the conference center where, except for restroom breaks, they never have to leave the conference center environs. Using barrier-type doorways as previously described can help to keep guests within a limited area, even when visiting a restroom. More often than not, restrooms are located in the building's core along with the fire stairways and the elevators. A conference center floor plan that considers the location of these various facilities and is designed to keep most visitors within a designated and controlled "visitors' zone" has gone a long way toward preventing intentional or accidental espionage. Figure 5.3 is a multi-purpose conference center plan.

Conference Rooms

Most frequently, conference rooms have been located to provide maximum service for operations, often without regard for intellectual security. Following are some suggestions for improving conference room security without compromising operational efficiency.

As with conference centers, locating conference rooms at the near-ends of elevator lobbies or corridors helps to keep visitors within relatively secure areas and close to restrooms. If having a conference center is not an option, a small conference room adjacent to a larger one, together with one or two telephone closets, might be a reasonable solution. (See Figure 5.2.)

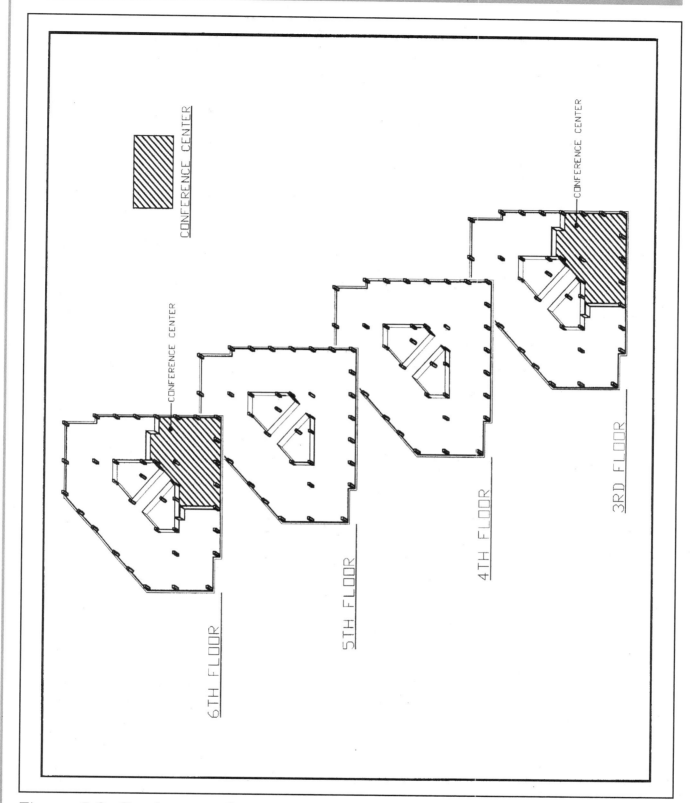

Figure 5.2: **Conference Centers on Non-Contiguous Floors**

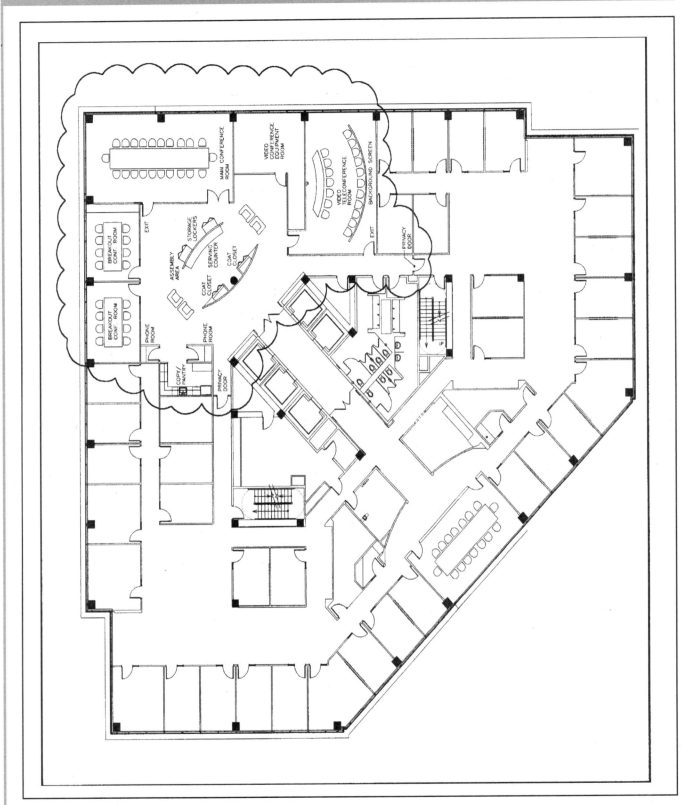

Figure 5.3: **Multi-Purpose Conference Center**

Visual Screening

Constructing a floor-to-ceiling screen wall in front of the conference center or conference room entrances helps to provide some visual security for those involved in the meetings. In addition to providing psychological barriers to a wandering stranger, screen walls can be highly attractive features at the ends of lobbies or main corridors. Screens of this type can cover double entrances, keeping both out of visitors' primary view. Figures 5.4A and B show two examples of privacy screening in conference room areas.

Acoustical Security

Acoustical security between the various conference and the VTC (video teleconference) rooms and telephone closets is critical. Windows within these spaces might be provided with protective drapes, in addition to blackout drapes that might be needed to darken the room for projection purposes. Acoustical security between the various conference and VTC rooms and telephone closets is also vital.

Supply air ducts are often insulated to prevent heat or cooling loss. The thermal insulation may also provide some added security benefit by absorbing sound and preventing conversations from being overheard in adjacent rooms. However, this is not usually the case with return air, which is sometimes handled through a ceiling plenum, in which case the entire ceiling is a duct for return air.

Usually designers specify conference room walls constructed from the floor to the structural deck of the floor above. They may even include some sound-absorbing insulation between the wall studs. It is recommended that all conference room walls be constructed based on a staggered stud, unbalanced design, as shown in Figure 5.5. However, even floor-to-deck staggered stud walls must have at least one large hole, perhaps two openings, one at each end, to provide for return air flow, and these become perfect conduits for transmission of conversations from the conference room to adjacent rooms or the corridor. This condition can be addressed by installing acoustical traps — nothing more than short, ducted returns — on the conference-room side of the openings required for return air. Often these traps can be constructed of a ridged, acoustical board, about five feet long, with one right-angle bend. A well-engineered and constructed acoustical trap should absorb most conversations, yet be large enough to permit sufficient return airflow. (See Figures 5.6 and 5.7.)

Depending on the assessed need for privacy, some or all of a facility's conference rooms might be located in areas without windows or with very limited windows to the outdoors. Conference rooms that have windows can utilize protective

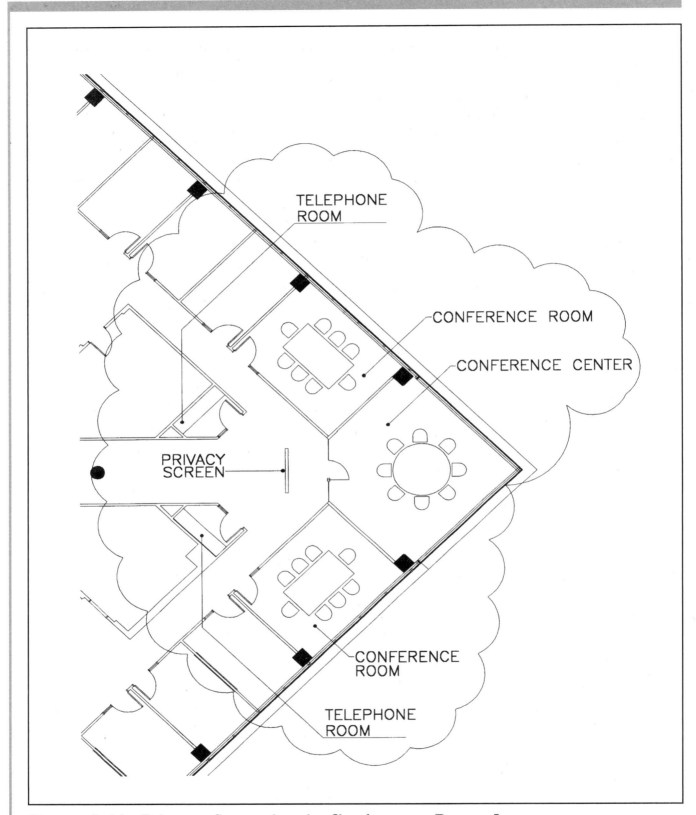

Figure 5.4A: **Privacy Screening in Conference Room Area**

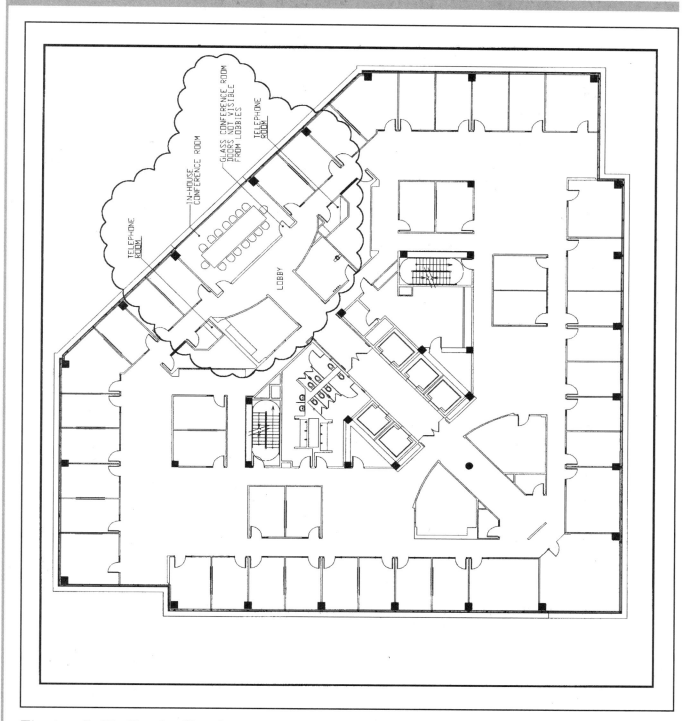

Figure 5.4B: **Basic Conference Center Plan**

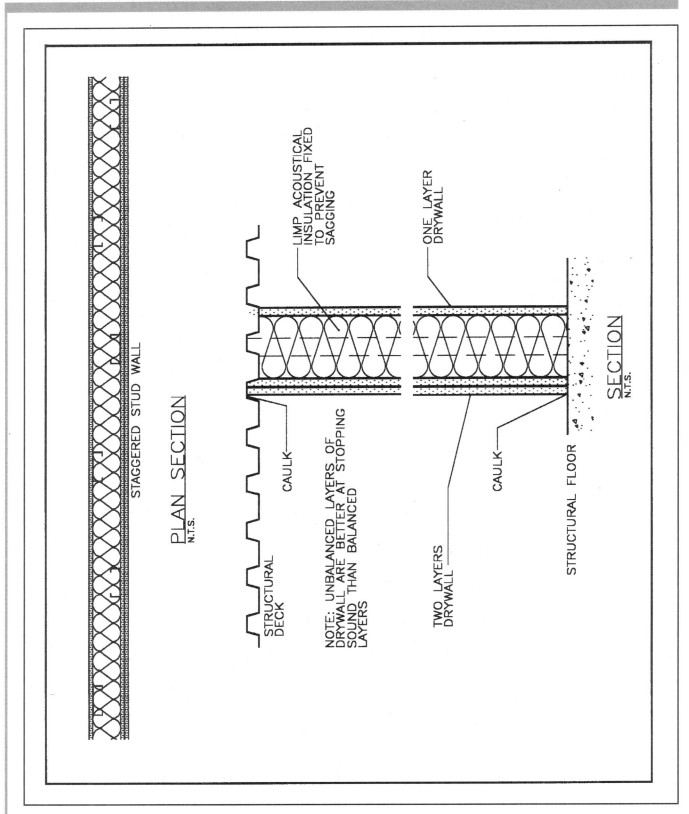

Figure 5.5: **Acoustical Wall Details**

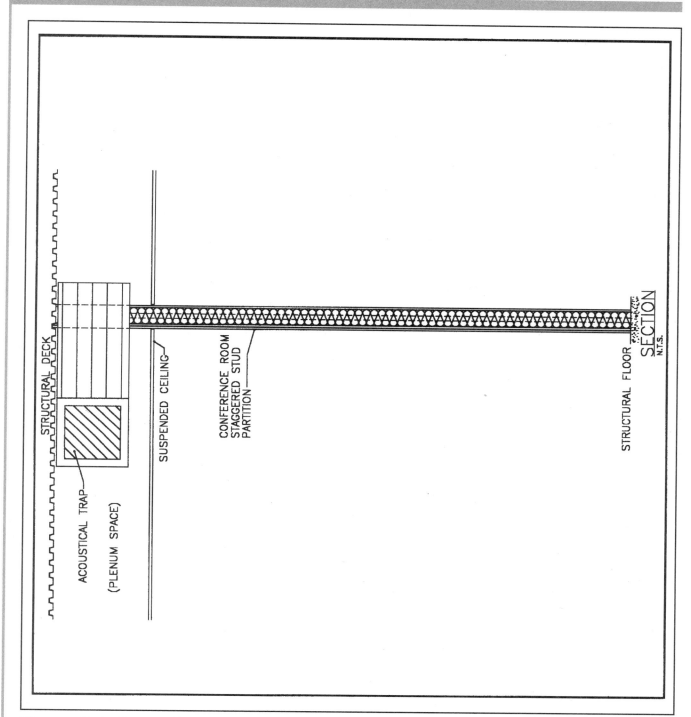

Figure 5.6: **Acoustical Trap**

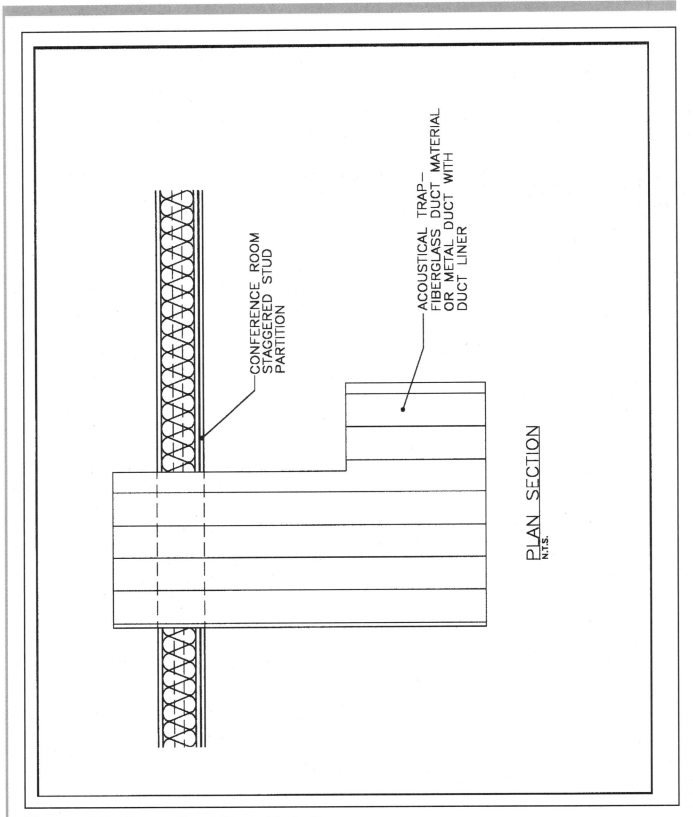

CONFERENCE ROOM
STAGGERED STUD
PARTITION

ACOUSTICAL TRAP—
FIBERGLASS DUCT MATERIAL
OR METAL DUCT WITH
DUCT LINER

PLAN SECTION
N.T.S.

Figure 5.7: **Acoustical Trap Details**

drapes, in addition to blackout drapes. High-tech listening devices are capable of picking up conversations through windows from a distance of 1,500 feet. Although such eavesdropping is most unlikely, some thought might be given to its possibility since the technology exists and is readily available to anyone seeking it. White-noise generators have been connected to windows or directed at them, causing the windows to vibrate, as a method of circumventing high-tech listening devices.

Other Interior Spaces

Controlling Space

Key personnel, such as CEOs and CFOs or others in sensitive or command positions, may be at higher risk as potential targets, especially from individuals who feel they have been treated unfairly by an organization. (See Chapters 1 and 2 for more on identifying potential targets and perpetrators.) Not only may the lives of these personnel be in danger, but those of co-workers or visitors within the general area who may be obstacles or random casualties of an attack.

An interior plan that anticipates this type of eventuality is neither difficult to create nor to construct. Placing senior personnel in areas accessible only through a series of security spaces such as vestibules, lobbies, and reception or waiting areas without direct line of sight or direct access, is a form of protective compartmentation. Designers might limit the use of heavy, tempered or laminated glass doors into private offices and office suite areas and substitute door-height sidelight windows instead.

Another form of compartmentation is the provision of transaction counters at a 48" height for receptionists and administrative assistants whose workstations are in open areas. These enclosures can provide some security from a visitor's prying eyes.

Use of copy centers is often extended to visitors who may then have an opportunity to pick through documents, which have been discarded or inadvertently left on copier plates. A trash shredder may be an inexpensive solution.

Mailrooms

When conditions permit, construction or placement of mailrooms and/or package delivery rooms would ideally be located in a separate building with its own HVAC system. If the mailroom must be housed within a highly occupied facility, attempts should be made to provide it with a separate HVAC system and walls, floors, and structural ceilings constructed to absorb bomb explosion within the room and to be as isolated as possible from highly occupied areas. (See Chapters 6 and 8 for more on mailroom security.)

IT Facilities

LAN, WAN, and IDF rooms should be located as close to the center of a building or floor as possible. If they must be along the interior perimeter of a floor, so-called, "hurricane walls" should be constructed along all glass lines. The use of elastomeric coatings on the occupied side of these walls will provide additional protection to personnel and equipment within the rooms.

Conclusion

This chapter explores some design approaches to security that can be incorporated into new construction and remodeling projects. Some precepts of security-conscious design involve traditional design elements, including ingress and egress, lighting, and factors for locating interior spaces. Others overlap into security systems and operations, as all elements of a security plan must work together to achieve an acceptable level of protection.

The next chapter delves into some of the potential threats, specifically chemical, biological, and radiological agents, and measures that might be taken to mitigate their effects. Chapter 7 follows with evacuation considerations and alert systems.

1. *See* www.nasatka.com and www.deltascientific.com

2. Prune Yard Shopping Center et al V. Robins et al., No. 79-289, Supreme Court of The United States, 447 U.S. 74; 100 S. Ct. 2035; 1980 U.S. LEXIS 129; 64 L. Ed. 2d 741.

Chapter Six

Chemical, Biological, and Radiological Agents

At this point, the organization should have developed its Emergency Response Plans, selected its Emergency Response Teams, and held some desktop training sessions. Other elements of emergency response may have been established as well, such as mapping evacuation routes; developing telephone trees; and creating vendor, consultant, and contractor lists. Before proceeding with the next steps — putting security features and procedures in place at the facility, it is helpful to consider the particulars of certain types of events or incidents, how they can affect a facility and its personnel, and what responses may be available. Once again, it is impossible to accurately predict what type of incident may occur, or when. Without knowing the full circumstances or timing of a potential event, the risk cannot be fully defined. Having some understanding of the perils may be useful in putting security provisions into context.

This chapter reviews some basic information on chemical, biological, and radiological agents (CBR) that have been recognized as potential weapons of terrorist networks. Brief guidance is provided on each of the major agents within each category. Footnotes throughout this discussion refer to a number of sources listed at the end of this chapter for more detailed information. Chapter 7 follows with emergency responses to crises that might involve CBR, acts of nature, or other types of events.

There may be nothing that can be done (by individuals outside of law enforcement or the military) to prevent a chemical or biological attack. It may seem that there is little we can do to protect ourselves from these agents, if they are used in an attack. However, there are things that are helpful to know that could not only save lives, but prevent injury and further contamination. Methods and equipment to close off and shut down outside air supplies, as well as filtering equipment (addressed in Chapter 8) provide some level of protection. Additional measures that can be taken are reviewed in the following section, along with basic information about the most likely CBR weapons, what they do, and how they can be delivered. This information has been gathered from a variety of sources.[1][2][3]

Biological Agents

There are dozens of biological agents that could conceivably be used as a terrorist or warfare weapon. There are only four or five that exist in a natural form and that, due to their lethality, would likely be the choice of terrorists. There are either vaccines and/or antidotes for all of these, provided they are diagnosed and treated promptly.

Anthrax

This may be the biological terrorist's preferred agent because it is many times more lethal than the most toxic chemical warfare agent. If a terrorist or a warring country could devise a perfect mechanism for distribution, a very small amount of anthrax, about 1 gram, could produce over 1,000,000 lethal doses.
A bacterium, anthrax occurs in nature, in soil, and infects herbivores. Most of the natural outbreaks in animals have been contained, and the disease now occurs only occasionally. Anthrax spores, under the right conditions, can remain dormant for decades.

There is a vaccine that can be used against anthrax, presently available only for individuals who are directly working with the bacteria in laboratories, are in the military, or are involved with known anthrax outbreaks, whether animal or human. Principal treatment is with ciprofloxacin (Cipro), dioxycycline, or penicillin. Treatment must begin prior to the outbreak of symptoms and must include vaccination.

If there is the remotest possibility of exposure to anthrax, multiple-layered, properly fitted HEPA (High Efficiency Particulate Air) facemasks can filter 99.99% of most aerosol and dry-type anthrax spores. However, most anthrax is contracted through the skin or mucus membranes. A long, thorough shower with soap and water can wash away 99.99% of the bacteria.

Anthrax in the Mailroom

Chapter 8 addresses mailroom security procedures and equipment. However, as mailrooms have been shown to be susceptible to anthrax contamination, the following section covers procedures and materials needed to address this hazard specifically in mailrooms.

Anthrax bacteria is spread as a powder or spores. Should a white powder appear to be leaking from an envelope or package, this event should be treated as if it contains anthrax spores. If the powder turns out to be harmless, the worst that could happen is that a few people are frightened and/or embarrassed. If it should turn out to be anthrax, following the appropriate procedures may save many lives.

Facility mailrooms should be stocked with a few emergency materials, listed below. The security staff should confirm the stock of these materials at least monthly. Missing materials may contribute to a loss of life.

- Zip-lock bags large enough to hold a good-sized envelope.
- Heavyweight trash bags with twist ties capable of holding a medium-sized package.
- Optional, but important: A large, sealed plastic bag containing the following:
  — A freshly laundered pair of coveralls, large enough to fit an average-sized man. Too large is better than too small.
  — A pair of inexpensive slippers to fit the same-sized person.
  — A couple of pair of latex gloves.
  — At least two plastic bags with twist tie closures large enough to hold all of a person's clothing and shoes.
  — A bar of strong soap.
- A generous supply of latex gloves. (Some mailroom personnel wear latex gloves at all times when sorting recently received mail.)
- A conspicuously posted sign containing:
  — The telephone number of the local FBI office.
  — The telephone number of the local police department.
  — The telephone number of the facility's or organization's security station or office.
  — The telephone number and exact location of the nearest hospital emergency room with the capabilities of handling bioterrorist events.
  — The list of instructions shown in Figure 6.1.

Bubonic Plague

This bacterium has been the cause of millions of deaths throughout history. A terrorist would likely transmit it either through an aerosol or through the distribution of fleas, which, once released, would seek out ground squirrels and rats as their hosts. The disease initially manifests itself in the form of buboes, or swelling of the lymph glands, with severe pain. The bubonic form is nearly 60% fatal. If untreated or not treated in a timely manner, the disease will progress to either a septicemic or

If You Think That Anthrax Is Present, Do the Following:

1. First, put on a pair of latex gloves.
2. Immediately place the suspicious envelope or package in a zip-lock or trash bag and close tightly. Do not shake or try to empty the envelope or package. Handle very gently.
3. Place the closed bag in a second zip-lock or trash bag and close tightly.
4. If you do not have zip-lock type bags or trash bags, cover the envelope or package with an emptied waste basket, multiple sheets of paper or cardboard, or a piece of clothing.
5. Call the FBI, the local police, and your security staff.
6. List all personnel in the room with you when the envelope or package was discovered and bagged.
7. Take the sign with the telephone numbers and the package containing the overalls, slippers, and bags with you.
8. Leave the room.
9. Close the door.
10. Find an associate or individual willing to assist you.
11. Instruct them to call the numbers on the sign, to confirm your previous call and to provide helpful directions to your location.
12. Orally, give the associate the names of those people who were in the room with you and instruct him or her to give those names to the authorities.
13. Do not let them touch the sign or the list, which may be contaminated.
14. Instruct the associate not to let anyone into the room until the notified authorities have arrived and taken over responsibility.
15. Go to the nearest restroom.
16. Do not touch your face, any other parts of your body or clothing.
17. Open the restroom doors with your body not with your hands.
18. Instruct anyone in the room to immediately leave and not to return or let anyone else into the room.
19. Using the restroom soap, wash your hands and arms in lots of warm to cool water using lots of soap.
20. Remove the plastic bags from the package with the overalls.
21. Remove all of your clothing and shoes and socks.
22. Place all of your clothing, along with the sign you have taken from the mailroom with the emergency telephone numbers, and the list of the other persons in the room, in one of the bags and close tightly.
23. Place the first bag in the second and close it tightly.
24. Remove the soap from the package.
25. Wash as much of your body as possible under the circumstances. This is no time for shyness. Your life may depend on your actions.
26. Remove the fresh coveralls and slippers from the package and dress.
27. Turn over the bags with your clothing, sign, and list to the authorities.
28. Go to the closest emergency room that has the capabilities to handle bioterrorism events.
29. Double-bag the overalls and slippers, as they may be contaminated, to deliver to the authorities.
30. Take a long, warm-to-cool shower, using lots of soap and shampoo. The priority is to shower or wash as quickly and as thoroughly as possible.
31. Think. Try not to panic. Panic will cause you to breath more deeply and more quickly. Your life and the lives of others may depend on your following these procedures precisely.

Figure 6.1: **Mailroom Instructions for Possible Anthrax Exposure**

pneumonic form, both of which are nearly always fatal. Once a human has contracted the pneumonic form of the disease, it can be transmitted through the respiratory system by kissing, sneezing, or coughing.

It is obvious that leaving the contaminated area as quickly as possible is the best way of avoiding contamination. Treatment can be through vaccination, the injection of streptomycin, or sometimes gentamicin, although avoidance of host sources is the best method of protection. These include known or possible victims of plague and any fur- or hair-bearing animals that might be carriers of fleas. Again, the use of multiple-layered, well-fitted HEPA masks is helpful in preventing inhalation of airborne bacteria.

Smallpox

Because it is a virus (specifically variola), there are no known antibiotics that will treat the disease. However, a smallpox vaccine does exist. Vaccinations can be effective even if administered four to five days after exposure, although full effectiveness would not be achieved for about two weeks. Some relief may be obtained through the administration of vaccine immune globulin (VIG). Smallpox, like anthrax, may be a bioterrorist's weapon of choice. At present there are four known types of smallpox:

- Classic — highly contagious with a death rate of about 30%.
- Hemorrhagic — with a death rate of 95–100%.
- Flat form — so-called because of the shape and feel of the lesions, with a death rate of nearly 100%, but affects a smaller population.
- Modified — more often affects those who have been previously vaccinated and will affect up to 15% of the exposed population.

The best protection may be to leave the area as quickly as possible, if allowed. Vaccination (both well before or within days of potential exposure) and HEPA facemasks (because the virus is carried in the air by droplets) may be somewhat effective against an inhaled virus. Because the virus can survive for long periods, protective clothing that can be safely destroyed is a must for emergency response and healthcare workers.

One of the great concerns about smallpox is that it may be a leading prospect for genetic re-engineering with a potential of rendering it nearly vaccine-proof due to the time required to develop a new vaccine, if one could be developed at all.

Deterrents to Biological Agents

The aforementioned biological agents are only a few, but perhaps the most significant of the possible bio-terrorists' weapons of mass destruction. One of the greatest deterrents to their use may be the fact that once the genie is out of the bottle, it may not be possible to put it back in and may turn around and infect the perpetrator. All of the aforementioned diseases are self-perpetuating, and the direction of the winds and of contaminated people will determine which way the disease spreads. Those responsible for releasing the contaminants may be become victims of their own terror.

Chemical Agents

Chemical weapons agents (CWAs) can be classified as one of four basic types:

- Blistering agents
- Blood agents
- Nerve agents
- Incapacitating agents

All four are liquids or vapors, i.e., constituted of droplets. The first three are reviewed below. (Incapacitating agents have rarely been used.)

Blistering Agents

Mustard gas is not a gas, but a sulfur mustard vapor made up of fine droplets. Sulfur mustard is slow to act during cool or cold weather, but very fast-acting during warm or hot weather. Its primary penetration is through inhalation, although as little as 7 grams on the skin can cause death in over half of those contaminated. It has an odor of onions or garlic. It is highly penetrable, easily passing through clothing, even rubber and skin, where it will cause a burning sensation, stinging, extreme pain, and blisters. An exposed person has about two minutes to be decontaminated through washing with mild soap and warm or cool water. Since sulfur mustard penetrates very quickly, decontamination, even early, will not prevent penetration where the agent has been in contact with skin, but will prevent further spread of the agent.

Washing the eyes with a mild saline solution is the preferred initial treatment for eye contamination. Further treatment with ointments to prevent the lids from sticking together is helpful. Eye damage may take between two and four months to heal.

Blood Agents

Cyanide (KCN) and arsine (H_3As) act on the body by preventing the cells of the body from absorbing oxygen from the blood. The reaction to blood agents and nerve agents, as described in the next section, would be the same. The only clue might be the smell of bitter almonds or garlic. Individuals stricken with cyanide poisoning would have cyanosis (bluish discoloration) of the lips and under the fingernails. Quick administrations of amyl nitride will tend to kick-start the body, hopefully long enough to help it to burn off the poisons. As with nerve agents, getting to fresh air quickly provides the best chance for survival.

Cyanide exists all around us, every day. Burning silk, rubber, plastic, some paper, and cigarettes can generate cyanide. Cyanide is found naturally in some fruits and vegetables, but it would require eating massive quantities over long periods to cause any real toxicity. It is commonly used in electroplating, photography, and the manufacturing of some plastics.

Nerve Agents

There are five basic nerve agents, the best known of which are tabun, sarin, and VX. Of these, VX is the most dangerous by a factor of 100–150. It is quite viscous, much like thick syrup. It need not be inhaled, but can be absorbed through the skin and even through clothing into the skin. All are similar to Raid® and Malathion, a now banned insecticide, which are much less potent. Most nerve agents work on the respiratory system, nervous system, musculoskeletal system, cardiovascular system, and central nervous system.

If a chemical weapons attack is thought to be occurring or to have occurred, the best course of action is to first and foremost remain calm. Panic will cause faster breathing and possibly increase the rate of inhalation. Next, it is important to assess what is happening. Did someone in a crowd spray something over the heads of people, or did an aircraft fly over, trailing a smoke-like emission? Are people in the area developing sudden headaches, difficulty breathing, or nausea? Is there the scent of new-mown grasses, hay, or fruit — especially apricots, or oil of camphor?

The quickest antidote or treatment is fresh air. If at all possible, find some sort of shelter from the vapors. Most of these materials are heavier than air and will sink to the ground, seeking the lowest spots possible. Therefore, if there is no shelter available, try to move either upwind or to one side of the contamination flow. Remember, remain calm and breathe slowly, but breathe as much "fresh air" as possible. Scrape off any blobs of moisture on skin or clothing. Try to find a means of washing or, better yet, getting a shower. Soap and warm water will rid skin of 99% of the agent. Do not scrub too hard, as this may do more harm than good.

Atropine is the preferred medication. It helps to open up the airways and counters nausea and vomiting. Given prompt decontamination and medication, most nerve agent toxicity can be ameliorated in a matter of hours.

Radiation

Radiation is all around us almost all the time. Sunlight's ultraviolet short waves can burn us; its longer infrared waves provide us with heat. We ourselves emit some radiation. Higher levels of radiation are found the farther north or the higher one travels. Finland has one of the highest levels of Radon, while Australia has one of the highest levels of outdoor gamma ray radiations. The United Kingdom has one of the lowest levels of natural radiation in Europe. Radiation in the form of x-rays is used to radiate cancers. It is both good news and bad news, depending on how it is used and delivered to the environment.

All radiation is emitted from an atom. Some atoms, such as carbon-12, are very stable, meaning that their nuclei are completely stable and never change. Carbon-12 will remain carbon-12 forever. Others, such as uranium, are elements whose multiple and various-sized nuclei (isotopes) are unstable. These atoms are constantly changing, giving off their excess energy in the form of radiation (a process known as radioactive decay), trying to achieve a stable condition. The radioactive rays emitted from the atom can be in the form of gamma rays, alpha particles, or beta particles. Some radioisotopes decay into new or different elements and, in the process, emit gamma rays, along with alpha or beta particle radiation, until they become a different element. Uranium-238 will decay, given enough time (in the billions of years) to lead-206, which is totally stable and no longer radioactive.

Radioactivity is measured in Becquerels (Bq), a modification of an older term, the Curie. The Bq permits the measurement of radioactivity and comparison of one radioactive source to another. This comparison helps us to better understand the relative significance of various forms of radioactivity, the good forms and the highly dangerous forms.

Sources of Radioactivity	Amounts in Becquerels
1 Adult human (100 Bq/kg)	7,000 Bq
1 Smoke detector	30,000 Bq
1 kg of low-level radioactive waste	1,000,000 Bq
1 kg of high-level nuclear waste, 50 years old, vitrified in glass	10,000,000 Bq

How Dangerous Is Radiation?

This is a "depends" question. As mentioned previously, radiation has many sources, such as sunlight, granite, radon emitted from soil, and others. Cosmic radiation comes from outer space, and the earth's atmosphere provides our only natural protection from it, especially at its thickest point near the equator. The absence or thinning of atmosphere, such as at the South Pole, is a real cause for concern. The three most frequently encountered forms of radiation are gamma rays, alpha particles, and beta particles. Neutron particle radiation is found only when fissioning (splitting) or fusioning (combining) atoms inside a nuclear reactor. Thick layers of concrete or water provide protection from neutron radiation.

Gamma rays are similar to x-rays, true rays with wavelengths like a sound wave. (X-rays are usually produced by a machine rather than from an atomic nucleus.) Gamma rays have great penetrating power and can pass through animal tissue. Heavy layers of concrete, lead, or water are used as protection.

Alpha particles consist of two protons and two neutrons. Because of their relatively large size, alpha particles quickly lose energy. They have little penetrating power and are stopped by the first layer of skin or a sheet of paper. However, if ingested through breathing or swallowing, they can affect the body. Since they lose energy quickly over a relatively short distance, they will produce less damage than some other forms of radiation.

Beta particles are electrons from an atom's nucleus. They are much smaller than alpha particles and are emitted from many radioactive elements. Their penetrating power is up to 1–2 centimeters of animal (human) tissue. Lead or aluminum sheets 3–4 millimeters thick will stop beta particles.

None of the above will cause the body to become radioactive, but they can cause radiation sickness, leukemia and other forms of cancer, and in some instances, mutations. To quantify how much exposure is okay versus how much is too much, units of measure called sieverts (Sv) and millisieverts (mSv) — one one-thousandth of a sievert — will be used.

3-mSv/yr ± is about the normal background radiation in North America to which everyone is exposed. 50-mSv is the lowest level at which cancer may be caused in adults. In some parts of the world, levels in excess of 50-mSv/ are normal, with little or no discernable effects on humans. 1,000-mSv (1 sievert) over a short period is likely to cause early radiation sickness, but is unlikely to be fatal. Above 1,000-mSv, over a long period, is likely to increase the risk of cancer at some time in the future. Between 2–10 sieverts in a short-term dose would cause severe radiation sickness with increasing likelihood that this would be fatal. An

117

exposure of 10,000-mSv (10 sieverts) for a short-term and whole-body dose would cause immediate illness, such as nausea and decreased white blood cell count, and subsequent death within a few weeks.

"Dirty Bombs"

A dirty bomb is device consisting of a conventional explosive material, such as dynamite, used with a binder material, such as sawdust saturated with nitroglycerin $[C_3H_5(ON)_2)^3]$, C4 (known as RDX, for Research Development Explosive — $C_3H_6N_6O_6$), TNT [trinitrotoluol or $CH_3C_6H_2(NO_2)^3$], which is detonated in combination with radiological material. The objective of a "dirty bomb" is to spread radiological material over a fairly large area. The area involved will depend on three factors: the size of the explosion, the amount of contamination spread by wind or drift, and the area affected by falling dust.

As with a thermonuclear device, the best course of action is to avoid panic, leave the area, get rid of the clothes you are wearing, wash, and try to create or locate a HEPA facemask. Dirty bombs are intended to create panic as well as injury. The chances of surviving a dirty bomb event without injury are quite good if panic is avoided.

What to Do Following a Radiation Explosion

An atomic bomb could be delivered by a rocket, aircraft, or even in a suitcase. In such an event, the only warning is likely to be the explosion itself. While these guidelines may seem anticlimactic, they are measures that could potentially reduce the risk of injury or death. Upon hearing the sound of an explosion, it's best not to look towards its source, but rather get down on the floor or ground and stay down, as there may be an enormous blast of air, possibly super-heated. Stay down after it passes. Similar to the action of a hurricane, the air blast will return from the opposite direction with almost equal force. After the second air blast, move away from the blast zone as rapidly as possible. Limiting your time in the contaminated area is extremely important, if not vital. Avoid panic, which could cause more injury than the blast itself. Get out of the clothes you are wearing. Try not to breathe the dust or ingest it through your mouth. Find some form of a facemask, preferably a multiple-layer HEPA mask, to prevent breathing any dust particles. Wash with lots of water. Get any dust off of your skin, especially out of your hair. The chances are that you will eliminate 95% of any radiological contaminant by following these simple steps.

If you are in an area where a nuclear power plant has been damaged (through a violent act or by an accident), leave the area and keep as much shielding between yourself and the radiation source as possible. Immediately taking a dose of potassium iodide may help in preventing thyroid cancer.

Conclusion

This chapter provides a brief review of the particular hazards of chemical, biological, and radiological agents, along with some possible means of ameliorating their effects. It is hoped that no facility will ever encounter these agents, but having some understanding of their properties may help in developing an overall security plan. It is important not to become overwhelmed or panicked by the prospect of a chemical, biological, or radiological attack. Knowledge of what can happen, balanced against what is really likely to happen and what may be done about it, together with some old-fashioned common sense, may lead to some effective protective measures that remain within budgetary reason. Chapter 7 follows with some guidelines for response in the event of an emergency situation involving these and other security and safety hazards.

[1] www.emedicine.com/emerg

eMedicine Journal, April 16, 2002, Volume 3, Number 4, Daniel J. Dire MD, FACEP, FAAEM, Edited by Edmond Hooker, MD; John T. VanDeVoort, PharmD, DABT; Michael J Burns, MD; John Halamka, MD; and Raymond J. Roberge, MD, MPH, FAAEM, FACMT; eMedicine Consumer Journal, April 25 2002, Volume 3, Number 4, Jeffrey L Arnold, MD, FACEP, FAAEM and Jeffrey L Arnold, MD, FACEP, FAAEM. Edited by Suzanne White, MD, Francisco Talavera, PharmD, PhD, Robert G Darling, MD, Jonathan Adler, MD, and Raymond J. Roberge, MD, MPH, FAAEM, FACMT.

[2] www.terrorismfiles.org/weapons; www.ciss.org
Various papers by Anthony H. Cordesman, Holder of the Arleigh A. Burke Chair in Strategy at Center for Strategic Studies and International Studies.

[3] www.uic.com.au/ral.htm
URANIUM INFORMATION CENTRE Ltd.
Melbourne, Australia

Chapter Seven

Responses to Emergency Events

The previous chapter reviewed a number of terrorist weapons—what they are, how to recognize them, and to some extent how to mitigate their damaging or lethal effects. This chapter addresses the emergency response processes for dealing with a crisis, of whatever nature. Included are evacuations, alert systems, emergency equipment, weather forecasting sources, and the provision of fresh air supplies.

Emergency Response Teams and Plans

Following are some important questions to ask regarding emergency response provisions.

- Does the facility or organization have a structured Crisis Management Team familiar with the various emergency response plans?

- Has the Crisis Management Team developed Departmental Response Teams and an Infrastructure Response Team (described in Chapter 4) and, if available, a Health and Safety Response Team to go into action immediately following an event?

- Has the Health and Safety Departmental Response Team, or Infrastructure Response Team, established procedures for dealing with an unexpected emergency? Has it been trained in developing different responses to different emergencies? (These teams' responses can be tested and evaluated by a designated monitor through actual walk-throughs, as well as "tabletop" or "desktop" practices which can be conducted without leaving a meeting room.)

- Are there well-developed emergency response plans in place to deal with differing types of emergencies? Are these plans designed to mitigate panic and disruption as much as possible, yet adequately address the emergency?

- Has the Health and Safety Departmental Response Team or Infrastructure Response Team selected fire or floor wardens and their substitutes, and have they all been trained? Has there been a recent fire drill with a critique?
- Is there a plan or procedure in place for locating injured personnel within the facility and directing others, such as EMS (Emergency Medical Services) personnel, to them?

All of the above items should be checked and reviewed, and updated annually. Portions relating to wardens and personnel locations should be reviewed monthly to ensure continuity and accuracy of information.

Full evacuation drills should be held at least once a year for both a fire condition and a storm condition. Desktop drills and actual evacuation procedures and drills should be reviewed, revised, and re-published so that all personnel are aware of any changes.

Evacuation

There are two basic types of evacuations. The first and probably the most common is the result of fire or fire-related events, such as smoke, and toxic agents (e.g., chemical fumes or airborne bacteria, such as anthrax). A second form of evacuation would be the result of a natural event such as an earthquake, tornado, or hurricane. Each type of evacuation has its unique conditions and requirements.

Evacuations as a Result of Fire, Smoke, a Bomb Threat, or Toxic Agents

Most people are familiar with fire drills, having experienced them since grade school. Elevators will automatically shut down during a fire alarm condition and may be operated only by fire department personnel. This means that building occupants must exit through designated "Exits," which will either lead directly outside or down a fire stair tower that leads outside. Most contemporary fire tower stairways are pressurized during a fire alarm condition. Consequently, doors into a fire tower stairway should never be propped open, even if it appears that by so doing, more people could evacuate more quickly. Propping open a fire stairway door reduces the internal pressure, which will, in turn, permit toxic smoke and gasses to enter.

If the evacuation is triggered by a bomb threat, there should be alternate evacuation procedures and routes defined in order to evacuate personnel via what may be considered a safer route. There should be practice walk-throughs to test the efficacy of the procedure. If possible, more than one alternate exit route might be considered in order to avoid predictable patterns, which could be observed and documented by terrorists.

The evacuation plan should include a method of controlling personnel once they are outside. This might include directing people to specified areas where they will be safe from danger, removed from the fire department's activities, and yet within communication of designated fire wardens.

Evacuations as a Result of an Act of Nature

Evacuation as a result of a natural event, such as a tornado or hurricane, is substantially different. First, the evacuation is more likely to be announced over a public address system than signaled by an alarm. Because this form of communication is less pronounced than a fire alarm with flashing lights and claxons, the evacuation team and/or floor wardens will have a more significant role to play. If the facility has an internal public address system or a zone paging system, the evacuation instructions can be communicated much more easily. This is assuming that there has been no damage to the facility's internal systems.

Evacuation Routes

- Are all egress or exit points clearly marked and visible day and night and in event of loss of power? Are they clear of obstructions?

- In the event of a power failure, are all electronically secured doors programmed to "fail" open? Fire exits and stairway doors *must* fail locked from inside the fire tower so that they will open into the fire stairway only, not out onto the floor. Remember, fire stairway towers are most likely pressurized during a fire alarm condition. Do not attempt to prop open one of these doors.

- If floors contain secured areas such as Local Area Networks (LAN) rooms or Intermediate Distribution Frame (IDF) spaces, are fire stairways or exits accessible at all times? Areas of congregation (such as elevator lobbies that might be secured from the rest of the floor area, but have no fire exiting tower or stairway within them) must be provided with an emergency exit system initiated by pushing on the exit doors for a specified period of time (usually 15 seconds) — even though those doors may be alarmed. These doors or their adjacent panels must be marked with signs describing how to exit through them. This is both a building and a fire code issue. Following is language typical of what must appear either directly on the door or immediately adjacent to it. The lettering must be clear and at least 1" in height:

> Emergency Only
> Push on Door Until
> Alarm Sounds.
> Door Can Be Opened
> Within 15 Seconds.

- Do all personnel know how to exit and where they are to congregate? (Sometimes this is a matter of local code.)
- Are passageways clear of all obstructions, trip hazards, and "head-knockers?" People rushing toward an exit that may be obscured by low light or smoke must not be impeded by bad housekeeping or poor safety practices.
- Have arrangements been made to quickly and properly aid in the evacuation of physically challenged people? Have their locations and particular disabilities been identified? Are there plans to deal with their differing needs?
  - If the Health and Safety Departmental Response Team, or Infrastructure Response Team does not know what kind of assistance an individual might need, they should ask. Even if these individuals respond that they will need no special assistance, it may still be a good idea to develop a special assistance plan. Sometimes even the strongest of us fall short of our expectations.
- If there are spaces that are designed and constructed as "smoke-free containment areas," does everyone know where these areas are and how to reach them? Are they marked as such?
- Has the facility had a recent fire drill, followed by a critique?

Alert Systems

This section reviews four basic types of alert systems:
- Conventional Public Address (PA) systems
- Zone Paging Systems
- Chain or Telephone Tree calling
- E-mail Systems

PA or Public Address Systems

This is a conventional, reliable type of system. Usually someone in Health and Safety, Security, or Human Resources will make an announcement over the PA system, informing all personnel within the PA system's sound range of a condition and what action they are to take. PA systems are readily available and easy, if time-consuming, to install. These systems are moderately expensive and require a multitude of speakers, usually ceiling-mounted, and a broadcasting station from which announcements can be made. They have a high reliability factor unless they are installed with non-locking, local volume controls, which can be lowered to a "mute" status. The difficulties with these systems are:
- Authority — Who has the authority to make the announcements? This is particularly important in a multi-occupant facility when not all of the occupants answer to the same authority.

- Liability — Who assumes the liability of miscommunication, false alarms, or an untimely or no announcement having been made?

Zone Paging Systems

These operate through the telephone system and are dependent on all, or nearly all, phones being equipped as speakerphones. In essence, they are an add-on to a phone system's hardware and software. The software empowers telephones to be used as voice input stations, or to act as if they were microphones in a PA system. The caller may have the ability to access every phone in a particular area, a single floor, or all floors, in one or all of a number of buildings through the use of dialing codes. The caller employs an access code, then a location(s)-to-be-called code. All telephones within the specified calling block are called, and their speakers activated. The caller relays the message and instructions. The message can be extemporaneous or prerecorded and repeated at selected intervals. Again, these systems require speakerphones, and compatibility of the zone paging system equipment and software with that of the existing phone system, but they are only moderately expensive (http://www.bogen.com; http://www.valcom.com; http://clarity.com).

Chain or Telephone Tree Calling

Most people are at least acquainted with chain calling, a pre-systematized list of personnel, each with a specific list of other personnel and their phone numbers whom they are to call and notify in an emergency. At each tier, people will be required to communicate some sort of vital information, such as the need to evacuate a facility, and where they are to go. Each individual in Group One calls each person on his or her list of three to five individuals, who are in Group Two. The Group Two individuals, in turn, call the people on their lists in Group Three, and so on until all personnel have been called. The defects in this system are the time required to complete the calling chain and failure to notify individuals who are not at their phones, which can cause a breakdown in the chain or require someone upstream in the system to undertake more than his or her share of calls.
The benefit is the low cost. It is an inexpensive, if not too reliable system.

E-mail Systems

The ubiquitous, in-house computer network system has become the favored instrument of communication. However, many people check their e-mails only once or twice a day, if that often. Furthermore, many people are often away from their desks, in conferences, at someone else's office, or have their e-mails forwarded to a remote site. E-mail is a very unreliable means of communication for emergency notification. There is no harm in putting an emergency notice out in the form of a pop-up e-mail warning message. In addition, IT can lock all networked terminals until the pop-up warning has been acknowledged or cleared. However, e-mail messages should not be relied on as the sole method of alerting facility users.

Shelter from Severe Weather

Hurricanes

Natural event evacuation plans differ from fire evacuation plans in that people most often seek refuge from windborne debris or possibly dangerously high water levels. Hurricanes contain winds starting at 74 miles per hour for a Category 1 hurricane to winds of 155 miles per hour and up for Category 5 hurricanes. Evacuation from the path of a hurricane may be essential even if the facility is not in a coastal zone facing tidal surges. Wind damage and the danger from windborne debris are the most lethal results of such storms. Hurricanes often sustain winds for hours and can spawn tornados. Fortunately, hurricanes usually move slowly. Forecasting an evacuation will be in the time frame of days or hours, not minutes. If in the path of a hurricane, and there are no safe places within its path, the only really safe thing to do is to evacuate and travel to an area not severely threatened. Hurricane evacuations are usually ordered on a county-by-county basis. They are most often mandatory. Making the wrong guess about a hurricane's path could mean slim chances of survival.

Tornados

Tornados are a much more localized natural event, sometimes possessing winds of up to 200 miles per hour. Again, the objective is to evacuate to a safe area. Tornados can move across ground at speeds of up to 80 miles an hour. Forecast warnings may only be within minutes of the strike. Weather forecasts or storm tracking will likely begin with a weather advisory. If weather conditions deteriorate, a tornado or storm "watch" may be issued. If conditions deteriorate even more and there develops a likelihood of a tornado, an official "tornado warning" will be issued. This is the time to seek shelter, hopefully below grade and out of the direct path of the storm.

Tornados move quickly and with enormous force. Wind forces are capable of picking up an automobile and carrying it for hundreds of feet or driving wheat straw through a wood plank door. Therefore it is critical that the safest refuges possible be available for all personnel. Multiple areas of refuge may be required, depending on the facility, the number of building occupants, and the facility's proximity to some form of storm shelter. Some of the best locations for refuge are in the first or second stories, or below grade in underground parking structures. Evacuation, prior to the impact can be made using elevators as well as stairs. The fire stair towers themselves are excellent areas of refuge for acts of nature.

Weather Forecasting Sources

Besides the Weather Channel on television and the Internet's http://www.weather.com, the National Oceanographic and Atmospheric Administration (NOAA) Web sites contain long-range and up-to-date weather information. These web sites could be included in both the Contacts file and/or e-mail notifications. It would be very wise to procure one or more radios with battery backup or hand-cranked portable radios capable of being tuned to the local (regional) NOAA weather broadcasts (http://www.noaa.gov; http://www.nws.gov; http://www.spc.noaa.gov).

Emergency Equipment

Having on hand, maintaining, and conveniently locating basic first aid equipment is not a high cost commitment. A life may be saved with a defibrillator or emergency oxygen supply.

- Are there first aid kits readily available, and does everyone know where they are?
- Are there people who know CPR and the Heimlich maneuver? Is it known who they are and where they are normally working? Can they be easily found in an emergency?
- Is a defibrillator on hand, and are there people in the facility who know how to use it? Again, is it known who they are and where they are normally working? Can they be easily found in an emergency?
- Are an oxygen supply and masks available?
- Are there graphics displays for every floor — posted and, ideally, in the hands of all personnel — showing the location of all exits, fire and smoke detectors, fire extinguishing materials, alarm boxes, areas of refuge, and first aid materials?
  - Have these graphics been shared with the local fire, police and EMS departments and, if in a multi-tenanted building, with the building management?
- Have emergency plans been coordinated with building management?
- Is all fire suppression equipment in good working order, and has a qualified contractor recently tested it? Keep in mind that normally the fire department has no interest in gas-type fire suppression systems, such as FM200 (heptafluoropropane). Just because the fire department has

recently inspected the facility, there is no assurance that the gas fire suppression systems are in working order.

- Is there a centralized communications or public address system protected by a hardened environment?

Health, Safety, and Security

A good place to begin any security program is with those whose primary responsibility is the health and safety of both internal personnel and visitors. If the organization or facility has no special group responsible for this function, the Facilities and Human Resources departments may have to take on this role and produce a health and safety guideline. An appropriate place to begin might be obvious health and safety concerns, some of which may be related to security.

Fresh Air and Lighting

Although fresh air and work lighting systems are not strictly security concerns, they are both related to security measures. For example, in addition to provision of adequate lighting for evacuation of a building, we may also need to think about providing backup power for work lighting after an emergency event. Emergency lighting for evacuation is a minimum requirement intended to enable people to get out of a structure on an emergency basis. The level of lighting required to resume work after an event (that may have knocked out the local electric power grid) is another matter entirely — especially if the organization is working in a paper and pencil mode. Most ambient work lighting in today's facilities is not only fluorescent, but 277 volts. Providing adequate emergency backup power for work lighting and other operational requirements can be complicated and costly. The only practical solution may be a backup generator system. Most are diesel motor-powered. Natural gas will work, but most gas utilities will not guarantee an uninterrupted supply. Fuel cells are presently available, but for the most part must rely on some form of a fuel reformer, such as natural gas, methanol, or gasoline, and at present, have a very high cost per kW when compared to a diesel-powered generator.

Fresh Air Supplies and Biological and Chemical Contaminants

Nearly all buildings today are required to provide fresh air. Under current building codes, minimum amounts of fresh air must be introduced into ventilating systems. The amounts or percentages of required fresh air depend on the type or use of a particular space when it is designed, and applications are submitted for building permits. The greater the people load in a given space, the greater the required quantity of fresh or outside air. The fresh air systems are essentially quite simple. Usually, there is a louvered outside air intake located on or near the top of the structure, or at least at mid-level. Usually roofs are inaccessible, except to those with keys or pass cards and are restricted to maintenance and building operations personnel only.

If a particular fresh air intake is perceived to be highly accessible and vulnerable to a biological or chemical attack, consideration might be given to relocating the intake to a higher or otherwise less accessible location, or providing some form of security, ranging from CCTV to actual 24/7 guards.

A fresh air duct or outside air duct is usually run from the outside air intake down through the building, off of which requisite quantities are tapped and distributed throughout the floors, on an "as needed" or code-required basis. A portion of the structure's total air volume is bled off through the toilet room exhaust systems. Smaller portions escape through doors to the outside. Occasionally, fresh air is introduced or augmented on a floor-by-floor basis. If there is a perceived unique threat to a facility, these sources of fresh air would have to be protected, or modified based on code requirements and constraints, location, and type.

With this simple description of an outside air (OA) system, it is possible to consider what can be done in the event of some form of a biological or "gas" attack. The appropriate security measures will depend on the assessment of risk probabilities.

If the facility is located in an area determined to be reasonably at risk, a decision may be made to provide automatic or manual shut-off of the outdoor air intake blowers. Since most outdoor intake louvers are fixed rather than dampers and actuators, fixed louvers could be replaced with dampers and actuators with a remote control that can both shut down the intake blowers and close the dampers.

Many building managers may have already closed off their OA systems as a means of reducing the energy costs required to dehumidify, heat, or cool air, relying on building leakage for so-called fresh air. This practice would be in violation of most code requirements and could cause health problems.

Most standard filtration systems currently employed in facilities are one of four basic types and efficiencies and usually are made of low-density fibrous materials that are often coated with an adhesive substance, such as oil. Most filter materials are made of foams or felted cloths, or mats of fiberglass or cellulose fibers. Chapter 8, "Security Systems and Devices," reviews the different particle filter systems currently in use in a section following "Safe Rooms."

The Air We Breathe

It is interesting to note that in the typical metropolitan area the outdoor air that is pulled into facilities contains some pretty nasty contaminants, such as nitrogen oxide (N_2O), sulfur dioxide (SO_2), ozone (O_3), formaldehyde (CH_2O), hydrogen sulfide (H_2S) and hydrogen chloride (HCl). Many of these same contaminants are present in the suburbs. The country air may have less of the previously mentioned contaminants, but may have ammonia (NH_3) from fertilizers and animal waste.

Interior spaces will most likely be off-gassing formaldehyde from carpeting and other fabrics (including clothing), paper and other materials, and will have an abundance of carbon dioxide (CO_2) from our own breathing. Clearly, simple particle filters, such as those used in home furnaces, are not capable of contending with these chemicals, to say nothing of a terrorist attack. Addressing this threat may involve a multi-faceted approach, including remote control capability for shutting down the intake blowers and closing the dampers, HEPA filtering systems, and relocation and/or protection of air intakes.

See Chapter 8 for more information on HEPA filtering systems.

Conclusion

This chapter outlines some basic emergency response procedures, including evacuations, alert systems, and use of shelters, as well as emergency equipment. The Emergency Response Teams, described in Chapter 4, would include these items in the plans they develop.

Chapter Eight
Security Devices and Systems

Controlling Access

Most security begins at the perimeter of a facility. The objective is to prevent unwelcome persons from gaining access. Because there are frequently a number of different access and ingress points, all should be inventoried and assessed. Just because a door is normally secured from the inside and is theoretically to be used only for exiting (such as an exit from a fire stairway), this does not mean that it is, in fact, secure. Without some form of monitoring, any such door is a way into the facility space. An assessment can begin at the bottom or street level of the facility, with a log prepared, floor-by-floor, of every entrance into any of an organization's occupied areas, moving up through the facility to the roof. (See Chapter 3 and the Appendix for more on auditing a facility in preparation for security enhancements.)

Unauthorized individuals (including those associated with the user organization) should be prevented from accessing certain areas. At the same time, however, it is important to be sensitive to the needs of personnel to move about the facility with as much freedom as possible. The location of secured doors and the type of security or locking devices selected should be based on consideration of these criteria:

- Preventing undesirable individuals from entering.
- Permitting personnel reasonable freedom of movement.
- Permitting selected or authorized personnel access to sensitive spaces, while preventing access to others.
- Providing controlled access to specific areas for guests, service personnel, and contractors.

- Determining the level of security desired for any given space or area.
- Determining the form of monitoring desired for any point of access. Monitoring options may include:
  — Electronic logs
    - In only
    - In and out
  — Real-time, digital display, and/or
    - Archival history data
  — CCTV
    - Real-time, display, and/or archival history data.
- Selecting doors and areas to be controlled, and/or devices appropriate to the level of security desired.

Worksheet for Selection of Security Devices

Figure 8.1 is an example of security device selection and cost analysis, in worksheet format, for an urban building. The analysis is separated into three segments: *Ingress and Egress, Special Areas*, and *Costs*. The first addresses ingress and egress control and monitoring, essentially from the outside of a facility. The second, Special Areas, addresses internal ingress and egress for areas within the facility over which there needs to be a level of control. The third segment assembles the various devices into a costing matrix and produces a typical, if simple, budget. (Note: An interactive version of this worksheet is available at http://www.rsmeans.com/supplement/bldgsecurity.asp)

In this example, the analysis would have begun with the building drawings. This process involved locating every point along the building perimeter that was either a point of ingress or a point of egress only, such as a fire exit door. The parking structure, truck dock, and freight elevator and its lower level lobby are all considered points of entry into the building. All of these points require some form of security. Some were determined to require accessing devices, while others required only monitoring to determine if doors were open or closed, or windows intact and secure. In using the worksheet in Figure 8.1, it was necessary to count by hand the number of devices designated (by initials) and to enter the totals for each device in the appropriate box. The same process was applied to special or interior areas, adding the various required devices as designated by initials and indicating the amounts in the appropriate boxes. Finally, these quantities were transferred to a summary cost sheet. The security providers' unit cost estimates for each device were added to develop aggregate device sums and totals, plus costs for the selected e-cards, miscellaneous costs, and a contingency.

Ingress & Egress Points
Control and Monitoring Devices

Ingress / Egress	Drive Ramp - Entering	Drive Ramp - Exiting	Elevator - Lobbies	Passenger Elevators	Truck Dock & Freight Elevator	Fire Stair No. 1	Fire Stair No. 2	Roof & Penthouse Access
X Control and **X** Electronic Monitoring Functions	**SG** Security grille. **DC** After-hours access device. **PB** Parking attendant booth. **PG** Parking gate control device.	**PG** Parking gate control device. **DC** After-hours door or grille control device.	24/7 access devices. **DC** Parking Facility. **DC** Building.	**EC** After-hours control device. Assume two in parking. Assume controlled five in building.	**EC** Control device. Assume one elevator. **DC** Controlled access into building. **DP** Direct Phone to Security Station.	Unlimited access to stairway. **DC** Controlled access to occupied spaces. **PR** Door "open" Alarm.	Unlimited access to stairway. **DC** Controlled access to occupied spaces. **PR** Door "open" Alarm.	**DC** Controlled access to roof & penthouse. Unlimited egress from roof & penthouse to fire stairway. **PR** Door "open" alarm.
Parking Facility Street Level	SG,DC	PG, DC	DC			DC, PR	DC, PR	
P1 & Truck Dock	PB, PG		DC		DC, DP	DC, PR	DC, PR	
P2			DC			DC, PR	DC, PR	
P3			DC			DC, PR	DC, PR	
P4			DC			DC, PR	DC, PR	
P5			DC			DC, PR	DC, PR	
P6			DC			DC, PR	DC, PR	
Elevators				EC, EC, EC, EC, EC	EC			
Main Floor			DC, DC			DC, PR	DC, PR	
2nd Floor			DC, DC			DC, PR	DC, PR	
3rd Floor			DC, DC			DC, PR	DC, PR	
4th Floor			DC, DC			DC, PR	DC, PR	
5th Floor			DC, DC			DC, PR	DC, PR	
6th Floor			DC, DC			DC, PR	DC, PR	
7th Floor			DC, DC			DC, PR	DC, PR	
8th Floor			DC, DC			DC, PR	DC, PR	
9th Floor			DC, DC			DC, PR	DC, PR	
10th Floor			DC, DC			DC, PR	DC, PR	
11th Floor			DC, DC			DC, PR	DC, PR	
12th Floor			DC, DC			DC, PR	DC, PR	
Roof & Penthouse						DC, PR	DC, PR	DC, PR, DC, PR
CC									0
DC	1	1	31			19	19	2	73
DP					1				1
EC				5	1				6
ES									0
PB	1								1
PG	1	1							2
PR						19	19	2	40
SG	1								1

CC = CCTV; **DC** = Door Control Device; **DP** = Direct Phone; **EC** = Elevator Control; **ES** = Emergency Call Station
PB = Parking Booth; **PG** = Parking Gate; **PR** = Prop or Door "Open" Device; **SG** = Security Grille

Figure 8.1: **Security Selection Worksheet, Page 1**

Special Areas
Control and Monitoring Devices

	Parking Structure Entrance CC CCTV at Truck Dock Man Door	Parking Levels and Generator Room with Tank Room	Elevator Lobbies	LAN Room	IDF Rooms	Executive Suite	Wire Transfer & Check Writing	Main Entrances and Reception Lobby	
X Control and **X** Electronic Monitoring Functions	**CC** After-hours CCTV camera and **DC** door control device activated. **CC** CCTV at Truck Dock man Door.	**ES** Emergency call Station with **CC** CCTV camera. Emergency call activated. **DC** Controlled access device and **PR** Door "open" Alarm.	**CC** CCTV cameras. Each lobby entrance.	**CC** CCTV cameras. Each entrance.	**DC** Control device. **PR** Door "open" Alarm.	**DC** Control device. **PR** Door "open" Alarm.	**DC** Control device. **PR** Door "open" Alarm.	**CC** CCTV cameras. Each entrance.	
Parking Facility Street Level	CC, CC, DC	ES, CC	CC						
P1		ES, CC	CC						
P2		ES, CC, DC, PR	CC						
P3		ES, CC	CC						
P4		ES, CC	CC						
P5		ES, CC	CC						
P6		ES, CC	CC						
Main Floor			CC, CC		DC, PR			CC, CC	
2nd Floor			CC, CC						
3rd Floor			CC, CC		DC, PR				
4th Floor			CC, CC						
5th Floor			CC, CC	CC, CC	DC, PR				
6th Floor			CC, CC						
7th Floor			CC, CC		DC, PR				
8th Floor			CC, CC						
9th Floor			CC, CC		DC, PR		DC, PR		
10th Floor			CC, CC						
11th Floor			CC, CC		DC, PR				
12th Floor			CC, CC			DC, PR			
Penthouse									
CC	2	7	19	2				2	32
DC	1	1			6	1	1		10
DP									0
EC									0
ES		7							7
PB									0
PG									0
PR		1			6	1	1		9
SG									0

CC = CCTV; **DC** = Door Control Device; **DP** = Direct Phone; **EC** = Elevator Control; **ES** = Emergency Call Station
PB = Parking Booth; **PG** = Parking Gate; **PR** = Prop or Door "Open" Device; **SG** = Security Grille

Figure 8.1: **Security Selection Worksheet, Page 2**

Security System

Security Provider's Costs

Device	No. of Units	Unit Cost	Total Cost	Notes:
CC = CCTVs—Color	32	1,000	32,000	1
DC = Door control devices or readers	83	3,000	249,000	
DP = Direct connection phone (set)	1	600	600	2
EC = Elevator control operation readers	6	7,500	45,000	
ES = Emergency call stations	7	1,500	10,500	
PB = Parking booth controls	1	5,000	5,000	
PG = Parking gates	2	3,000	6,000	
PR = Prop or "Door Open" monitoring	49	1,250	61,250	
SG = Parking structure grille access device	1	6,000	6,000	
e-cards	500	10	5,000	3
Subtotal			**420,350**	
Misc. costs at 8% to 10%	1	42,000	42,000	4
Total all Costs			**462,350**	

Miscellaneous Costs	Hours/Feet	$/Unit	Cost	
Mounting Board—hours	4	80	320	5
3/4" EMT Conduit—feet	600	4	2,400	6
Dedicated 120 V, 20 Amp Outlets	4	52	208	7
Lighting for Equipment Closet	2	80	160	8
One time cost to install 2-ADSL circuits	1	200	200	
Total Miscellaneous Costs			**3,088**	
Total all Installed Costs			**510,726**	
Annual Expenses				
Security provider system annual maintenance			25,221	
Provider's annual system monitoring (Operations)			42,000	
Voice grade plus data dedicated telephone circuits (2)		65	130	
Total all Annual Expenses			**67,221**	

Notes:

1. Color to monochrome, deduct about $400 per camera
2. At truck dock man-door
3. This is a generic card neither a prox nor smart-card
4. Contingency and miscellaneous costs
5. Required for provider's control panels
6. Required for cables in exposed areas
7. Required for provider's control panels
8. Required for provider's control panels

Figure 8.1: **Security Selection Worksheet, Page 3**

Associated Labor Costs

Security providers usually do not perform general electrical work, such as installing a mounting board (on which they will mount their equipment), nor conduits needed for their cables, especially in exposed areas, such as parking facilities. These costs (which can also be recorded on a spreadsheet such as Figure 8.1) must be obtained from the facility's electrician. These items together comprise a fairly reliable estimate of installed costs of a security system.

Maintenance and Monitoring Expenses

The security provider will most likely have two annual expenses, one for system and equipment maintenance, and the other for monitoring the system on a 24/7/365 basis. Whether an outside provider monitors the facility's systems or it is done in-house, it may be wise to have at least two sites, possibly three, at which monitoring will take place. One should be at the public security desk, a second in the security director's office, and a third at a 24/7/365 monitoring station. (See Chapter 5 for more on security monitoring locations.)

Review of Security Devices and Systems

The security industry has developed a vast array of devices and systems to assist in protecting people and property. The remainder of this chapter offers brief descriptions of many of these items and what they do. The products are grouped by function, starting with barriers. (Note: More information and potential suppliers of many of these products can be found in the endnotes at the end of this chapter, as well as in the "Resources" section at the back of the book.)

Barriers
Fences

One of the simplest forms of control and protection is a wall or fence. Fences are still one of the most cost-effective and efficient forms of access and egress control. They are relatively inexpensive to acquire, simple to install, and effective in preventing people from entering or leaving specific areas. Fences or walls are nearly a must for facilities such as airports, marine installations, generating facilities, water treatment plants, storage yards, pumping stations, and other such facilities. Fences can be monitored through the use of either copper or fiber optic cables and intrusion detection sensors (http://www.fibersensys.com).

Walls

Walls can provide protection similar to that of fences, with the added benefit of visual privacy and acoustical screening. Walls are one of the oldest forms of protection devised by man. Some of the more famous ones include the Great Wall of China and Hadrian's Wall in England. There is even a wall in Savannah, Georgia, which legend has it was constructed to prevent ghosts from a haunted house from getting into the house next door. Wall construction is generally more costly than fencing and requires more time for installation. Today most barrier-type walls are constructed of concrete masonry units (CMUs), brick, cast-in-place concrete, natural stone, stucco, or combinations of materials. Walls can lend themselves to creative design solutions and can be made attractive with little added cost. They too can be monitored with intrusion detection systems.

Low Wall Barriers

Low-rise walls or barriers are available prefabricated in a multitude of designs, similar in functional design to highway median barriers. These barriers are available in many colors and stone finishes, usually in 4'-12' lengths and approximately 3' heights. Designs range from classical Greek panels to balustrades, to contemporary and others. They can be anchored to new or existing concrete or asphalt surfaces.

Planters, Bollards, Pilasters, and Spheres

In the same category with low-rise walls are architectural planters, bollards, pilasters, and spheres available in a variety of colors and stone finishes, with waterproof and anti-graffiti sealers. Like low wall barriers, these features can be anchored in concrete or asphalt paving surfaces or to sub-surface anchor blocks set in landscaped planting or lawn areas. Most manufacturers of these products can assist a user in selecting barriers and anchoring techniques to meet U.S. government anti-ram criteria ranging from stopping a vehicle traveling at 30 miles per hour within 50'-70', to stopping a vehicle traveling at 50 miles per hour within 3'.

Planters are available in a wide variety of shapes and designs from classical to contemporary, ranging in size from 30"-42" in height, and from 3'-6' in diameter, or side-to-side. Planters have the advantage of being not only highly effective barricades, but planted and properly maintained, can be attractive additions to a plaza or building entrance.

Bollards are usually smaller in size than planters or pilasters and are the workhorse of the individual barricade. They, too, are anchored by pinning, using internal steel pipe columns or bent reinforcing rods set into concrete. Bollards sometimes function as directional or informational signs. Bollard sizes range from 30"-48" in height, and from 10"-24" in diameter, or side-to-side.

Pilasters and Spheres are the no-nonsense "big guys" of barricades. As with planters and bollards, they are available in a variety of material colors and stone and sealer finishes. Often these are massive elements, with pilasters ranging in size from 6' to 6'-6" in height, and from 27"–32" across, and spheres measuring between 36"–48" in diameter. Pilasters can be acquired in design looks ranging from a simple column, base and cap, to coined, fluted, paneled, and cut stone, among others (http://www.durastone.com).

Mechanical Barriers
Gates

Mechanical gate barriers are becoming a more accepted and common means of pedestrian and vehicular control. They are no longer just the simple barrier arm-type often seen at railroad crossings and parking lot entrances and exits. Wherever fences or walls are installed, there must also be gate systems to allow ingress and egress. The value of security is only as good as the building site managers' ability to control those access points. Mechanically moving gate systems have progressed to the use of keypad, e-card, and other forms of access devices. Slide gates slide open, either to one side of the access point or to both sides. Swing gates also may open to one or both sides of the access point. Vertical lift gates are frequently used in large crowd control, but are more often employed in industrial environments and parking lots. Most systems are hydraulically driven and contain their own UPS backup power batteries.

Swing gates can open or close in 14–30 seconds, depending on their width and weight. Slide gates open or close at a rate of about one foot per second, although if speed is a special requirement, there are slide gates available that can open or close at a rate of over two feet per second. The barrier arm-type gates can open at rates from two to eight seconds and can close at similar rates, from three to eight seconds. Where overhead capacities are generous, lift gates may be the most cost-effective choice. They can be installed in widths up of from 10'–80' and can be opened to full height at a rate of about one foot per minute. Lift gates can be designed and manufactured as attractively as either swing or slide gates.

Restricted access vehicular gates are rated as meeting or exceeding UL325 Class IV, "for use in a guarded industrial location or building, such as an airport security area or other restricted access location not servicing the general public, in which unauthorized access is prevented via supervision by security personnel."

A Word of Caution: Mechanical gates are powered mechanical devices and can develop their own potential risks, either through their mechanical operations or entrapment (http://www.hy-security.com).

Vehicle Security Barriers

Vehicle security barriers offer a high-degree of security protection and are engineered primarily for the prevention of vehicle penetration. Most of these devices are built into a road or driveway bed and have two normal operating conditions: "Normal Closed," in which case the barrier is closed when there is an apparent need to prevent a vehicle from entering a private space, and "Semi-Open," which allows vehicles to pass only after having been authorized. The most common of these barriers are the anti-pass-back tire penetration devices found at most rental car lots at airports. However, these barriers are also available up to 12' high and capable of stopping most vehicles. Some are portable, tow-behind units, which can be set up by two people in about 15 minutes. Note: Improper operation where the barrier is activated without human intervention can result in injury or even death (http://www.armrservices.com; http://www.nasatka.com).

Window Protection

Chapter 5 (in the section titled, "Absorption") touched on the dangers of shattering window glass and the properties available in safety window glass and films. The following section delves further into this subject. Glass may present one of the greatest risks because it is such a common material, both on the exterior and interior of the building.

Interior Glass

Interior glass is used with greater frequency both to provide visual contact between people (such as supervisors and department personnel or associated parties) who require acoustical or hygienic privacy or separation, yet have a need to observe activities through an interior window. To create "greener" buildings, more glass sidelights next to doors, transom glazing at the tops of partitions, and glass partition walls have been incorporated into building designs in an attempt to harvest and distribute light and save energy. With the current concerns for protection from the ballistic nature of flying glass (which may result from an explosion or a natural phenomenon, such as a tornado), it is important to weigh the benefits of interior glass versus potential hazards. To review the options, it helps to know more about the types of available glass, for both interior and exterior use. There six or seven basic types, which are explained briefly below.

Types of Window Glass

Annealed or Float Glass (AG) Nearly all glass begins as float glass, that is, liquid or molten glass poured onto a bed of molten tin. The tin, being heaver than the glass, remains on the bottom, and the glass "floats" on top. The molten tin, undisturbed by any motion, remains absolutely flat and extremely smooth. The molten glass flows out to become a sheet, consistent in thickness and with its upper surface equally as smooth as the bottom surface floating on the tin. The tin, having a much lower melting point, remains molten while the glass begins to cool and harden. When sufficiently cooled and set, the glass is pulled from its tin bed and fed into a chamber where it slowly cools. This cooling, or annealing, process leaves the glass with only slightly compressed surfaces. When there is a failure from too much pressure, such as wind load or a smack from the back of a chair, or if there is too much heat on one side and too much cold on the other, the glass shatters into large, irregular pieces with razor-sharp edges. Most common window glass is of this type. Annealed glass will break at 0.2 psi of overpressure.

Heat-Treated Glass or Thermally Tempered Glass (TTG)

Thermally tempered glass, more commonly known as *tempered glass*, is annealed glass that is subjected to heat-treating. Monolithic, or annealed, glass is heated to 1150°F. Cool air is then blown across the both surfaces simultaneously, which rapidly cools the exterior skin of the glass, causing it to try to shrink. The two inner portions of the glass right under the outside surfaces remain fairly stable, while the innermost core remains stressed. The result is five layers. The two outer layers are under compression from shrinking, while the two next layers are fairly stable or neutral, and the inner layer is under stress. The layers are most often about equal in thickness. When this glass breaks, it does so in small cubes, or "dice." If properly heat-treated so as to meet certain ASTM, ANSI, and CFR requirements, the glass may be labeled as a safety glazing material or "tempered glass." This label is usually found etched into the glass in one of the corners of the sheet. Tempered glass will break at 0.8 psi of overpressure.

Heat-Strengthened Glass (HSG)

Heat-strengthened glass is similar to tempered glass. However, the tempering process has not produced the requisite surface compressions of tempered glass. Heat-strengthened glass is inconsistent in treatment and, as a result, may shatter in patterns similar to annealed glass. There is no industry standard for heat-strengthened glass. Heat-strengthened glass, also known as "double-strength glass," breaks at .04 psi of overpressure.

Chemically Strengthened Glass

Chemically strengthened glass is not normally used as a window glass even though it can achieve strengths equal to tempered glass. It is quite costly and is more often used in special industrial applications. When shattered, it responds more like monolithic or annealed glass, rather than tempered glass.

Laminated Glass (LG)

Laminated glass was discussed in Chapter 5 (under "Absorption") as a design approach to security, but will be briefly reviewed again in this section. It is sometimes called *safety plate glass*. It consists of two layers of glass, not necessarily of the same thickness, bonded together under a pressure of about 250 psi at a temperature range of 250°F to 300°F with an interlayer of polyvinyl butyral (PVB). Usually, laminated glass is made of annealed glass, which shatters into large, sharp shards. The shattered pieces will likely adhere to the interlayer, which will prevent them from becoming dangerous. Laminated glass can also be made using heat-treated glass, when required. An automobile windshield is made of two layers of thermally tempered glass laminated together with a single interlayer of PVB. The combined strengths of the tempered glass and the PVB interlayer give automobile windshields their inherent strength.

Insulated Glass Insulated glass, sometimes known as *thermo pane glass,* is fabricated of two layers of glass, either heat-treated or monolithic, set into a special frame that seals the space between the two layers of glass. The sealed, interstitial space may contain a low-conductance gas, such as argon or krypton, which are both safe and inert. In addition, one of the two interior surfaces of the glass may be coated with a metallic oxide, which can reflect up to 90% of heat energy. Which of the two surfaces is coated depends on whether the system is in an environment that is predominantly heated, or one that is predominantly cooled. Again, unless specifically required by building codes, one or both layers of glass may be monolithic, which means that shattered glass can present a high risk.

To this point we have reviewed types of window glass that may or may not be inherently dangerous in the event of breakage, especially from explosion, extreme wind pressure, or flying debris. Heat-treated glass presents a greatly reduced threat of ballistic injury, but only to the extent that the small pieces, or "dice," are not projected at high velocity. Laminated glass is, by far, the safest window system of those that are commonly available, but it has a comparatively high cost, especially if it is used in combination with an insulated system.

Bullet-Resistant Glass Lexan®, a product of GE Structured Products, is a typical polycarbonate sheet product used in the manufacturing of bullet-resistant glass systems. These systems are comprised of multiple layers of glass and polycarbonate sheets. Both the glass layers and the polycarbonate layers can be of varying thicknesses and numbers of layers. Some bullet-resistant glazing systems can be manufactured of either a single layer or multiple layers of just polycarbonates, with no glass involved at all. These systems usually require specially designed frames and are very expensive to acquire and install. Consequently, they are usually installed only where a high degree of security is required (http://www.lexan.com).

Films

One common and now highly developed method of protection from heat is through the use of retro-applied films. Mylar®, a Dupont product, is one of the oldest, if not the oldest of the polyester-based films. Until recently, residential and commercial use of these films has been by application directly to the inside of a very clean, very wet glass surface with the edges of the film trimmed to the window frame. A release liner is removed from the adhesive surface of the film, and the excess water is squeegeed from between the glass and the film.

The initial intent of this film was to control solar-heat transmitted through the glass, with a resulting reduction in air conditioning costs. These applications go back to the 1960s. Over time, some of the films failed. The thin, reflective coatings were comprised of tiny, interspersed dots of metal (often silver), and those dots would begin to migrate towards one another, forming large areas of reflective material, with some clear film. Some films began to peel off of the glass. Nonetheless, the industries supporting window films have since developed their products to high levels of performance and reliability.

More recently, the widow film industry has taken an additional direction toward protecting window glass from the hazards of flying debris. These films, called fragment retention films, or FRF, can protect glass from deliberate acts of violence in the form of explosions, vandalism, or attempted break-ins—and from wind pressures and wind-blown objects. The use of films as a means of protection from wind pressures and wind-blown objects resulted from building code changes, which have begun to require protection against ballistic objects carried by extreme wind velocities. These building code changes are in response to the Federal Emergency Management Agency's (FEMA) insurance requirements designed to reduce insured damage as a result of natural disasters. The film must be applied in conjunction with a properly engineered and installed frame system capable of holding the film in place when stressed by a severe impact. Properly installed, a film and frame system not only serves to prevent intrusion of ballistic-like objects, but will also substantially limit the hazard of flying glass shards. Window films are produced in various thicknesses, ranging from 1.7 mils for solar (1 mil = 0.001 inch); safety films starting at 4 mils thick; and security film starting at 7 mils. The thickest film commercially available is about 15 mils.

A Few Words of Warning In considering the use of window films for thermal and or security control, it is important to work with an experienced and reliable contractor. Due to the nature of heat or solar reflectivity, applying the wrong reflective film to the inner surface of insulated glass (dual panels) can often cause a sufficient expansion of the gas sealed between the two glass layers to cause one of the layers to crack, or the system's seal to be broken—an expensive mistake. This problem has become more common as more and more homes and offices have insulated glass windows. Fortunately, manufacturers and installers have become very aware of the problem and can recommend filming solutions that should prevent this damage. It is best to ask the contractor about the particular film that is being specified. There are specially tinted films that do not cause enough heat reflection to create a system or glass failure and can still provide some heat control, almost total ultraviolet control, and a great deal of impact security.

Another consideration in the use of films is the potential for adhesive limitations. The adhesives bonding the film to the glass will at some point begin to break down, causing the film to delaminate from the glass. Recent improvements in adhesives have extended the bonded life of films into the realm of 15+ years.

A third difficulty, particularly with some of the early films, was a tendency for the reflective or coloring materials (applied to the film to give it its reflectivity or color) to begin to separate (through molecular adhesion) into small dots of material. The result is a reduction in heat reflectivity and therefore a decreased effectiveness of the film (http:www.glasslock.com; http://www.3M.com).

Fabric Screening Systems, or Blast Curtains

Chapter 5 touched on the use of specially fabricated window draperies, capable of stopping glass window shards that might result from explosions, wind pressure, or wind-blown debris. Two different systems are available, both of which use specially constructed fabrics fixed at the head, or top, of the window. Here the similarities end. One system is fixed at both the head and at the bottom of the window, much like a solar screen. It is available in two configurations, one of which is designed to catch the glass shards through tension and to reject the glass back in the direction from which it came, at the same time letting the gas and air pressures dissipate through the fabric mesh.

The second configuration acts more like a net, again dissipating the gas and air pressures through the mesh and absorbing the shards and shock as the mesh "bags" with the pressures and catches the flying glass (http://www.BlastShield.com). The second system also uses specially manufactured fabrics to catch ballistic glass shards and to dissipate explosion forces. However, this system has more of a drapery appearance, being fixed at the head, but not at the foot. Excess material, at three times the width and twice the height of the primary window coverage, is folded into a special "trough," which is fixed at the windowsill or the bottom of the drape. This excess material also "bags" into the room, absorbing the gas and air pressures, and at the same time netting the glass shards. As the pressures dissipate, the fabric relaxes, and the glass shards drop into the trough. Both of these products meet the GSA criteria for glass hazard mitigation. Both are fabricated of polyester-enhanced fibers, some of which achieve tensile strengths as high as ten times that of steel wire (http://www.safetydrape.com).

HVAC Security
Safe Rooms

Over the years, cigarette smoking has become a less acceptable practice, particularly around other people. Initially employers tried to designate a special area for their smokers, but without doors, these areas permitted too much secondhand smoke to spread into adjacent areas, to the discomfort of non-smoking employees. Eventually, special lounges or smoking rooms were made available for the smokers. Problems and complaints continued as the concentration of smoke was sucked into the return air system and then returned throughout the facility through the HVAC system. In addition, the heavy smoke load within the designated space was even more than many of the smokers wanted to experience.

The industry, ever ready to fill a need, began to develop air-handling equipment to eliminate the smoke. Three different solutions have evolved: charcoal filtering systems, ultraviolet light, and ozone generation. Manufacturers began providing units of varying sizes and capacities, eventually producing models that could be used in larger and larger spaces, such as restaurants and bars, some portable, some ceiling-hung, and others large enough to handle complete facilities. The cleaned up "smoke-filled rooms" have now evolved into special rooms capable of providing havens from biological and chemical contaminants through the use of these purifiers.

Activated charcoal can filter with up to 99.99% efficiency. Ultraviolet light can decontaminate many of the toxic particles trapped in the activated charcoal filter. Care must be taken to avoid overexposure to UV, which can cause painful eye irritation, sunburn, and skin cancer. Most frequently, the ultraviolet waves are contained within the equipment to prevent direct exposure to building users.

Ozone is a gas and a form of elemental oxygen. Oxygen is inherently stable and exists as diatomic molecules (O_2). However, molecules of ozone contain three oxygen atoms (O_3) and are inherently unstable. Ozone is a very irritating and toxic gas, and is very reactive, which is what makes it such a powerful bactericide. It is also an extremely powerful oxidizing agent. It is oxygen that bleaches clothes with chlorine bleach, or teeth with hydrogen peroxide (H_2O_2). Because ozone is so caustic, it, too, like ultraviolet, can be dangerous. It is also a gas and cannot be contained while decontaminating air. The amount of ozone generated and distributed in the air must be carefully regulated so as not to cause lung damage to those who breathe it. Ozone filtering equipment is available with features that can continuously sample the air within a room, as well as regulate the amount of ozone it generates.

While safe rooms are limited in area due in part to the limits of ultraviolet decontamination of the filters and the need to limit the quantity of ozone injected into the air stream, they may be as reliable a "safe haven" as one might find given a bio-terrorist event. Air filtering systems are also covered at the end of Chapter 7 in context of providing clean air in an emergency situation (http://www.hivroom.com).

Particle Filter Systems

Some protection from chemical, biological, or radiological and other substances can be offered by filtration systems. Most standard filtration systems currently employed in facilities are one of four basic types and efficiencies and usually are made of low-density fibrous materials that are often coated with an adhesive substance, such as oil. Most filter materials are made of foams or felted cloths, or mats of fiberglass or cellulose fibers.

There are four fundamental types of filter systems in use today, with elaborations and combinations that can result in complex and highly efficient filtration systems. The basic types are:

1. **Straining:** Fairly inefficient, traps particles larger than the spaces between the fibers.

2. **Impingement:** Most common, still low-efficiency. Particles get stuck or hung up on the filter's fibers, which are usually coated with an adhesive.

3. **Interception:** Medium efficiency. Particles bounce around from one fiber to another until they adhere to a fiber or fibers.

4. **Diffusion:** Good efficiency. Tiny particles are churned in the air stream and collide with molecules of the air itself (called a Brownian Movement), causing the particles to eventually attach themselves to a filter's fiber.

These kinds of filters will handle most airborne dust, some vapors (a liquid converted to a gaseous state), and some forms of chemical weapons.

There are two non-standard or less common types of filtering systems available. They are adsorption condensation and chemisorption. These are fairly large systems with a higher first cost and are more costly to operate than the more basic systems. The filters they require have a comparatively short life span.

Adsorption Condensation: There are two variations:

- The older design consists of a tray or trays of activated charcoal called a *sorbent,* through which the air stream is directed. These filters were messy to install and change, as the charcoal tended to drift out of the tray and spread itself all over the place.

- The newer designs have the sorbent charcoal encased in a mesh. These newer types are far easier to change and far less messy. They are also able to use a so-called "small geometry" charcoal, which has a higher and faster adsorption rate. These filters function by trapping particles and absorbing vapors in the charcoal by diffusing the vapor particles and converting the vapor back into its liquid state, where it is absorbed by the charcoal. The used charcoal is ultimately disposed of. Because the diffusion process is not instantaneous, there is a limit to the amount of vapor that can be absorbed in a given time period. In other words, this form of filter can be overwhelmed by a large quantity of vapor.

Chemisorption: This system is similar to adsorption condensation in that there is an activated charcoal base. However, if a reagent is added to the activated charcoal, the vapor particles or gas molecules will tend to bond to the sorbent. The reagent will then cause the vapor or gas to be converted to a different, benign chemical compound. Some of these converted compounds will remain bound to the sorbent; others, such as water and carbon dioxide, will be released into the air stream. Typical reagents are potassium permanganate, silica gel, or activated alumina. Chemisorption is comparatively slower due to the complex nature of the chemical processes.

The two above systems, both of which primarily utilize activated charcoal as a sorbent, are expensive to operate on a 24/7 basis. Those utilizing a true HEPA (High Efficiency Particle Arresting) filter system require a pre-filter to prevent a too rapid clogging of the fiber geometry. Packaged systems or processes are available that can provide chemical, bacteriological, viral, and radioactive product responses. These systems have capacity limitations due to the limits of air flow (cubic feet per minute) that they can accommodate.

Some systems have the capacity to generate controlled quantities of ozone (O_3), which can decontaminate very large spaces over a period of time to allow for sufficient air turns. As previously mentioned, ozone is highly corrosive to lung tissue, particularly in quantities in excess of .1 ppm. Safe levels of ozone are in the range of .05 ppm and below. Use of ozone as a decontaminating agent must be by people with expert training, with no others in the area being treated. The federal government, in some locations, is considering the use of ozone as a decontaminating agent (http://www.tbisolation.com; http://www.surroundair.com).

Identification Systems
Biometrics: Current Availability and Future Trends

Biometrics are electronic methods of identifying and authenticating a person's identity through the confirmation of his/her physiological or sometimes behavioral characteristics. Techniques in use and/or development include fingerprint matching, iris and retinal scanning, facial recognition, hand geometry matching, voice recognition, and even vein matching.

The next section addresses fingerprint matching and, to a lesser degree, iris and retinal scanning and facial recognition. It also touches on hand geometry and vocal recognition. Before delving into any particular system, it is important to spend a moment considering what is required in terms of reliable identification and authentication. If an organization is not engaged in highly classified, financial, or physical risk-intensive functions, the preferred systems will be those that function in minimum response times.

In reviewing both the facility's needs and options, the ultimate objective should be an integrated or "enterprise" system. This means permitting only authorized personnel into the facility, and permitting only specially authorized personnel into special areas (such as LAN rooms, spaces where highly sensitive information is being processed, money counting rooms, clean rooms, and biological or chemical processing rooms). There might also be a need to restrict access to certain computers and/or to specific files and functions, such as "read only" authority. Chances are that an ID database configured by the internal security department or consultant for access purposes will not be compatible with an ID database configured by the organization's IT department. (See Chapter 9 for more on systems integration.) Finally, depending on the organization's risk assessment, the costs of installing and maintaining these systems will play a major role in the type of biometric devices selected.

Fingerprint Matching

Among the electronic fingerprint matching techniques currently in use are the **minutia-based** technique and the **correlation** technique. Both correlation and minutia-based technologies locate numerous points on a fingerprint that differ from a consistent pattern and then map them into a unique geometric *template* that can be plotted and measured from point to point, converted to computer code, and stored as a template. Minutia techniques match the minute points of a fingerprint that differ from a "normal" or common pattern. Because of the number and variances of minutia points, if a fingerprint is of a poor quality due to dirt or lack of consistent sizing, a faulty match may result in either a "false reject" or a "false acceptance."

The correlation technique depends on matching or correlating specific points. Points stored on a template in the database are matched with those captured at the point of access. This technique has difficulties due to lack of precision and rotation. In other words, if the stored print and the print to be matched differ as to a precise location of a registration point, or are affected by image translation and rotation, left to right or right to left, the result may be a "false reject" or a "false acceptance," as can occur with the minutia-based technique.

Those working in the industry are attempting to combine various matching techniques in order to increase accuracy. Improvements include computer-enhanced "acquisition" or "sensor" fingerprints. A fingerprint-based authentication system must achieve a very low False Reject Rate (FRR), as well as a low False Acceptance Rate (FAR). If there is a high FRR, the efficiency of a biometric authentication system is severely

Background Checking

In attempting to attain reliable identification and authentication of those who enter a facility, it is crucial to incorporate background checking into the plan. Background checks are not security devices or protective construction elements, as are the other topics in this chapter, but are noted here because they are so integral to a successful security system.

The first requirement in any identification system, and also its weakest link, is finding out if people are who say they are, and what their backgrounds really are. ("I know who I am, but do you really know that I am who I say I am?") During 2001, 900,000 people had their identities stolen in the United States. It is possible to secure multiple Social Security numbers, which provides the ability to secure multiple drivers' licenses. The Immigration and Naturalization Service has acknowledged losing track of 547,000 foreign national students. The maintenance worker

invited into Elizabeth Smart's home to perform part-time work had 18 felony convictions.

It is paramount that thorough background checks of all personnel be conducted and authenticated. Checking references may not be enough, and may in fact yield nothing due to dishonesty or reluctance to provide information. If a former employee or associate is given a bad reference (even though facts are accurate) and he or she is consequently denied a particular job, the reference provider could face a lawsuit for defamation of character. If, on the other hand, the same former employee, discharged for cause, is given a favorable reference that leads to new employment, and turns out to be a criminal, the new employer may be able to sue for providing false or misleading information.

Background checks are not expensive. In-house security personnel are capable of performing some background checking

limited. If there is a high FAR, unauthorized individuals may be gaining access. Given the probable variables in sensing devices, potential transmission line noise, or even the displacement of image due to the pressure applied by the individual whose print is being scanned, it becomes very difficult to achieve perfect success with any one technique. Yet, even though it is estimated that close to 5% of the population does not have a readable fingerprint, biometric fingerprint identification and authentication remains at the top of the list as one of the more practical, cost-effective, and universal systems available.

One of the greatest drawbacks of fingerprint identification is that it appears to be privacy-intrusive. One way to preserve privacy is to store the template of an individual's fingerprint, rather than the print itself. A template is what is stored in most databases and is more than adequate for one-to-one or one-to-many matching. However, the use of templates only may be changing. Given the trends toward interrelated identification databases, full fingerprint databases may be more commonly used.

directly. Firms specializing in background checking can provide on-line background checks, probably in far greater depth and accuracy than most organizations' in-house security personnel. These firms can also perform the check in less time and for less cost than the cost of an internal security officer's research time or human resources personnel's face-to-face interview. Using qualified, independent background providers also helps protect internal personnel from liability exposure. Considering that hiring and then losing an employee for cause—or for any reason—will cost about 25% of that employee's annual salary, it is apparent that doing it right the first time is the better practice (http://www.choicepoint.net).

Risk Assessment and Background Checking

The type of employer and the particular job function determines how intensive or invasive the background check should be. Risk assessment is an evaluation of both financial and physical risk. An individual with a history of violent crime may pose a physical threat to fellow employees. An applicant who falsifies academic or work qualifications may pose a risk such as malpractice or loss of funding for the organization.

Pre-employment background checks have become a necessity for employers and must extend to part-time workers, including contract workers and consultants. Interestingly, many workers think that their employers should be conducting more stringent background checks. (See the end of this chapter for more about privacy and security.)

Difficulties with Fingerprint Databases Fingerprints are collected and stored every day by the thousands. They are collected in some driver's license applications or renewals, facility accessing systems, criminal arrests, job applications, military enlistment, and other situations. The FBI has about 70,000,000 fingerprints in its growing database. It is obvious that some form of indexing or classifying fingerprints is needed, and with some consistency from one database to another, in order to cut down the time required to search through these huge databases. True, more powerful and faster computers can handle searches in minimal time, but the cost of these computers and their related software and support is very high. Fortunately, there is an indexing system that can be adapted to a computer system, which employs a set or bank of filters called Gabor filters, which have the capacity to establish patterns of pixels, which are similar and can be used to classify various fingerprint patterns.

There are five basic patterns used in classifying fingerprints. These five patterns are *whorl, right loop, left loop, arch, and tented arch.* Combining certain patterns, such as arch and tented arch classifications, can improve classification accuracy from 90–94.8%, and by adding a reject option, a classification accuracy of 97.8% can be achieved. Currently, fingerprint scanning is by far the least costly, if not the absolute in reliability. This indexing system method rarely produces a false acceptance, but it can produce about a 3% false-rejection. Iris scanning systems, covered later in this section, can achieve false-rejection rates at 0%.

Hand Geometry

The human hand is not as unique as are fingerprints, retinas, or irises. However, combining features, such as the finger lengths (and comparative lengths of one finger to another on the same hand), thickness of fingers, and width and length of palm, can provide fairly accurate templates for authentication, if not enough for identification. Because hand geometry scanning is so much easier to acquire and to scan for verification purposes, it has the value of simplicity and speed. When combined with another biometric system, such as a fingerprint scan, it can be a useful tool where frequent authentication is needed.

Vocal or Speech Recognition

Speech patterns and sound emissions in humans are based on physiological features of the individual's speech production system, cultural influences, speech habits, gender, age, physical condition, and a host of collateral influences. To create a database of voice patterns and sounds is a complex and time-consuming project. Just recording a voice for identification or verification purposes is time-consuming. The odds of achieving a match are reduced by the many physical influences that can distort a person's speech, including fatigue, illness, aging, and smoking.

Voice recognition is being used for computer control and for text input. Once the voice and speech characteristics are captured and converted into a recognition program, these systems are capable of transcribing speech into text at a rate of up to 160 words a minute. This is not biometric security.

Facial Recognition

Facial recognition systems analyze images of human faces by measuring such characteristics as the length of the nose, distance between the eyes and/or eyeballs, and angle and width of the jaw. Well over a hundred modeled features may be used to create a template. As with any other biometric system, an individual's facial scan is compared to his or her template for authentication purposes, which may be called "one on one" matching.

Facial scanning is fraught with difficulties as either an authentication or an identification system, unless operated in a situation with limited focus, such as in a Las Vegas casino, where monitoring for known cardsharps or card-counters might employ a relatively small database. Even then, facial recognition databases must be constantly updated when there are differences in lighting or camera angles. Changes in people's appearances such as hairstyles, beards or moustaches, and weight gain or loss all interfere with facial scanning.

Retinal Scanning

The retina is at the very back of the eyeball and requires an infrared light to penetrate through the pupil to scan it. First, the retina is scanned to map the vascular patterns for the database. Then the retina is scanned each time it is necessary for identification or authentication. Retinal scan identification and authentication technology is credited with being the most reliable of all of the biometric systems. However, the difficulties in capturing the initial template against which to compare, along with the follow-up difficulties in capturing the comparison image, render retinal scanning systems cumbersome to use, unless they are necessary and employed in a very high-security environment.

Iris Scanning

Iris scanning is another matter entirely. Along with retinal scanning, it is likely the most reliable method of identification and authentication. The iris, or colored portion of the human eye, is formed at birth, fixed by the age of two years, and barring injury, never changes during one's lifetime. An individual's left eye is different in many respects from the right eye, once in a while even in color. An individual iris has over 200 characteristics that can be mapped and assigned geometric relationships. The resulting electronic template is recorded in the database. Usually both eyes are photographed and recorded, so that the resulting electronic image characteristics could be as high as 400 or more. Because an infrared camera captures the images, high-intensity lighting is not required. The odds of a false acceptance are about 1 in 1.2 million. The process is reported to take a mere three seconds, including a check for the normal continuous fluctuation in pupil size. Eyeglasses, tinted glasses, dark glasses, and some contact lenses can interfere with capturing a clear, matching image.

Photographing the eye for the initial database template takes only a few seconds. Mapping and processing the image into a template takes a few minutes. Thereafter, comparison images are captured at a glance and take only two to three seconds. Personal experience with iris scanning has demonstrated a time of ten seconds for finding a match and permitting access (opening a door). The lag time depends on a number of systems configuration factors, such as the size of the database being interrogated. Compared to biometric fingerprint systems, iris scan systems are quite expensive and respond much more slowly. However, they are assuredly at the high end when it comes to conclusive identification and authentication.

Multi-Modal and Biometric Systems

It should be apparent by this point that there is no such thing as the perfect biometric system. Some systems are extremely accurate, but a little slow. Others lack reliability or are too unwieldy or costly to install or to operate. Multi-modal (as in multiple-modes) systems offer some strong performance enhancements. By combining two or more biometric systems, it may be possible to overcome some of limitations inherent in a single system, especially in those instances where a high degree of identification and/or authentication is required.

An alternative to a pure biometric multi-modal system is a system that combines a biometric system with a "smart" card, which, to this point, has been grouped with other types of e-cards, but will be explored shortly.

Access Systems and Devices

To understand how an effective security identification and authentication ingress or ingress/egress accessing system can work, it is helpful to first take a brief look at its elements, keeping in mind the salient aspects of identification and authentication. First is the simple, magnetically encoded, "swipe," credit card. This is nothing more than a simple identification card that represents the holder or user of the card. There is usually a space on the back of the card for that individual's signature. Hopefully, the holder and user of the card is really the person to whom the card was issued. The card does not really identify the individual as the authorized cardholder, because it fails to authenticate that the person representing him or herself as the authorized cardholder is, in fact, that individual. This type of card has only one element of authentication, the signature, which is easily forged and rarely examined by the person approving the credit card transaction.

A bank or Automatic Teller Machine (ATM) card, on the other hand, requires the knowledge and use of a Personal Identification Number (PIN). The card identifies the individual wishing to perform some form of banking transaction, and the PIN (which only the authorized user is supposed to know) is the form of authentication. This is clearly a far more secure system than the simple credit card, which relies on a signature only for authentication.

Any good accessing system—whether controlling access to a facility, special area, computer (or particular files on the computer), or special equipment, must be able to identify and authenticate before authorizing access. The security and reliability of the system depends on the reliability of the identification system.

Basic System Components and Workings To understand the facility or organization's system needs, it is important to understand the basic system components, what they do, and how they do it. Access systems are basically a simple loop, which, in very simple terms, engages in the following exchange:

"May I access this door?"

The system responds with, "Who are you"?

"I am Joe Smith."

"Prove it."

"OK, here is my authentication." (In this instance, a PIN.)

"Yes, you seem to be Joe Smith. I'll now unlock the door."

The door unlocks, and Joe Smith goes through. This process can take between a fraction of a second and a few seconds, depending on the complexity of the authentication process.

The pieces and parts of the system start with the identification tag, which displays Joe Smith's company name or other affiliation, perhaps his title or function, and probably his photograph. This information is printed on the outside of the card. For the moment, we will assume Joe's ID card to be a magnetic stripe type. (Although magstripe identification/access cards are becoming less frequently used for this purpose, they probably still represent the majority of the systems in use. Conversion to a so-called "smart card" is costly.) The card is the electronic key to the system. Joe presents his card to a reader adjacent to the door, in this instance a swipe reader. He then inputs his PIN using a keypad. The reader "reads" the information encoded in the magnetic stripe on the back of the card, which may be little more than an encrypted identification number. A data cable connected to a remote computer database transmits Joe's transmitted ID number, the keypad PIN entry, and the identification of the particular door to which he is seeking access.

Joe's ID number is sequentially located and matched to his ID number in the database. The transmitted PIN is matched to his PIN in the database file, thereby confirming that the person requesting access is authorized. Joe's database file contains a list of doors, facilities, devices, or other integrants for which he has been granted access authorization. If Joe is authorized to enter this door, the computer sends a signal (via cable) back to the door, which either releases the latch or shuts off the magnetic lock, so that he can enter.

There are many and varied components, including cards (technically called "tags") that can be substituted at the input end of the system. The following section is a brief review of the most common types. With one exception, nearly all access systems work on the same principle and rely on identification and authentication.

Identification Cards, Tags, and Badges

ID, or Identification Badges, are among the oldest and most common type of device used to identify individuals. They range all the way from the basic "Hello My Name Is," pressure-sensitive, stick-on label, to a pinned-on badge identifying the wearer by name with, possibly:

- His or her photograph,
- Company, unit or other affiliation,
- Color-coded background for further identification,
- Date and duration of authorization, etc.

As mentioned earlier, temporary badges are inexpensive and provide some level of acknowledgement of authorized entry into a facility or environment. They can range in material and prominence from metal (a police-type badge) to plastic or paper. However, if someone is intent on an unauthorized entry, temporary badges are relatively easy to obtain and duplicate.

Magnetic Cards, Fobs, and Tags

The next step up from a simple ID badge is the magnetic stripe or swipe card, used in the "Basic Systems Components" access example earlier in this section. Magnetic cards are similar to credit cards or other contact proximity or "Prox" cards that must be inserted into, or come in contact with a reader, such as a the plastic hotel keys inserted into hotel room door readers.

Often a magnetic stripe card is combined with a contact or contact-less Prox card to form a multi-technology card. Contact-less Prox cards are technically referred to as the *ISO II (1386) (International Organization for Standardization) card.*

The stripe on the back of a credit card is a magnetic stripe, which may be called a magstripe. This magstripe is made up of tiny **iron-based** particles imbedded in film. Each iron particle is a tiny iron bar, which is magnetized and forms a bar magnet.

The magstripe can be coded by magnetizing the magnetic bars in north or south polar directions. Data is written or coded through a process that sets the direction or polarity of each bar so that some bars face the north, and others face south. As the card is swiped or drawn past a reader head, there will be a series of changes in the magnetic field that can be read by the card reader. There are two magnetic directions or fluxes, which are read as the coding reverses the magnetic bars. The result is a strip, or line, of magnetic impulses, based on the fundamental binary code system of 0's and 1's used by computers.

Mag cards all have three stripes or fields contained within the black stripe on the back of the card. Each is about 1/10" wide, and they are stacked one above the other and are usually designated as A, B, and C or 1, 2, and 3. Bank or ATM cards are very much alike in the type of information contained in each stripe, as specified by ISO/IEC standard 7811. Credit cards typically use only tracks 1 and 2, track 3 being a bit more discretionary, containing information peculiar to the cardholder.

A Brief Word of Warning About Mag Cards These cards can be easily, accidentally de-magnetized by:

- Getting them too close to magnetic catches on a purse or billfold.

- Getting them too close to the Electronic Article Surveillance (EAS) tag de-magnetizers (used in retail stores to de-magnetize a security tag attached to merchandise, which if not de-magnetized, sounds an alarm as one tries to walk out of the door).

Radio Frequency Identification (RFID)

A second form of ID card is the Radio Frequency Identification (RFID) card. As the name implies, this type of card employs radio waves as a means of communication between it and a card reader. RFIDs function in a similar way to mag cards in that they identify the cardholder via a card reader, which in turn, matches the holder's ID with a database. Once it is matched, the cardholder is permitted access to the device, function, or space tied to the particular card reader. In a simple system, authentication depends on the concept that the cardholder is the authorized person. What sets RFID cards apart is that they do not have to come in contact with anything to be read. One is required only to bring the card into proximity to a reader in order to establish communication.

Proximity (Prox) Cards

Passive RFID Cards There are two basic types of Prox or RFID cards: passive and active. Passive RFID cards have no internal power supply and rely on the power transmitted to them by the reader, through radio waves. Consequently, a passive card's effective proximity range is quite short—usually only an inch or so. The advantage is that they have no battery to run down, can last for years, and are relatively inexpensive to acquire.

The physical card is the usually the same size and shape of a mag card. The cards are formed by laminating two layers of PVC together with a loop or coil band of copper (shaped like a rectangle with rounded corners) between the layers. The copper shape is merely a loop antenna capable of receiving a signal from the reader. Connected to the antenna is a small, flat computer chip (about 1/8" square) in which the user identification data are stored. Usually, the stored data include a facility code identifying the physical location of the reader (often in two parts, such as a city code and a building code) and the individual's identification number, which is likely to be encrypted so that only the recipient computer or reader can de-crypt it.

Passive cards are usually programmed only once with between 32–128 bits of data. The difference in bit structure is usually related to the size of the encryption algorithm.

Active RFID cards receive their power from a battery inside them. Because they carry their own power supply, they are usually of a read/write type, can carry up to 1 MB of memory, and have a much longer read/transmit range. Active RFID cards are nearly always of the Smart Card variety, which means that, in addition to having their own internal power supply, they also have a "smart" chip which can function as a miniature computer and can be programmed to store quantities of data, match data, and transmit data. Smart cards are clearly going to be thicker, heavier, have a shorter useful life due to the life of the battery, and cost a good deal more. However, it is important to consider how they can be used.

The RFID card or "tag," as it is often referred to, is actually a transponder (transmitter-responder). It receives a request for information contained within its memory from a reader or interrogator, which is constantly sending out signals requesting information (polling) from any transponder within its receiving range. The tag responds with the requested information. If it is a passive card, the response can travel only a short distance (inches), as the energy received by its antenna is quite weak. If card is an active-type, its range can be up to 90'. Whether the card is passive or active, transmission and response are not hindered by fog, rain, snow, dirty cards, non-metallic paint, or the like, as transmission is by radio wave and will travel through the air, even in a vacuum. Response times are up to 1/10 of a second.

RFIDs When Part of Multi-Modal Systems Returning to the problem of identification and authentication, let's consider that the facility may be using a multi-modal system of an encrypted ID number with a fingerprint or a numeric/fingerprint reader. Let's assume that it has both the encrypted ID number and the template of the user's fingerprint encoded in the smart card. The user approaches a storage unit to secure some highly expensive materials. The reader at the door of the storage unit can read both the ID number encoded in the smart card's memory and the fingerprint of the individual attempting to gain entrance, and can convert that data to a template as it is being read. The reader, through its connection to its database, merely has to match the ID number, which it received from the smart card, to its database. The smart card now matches the internally stored fingerprint template to the one just read. Identification and authentication are confirmed from the database and a second source—and the database has not been loaded up with fingerprint templates.

One could also approach the problem from the reverse end, depending solely on the fingerprint match within the smart card to authenticate identification. This assumes that there can be only one fingerprint match, and that the individual is identified by his or her fingerprint.

Paper Batteries At this time, most smart cards are still passive. This does not reduce their "smart" capabilities, but merely limits their transmission range to an inch or so. Some versions of smart cards with internal batteries are currently in use as

"EZ-Passes," such as those used to pass through tollgates on the highway. These are fairly large and would not be feasible for a personal ID card. However, there are solutions being perfected for making either standard Prox cards or smart cards active or powered. One solution nearing practical application is the paper battery.

It is difficult to imagine a battery small and light enough to operate within a slightly fattened credit card-sized Prox card. The paper battery will be made of three thin layers of paper on which will be silkscreen-printed a cathode layer, an electrolyte layer, and an anode layer, in addition to power contact or connection points—one positive, the other negative.

Both the cathode and the anode will consist of inks composed of zinc and manganese dioxide (MnO_2). One paper cell will be about .05 millimeter thick and will generate about 1.5 volts of electricity, about the same as standard watch batteries. Multiple layers of paper batteries can be stacked to produce more power. The paper battery is considered a dry system, which precludes the need for a casing and permits the battery to have great physical flexibility. Fabrication of the battery takes place during the same manufacturing process as the device in which it is to be used.

Closed Circuit Television (CCTV)

Closed circuit television is technically no different from commercial television, in that it consists of a camera or cameras that take pictures, a transmitter that sends the pictures out as radio waves or over a cable and a receiver, and usually a cathode ray tube (CRT). The more common security-related CCTV systems do not include sound, which makes them easier and less costly to install.

CCTV does not enjoy universal acceptance in the security world. Facility owners seem to be more enthusiastic about its value than many security professionals. To understand this apparent dichotomy, it helps to take a look at what CCTV can do, what it cannot do, and the different ways in which it can be employed. CCTV is very effective at continuously viewing one thing, such as an entrance door. The difficulty is in deciding what to do with the pictures that are received. Is the purpose to:

- Continuously monitor those individuals entering and leaving the facility?
  - If so, what are we looking for?
  - Who is available to continuously view the monitor?
  - What happens if they see the activity, person, or whatever it is that they are looking for?

- Simply record pictures of individuals entering or leaving the facility?
  — Why?
  — What will be done with the recorded images?
  — How long will the images be archived?
  — Who is going to view the images, and what will they be looking for?

Valid Applications for CCTV

There are a number of valid venues for the use of CCTV as part of a security plan. A few are listed below:

- Hospitals
  — Major entrances and stairways
  — Intensive care units or intensive care patients
  — Surgical training theaters
  — Specific forms of diagnosis
  — Patient floor passageways
  — Emergency room entrances and waiting rooms
  — Psychiatric entrances and wards, and prison wards and rooms
  — Gas (oxygen, nitrogen, carbon dioxide) storage tanks and distribution piping
  — Mechanical/Electrical rooms, truck docks, etc.
- Schools and Campuses
  — Major entrances and stairways
  — Hallways
  — Mechanical/Electrical rooms, truck docks, etc.
  — Cafeterias and major areas of assembly
  — Driveways and parking lots
  — Walkways and dormitory entrances, etc.
- Hotels and Motels
  — Entrances and stairways
  — Elevator lobbies
  — Reception desk
  — Mechanical/Electrical rooms, truck docks, etc.
  — Parking structures and porte-cocheres, etc.
- Casinos
  — Entrances and stairways
  — Cashiers
  — Cash counting rooms
  — Gaming tables
  — Slot machines

— Entrances and fire exits
— Mechanical/Electrical rooms, truck docks, etc.
— Parking structures, porte-cocheres, etc.

- Banks and Other Financial Institutions
  — Entrances
  — Cashiers and tellers
  — Safe deposit box vaults
  — Cash counting rooms
  — Cash vaults
  — Banking floors, etc.
  — Parking sturctures and lots
  — Mechanical/Electrical rooms, truck docks, etc.
- Retail, Convenience Stores, and Food Service Establishments
  — Entrances and fire exits
  — Cashiers
  — High-cost merchandise counters and areas
  — General selling floor areas
  — Dressing room and locker room—lobbies only
  — Serving and food storage areas
  — Freezer and refrigerator storage rooms
  — Mechanical/Electrical rooms, truck docks, etc.
  — Parking lots, entrance walkways and drives, etc.
- Utilities and Manufacturing
  — Fence lines
  — Grounds entrances
  — Truck docks and receiving areas
  — Storage tanks and pumping stations
  — Mechanical/Electrical rooms, truck docks, etc.
  — Transformers
  — Inventory and tool yards
  — Rail sidings and unloading/loading docks
  — Parking lots, entrance walkways and drives, etc.
  — Hazardous materials storage and transmission facilities, etc.
- Office Buildings
  — Entrances and fire exits
  — Reception desk and areas

- Elevator lobbies
- Mechanical/Electrical rooms, truck docks, etc.
- Hallways
- Cafeterias and major areas of assembly
- Parking lots, entrance walkways and drives, etc.

As stated above, there are only two fundamental functions of CCTV:

- Real-time observation, which requires people watching monitors either all the time or on call.
- Archival retrieval, which requires some sort of trigger or demand to cause security personnel to search through recorded, televised material.

One might argue that the apparent threat of being observed is also a valid function of CCTV, but if the threat were all that is needed, dummy cameras would suffice. If the organization is serious about observation, it must provide observation. There are a number of variations to real-time observation and archival, such as motion detectors that can sound an alarm and cause cameras to begin filming and recorders to begin recording at the sign of any unrecognized motion. An attendant at the monitoring station can immediately zoom in on the motion and identify the anomaly as friendly or hostile while recording the event for future identification purposes. A teacher can call the office and report a stranger in a particular school corridor. The office personnel can then isolate a camera in the area and monitor and/or record the individual's behavior.

If multiple cameras are viewing multiple areas, the questions become more complex, particularly if the cameras are capable of panning and/or tilting, resulting in views of larger areas and increasing detail. These are all fundamental questions that need to be carefully resolved before making a commitment to a major investment in a CCTV system. These systems are expensive to purchase and even more expensive to install, as well as cost- and time-intensive to employ and keep up to date.

Once it has been determined that CCTV is a suitable and worthwhile system for an organization or facility's security needs, the next question is which areas or functions should be covered by the system? What does the system need to report and during what time periods? Because the equipment is costly and there are so many variables, it is important to consider the additional areas or functions that might need to be added in the future. The trick is not to acquire more equipment than is needed at this time, but not to cut off future expansion of either quantity or capability. Once the CCTV system's purpose, place, and use have been determined, the next step is considering what kinds of equipment to acquire and how to use it.

Equipment

There are two basic television systems. The old standby that has been around for many decades is the analog system, which many still use at home. The second and newer system is digital television. In selecting CCTV equipment for a security system, it is important to understand the differences between analog and digital and their advantages and disadvantages. Digital TV is much more costly than analog, but its substantial advantages may outweigh the cost differential.

Analog TV Analog television, in its original form, is based on standard radio wave technology, the same technology that is used by wireless phones, microwave ovens, the original cell phones, radios, and garage door openers. Analog systems employ radio waves in the 54–890 MHz range, in other words, radio frequency waves from 540,000–890,000 cycles per second. Analog television cameras record pictures at a rate of 30 frames per second, and transmit them either through cyberspace or by cable to a television monitor, where they are "painted" on a phosphor-coated screen 60 times per second. Only half (every other) of the lines are painted per frame. (Thirty frames per second can be viewed.) This technique is called "interlacing" and is the standard used in analog TV. Fortunately, the human eye is very tolerant and sees the progressive frames as a continuous motion.

Computer monitors use another painting technique, called "progressive scanning," This method paints every line 60 times per second, providing a much more stable picture with far less flicker. (This is one reason why a TV screen does not work well as a computer monitor.) Analog images must be stored on videotape and viewed on the same type of VCR as used to watch movies at home.

Digital Television Digital television is different from analog TV in nearly all respects. Digital cameras record their frames not in sine waves as do analog cameras, but in a binary code system of 0's and 1's as used in computers, similar to the system mentioned earlier in this chapter for digitally coded magnetic cards. Digital signals are transmitted to a receiver, either by a satellite transmission to avoid line-of-sight interference due to the earth's curvature, or by cable. Analog signals can be substantially compressed, but digital signals can be compressed further, resulting in the ability to store a large amount of graphic data in a computer format such as a floppy disk or a hard drive. From a viewing standpoint, real HDTV (High Definition Television) produces a much sharper picture due to fact that digital TV monitors employ 1,920 lines of pixels (wide) by 1,080 pixels (high), or a total of 2,073,600 pixels per screen. Analog uses 704 pixels (wide) and 480 pixels (high) for a total of 337,920 pixels per screen, a difference of slightly more than 6 to 1.

Image Enhancement and Thermal Imaging Both analog and digital systems are available in monochrome or color. Additional options include low-level light or image enhancement and/or thermography or infrared viewing. These cameras can be invaluable in the right situations due to their high levels of capability. Low-level light viewing or image enhancement is based on two camera capabilities:

- First to view some of infrared light rays that border the visible light spectrum and
- Second, to enhance what low level visible light might be available, such as moonlight or even starlight, permitting the CCTV system a good deal of nighttime capability.

Thermal imaging or infrared cameras are of two types:

- Un-cooled, which are the most common and can view temperature differentials as low as -4°F, and
- Cryogenically cooled, which can view temperature differentials as small as -0.2°F, as far away as 1,000'.

Thermal images are not as crisp as an actual black and white or color photograph. Neither low-level light enhancement nor thermal imaging technology is well qualified for identification purposes. However, they are excellent tools for large area or fence line security viewing or for spotting movement on dark nights, in fog, heavy snow, and rain.

Hybrid CCTV Systems

A CCTV system can be assembled from a simple $100 analog camera with fixed pan and tilt, displaying only a single, real-time image on a simple, small screen analog TV monitor with the images stored on a VCR tape. Or it can be a multi-camera system with multi-paced refreshing, either full digital or analog, digitally converted, compressed, transmitted by Web, phone line or broadband, buffered and stored to await viewing, or stored in a computer file. Or it might be any number of combinations in between. The point is that selecting a CCTV system need not be all one or the other system, but a combination with features selected to meet particular needs.

Making the Selection

Keeping in mind the fact that the only two reasons for using CCTV are to view an area or thing on a real-time basis and/or to be able to store or archive images for viewing at a later time, it becomes apparent that digital provides not only a far better image than analog, but greater storage capacity and retrieval of highly compressed images through a computer system on floppies or hard drives. However, these attributes come at a high cost, which can only be justified if the needs assessment so indicates. Selection should be based on a hard-nosed evaluation of the organization's real needs, with a cautious eye to the future.

Access Systems and Doors

The most common doors in commercial facilities are plain 6'-8" high doors (sometimes called "leaf doors") of the type found in homes. Commercial doors, depending on their locations, are frequently required by building code to be fire-rated. Residential doors, on the other hand, are not likely to be fire-rated, other than those that separate an attached garage from the house. Commercial doors are either of solid-core wood or steel, while most residential interior doors are either paneled doors or hollow core. Another difference in residential versus working-world doors is likely to be the locking mechanism. The locks on residential exterior doors are likely to be heavy-duty, key-operated, with anti-bypass pins, plus a deadbolt. Because of the need for a high level of mobility in larger commercial facilities, electronic keys are more likely to be used than the brass, aluminum, or steel keys on house doors. (Keying devices are covered later in this chapter.)

When considering exterior and interior doors, there are a number of options available for commercial use. Main entrance doors are likely to be constructed of thick or laminated glass with a metal frame that holds the hinges and locks. These primary exterior doors are usually unlocked during normal business hours. Some interior doors may be in a locked status at all times.

Exterior Doors

Revolving Doors and Security Booths These can be free revolving or access-controlled and might have anti-piggy-backing, tailgating, and pass-back capabilities. They can be equipped with a variety of standard and optional capabilities, such as torque control, tamper reporting, fire/emergency egress facility, and UPS backup. In addition to being an extremely efficient security door, revolving doors are a highly energy-efficient means of ingress and egress and can interface with many standard access control systems. This type of door may provide one of the highest levels of main ingress/egress security available, but it does not accommodate large or bulky bundles or packages. Consequently, a side door is usually required for individuals transporting such items (http://www.safesec.com; http://www.gunnebo-omega.com).

Bi-Fold Doors Bi-fold doors are rarely used in conventional commercial applications, but are gaining popularity in the retail industry due in part to their simplicity of design and low maintenance. Because of their light construction, however, they are not very secure.

Large, Full-Height Turnstiles Full-height turnstiles include the one-way, prison-looking devices used in the exits of some subway platforms—or they can be an attractive alternative—a high-flow, good security, one-direction, glass passage control door-set that opens in the direction of the correct passage. This latter type of door is not, in fact, a turnstile, because the narrow pair of doors open in the same manner as a standard door.

Sliding Doors Sliding doors are occasionally used for ingress and egress to facilities, but they are more often used in an architectural context because, from a security standpoint, tailgating and piggybacking are nearly impossible to control. Again, sliding doors are more likely to be found in a retail environment.

Overhead Doors and Grilles Overhead doors and grilles are primarily used for large openings such as truck docks, parking facilities, or stadium entrances. Because of their slow opening and closing cycles, once they are opened, they usually remain open until a pre-determined closing time. Ingress accountability is handled through other means.

Interior Access Controls

Walk-Through Metal Detector The metal walk-through detector, is not often used in a conventional commercial/industrial environment where personal property frequently contains metal, and identification and authentication of individuals is of prime importance. However, metal detection is of major importance in facilities such as airports, boarding ships, public buildings (including courthouses, sports and entertainment facilities, schools, and others), and other types of government institutions. These devices are the unattractive arches we see in airports that can beep at watches, belt buckles, shoe eyelets, or costume jewelry. Although they can be programmed to detect different zones (usually 8 zones above the floor), with or without overlapping, experience shows that the variety in the heights of individuals renders multi-zone detection less than ideal. Nonetheless, if programmed for a more uniform and reasonable detection level, metal detectors do provide excellent early warnings. Metal detectors require not only personnel to monitor them, but also the availability of personnel who can be called upon to act if a weapon is detected (http://metorexsecurity.com).

Turnstiles, which are not actual doors, consist of two pedastals, about 38–39" high, that make up their sides, with some form of rotating or retracting internal rod or barrier. Taller glass entry gates are available up to 74" high. The "throats," or passageways, through the stiles can range from about 18–39" to meet ADA requirements. Access speeds through the stiles can range up to 1,800 people per hour and can function bi-directionally. Most can use standard access control systems. Turnstile systems are excellent devices for controlling ingress and egress personnel flow. When interfaced with many standard access control systems, especially multi-modal systems, they can identify, authenticate, and provide access for large numbers of people at reasonable levels of security.

Mechanical Locks

Mechanical locks are available with between 1–7 pins, and from single- to dual-milling. As old-fashioned as they may seem in today's high-tech world, they are still one of the most reliable and security devices available. Doors with electronic or multi-modal access control systems should still have a mechanical lock in the event of a power loss which would cause the electronic access devices to fail in an "open" mode.

Cyber Locks

Cyber locks are essentially a lower-cost electronic system. These lock cylinders can probably replace the 6-pin mechanical cylinders in existing doors—whether they are a lever-type, standard interchangeable core (IC), IC in a knob, mortise lock, or a rim lock. The key itself is rather large—about 2.5" long by about 1.5" wide, and about 1" thick—containing its own battery. The lock within the door must be programmed with a special key, which is, in turn, programmed as a master cyber key by a device connected to a computer. The door lock has no power source within itself, but receives its necessary power from the user's cyber key. These locks can be programmed to accept specific keys, on specific days, between specific hours on those days, and even to require two user keys for access. User keys can be programmed to match specific locks, days, and times. Door locks can be connected to a control device connected to the computer that can identify a key user, date, and time of access or attempted access, and the results of an access attempt, such as access permitted, denied (wrong day, wrong time, expired authorization, lost key reported, etc.). This system must rely on the assumption that the key holder (identification) is the actual authorized holder (http://www.videx.com).

Electronic Locking Systems

There are two basic types of electronic locking systems currently in use:

- magnetic locks
- electronic mortise locks

Maglocks, or magnetic locks, are not locks in the strict sense of the word, but rather simple holding devices. They consist of an electrically powered bar electromagnet, usually fastened at the top of a doorframe, and a steel plate fastened at the top of a door.

The electromagnet, in its normal energized state, holds the door in a closed position. Maglock holding capacities usually range from 600 pounds of holding or negative pressure to 1,800 pounds of negative pressure. As the accessing device receives an approved signal, the electricity is switched off to the electromagnet, and the door is free to open. Once the signal is ended, the magnet is re-energized, and when the door closes, the electromagnet again grips the door and holds it in place. During a power failure or fire alarm, the system will fail in a free-to-open condition. In the event that there are double doors, usually one long electromagnet will hold both doors closed. When de-energized, both doors are free to open.

There are two types of electrically disengaged locks, whether cylinder, tube, or mortise. With the older type, the lock itself is electrified, and the latch is withdrawn from the mortise, thus permitting the door to open. When the lock receives an approved signal, a solenoid within the lock retracts the latch, and the door is permitted to open. The difficulty with this type of electric lock is that the door itself must be wired to a power source as well as to a signaling device. It is difficult enough to get power and signal to a door that is constantly opening and closing (which results in constant changing connection distances and configurations), but now the power and signal must be run through or over the surface of the door to the lock. However, a great many locks of this type are still in use and continue to be installed.

A more current type of electric lock is the powered mortise. In this version, a signal is sent to the mortise itself, first causing a plate within the mortise to be pulled out of the way of the latch pin. At almost the same time, a solenoid plunger pushes the latch clear of the mortise cavity, permitting the door to open. When the signal is no longer being received, the mortise plunger withdraws, and the fingerplate returns to its appropriate position. The door closes, the latch is again located in the mortise, and the dead latch pin returns to its mortise position. In the event of a power failure or fire emergency, most doors fail in the open position, the exception being doors within fire stair towers which can open into a fire tower, but not out of a tower onto intermediate levels. (They generally open from the fire tower only at ground level or some other safe area.)

All electronically controlled locking systems automatically release doors when approached from inside using mechanisms such as an electronic eye, infrared or motion detection. When a door is approached, the electronic eye notes the presence of an object and releases the door. When the object has passed out of "view," the door automatically returns to a locked mode, which is completed when the door actually closes.

A Word of Warning If doors do not have doorstops or an astragal, a long-handled, feathery-type tool can be inserted between the door and the doorframe, which may be viewed by the electronic eye and cause the door lock to release (http://www.securition.com).

Accessing Devices for Locks

Once a door or access to a computer or its internal files (or anything else that should not have general access) has been secured, means must be provided for authorized access. This is accomplished with a device that recognizes or reads an identification code, sends a signal to the door or other device, and then electro-magnetically (or through an electronic switch or code) releases the door or permits access. The basics of signal loops have already been covered under "Identification" earlier in this chapter. Usually a binary code identification entry is conveyed to the database, authentication is verified through a data match, and an approval is signaled back to the device for which access is being requested. The door is opened electronically or electro-magnetically. The following is a brief look at some of the more generic accessing devices presently available.

Keypads

There are two basic types of keypads. The first is integrated into the door handle and lock system and is essentially mechanical in nature. Pressing the correct numbers unique to this particular door, in the correct sequence, will mechanically release the lock, and the door can be opened. The second type of keypad is also combined with the lock, but requires input of a personal ID number which is matched by a connected database to a like number programmed into the keypad-lock device. If a match is found, the door lock is released. These doors must be able to be exited for fire alarm conditions from the inside by merely turning a lever and opening.

Keypad Readers

Keypad readers are most frequently located on the strike side of a door. They are connected to a database that can receive an individual identification number input into it (converted to binary code), authenticate the number, and signal the door to open.

Proximity Readers

Proximity readers are, like almost all readers, mounted on a wall or mullion on the strike side of a door. These readers work with proximity, or Prox, cards, reviewed earlier in this chapter. Proximity readers can be capable of reading and matching an inquiry from a Prox card directly, or they may depend on having to access a PC running in the background. Unless the installed system uses wireless technology, the reader is hard-wired to a PC database, frequently through an interim controller. Prox readers have effective signal and read ranges of from 1–2" up to 24". Some of the more recent Prox readers are quite attractive and can have a corporate logo embedded in the read face.

Swipe Readers

Swipe readers function in the same manner as Prox card readers, with the exception that the user must swipe his or her card through a slot in the reader in the same manner as the clerk swipes credit cards in the grocery store. The essential difference is that the code embedded in the card is in magnetic code, which will have to be converted to binary code to be downloaded to a PC.

Biometric Readers

Biometric readers are likewise mounted on the strike side of the door. Covered earlier in this chapter, there are a variety of biometric readers, fingerprint scanners, hand scanners, iris and retinal scanners, facial scanners, and vocal or voice recognition devices. Because of the difficulties of scanning and then developing a template of the feature being scanned, most of these readers rely on identification and authentication by a PC database. Most of these types of biometric readers have reliability concerns due mostly to mis-reads, especially when used as stand-alone systems. Nonetheless, when it comes to authentication, a confirming match of an individual's physical features is far superior to any card or PIN available.

Multi-Modal Readers

Multi-modal technology, also addressed earlier in this chapter, combine an identification number (whether a PIN or read from a card) with a biometric feature, which is pretty tough to counterfeit. Combining an ID number with a hard-to-convert template feature is highly efficient. The PC can almost instantly locate the appropriate identification file. The required template is instantly available to be matched to the one having just been scanned at the reader. Unless there has been a very poor scan and read, the sought-after authentication is made.

Wireless Readers

As wireless technology (radio frequency) advances, communication between readers or interrogators and locks (whether through a remote-mounted reader like the Prox or swipe readers, or like a keypad-integrated door lock) is becoming more practical. Wireless accessing systems are available, with batteries that power both the integrated reader/door lock installed system and a remote reader. Elevators can be operated using wireless technology through the use of remote antenna modules. Transmission distance between interface modules (which can control 2–4 transceivers, or door readers, per interface module) is about 200' in a conventionally constructed building. Some manufacturers are developing wireless systems using RS-485 technology that will be capable of handling up to 32 transceiver readers per interface module. In turn, the interface modules are hardwire-connected to conventional access control panels, which are connected to a PC (http://www.recognition-source.com).

Prop Sensors and Alarms

Most door accessing systems are equipped with some form of sensing capability, which monitors whether the door that has just been opened has closed and latched after a set period of time (usually seconds), in other words, not *propped* open. Often the sensing system is connected to an audible alarm that sounds if the door is not closed within the set time period. In the case of a mortise lock, the door must be fully closed, and the latch fully extended into the mortise in order to complete a "door-closed" condition. In the case of a magnetic-type lock, two electrified metal plates (one attached to the door, and one attached to the frame) must come in direct contact with one another to complete an electrical circuit and meet the "door-closed" status. If the Prop circuits are not completed within the specified set-times, the monitoring or operations center real-time computer system will signal the operator that there is an open-door condition. The operator should then notify an appropriate person that there is a problem. Prop-type alarm systems can also be installed to signal a water leak; broken windows; or failed heat, or cooling systems, including temperature rises or drops, loss of power, and tripped intrusion sensing devices, such as infrared, motion detectors, etc.

Mailroom Security Devices and Cautions

The mailroom in almost any organization may be the weakest chink in its security armor. If the organization is large enough to have a mailroom, it is likely that it will handle hundreds, if not thousands, of pieces of mail and courier-delivered envelopes and parcels every day. Mailrooms, by the nature of their functions, are most frequently staffed by junior level personnel and considered a lower level function. Consequently, it may be difficult to focus attention on the mailroom as a focal point for security. However, a number of steps should be taken to reduce the risk of hazards entering a facility through its mailroom. Since this topic is as much about security procedures as it is about devices, the following guidance is interjected on what to watch out for, along with some useful inspection devices. These are items that an organization might consider purchasing and installing as part of its overall security equipment.

A Note on Mailroom Awareness

In considering mailroom security, one should take a second look at the particular organization or facility's potential for risk incidents and their sources, as addressed in Chapter 3. If new construction or remodeling are part of the security plan, design considerations such as those noted in Chapter 5 should be applied to mailrooms. The next step is to begin a program to educate personnel who deal with mail and parcel delivery. All mailroom personnel should be regularly reminded—with reviews and re-reviews of safety procedures—of the potential for hazardous items coming into the mailroom, and what they should do if they think an item is potentially dangerous. Awareness, education, and re-education are among the best forms of security. The correct assessments must be made every time, all of the time. A terrorist needs to be right only once.

What to Watch for in Mailrooms A number of clues can be a tip-off to a possible threatening or dangerous letter or parcel.

1. A hand-delivered letter or parcel.
2. An envelope that is excessively stiff or bulky.
3. An extra heavy envelope for its size.
4. An envelope that seems to be out-of-balance, heavier at one end than the other.
5. An envelope or parcel with a peculiar odor, such as perfume, shaving lotion, gasoline, paraffin, fruit, almonds, or chemicals.
6. An envelope or parcel emitting a powdery substance. (See Chapter 6 for mailroom security procedures in the event anthrax is suspected.)
7. An envelope or parcel with excessive dirt or finger marks on the outside.
8. Parcels that appear to be inexpertly wrapped or have excessive amounts of wrapping, tape, or string.
9. A parcel having cuts or tears in the wrapping, exposing foil, cords, or wire.
10. An envelope or parcel postmarked from a different location than the return address.
11. An envelope or parcel bearing out-of-country postage or return addresses, especially from unknown places or with an unknown or unrecognizable name.
12. An envelope or parcel with no return address.

13. An envelope or parcel with an address made from letters or words cut out from some form of printed materials, such as magazines, newspapers, business cards, or printed labels.

14. An envelope or parcel with the address inexpertly typed, with typing or spelling errors, typed all in capitals, etc.

15. An envelope or parcel that appears to have excessive postage for its weight.

16. An envelope or parcel that is incorrectly addressed, or with unusual address sequencing or directions.

17. An envelope or parcel with special instructions such as "Fragile," "Urgent," "Rush," "Open Here," "Personal," "Very Personal," or "Confidential."

18. An envelope or parcel addressed to an unknown party, or to an individual who has not been with the organization for some time.

The above-described envelopes and parcels may or may not contain explosive, incendiary devices or booby traps. Bombs and incendiary devices are self-explanatory. Booby traps are designed to cause injury or death. One type consists of a conventional, soft pouch-type envelope, which is clearly intended to be opened at one end only. The recipient opens the pouch, inserting their fingers to extract the contents. Internal flaps prevent the fingers from being withdrawn and razor blades severely lacerate the fingers. Some animal rights extremists have used this device. A similar device contains a form of hypodermic, which can inject small amounts of blood containing AIDS or other infectious disease.

Mailroom Inspection Devices

There are a number of mailroom inspection devices available for X-raying envelopes and parcels. The need to acquire one of these devices will depend to some extent on the organization's assessment of how vulnerable it might be to a mail threat. Considering the low cost of some inspection devices, it may be best to err on the side of acquiring too many, rather than do nothing. There are tabletop detecting devices that operate at 110V, weigh less than 20 pounds, and can sense—at high speed— envelopes and packages up to 2-½" thick by 16" wide, with UPS (uninterruptible power supply) backup. Smaller units like these sound an alarm when metal or explosives are detected. Larger units can handle parcels up to 13" x 22" x 21", which could include large bundles of envelopes or multiple packages. Contents are displayed on a TV monitor. These units are mobile and require 110V or 230V power. There are portable or even small track-mounted type units for remote x-ray scanning requirements (http://www.scanna-msc.com).

Emergency Communications

Throughout this book communications, in one form or another, have been noted as an essential component of an organization's ability to continue to function in the event of a security-related incident. It is important for those concerned with security to also realize that not all communication needs are solely within spaces that have a functioning PBX or regular phone lines. Many locations within and outside of facilities may have emergency communication needs that most likely will not be served by a conventional desk or wall phone. These areas and spaces might include:

- Elevators and elevator machine rooms
- Mailrooms and parcel delivery rooms
- Mechanical rooms
- Generator rooms
- Loading docks and rail sidings
- Electrical switch rooms
- Parking structures—above and below grade
- Parking lots
- Campuses—academic and business
- Dormitories
- Hospital and clinic corridors and emergency room lobbies
- Shopping malls
- Hotel and motel corridors and entries
- Guard stations
- Refineries
- Factory floors
- Fire stairways

The above locations are places where hazardous functions are being carried out or where someone may find themselves at risk, either from a work, environmental, criminal, or terrorist occurrence—or because they are isolated, and normal communications—even cell phones—may fall short. Parking lots have become the leading sites for criminal assault and theft. Moral, legal, and statutory demands require the provision of a high degree of security for personnel, customers and visitors, regardless of their identity or the organization's interest in their presence.

There are an abundance of specially designed emergency phone systems presently available to fit almost any type of condition— wall-hung, towers with or without CCTV, blue strobe lights, etc. They can possess a single "Emergency" button, which instantly communicates with the main security station, or two buttons, one for dire "Emergency" and the other often labeled "Information," which can be used in the event of a dead battery or a flat tire. Most systems have "polling" features that confirm the operating viability of each unit every minute or so.

In light of potential liability, a corporate general counsel was asked if emergency communication, blue light towers should be installed in a semi-public, below-grade parking structure, even though security personnel might not be able to reach the site of an assault in time to prevent it. His answer was, "Absolutely. I would rather err on the side of not being able to get to a problem in time than to not have had the opportunity to try" (http://www.talkaphone.com; http:///www.aiphone.com).

A Word About Privacy and Security

Many of the techniques and devices reviewed in this chapter pertain to identification and authentication. As society and the world become more perilous, we seek more protection during travel and in our communities, work places, and homes. Outside of our homes, positive identification becomes less certain. It is not our intention to delve into the controversy of individual privacy versus the invasive, "big brother" approach. However, since 9/11, and even before, privacy versus risk, and risk versus security has been a major concern.

It is generally accepted that the banker who is considering a substantial loan for a new car or home is going to require an in-depth review of an individual's current credit history, but does an employer need to have this sort of information? The life insurance company preparing to sell someone a million dollar policy is surely interested in the current state of that individual's health, but is it entitled to access his or her genetic makeup or that of his or her parents or siblings? Is an employer entitled to any more knowledge about employee's or potential employees' health than the information that relates directly to their ability to perform their designated work? The responses to these questions vary widely depending on many factors, such as the level of security actually required and the authority or responsibility to be vested in the employee. Of this much we can be assured: background checking of all employees is now, or soon should become a standard practice. Individuals are entitled to certain levels of privacy in the workplace, but they are not entitled to be anonymous.

It has become fairly well established that the employer has the right to know his or her employee's background and, under special conditions, to request physical examinations, psychological testing or interviews, and drug tests. However, the employer in possession of this information must deal with it in a manner that respects the employee's privacy and dignity. Practices such as monitoring telephone calls, e-mails, and Internet usage, or reviewing work performance must be done fairly, evenhandedly, and within standard company policies that have been communicated to all employees. All personnel, financial, employee assistance, medical, psychological, compensation or pension and profit sharing records must be kept strictly confidential. A recommended white paper on this subject can be found at http://www.choicepoint.com.

Conclusion

This chapter has covered a wide range of security devices and construction solutions — from CCTV biometric identification systems to physical barriers, such as walls, bollards, and window films. Selection of the appropriate items will be an outgrowth of the assessment process described in Chapter 3, the design and procedure considerations in Chapter 5, and the organization's budget constraints.

Chapter 9 also ties into this process, as consideration is given to the integration of building systems, a process that may appear complex, but can actually be one of the more cost-effective and valuable security procedures available. Part Two of this book provides cost data for purchase and installation of most of these devices and systems.

Chapter Nine

Integration of Security and Related Systems

By David Owen and T. K. Gaughan

Note: This chapter includes a number of terms, technical descriptions, protocols, and standards, some of which have been previously defined. A mini-glossary appears at the end of this chapter for quick reference.

Information Technology Security

This chapter will not attempt to deal with Information Technology (IT) security from the point of view of the IT specialist. Assembling and installing, maintaining, modifying, protecting, and, as necessary, rebuilding or restoring an IT system or composite of systems are all functions that, thankfully, fall to IT specialists and their Chief Information Officer (CIO). However, the IT department must be provided with some basic infrastructure needs, support, protection, or security for its:

- Local Area Network/Wide Area Network (LAN/WAN) systems and facilities Datacom and telecom cable networks.
- Intermediate Distribution Frame (IDF) rooms.
- Uninterruptible Power Supply (UPS) and Emergency Power Supply (EPS) or Backup Power Supply (BPS) equipment.
- Power Distribution Unit (PDU) equipment.
- Heating, ventilating, and air conditioning (HVAC) equipment maintenance and operation.
- Code-mandated fire suppression and alarm systems and monitoring.
- Other fire suppression equipment, particularly those using heptafluoropropane (such as Great Lakes Chemical Corporation's FM-200® system), which is rarely, if ever, inspected or monitored by local fire departments.

It may be argued that the construction, modification, and maintenance of some of these spaces and equipment should properly fall within the scope of the maintenance department, corporate services, or facilities management group. Perhaps so, but the day-to-day physical security and monitoring of such vital and costly facilities and equipment may well be assigned to the security department, working in close alliance with IT. There are important reasons for such an assignment.

- First, the security department's single concern is security.
- Second, the security department will almost certainly be an internal resource and operation with a physical presence 24/365, just as IT is a 24/365 operation.
- Third, security often has backup monitoring in the form of off-site or external resource monitoring via a contractor or department, also 24/365.

This arrangement does not suggest that the IT department should not have independent or collateral monitoring, as well as automatic notification systems and perhaps its own security officer. However, IT security officers are often more concerned with data, file, and systems integrity than physical infrastructure security (i.e., who is accessing the facilities). The IT department may wish to receive frequent print-outs of who accesses portions of the IT physical facility, and the times they arrived and left — both the date and time of day.

Some of the more sophisticated IT systems are likely to have three different "hot sites" at which data is simultaneously "saved" on multiple storage devices in a Storage Area Network (SAN) architecture through time fiber channel switching. Such systems ensure that data will be protected and always available. However, data recovery depends on having a place for the recovered data to go. In the event of significant damage to the facility that results in a disruption of Datacom and/or Telecom service, recovery efforts will not be automatic, as is "hot site" data backup.

Infrastructure recovery following a security event could take a significant amount of time. Very likely, responsibility for recovery will be divided between IT and Facilities Management. IT will probably handle the acquisition, installation, and testing of all equipment and systems (including cabling) and data restoration.

When it comes to the installation of cables in the new or re-built facility, IT may wish to deal with its own subcontractor and have its own project resources follow the design, installation, punch-down, continuity testing, and signal integrity verification. Project control should reside with Corporate Services or Facilities Management, which will have overall responsibility for the facility construction or reconstruction. Failure of Facilities Management to control coordination of work can lead to misunderstandings, delay of the work performance, and possible conflict between departments. Many IT department personnel lack knowledge of construction project budgeting procedures, which may be one of the most compelling reasons for having Facilities Management as the coordinating entity.

Monitoring

It is important to review the ways in which security systems are currently monitored, and how to integrate what may seem to be disparate systems into one. An integrated system provides for monitoring of a large number of conditions and terminal points through a system of alarms; automatic actions; and cognitive, decision-based actions taken by systems operators.

Many security professionals prefer on-site monitoring by internal resources. This is particularly true if the security installation is large enough to be able to employ a sufficiently large and qualified staff, such as some government agencies. Such a staff would include backup personnel to cover illnesses, vacations, or other absences in order to ensure monitoring, real-time, full-time, 24/365. If the organization is large enough to be able to recruit full-time people for this task, the system may be more reliable and responsible, but there are still challenges. For smaller organizations, urgent and frequent demands on the security officer and his/her associates are so frequent that trying to maintain a full-time person in the security office (in an attempt to render it a primary 24/365 Command and Control monitoring site) is an objective not often achieved. If real-time surveillance is the objective, it may not be achieved when there are "windows" of unobserved time. Because many organizations cannot afford or do not wish to invest in their own full-time or 24/365 personnel, they utilize outside contractors to monitor their security systems.

A Word of Clarification Before moving too far along in the review of on-site and/or monitored systems, it is important to define some key terms as they are used in this chapter. As previously stated, a proprietary system is one that is exclusively monitored and maintained on-site. The difficulty comes with the term "monitor," which can have a number of different meanings:

- The VDT (CRT or plasma screen) used with computers.
- The person stationed at the VDT, viewing CCTV pictures, data transmissions from terminal points, and instructions.
- A terminal device, such as a CCTV camera or an infrared or motion detector, more properly termed, "detecting devices."
- Automatic monitoring of the condition or the different components of hardware and software.
- "Monitoring Station"–workstations, owner- or user-operated or outsourced to contract monitoring companies.

Proprietary or On-Site Systems

If an on-site system is selected, the next questions are where to locate the monitoring station or stations, and how much authority should be given to its numerous operators. Their actions include system commands, and manipulation or analysis of the many files that will be available within the integrated system. If the operator is seated at a reception/security station, he or she should be able to issue security passes to individuals whose identifications may already be stored in one of the databases. It follows that the monitoring operator would have to have access to some system files and possibly to enter or update information about a visiting guest.

One of the problems with this arrangement is that sitting at a security desk for hours at a stretch, even with periodic breaks, is likely to be extremely boring. This, together with a probable low wage scale, results in high turnover in these positions. As a result, these personnel may be transient, with low levels of interest and motivation. Therefore, the possible risk of error or collusive behavior could be fairly high. In addition, given the direct and indirect costs of full-time employees, there is likelihood that, without an assessed high-risk need, the cost-benefit ratio could not be justified. Even when using contract security personnel for the reception/security station, many of the concerns relative to turnover, boredom, absenteeism, and improper or even criminal behavior, will remain. However, it is easy to pick up the phone and order a new or replacement security person from a contractor, and it may be somewhat more cost-effective. Many commercial security companies provide well-vetted, professionally qualified personnel.

As to the issue of monitoring the system (looking at the VDT monitor) with its CCTV camera transmissions or other devices and conditions for alarms, it is important to realize that a security person at the reception desk would not likely be able to handle the ebb and flow of visitors while simultaneously providing a reasonable level of observation. A second monitoring workstation (on- or off-site) may be required. The question is, what is the best solution? In a true on-site proprietary system, when an event alarm is received, a security person or persons will observe the alarm and evaluate what action to take. (Such action will be in keeping with previously prepared instructions, if appropriate to the situation. If there is no standard protocol for the event, the security person must act on his/her judgment.) The answer might be a primary or Central Command Security workstation where security officers are located, and where a second staff of individuals is monitoring the total system. This then becomes a multi-tiered type of monitored system.

The type, location, and number of monitoring and/or active security workstations an organization utilizes will depend on:

- The size of the organization.
- The aspects of security it elects to control and monitor.
- The location(s) of the various sites to be monitored.
- How much of the required personnel the organization wishes to have as direct employees, and how much it chooses to contract.

The mix can be varied based on different risk assessments and monitoring and control philosophies. Examples include:

- One security/reception workstation.
- A security/reception workstation, plus a Central Command Security station.
- A security/reception workstation, plus a Central Command Security station and an outside contractor monitoring company.
- A security/reception workstation, plus a Central Command Security station, plus a related or proprietary station or stations, off-site in a remote location (perhaps in other cities or countries).

Off-Site Monitored Systems

Off-site monitored systems are those whose functions are monitored by propriety, related, or even contracted third parties through either a dedicated high-speed data communications link or a dial-up connection. These second or third parties can either be the company's own personnel or a contract monitoring company.

Components of Security Monitoring Stations

To briefly review, there could be the following monitoring/control locations:

- In-house security/reception station.
- Central Security Command Center on-site.
- Off-site, secondary, or contract site location(s).

Each of the security monitoring stations may involve the following:

- One or more workstations with internal storage capacity, video and data communication interfaces, display (e.g., CRT or flat panel), keyboard, mouse, and printer (usually shared or networked).
- Operating system (OS) and applications software with password-protected user permission settings for data access/retrieval and entry, and full override systems monitoring, command, and control.

- Multi-line telephone instrument.
- Mobile radio handset ("walkie-talkie").
- Telecom and Datacom connections:
  — From terminal points to control panels via cable, fiber, or wireless.
  — From control panels to LAN or WAN via cable or fiber.
  — To central monitoring site or outsourced contractor or off-site department via dial-up or fiber.

Integration and Enterprise Security and Safety

What happened to the eight-hour day and the five-day work week? Unlike the 10-½ oz "pound" of coffee, or the 1-¾ quart "half-gallon" of ice cream, which continue to shrink, the concept of the 40- or 36-hour work week continues to stretch. Most organizations, such as banks, insurance companies, manufacturers, hotels, and even coffee houses, are now national operations, frequently in multiple countries. Their real time is, in fact, 24/7/365. This expansion of functional working time extends into every aspect of life, including work, and most assuredly into security and safety. Organizations spend massive amounts of time and money considering and developing ways to increase efficiency, improve communications, and to reach for the Holy Grail of a homogeneous enterprise-wide solution. Why? Because management realizes the benefits of improved productivity through economies of scale and efficiency in synergistic operations.

When looking at the many and often disparate safety and security systems in place or under consideration, it may be time to join the "e-mentality," consider a holistic plan, and design an enterprise solution for safety and security systems. In the security world, this solution is referred to as "integrated systems." Systems are more often physical and intelligent, both passive and active (i.e., comprised of hardware and software such as wires or cables; locks; access, smart, or proximity cards; bells; doors; prop devices and alarms; water detection devices; fire alarms and smoke detectors; closed circuit television cameras; transmission equipment; and infrared and motion detectors). As a result, within each area of interest, if not responsibility, are many distinct systems, some freestanding and often unable to communicate with more than one other device.

Integration is not an easy task. Because a lot of different systems are likely to be employed as mentioned above, it is possible that there are not many organizations truly qualified to produce an integrated system of acceptable quality. The task becomes even more formidable if a company wants to add monitoring of its building power, AC, HVAC, and IT devices and systems. One security provider in New York City has said that there are probably only two or three providers within the greater New York metropolitan area with the capability of integrating all of these systems.

Since 9/11, many organizations are just beginning to look beyond their cyber security systems to physical safety and security systems for integration implementation and budgeting. Yet another reason for integration may be insurance. Traditionally, physical property is insured against loss. If a water line supplying an AC unit or pantry floods the Chief Executive Officer's (CEO) office and runs for a half-hour before it is discovered and shut down, the office has become a small pond, its files soaked, furniture and artwork ruined, and favorite memorabilia destroyed. Is it really possible to believe that all is well in such a circumstance because there is insurance in place? The best (and the cheapest) insurance is to catch an accident early enough to prevent damage, which no amount of insurance might be able to cover.

Generally, unless there are water detectors, such as those frequently located under raised floors in data centers, a broken sprinkler line in any office may be an unmonitored system, because the usual fire suppression or fire detection system is often monitored only by the local fire department — and they may receive an alarm signal only if there is an actual fire or a sprinkler head goes off, or if a detector has sensed smoke.

Unless the system is addressable, it is not until the fire department has entered the building and found the fire alarm control panel at the fire command station or fire enunciation panel, that they will even know the location of the fire within the building. There has got to be a better way, if not from the fire department's point of view, at least from the organization's. That way is a fully integrated, 24/365 monitored safety and security system, with immediate notification to designated individuals.

What Components Should Be Integrated?

Terminal Devices

For this discussion, a number of terminal devices will be grouped together, including such items as access devices, door lock status devices, IR devices, motion detectors, smoke and heat detectors, water detectors, glass breakage detectors, temperature sensors, and on/off status devices. What each terminal device will require in the form of communications will depend on what it is designed to do, and its planned application. Some units will require nothing more than device identification—in addition to "this is who I am," a status-polling and/or "I'm OK" signal, or an "I'm not responding" condition and alarm.

Some "smart" terminals possess a considerable amount of pre-programmed intelligence, such as identification codes, date and time of day capability, "false access" condition, a "tamper" condition, "prop" condition, etc., together with information received in the ordinary course of its function, such as an individual's identification number or a facial, fingerprint, or iris template. The terminal must be capable of transmitting this information to its Intrusion Control Panel when called upon.

Control Panels

Higher quality control panels are both interactive and semi-interactive, and will sometimes receive an alarm and merely send it along to the central station. In other situations, they may receive a motion alarm, automatically signal a specific CCTV camera to turn on and to start recording, and at the same time send the alarm and its instructions on to the Central Command station PC, which can now take over and employ any necessary tilt, pan, and focus instructions as necessary. Control Panels can receive and transmit data to a number of terminal devices of differing functions. However, many control panels are so manufacturer-oriented (i.e., proprietary) as to be incapable of true integration with devices or software produced by others, which is why prudence in the selection process is necessary. An integrated system requires control panels that are not just access-related, but can accommodate data input from other types of devices. When moving toward integration, this need becomes increasingly important.

Integrated Components

The following elements should be considered in an integrated system. (Some may seem unrelated to security, but their inclusion in a fully integrated security system is beneficial for all parties, no matter how diverse their areas of interest or responsibility.)

- Access Control
- CCTV
- Fire and Life Safety
- Building and Mechanical Systems
- IT Equipment
- Transmission Media
- Interface Control

Primary Access Control

The security industry appears to be at the forefront of supplying advanced terminal devices, control panels, and systems architecture for managing and monitoring multiple points with diverse functions. Access control must deal with a multitude of devices and types of devices from proximity card reader to biotech type readers functioning as access control points and/or monitoring points. It will be simpler, and probably less costly, if one vendor supplies all of these devices (and their related control panels and reporting software). Systems compatibility at this level is important. Fortunately, most hardware interfaces will be RS-232

(TIA/EIA-232) or RS-485 (TIA/EIA-485) at control panels. The most commonly used logical interface (i.e., signal format) is TCP/IP (Telecommunications Control Protocol/Internet Protocol). RS-232 is a single-device interface to a single control panel and is less costly than a panel configured with an RS-485 interface. A single RS-485 control panel will handle up to 32 devices. (TCP/IP is addressed later in this chapter in the sections on Transmission Media and Interface Control.) Following is a short list of the various terminal points the security system will be called on to handle:

- Building(s) ingress and egress points
- Access – PIN, Swipe, Proximity, Biotech
- Egress – PIN, Swipe, Proximity, Biotech
- Intrusion – Prop Alarm detection
- Tampering
- Glass breakage

Secured Spaces Ingress and Egress

There are no essential differences between internal secured spaces and building ingress and egress, except that there may be no security person at the entrances to secured spaces, such as data centers or LAN or WAN rooms, IDF rooms, secured storage spaces, computers, and secured data (e.g., databases and personnel files) stored in some computers. One of the more significant differences might be an intense interest in who is leaving—and at what time—in addition to who is entering secured areas.

- Access – PIN, Swipe, Proximity, Biotech
- Egress – PIN, Swipe, Proximity, Biotech
- Intrusion – Prop Alarm, Motion, and IR detection
- Tampering

Elevators

Elevator control, especially after normal working hours, is one of the more effective methods of security control. Elevator control points can and should have different security controls from the main entrance, passenger elevator lobbies, and secured spaces. Not everyone may need to have the same freedom of access to freight elevators as passenger elevators. Freight elevators are often in back areas of building cores with lobbies emptying onto floors that contain potentially dangerous machinery and equipment.

- Elevator cab access – PIN, Swipe, Proximity, Biotech
- Elevator floor selection – PIN, Swipe, Proximity, Biotech

CCTV

CCTV systems begin with one or a number of camera types with different features such as black and white, color, and IR (infrared). Some cameras are fixed in one position and send an image of one location. Others provide pan (side-to-side) movement, tilt, focus, and/or zoom controls. Analog cameras acquired with no control capabilities require only a coaxial cable. If control is necessary, a pair of control wires is also required. Coaxial cable (bundled with sets of power and control wires) is readily available from a number of CCTV providers. Some cameras may operate full- or real-time. Some may be turned on by a command — either manually input by an operator, or by an automatic command as the result of a motion, sound, or detection of a rapid rise in heat, which might activate an infrared camera. The most basic determinations prior to selecting the correct camera type include what is to be observed, how the images will be used, and how long the images need to be retained. Some of these questions were reviewed in the section on CCTV in the previous chapter. Once a facility or organization's risk assessment has been made, it will be possible to develop a reasonable idea of what needs to be observed, how, and for how long.

Cameras

As already stated, the system may require analog cameras that have control—tilt, pan, zoom, etc. Digital cameras are also a possibility, but are not necessary unless their features, image resolution and very high definition (more pixels per screen), are required and meet budget limitations. System interfaces will be RS-232 (TIA/EIA-232) or RS-485 (TIA/EIA-485) using TCP/IP as the control signal format. The video signals from multiple cameras can either be connected to a workstation or combined (i.e., multiplexed) into one signal through a video hub device. A couple of levels of sophistication for the overall system will be discussed, each having its merits and limitations.

A Basic CCTV System

In all of the following situations, it is assumed that there is an existing computer. If a video capture board is installed in the workstation, the coax cables can be attached from the cameras to receive the video signals directly from each camera. These boards usually come in 4, 8, and 16-port configurations. The video capture board converts the video stream into digital MPEG (Moving Picture Experts Group), which can be understood by the computer. Once the video images are in the computer's hard drive, they can be monitored, stored, and played back, and tape can be made available to a remote station, as well as forwarding it via the network or modem. While this is a simple system, it consumes vast amounts of computer processing and storage capacity. In addition, the computer has to be in an always-on status to receive the video stream. It is not likely to be very fast, but it may be adequate for the particular anticipated risk.

A Step Up: Hubs, Video Transmitters, or Video Senders

Video transmitters are specialized hardware. They are, to some extent, similar to access control panels. Many of the control functions handled by computer software in the previously described more basic system, are addressed by the video transmitter. These functions are handled via integrated circuits, which result in increased performance and processing speed, using less computer processing capacity. Video transmitters are normally equipped with four ports and can handle remote cameras at close to live speed. However, recording is still done by VCR or on a hard drive in MPEG format.

The Next Step Up

This step progresses into more automated control and especially into digital recording. A DVR (Digital Video Recorder) can be used to record onto a DVD (Digital Video Disk) formatted optical disk, instead of VHS/VCR magnetic tape. This allows for storage of much more media. To appreciate some of the differences between DVD recording and VCR recording, it is important to understand a little bit about how VCR recording is most often performed. First, in order to preserve tape, recording can be done in "time-lapse" mode. Time-lapse mode records only (n) number of frames out of the 30 frames per second that are transmitted, therefore saving (n) percent of the total transmission, which is why the images are jerky. Time-lapse mode saves tape capacity so that a full 24-hour period may be recorded before changing tapes. One 60-gigabyte (one GB = one billion bytes) drive can record 100% of the transmissions for one week. There are now digital DVRs on the market capable of recording one terabyte (one TB = 1,000 billion bytes) of data. Such storage capacity allows for the recording of 100% of the video signal over a period of time (i.e., full motion versus time-lapse).

Some Digital Video Recorders have a number of highly flexible features, such as multiplexing 16 security camera signals, or monitoring one camera while playing back recorded media. Some will record only when activated by a detected motion. Some records can transmit a live video signal to a user station when triggered by a detected motion, and record weeks of media without maintenance. However, not all DVRs come with all of these features. Considering the efficiency of DVRs and their constantly declining costs, they may be one of the more cost-effective options.

The Top of the Line

If very high definition images are needed for an end product, an all-digital system using digital cameras will not only produce much clearer images, but decrease the size of the files. These systems are currently somewhat more costly, but are coming down in price. Implementing analog cameras now and converting to digital cameras as part of a system upgrade in the future may be a fiscally prudent decision worth the money and effort.

Fire and Life Safety Systems

Fire and Life Safety will most likely be the first systems to consider for inclusion with security in an integrated system. However, there are some very early words of warning. First, most fire departments insist that they are the ones to receive all alarms, with few exceptions, through their central station. Their functions are fire code-driven. Second, they may or may not permit monitoring of the in-house fire alarm panel at a secondary receiving station. It will be necessary to contact the authority having jurisdiction (AHJ) and secure permission. This may be the Fire Chief or the Fire Marshal. Once the AHJ is satisfied that the monitoring system is non-intrusive and will not affect the primary system to the Fire Department's Central Station, permission to monitor the fire alarm panel is generally granted.

Fire Alarm Panel

The fire alarm panel has a host of similar functions that it is called on to perform. Since all functions must work together, there is no primary or secondary level. However, it is important to recognize the principal functions, whether from the terminal end or the alarm/activate end of the system.

There are two basic types of fire alarm panels: conventional and addressable. A conventional panel is most likely to be used in a smaller facility, since it has limited terminal-point identification capabilities. It will identify a building zone, but not a specific detection device. (An addressable panel is capable of identifying both the zone and the device.) All fire alarm panels have supervisory capabilities using polling or "pinging" signals. Many of the newer types have runaway dialer protection, that is, the panel recognizes that it has dialed the Fire Control Center a number of times and stops the dialer from continuous redialing.

Smoke Detectors and Terminal Detection Devices

There are two types of smoke detectors: photoelectric and ionization, which represent the terminal end of the system. Although very different in their workings, both rely on the presence of smoke within their chambers (to interfere with either a beam of light or an electrical charge) to send a signal to a Digital Alarm Communication Receiver, which, in turn, will set off a series of actions, such as sounding an audible alarm, a strobe light, a recorded evacuation command, a sprinkler initiation command, starting a pressurization fan, shutting down air-handling systems, etc. Alarm signals are sent to the Fire Department's Command Center, and (with appropriate approval) an alarm signal is sent to the Security Command Center workstation with a possible audible alarm.

In addition to smoke detection devices, terminal detection devices may be able to sense the presence of an abnormal heat rise (usually from a fire), the opening of a fire sprinkler head, or the charging of a pre-action system. Whatever signals the fire alarm panel receives and responds to, personnel will want to know as soon as it happens.

Building and Mechanical Systems Status

Not all, or even many, facilities have Building Management Systems or Energy Management Systems. With the focus on security, this discussion will begin by citing some of the critical pieces of mechanical and electrical equipment, and what is important to know about them at all times and why.

Central HVAC Systems

- Internal Air Circulating Blowers: *On or Off.* In the event of a fire, they must be shut off to prevent the supply of oxygen to exacerbate the fire. During normal operations, personnel wants to be assured that the environment is at an agreeable comfort level, and that they receive an adequate supply of fresh air.

- Fresh Air Intake Mechanical Louvers: *Open or Closed.* While not normally required for fire and life safety needs, the ability to close fresh air intake louvers (if they are not fixed and can be closed) could be an important security process in the event of a chemical or biological hazard or attack.

- Fresh Air Intake Blowers: *On or Off.* As is the case with the internal air-handling blowers, the fresh air blowers should shut down in the event of a fire so as to not provide additional oxygen to the fire. Shutting down the fresh air system is another way of mitigating a chemical or biological hazard or attack.

Condenser Water Towers and Pumps: *On or Off*

- Today more and more facilities up to and in excess of 200,000 S.F. are being cooled through the use of condenser water systems and packaged AC units. LAN/PBX/PDU and other electrical equipment rooms, IDF rooms, and UPS rooms may be subject to AC systems shutdown when condenser water flow is interrupted. Without air-conditioning, most of these rooms can reach a "systems failure" temperature in 30 minutes or less.

- Nearly all of the newer, packaged AC units must be manually restarted when shut down due to high head pressures (lack of cooling water). AC equipment manufacturers consider this manual restart requirement a feature designed to protect the equipment from damage due to repeated automatic restarts.

- From the standpoint of protecting vital IT equipment and logic systems, it becomes critical that the Security Command Center workstation receive an immediate alarm signal with a possible audible alarm when AC units fail to operate. Notification can be made by one of a couple of ways, signaling that:
  — The AC unit has gone off on high head pressure, and there has been a temperature rise above a given set-point in any of the above-cited rooms;
  — The condenser water-circulating pumps may have shut down;
  — During a switching process from the No. 1 set of pumps to the No. 2 set, the incremental AC units have shut down due to high head pressure.

This is a critical set of alarms, more often than not ignored by security departments and managed solely by building management and maintenance personnel (who, on a Saturday night, may not be readily available).

Other Building Systems

- A few other basic systems deserve attention as potential risks. Monitoring these systems for status—and being able to receive alarm signals from them in the event of an abnormal condition or activity—provides real-time knowledge of critical systems, such as:
  — Generators: *Standby/Not Available*
  — Water Detection Devices: *Presence Alarm*
  — Fire Pumps: *Standby/Not Available*
  — Dual Action and/or Dry Pipe Sprinkler Systems: *Standby (System Dry)/Charged (System Wet)*
  — Main Telephone Company Switch: *Operating/ Not Operating*

Because nearly all of these terminal nodes are similar in function to access points, the selection of compatible interface control panels and protocols is not only logical, but also an effective life cycle and management cost control.

IT System Supervisor or Network Control Center

Most IT departments are accustomed to operating 24/365. This, together with their reliability linked directly to an organization's ability to function, means that the slightest breakdown or interference with operations is a real emergency. Because IT departments have long recognized their responsibility and dependence on environmental conditions and status, they are apt to have some form of alarm and notification system already in place. This fact should not preclude having most or all of the IT monitoring and notification systems incorporated into an integrated security system. IT's security concerns can be separated into two groups: *physical-passive* and *physical-active*.

Repeating the approach taken with Access Control and Building Systems, the utilization of access point terminal devices, interface control panels, and protocols remains appropriate and cost-effective.

Physical-Passive

- FM200: *Charged/Discharged* (Depending on the installed system, this status may or may not be able to be monitored.)
- Water: *Presence Alarm*
- Uninterruptible Power Supply (UPS): *On/Off*
- Backup (Emergency) Power Supply: (EPS or BPS) *Standby/Not Available*

These last three items are the same as in building systems monitoring. Given the critical nature of IT systems, it would not be unusual for them to be monitored by building management, security, and IT. One integrated system with a primary or command workstation, and two, three, or another designated number of secondary stations, would be more efficient and result in fewer conflicts of data.

Physical-Active

Within an IT environment, there are likely to be numerous physically active and operating devices, any one of which, if not operating as it should, could cause functional and/or economic stress. Given the possible high cost of failure in IT system function, an electronic and human monitoring system for some or all of it may be wise.

- PBX Switch: *Operational/Not Operational*
- Routers and/or port cards: *Operational/Not Operational*
- Servers: *Operational/Not Operational*

Transmission Media

A transmission medium is simply the path over which a signal is transferred (transmitted) between two or more points. There are several types of transmission media: fiber optic cable, metallic cable (e.g., CAT 5E and coax), and wireless [mobile/cellular radio, satellite, line-of-sight microwave, omni-directional radio frequency (RF), line-of-sight optical laser, etc.]. It is important not to confuse the transmission media type(s) with the signal format. For example, a broadcast radio signal format may be amplitude modulation (AM) or frequency modulation (FM), while the transmission medium may be either satellite or omni-directional RF. A standard digital network signal format is Telecommunication Control Protocol/Internet Protocol (TCP/IP), while the signal path may be comprised of various transmission media. The transmission media external to a building is termed "Outside Plant," and the transmission media internal to a building is termed "Inside Plant."

Interface Control

In simple terms, interface control is the practice of identifying and documenting both the physical and logical system interfaces used to interconnect the various pieces of equipment. Interface control is important for several reasons:

- **Equipment Selection/Acquisition** While several products are available that perform essentially the same functions (e.g., various types of motion detectors), interface compatibility should be a part of the selection criteria. Avoid products that use manufacturer's proprietary or product-specific interfaces, as they may lack compatibility with the rest of the system. The objective is to select/acquire products with physical and logical interfaces common to the other elements of the total system.

- **Integration** Applying interface control practices to all of the elements of the system will ensure that the system can be readily integrated without requiring additional equipment for converting the physical or logical interfaces to a system standard. Thus, interface control practices will minimize the costs and complexity of system integration. Furthermore, interface control is a means of ensuring that future changes (e.g., additions and upgrades) can be easily integrated into the system.

- **Maintenance** Utilizing interface control should reduce long-term integrated system maintenance costs by precluding proprietary logical and/or physical interfaces. System life-cycle costs are minimized by cost avoidance in the areas of system maintenance support contracts, system changes and upgrades, and specialized training for facilities/security personnel.

- **Systems Management** For proper management of an integrated system, one should know and document the physical and logical interfaces used, just as one should know and document all of the various types of equipment comprising an integrated system.

Deciding Which Systems to Integrate, and When

In considering the order in which systems may be integrated, there are different approaches. Because there are more problems with failed or non-operating building systems than instances of fires, the choice of a sequence would be as follows:

- Security system
- Building and mechanical systems
- Fire and life safety systems
- IT systems
- Others

A strict security point of view might opt for:

- Security system
- Fire and life safety systems
- Building and mechanical systems
- IT systems
- Others

From IT's point of view (keeping in mind that the focus is security):

- Security system
- IT systems
- Building and mechanical systems
- Fire and life safety systems
- Others

Much of the organization and implementation of an integrated system is both physical and logical. Figure 9.1 is an organizational chart, followed by some comments that may be of assistance.

The solid black lines represent physical connections, while the dotted lines represent the logical connections.

It is important to note that a digital video signal may be in a TCP/IP format (i.e., logical interface) for transmission. However, depending on factors like transmission capacity and distance, the result may be near-real-time versus actual real-time display of the images—which could be a major factor in the decision-making.

Conclusion

This final chapter has addressed many facility elements that were introduced earlier in the book, including security system components such as CCTV, as well as other building systems. The focus here is potential integration of these systems—for more reliable, 24/7 performance and cost-effectiveness. It is important to be aware of the potential (and the limitations) for integration of components during security system design, so that appropriate equipment is selected for current and future needs.

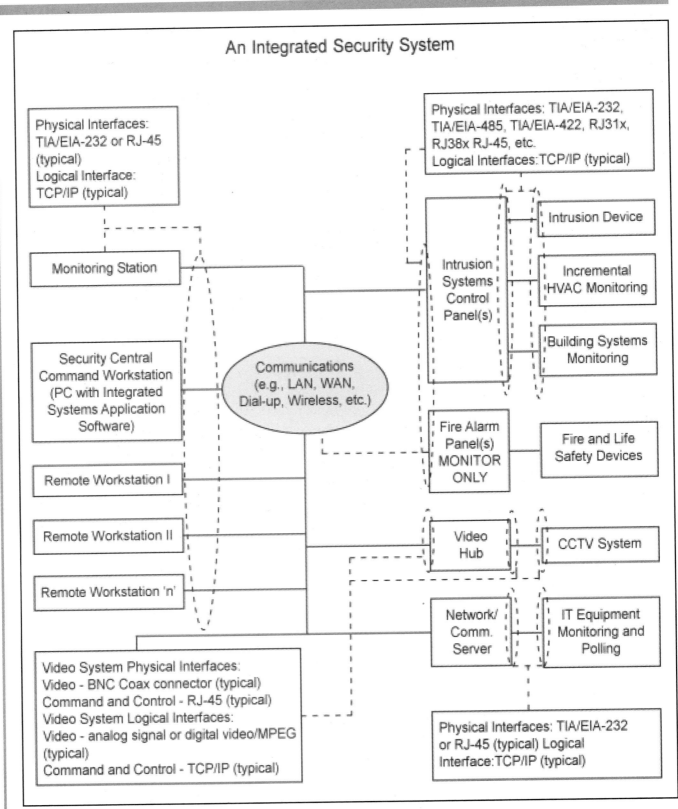

Figure 9.1: **An Integrated Security System**

Glossary of Building Integration Systems Terms

AM Amplitude modulation. A method of signal transmission in which information encoding is accomplished by varying the signal amplitude of a single frequency. The AM radio spectrum is from 535 kilohertz to 1.7 megahertz.

BNC Bayonet naval connector. A twist-lock, bayonet type connector assembly typically used with coaxial cables.

CIO Chief information officer.

CAT 5E Category 5E (or Cat 5E) A classification of network cabling that meets a recognized EIA specification for signal transmission capacity. The typical configuration is four twisted pairs of copper wire conductors. Cat 5E cable is used for data rates of up to 1,000 Mbps.

Coax Coaxial cable. A communication cable usually consisting of a solid copper conductor centered in a plastic core frequently wrapped by a braided metallic sheathing and covered by an outer insulation. The braided metallic sheathing is electrically grounded to reduce radio frequency (RF) emanations and external signal interference.

CCTV Closed circuit television.

CRT Cathode ray tube. The screen component of a computer monitor (or TV set).

DVD Digital video disk. A compact disk on which video images are digitally recorded.

DVR Digital video recorder. A device used to record digital images.

EPS or BPS Emergency power supply or backup power supply. Usually a diesel (or other fuel) powered generator used as the secondary power source engaged during extended primary power outages. There are other definitions for these abbreviations.

FM Frequency modulation. A method of signal transmission in which information encoding is accomplished by varying the signal frequency over a controlled bandwidth. The FM radio spectrum is from 88 megahertz to 108 megahertz.

GB Gigabyte (giant byte). A measure of digital capacity equal to one billion bytes.

Hot Site A term that identifies a facility as actively operational (i.e., not in a "standby" operational mode).

IDF Intermediate distribution frame. A communications cable management and distribution point located between the terminal devices (e.g., workstations) and the MDF.

IR Infrared.

IT Information technology. **IS** Information systems. **MIS** Management information systems.

LAN Local area network. A computer network spanning a local or small area.

MDF Main distribution frame. A communications cable management and distribution point located between the incoming lines (i.e., the Service Delivery Point or SDP) and the IDF.

MPEG Moving picture experts group. A compression process enabling computers to store video images. There are 3 MPEGs: 1, 2, and 4, with the lowest form of compression being MPEG-1 and the highest MPEG-4.

OS Operating system. Most commonly used in reference to the software platform used in a computer.

PBX Private branch exchange. An in-house telephone switching device used to switch between a limited number of outside lines to multiple in-house terminal equipment devices.

PDU Power distribution unit. An assembly, with surge suppression capability, used for distributing power in an equipment room.

PIN Personal identification number.

Plasma Display or Screen A flat panel display consisting of neon/xenon gas mixture between two glass plates and functioning as a CRT.

RF Radio frequency. An electromagnetic signal within the radio spectrum, characterized by radio wave propagation.

RJ-45 Registered jack type 45. An 8-pin, keyed miniature connector assembly typically used on cables for connecting a computer to a local area network.

RJ-38x Registered jack type 38x. An 8-position, non keyed miniature connector assembly typically used for connecting alarm circuit cables to devices.

RS-232 (TIA/EIA-232) Recommended standard (RS). Approved by the Electronics Industries Alliance (EIA) and the Telecommunications Industry Association (TIA) for serial interface between one driver (a PC) and one receiver can be a 25-pin, 15-pin, or 9-pin connector for cable lengths of 50–200 feet.

RS-485 (TIA/EIA-485) Recommended standard (RS). Approved by the Electronics Industries Alliance (EIA) and the Telecommunications Industry Association (TIA) for serial interface between up to 32 drivers (PCs) and up to 32 receivers. Can be 2-wire or 4-wire mode with distances up to 4,000 feet.

SAN Storage area network. A system of storage devices, such as magnetic disks, connected by a high-speed data network for simultaneous, real-time data storage.

Status Polling An automated process of periodic operational status queries and responses (e.g., alarm conditions) between a central control point and the connected remote/peripheral devices. The arrangement may be a master/slave configuration in which a controller queries remote devices for data. A polled device responds with data (e.g., a change in sensor conditions) or a null condition, and the controller polls the next device.

TB Terabyte (monster byte). A measure of digital capacity equal to 1,000 billion bytes

TCP/IP Telecommunications control protocol/internet protocol. Addressing schemes for transmitting data. IP sends packets of data into a system without a direct link; TCP establishes a virtual direct connection between a source and the intended destination. TCP/IP combines both systems.

UPS Uninterruptible power supply. A rechargeable battery assembly, connected between the primary power source (e.g., commercial power) and the terminal equipment, used for maintaining power to the connected equipment during short-term primary power outages. Sizes vary from a small battery pack for individual device (e.g., a desktop computer) to a large bank of batteries for an entire equipment room.

VCR Video cassette recorder. A device for recording and playing video images and sound on a videocassette.

VDT Video display terminal. A computer monitor usually capable of graphics display.

VHS Video home system. A process of transcoding a media file from one format to another.

WAN Wide area network. A system of LANs connected together over a wide area.

Part Two
Security Cost Data

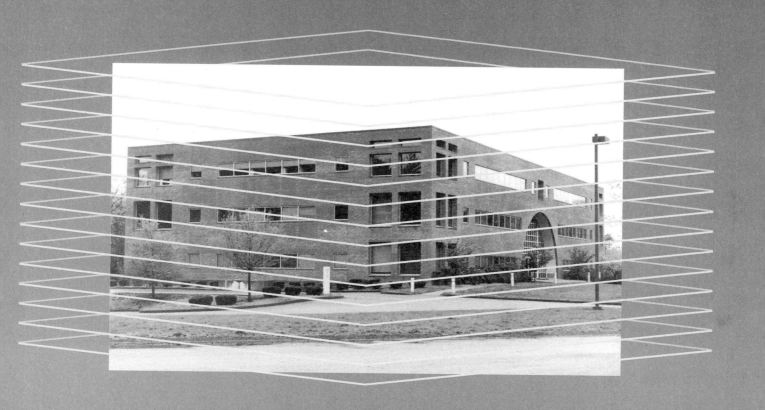

Cost Data

Introduction

The costs in this section include many security devices and construction materials appearing for the first time in Means data and researched specifically for this book. Other cost items address conventional building components that are either required elements in security systems, or that have properties that enhance security.

The selection of items is based on the editors' judgment and review of available products and recommended approaches. **Security devices** range from items such as CCTV cameras, electric gates and biometric identification equipment — to alert and alarm systems, chemical and biological detection systems, metal detectors, anti-eavesdropping sound conditioning systems, and more. The **construction materials and systems** are included to support security-conscious design. Examples are reinforced concrete and brick walls; barriers, such as bollards, retaining walls, and planters; bullet-resistant wallboard and glass; and filters and low-leakage dampers for HVAC systems. Additional equipment includes items such as bullet-resistant guardhouses to HEPA filtering machines, and many others.

Security Design and Estimating Considerations

It should be noted that since Means data is organized according to the CSI MasterFormat, some security items that will be used together in one system may be found in different divisions, according to their MasterFormat categories. For example, most of the glazing, or window, information is in Division 8, but bullet-resistant glass is in Division 11, under 11038, Bank Equipment. Similarly, active and passive vehicle barriers are covered in three locations — under 02945 Planting Accessories, 02840 Wall/Road/ Parking Appurtenances, and 13710 Security Access. (Note that steel cabling should be included as well as deadman anchors for interconnecting Jersey barriers and tying them to the ground. Also, planters and bollards without a ground connection provide a barrier against stationary vehicle bomb attack, but they should be connected at a prescribed depth in the ground in order to provide a barrier to the moving vehicle bomb tactic.)

The use of exterior plants for security-conscious landscaping should be combined with the outdoor security lighting plan to not only direct the flow of pedestrian traffic for those accessing the site, but also to minimize shadows and maximize visibility for security personnel. The plants listed in this cost section include ground covers and shrubs and help support differing approaches to security. One approach is maintaining a clear zone around a building with low plant growth. Others include blocking line-of-sight from the street, and installing dense or thorny shrubbery that resists penetration and serves as a security fence.

An important consideration that is not directly addressed in the cost data is protection of HVAC air intakes from sabotage with chemical or other harmful contaminants. Relocation of intakes to a high, out of reach location on the building—or creating a physical barrier that allows air flow, but minimizes vulnerability—is strongly recommended. If neither of those approaches is possible, procedural solutions are recommended, such as providing monitored CCTV coverage, security fencing, or guards to prevent access to points of vulnerability. Chapters 7 and 8 have more on air intakes, along with many other security devices and systems.

More information on these items can be obtained from the organizations and manufacturers listed in the Resources section in the appendix at the back of this book. The listed Web sites include product information, industry recommendations, and guidance from government agencies. The appendix also includes an audit checklist that can be used to review a facility's current level of security and to record the specific improvements needed to enhance the level of protection.

Table of Contents

The following pages provide information on the development of Means cost data and guidance for applying it.

Quick Start

If you feel you are ready to use this book and don't think you need the detailed instructions that begin on the following page, this Quick Start section is for you.

These steps will allow you to get started estimating in a matter of minutes.

First, decide whether you require a Unit Price or Assemblies type estimate. Unit price estimating requires a breakdown of the work to individual items. Assemblies estimates combine individual items or components into building systems.

If you need to estimate each line item separately, follow the instructions for **Unit Prices.**

If you can use an estimate for the entire assembly or system, follow the instructions for **Assemblies.**

Find each cost data section you need in the Table of Contents (either for Unit Prices or Assemblies).

Unit Prices: The cost data for Unit Prices has been divided into 16 divisions according to the CSI MasterFormat.

Assemblies: The cost data for Assemblies has been divided into 7 divisions according to the UNIFORMAT II.

Turn to the indicated section and locate the line item or assemblies table you need for your estimate. Portions of a sample page layout from both the Unit Price Listings and the Assemblies Cost Tables appear below.

Unit Prices: If there is a reference number listed at the beginning of the section, it refers to additional information you may find useful. See the referenced section for additional information.

- Note the crew code designation. You'll find full descriptions of crews in the Crew Listings including labor-hour and equipment costs.

Assemblies: The Assemblies (*not* shown in full here) are generally separated into three parts: 1) an illustration of the system to be estimated; 2) the components and related costs of a typical system; and 3) the costs for similar systems with dimensional and/or size variations. The Assemblies Section also contains reference numbers for additional useful information.

Determine the total number of units your job will require.

Unit Prices: Note the unit of measure for the material you're using is listed under "Unit."

- Bare Costs: These figures show unit costs for materials and installation. Labor and equipment costs are calculated according to crew costs and average daily output. Bare costs do not contain allowances for overhead, profit or taxes.

- "Labor-hours" allows you to calculate the total labor-hours to complete that task. Just multiply the quantity of work by this figure for an estimate of activity duration.

Assemblies: Note the unit of measure for the assembly or system you're estimating is listed in the Assemblies Table.

Then multiply the total units by . . .

Unit Prices: "Total Incl. O&P" which stands for the total cost including the installing contractor's overhead and profit. (See the "How To Use the Unit Price Pages" for a complete explanation.)

Assemblies: The "Total" in the right-hand column, which is the total cost **including the installing contractor's overhead and profit.** (See the "How To Use the Assemblies Cost Tables" section for a complete explanation.)

Material and equipment cost figures include a 10% markup. For labor markups, see the inside back cover of this book. If the work is to be subcontracted, add the general contractor's markup, approximately 10%.

The price you calculate will be an estimate for either an individual item of work or a completed assembly or *system.*

Compile a list of all items or assemblies included in the total project. Summarize cost information, and add project overhead.

Localize costs by using the Location Factors found in the Reference Section.

For a more complete explanation of the way costs are derived, please see the following sections.

Editors' Note: We urge you to spend time reading and understanding all of the supporting material and to take into consideration the reference material such as Crews Listing.

Unit Price Pages

Assemblies Pages

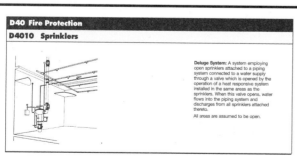

How to Use the Cost Data: The Details

What's Behind the Numbers? The Development of Cost Data

The staff at R.S. Means continuously monitors developments in the construction industry in order to ensure reliable, thorough and up-to-date cost information.

While *overall* construction costs may vary relative to general economic conditions, price fluctuations within the industry are dependent upon many factors. Individual price variations may, in fact, be opposite to overall economic trends. Therefore, costs are continually monitored and complete updates are published yearly. Also, new items are frequently added in response to changes in materials and methods.

Costs—$ (U.S.)

All costs represent U.S. national averages and are given in U.S. dollars. The Means City Cost Indexes can be used to adjust costs to a particular location. The City Cost Indexes for Canada can be used to adjust U.S. national averages to local costs in Canadian dollars.

Material Costs

The R.S. Means staff contacts manufacturers, dealers, distributors, and contractors all across the U.S. and Canada to determine national average material costs. If you have access to current material costs for your specific location, you may wish to make adjustments to reflect differences from the national average. Included within material costs are fasteners for a normal installation. R.S. Means engineers use manufacturers' recommendations, written specifications and/ or standard construction practice for size and spacing of fasteners. Adjustments to material costs may be required for your specific application or location. Material costs do not include sales tax.

Labor Costs

Labor costs are based on the average of wage rates from 30 major U.S. cities. Rates are determined from labor union agreements or prevailing wages for construction trades for the current year.

- If wage rates in your area vary from those used in this book, or if rate increases are expected within a given year, labor costs should be adjusted accordingly.

Labor costs reflect productivity based on actual working conditions. These figures include time spent during a normal workday on tasks other than actual installation, such as material receiving and handling, mobilization at site, site movement, breaks, and cleanup.

Productivity data is developed over an extended period so as not to be influenced by abnormal variations and reflects a typical average.

Equipment Costs

Equipment costs include not only rental, but also operating costs for equipment under normal use. The operating costs include parts and labor for routine servicing such as repair and replacement of pumps, filters and worn lines. Normal operating expendables such as fuel, lubricants, tires and electricity (where applicable) are also included. Extraordinary operating expendables with highly variable wear patterns such as diamond bits and blades are excluded. These costs are included under materials. Equipment rental rates are obtained from industry sources throughout North America—contractors, suppliers, dealers, manufacturers, and distributors.

Crew Equipment Cost/Day—The power equipment required for each crew is included in the crew cost. The daily cost for crew equipment is based on dividing the weekly bare rental rate by 5 (number of working days per week), and then adding the hourly operating cost times 8 (hours per day).

General Conditions

Cost data in this book is presented in two ways: Bare Costs and Total Cost including O&P (Overhead and Profit). General Conditions, when applicable, should also be added to the Total Cost including O&P. The costs for General Conditions are listed in Division 1. General Conditions for the *Installing Contractor* may range from 0% to 10% of the Total Cost including O&P. For the *General* or *Prime Contractor*, costs for General Conditions may range from 5% to 15% of the Total Cost including O&P, with a figure of 10% as the most typical allowance.

Overhead and Profit

Total Cost including O&P for the *Installing Contractor* is shown in the last column on the Unit Price pages of this book. This figure is the sum of the bare material cost plus 10% for profit, the base labor cost plus total overhead and profit, and the bare equipment cost plus 10% for profit. (See the "How To Use the Unit Price Pages" for an example of this calculation.)

Factors Affecting Costs

Costs can vary depending upon a number of variables. Here's how we have handled the main factors affecting costs.

Quality—The prices for materials and the workmanship upon which productivity is based represent sound construction work. They are also in line with U.S. government specifications.

Overtime—We have made no allowance for overtime. If you anticipate premium time or work beyond normal working hours, be sure to make an appropriate adjustment to your labor costs.

Productivity—The productivity, daily output, and labor-hour figures for each line item are based on working an eight-hour day in daylight hours in moderate temperatures. For work that extends beyond normal work hours or is performed under adverse conditions, productivity may decrease. (See the section in "How To Use the Unit Price Pages" for more on productivity.)

Size of Project—The size, scope of work, and type of construction project will have a significant impact on cost. Economies of scale can reduce costs for large projects. Unit costs can often run higher for small projects. Costs for projects of a significantly different size or type should be adjusted accordingly.

Location—Material prices in this book are for metropolitan areas. However, in dense urban areas, traffic and site storage limitations may increase costs. Beyond a 20-mile radius of large cities, extra trucking or transportation charges may also increase the material costs slightly. On the other hand, lower wage rates may be in effect. Be sure to consider both these factors when preparing an estimate, particularly if the job site is located in a central city or remote rural location.

In addition, highly specialized subcontract items may require travel and per diem expenses for mechanics.

Other factors—
- season of year
- contractor management
- weather conditions
- local union restrictions
- building code requirements
- availability of:
  - adequate energy
  - skilled labor
  - building materials
- owner's special requirements/restrictions
- safety requirements
- environmental considerations

Unpredictable Factors—General business conditions influence "in-place" costs of all items. Substitute materials and construction methods may have to be employed. These may affect the installed cost and/or life cycle costs. Such factors may be difficult to evaluate and cannot necessarily be predicted on the basis of the job's location in a particular section of the country. Thus, where these factors apply, you may find significant, but unavoidable cost variations for which you will have to apply a measure of judgment to your estimate.

Rounding of Costs

In general, all unit prices in excess of $5.00 have been rounded to make them easier to use and still maintain adequate precision of the results. The rounding rules we have chosen are in the following table.

Prices from ...	Rounded to the nearest ...
$.01 to $5.00	$.01
$5.01 to $20.00	$.05
$20.01 to $100.00	$.50
$100.01 to $300.00	$1.00
$300.01 to $1,000.00	$5.00
$1,000.01 to $10,000.00	$25.00
$10,000.01 to $50,000.00	$100.00
$50,000.01 and above	$500.00

Final Checklist

Estimating can be a straightforward process provided you remember the basics. Here's a checklist of some of the items you should remember to do before completing your estimate.

Did you remember to ...

- take into consideration which items have been marked up and by how much
- mark up the entire estimate sufficiently for your purposes
- read the background information on techniques and technical matters that could impact your project time span and cost
- include all components of your project in the final estimate
- double check your figures to be sure of your accuracy
- call R.S. Means if you have any questions about your estimate or the data you've found in our publications

Remember, R.S. Means stands behind its publications. If you have any questions about your estimate . . . about the costs you've used from our books . . . or even about the technical aspects of the job that may affect your estimate, feel free to call the R.S. Means editors at 1-800-334-3509.

How to Use the Unit Price Pages

The following is a detailed explanation of a sample entry in the Unit Price Section. Next to each bold number below is the item being described with appropriate component of the sample entry following in parenthesis. Some prices are listed as bare costs, others as costs that include overhead and profit of the installing contractor. In most cases, if the work is to be subcontracted, the general contractor will need to add an additional markup (R.S. Means suggests using 10%) to the figures in the column "Total Incl. O&P."

1 Division Number/Title (05500/Metal Fabrications)

Use the Unit Price Section Table of Contents to locate specific items. The sections are classified according to the CSI MasterFormat (1995 Edition).

2 Line Numbers (05580 900 0100)

Each unit price line item has been assigned a unique 12-digit code based on the CSI MasterFormat classification.

Level One - CSI-MasterFormat Division
Level Two - CSI

05500
05580-900-0100

Means 12-digit Line Number
Level Four - Means
Level Three - CSI

3 Description (Window Guards, etc.)

Each line item is described in detail. Sub-items and additional sizes are indented beneath the appropriate line items. The first line or two after the main item (in boldface) may contain descriptive information that pertains to all line items beneath this boldface listing.

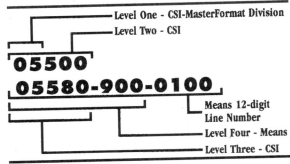

05500 | Metal Fabrications

05580 | Formed Metal Fabrications

		CREW	DAILY OUTPUT	LABOR-HOURS	UNIT	MAT.	LABOR	EQUIP.	TOTAL	TOTAL INCL O&P
900										900
0010	**WINDOW GUARDS**									
0015	Expanded metal, steel angle frame, permanent	E-4	350	.091	S.F.	15.95	3.31	.22	19.48	24
0025	Steel bars, 1/2" x 1/2" and 5" O.C.	"	290	.110		11.05	3.99	.27	15.31	19.70
0030	Hinge mounted, add					32			32	35
0040	Removable type, add					20.50			20.50	22.50
0050	For galvanized guards, add				S.F.	35%				
0070	For pivoted or projected type, add					105%	40%			
0100	Mild steel, stock units, economy	E-4	405	.079		4.33	2.86	.19	7.38	10.15
0200	Deluxe		405	.079		8.90	2.86	.19	11.95	20
0400	Woven wire, stock units, 3/8" channel, 3' x 5' opening			.800	Opng.	117	29	1.97	147.97	
0500	4' x 6' opening			.842		187	30.50	2.07	219.57	
0800	Basket guards for above, add					160			160	176
1000	Swinging guards for above, add					55			55	60.50

Crew (E-4)

The "Crew" column designates the typical trade or crew used to install the item. If an installation can be accomplished by one trade and requires no power equipment, that trade and the number of workers are listed (for example, "2 Carpenters"). If an installation requires a composite crew, a crew code designation is listed (for example, "E-4"). You'll find full details on all composite crews in the Crew Listings.

- For a complete list of all trades utilized in this book and their abbreviations, see the inside back cover.

Crews

Crew No.	Bare Costs		Incl. Subs O & P		Cost Per Labor-Hour	
Crew E-4	Hr.	Daily	Hr.	Daily	Bare Costs	Incl. O&P
1 Struc. Steel Foreman	$37.65	$301.20	$68.35	$546.80	$36.15	$65.65
3 Struc. Steel Workers	35.65	855.60	64.75	1554.00		
1 Gas Welding Machine		78.80		86.70	2.46	2.71
32 L.H., Daily Totals		$1235.60		$2187.50	$38.61	$68.36

Productivity: Daily Output (405)/Labor-Hours (0.079)

The "Daily Output" represents the typical number of units the designated crew will install in a normal 8-hour day. To find out the number of days the given crew would require to complete the installation, divide your quantity by the daily output. For example:

Quantity	÷	Daily Output	=	Duration
3240 S.F.	÷	405/ Crew Day	=	8 Crew Days

The "Labor-Hours" figure represents the number of labor-hours required to install one unit of work. To find out the number of labor-hours required for your particular task, multiply the quantity of the item times the number of labor-hours shown. For example:

Quantity	x	Productivity Rate	=	Duration
3240 S.F.	x	0.079 Labor-Hours/ S.F.	=	256 Labor-Hours

Unit (S.F.)

The abbreviated designation indicates the unit of measure upon which the price, production, and crew are based (S.F. = Square Foot). For a complete listing of abbreviations refer to the Abbreviations Listing in the Reference Section of this book.

Bare Costs:

Mat. (Bare Material Cost) (4.33)

The unit material cost is the "bare" material cost with no overhead and profit included. *Costs shown reflect national average material prices for January of the current year and include delivery to the job site. No sales taxes are included.*

Labor (2.86)

The unit labor cost is derived by multiplying bare labor-hour costs for Crew E-4 by labor-hour units. The bare labor-hour cost is found in the Crew Section under E-4.

Labor-Hour Cost Crew E-4	x	Labor-Hour Units	=	Labor
$36.15	x	0.079	=	$2.86

Equip. (Equipment) (.19)

Equipment costs for each crew are listed in the description of each crew. The unit equipment cost is derived by multiplying the bare equipment hourly cost by the labor-hour units.

Equipment Cost Crew E-4	x	Labor-Hour Units	=	Equip.
$2.46	x	0.079	=	$.19

Total (7.38)

The total of the bare costs is the arithmetic total of the three previous columns: mat., labor, and equip.

Material	+	Labor	+	Equip.	=	Total
$4.33	+	$2.86	+	$.19	=	$7.38

Total Costs Including O&P

This figure is the sum of the bare material cost plus 10% for profit; the bare labor cost plus total overhead and profit; and the bare equipment cost plus 10% for profit.

Material is Bare Material Cost + 10% = 4.33 + 0.43	=	$ 4.76
Labor for Crew E-4 = Labor-Hour Cost (65.65) x Labor-Hour Units (0.079)	=	$ 5.19
Equip. is Bare Equip. Cost + 10% = 0.19 + 0.02	=	$ 0.21
Total (Rounded)	=	$10.15

01500 | Temporary Facilities & Controls

01540 | Construction Aids

		CREW	DAILY OUTPUT	LABOR-HOURS	UNIT	2003 BARE COSTS MAT.	LABOR	EQUIP.	TOTAL	TOTAL INCL O&P
500	**0010** **PERSONNEL PROTECTIVE EQUIPMENT**									
	0015 Hazardous waste protection				Ea.	206			206	226
	0020 Respirator mask only, full face, silicone					30.50			30.50	33.50
	0030 Half face, silicone					4.29			4.29	4.72
	0040 Respirator cartridges, 2 reg'd/mask, dust or asbestos					4.13			4.13	4.54
	0050 Chemical vapor					8.70			8.70	9.60
	0060 Combination vapor and dust					400			400	440
	0100 Emergency escape breathing apparatus, 5 min					465			465	510
	0110 10 min					1,500			1,500	1,650
	0150 Self contained breathing apparatus with full face piece, 30 min					2,425			2,425	2,675
	0160 60 min					805			805	885
	0200 Encapsulating suits, limited use, level A					180			180	197
	0210 Level B				Pr.	4.77			4.77	5.25
	0300 Over boots, latex					9.45			9.45	10.40
	0310 PVC					50			50	55
	0320 Neoprene					5.35			5.35	5.85
	0400 Gloves, nitrile/PVC					28			28	31
	0410 Neoprene coated									

01560 | Barriers & Enclosures

		CREW	DAILY OUTPUT	LABOR-HOURS	UNIT	2003 BARE COSTS MAT.	LABOR	EQUIP.	TOTAL	TOTAL INCL O&P
100	**0010** **BARRICADES** 5' high, 3 rail @ 2" x 8", fixed	2 Carp	30	.533	L.F.	11	16.85		27.85	38.50
	0150 Movable	"	20	.800		11	25		36	51.50
	0200 Precast barrier walls, 10' sections	B-6	240	.100	Ea.	28	2.68	.91	31.59	36
	0300 Stock units, 6' high, 8' wide, plain, buy				Ea.	435			435	480
	0350 With reflective tape, buy				"	525			525	580
	0400 Break-a-way 3" PVC pipe barricade				Ea.	305			305	335
	0410 with 3 ea. 1' x 4' reflectorized panels, buy					72			72	79
	0500 Plywood with steel legs, 32" wide					6			6	6.60
	0800 Traffic cones, PVC, 18" high					18.25			18.25	20
	0850 28" high									
	0900 Barrels, 55 gal., with flasher	1 Clab	96	.083		52	2.05		54.05	60
	1000 Guardrail, wooden, 3' high, 1" x 6", on 2" x 4" posts	2 Carp	200	.080	L.F.	.93	2.52		3.45	4.96
	1100 2" x 6", on 4" x 4" posts	"	165	.097		1.79	3.06		4.85	6.75
	1200 Portable metal with base pads, buy					15.50			15.50	17.05
	1250 Typical installation, assume 10 reuses	2 Carp	600	.027		1.60	.84		2.44	3.07
	1300 Barricade tape, polyethelyne, 7 mil, 3" wide x 500' long roll				Ea.	25			25	27.50
	2030 Barricades, interlocking fence type, galv, 41" H x 85" L	2 Clab	30	.533		139	13.15		152.15	174
	2040 Barrelcades, plastic, stackable, 40" H x 24" Dia, w/rubber base		60	.267		75	6.55		81.55	93
	2050 Barricades, collapsable, plastic, fold-down type, 45" H x 25" W x 46" D		40	.400		88	9.85		97.85	112
	2060 Optional flasher for, 6V, 7" amber lens, with bracket	1 Clab	70	.114		25	2.82		27.82	32
	2070 Plastic, A-frame type, 42" H x 6' long	2 Clab	40	.400		129	9.85		138.85	157
	2080 42" H x 8' long	"	40	.400		149	9.85		158.85	179
	2090 Plastic, two-piece, 3-8' long boards, 5' H	1 Clab	25	.320		209	7.90		216.90	242

		CREW	DAILY OUTPUT	LABOR-HOURS	UNIT	2003 BARE COSTS MAT.	LABOR	EQUIP.	TOTAL	TOTAL INCL O&P
800	**0010** **WATCHMAN** Service, monthly basis, uniformed person, minimum				Hr.					8.20
	0100 Maximum									14.85
	0200 Person and command dog, minimum									10.80
	0300 Maximum									16.05
	0500 Sentry dog, leased, with job patrol (yard dog), 1 dog				Week					210
	0600 2 dogs				"					290
	0800 Purchase, trained sentry dog, minimum				Ea.					850
	0900 Maximum				"					2,000

01900 | Facility Decommissioning

01910 | Hazardous Material

300	0010	**HEALTH AND SAFETY**	CREW	DAILY OUTPUT	LABOR-HOURS	UNIT	MAT.	LABOR	EQUIP.	TOTAL	TOTAL INCL O&P	
							2003 BARE COSTS					
	8000	Radiation monitoring/health physics equipment										300
	8100	Personal dosimetry										
	8110	Audible alarms										
	8111	Ratemeter, w/clip, x and gamma, 500 mr/hr threshold				Ea.	195			195	215	
	8112	Ratemeter w/belt clip, x and gamma, adjustable					195			195	215	
	8113	Ratemeter and dosimeter w/belt clip					165			165	182	
	8114	Badge size clip-on alarm, alpha					440			440	480	
	8115	Badge size clip-on alarm, alpha-beta-gamma					555			555	610	
	8116	Badge size clip-on alarm, gamma					480			480	525	
	8117	Badge size clip-on alarm, additional cost for LED					8.20			8.20	9	
	8118	Badge size clip-on alarm, additional cost for banana plug					30.50			30.50	33.50	
	8119	Badge size clip-on alarm, additional cost for LED and ear					35			35	38.50	
	8150	Pocket ion chambers										
	8151	Quartz fiber, gamma and x-ray low E level, 0-500mr				Ea.	168			168	184	
	8152	Quartz fiber, gamma and x-ray medium E level, 0-20r					130			130	143	
	8153	Quartz fiber, gamma and x-ray high E level, 0-600r					158			158	173	
	8154	Fast neutron, 0 - 200mrad					147			147	161	
	8155	Thermal neutron, 0 - 120mrem					945			945	1,050	
	8156	Line operated charger (110V-AC)					141			141	155	
	8157	Battery powered charger					178			178	196	
	8158	Desk top calibrator					4,975			4,975	5,475	
	8159	Dosimeter viewer-charger					8,475			8,475	9,325	
	8161	Multiple calibrator, 75 dosimeters maximum					13,000			13,000	14,200	
	8162	Characterized direct reading dosimeter kit					4,075			4,075	4,500	
	8163	Plastic protective end caps (set)					5.45			5.45	5.95	
	8164	NRC approved dosimeter log book					40.50			40.50	44.50	
	8165	Pocket ion chamber alligator clip					251			251	276	
	8166	Dosimeter clip remover tool					153			153	168	
	8167	100 hole tray					46			46	50.50	
	8168	LED light source with battery					8.45			8.45	9.30	
	8400	Dosimetry systems, electronic										
	8410	Dosimeters										
	8411	Electronic dosimeter				Ea.	495			495	545	
	8450	Readers and components										
	8451	Electronic dosimer reader, remote sta w/ltd cap				Ea.	3,200			3,200	3,525	
	8452	Electronic dosimer reader, health physics sta w/exp cap					6,800			6,800	7,475	
	8453	Automatic electronic dosimeter calibrator	W-1	.50	76		4,200	2,400	174	6,774	8,475	
	8454	Personal computer system including color monitor					11,500			11,500	12,600	
	8455	Dosimetry system software					5,275			5,275	5,800	
	8500	Dosimetry systems, thermoluminescent (TL)										
	8510	TL dosimeters										
	8511	One element badge				Ea.	20.50			20.50	22.50	
	8512	Two element badge					31			31	34	
	8513	Three element badge					37			37	40.50	
	8514	Four element badge					51.50			51.50	57	
	8515	Neutron badge					31.50			31.50	34.50	
	8516	Ring w/basil chip					12.45			12.45	13.70	
	8517	Wrist bracelet w/basil chip					9.90			9.90	10.90	
	8518	Personal badge w/o chip					8.80			8.80	9.70	
	8519	Ring w/o chip					1.27			1.27	1.40	
	8521	Wrist strap w/o chip					.72			.72	.79	
	8540	TL readers and components										
	8541	Manual, economy w/o printer, one element	R-24	8	1.250	Ea.	12,600	47.50		12,647.50	14,000	
	8542	Manual, economy w/mini-printer, one element		8	1.250		13,500	47.50		13,547.50	14,900	
	8543	Manual, w/mini-printer, one element		8	1.250		14,900	47.50		14,947.50	16,500	

01900 | Facility Decommissioning

01910	Hazardous Material	CREW	DAILY OUTPUT	LABOR-HOURS	UNIT	2003 BARE COSTS				TOTAL INCL O&P	
						MAT.	LABOR	EQUIP.	TOTAL		
300 8544	Manual, 2, 3, or 4 element cards, base	R-24	8	1.250	Ea.	29,000	47.50		29,047.50	32,000	300
8545	Manual, 2, 3, or 4 element cards, w/ID	↓	8	1.250		33,000	47.50		33,047.50	36,400	
8546	Manual, 2, 3, or 4 element cards, w/options	R-30	8	3.250		31,300	97		31,397	34,600	
8547	Automatic, 50 card, base model		8	3.250		35,300	97		35,397	38,900	
8548	Automatic, 50 card, w/options		8	3.250		40,400	97		40,497	44,600	
8549	Automatic, 200 card, base model		5	5.200		53,500	155		53,655	59,000	
8551	Automatic, 200 card, w/options	↓	5	5.200	↓	67,000	155		67,155	74,000	
8800	Personnel monitoring										
8830	Hand and foot monitors				Ea.	240			240	264	
8831	Beta, gamma hand monitor					390			390	430	
8832	Alpha hand monitor	W-1	.25	152		15,800	4,800	350	20,950	25,100	
8833	Beta, gamma hand and foot monitor	"	.50	76	↓	18,700	2,400	174	21,274	24,400	
8834	Alpha, beta, gamma, hand and foot monitor										
8840	Whole body/portal monitors										
8841	Portal, w/GM detectors, manual read	R-30	.50	52	Ea.	8,000	1,550		9,550	11,200	
8842	Portal, portable, w/scint det, computerized	"	.50	52		13,800	1,550		15,350	17,600	
8843	Portal, w/plastic scint detectors, computerized	W-1	.25	152		27,300	4,800	350	32,450	37,700	
8844	Portal, w/gas flow proportional det, computerized		.50	76		32,800	2,400	174	35,374	39,800	
8845	Portal, w/beta detection, computerized control, enclosed		.25	152		31,000	4,800	350	36,150	41,800	
8846	Whole body, internal contam., computerized	↓	.50	76		88,500	2,400	174	91,074	101,500	
8847	Calibration programming for computerized monitors				↓	250			250	275	

02100 | Site Remediation

02110 | Excavation, Removal & Handling

			CREW	DAILY OUTPUT	LABOR-HOURS	UNIT	2003 BARE COSTS				TOTAL INCL O&P	
							MAT.	LABOR	EQUIP.	TOTAL		
300	0010	HAZARDOUS WASTE CLEANUP/PICKUP/DISPOSAL										300
	0100	For contractor equipment, i.e. dozer,										
	0110	Front end loader, dump truck, etc., see div. 01590-200										
	1000	Solid pickup										
	1100	55 gal. drums				Ea.						
	1120	Bulk material, minimum				Ton					220	
	1130	Maximum				"					165	
	1200	Transportation to disposal site									550	
	1220	Truckload = 80 drums or 25 C.Y. or 18 tons										
	1260	Minimum				Mile						
	1270	Maximum				"					2.50	
	3000	Liquid pickup, vacuum truck, stainless steel tank									4.40	
	3100	Minimum charge, 4 hours										
	3110	1 compartment, 2200 gallon				Hr.					110	
	3120	2 compartment, 5000 gallon				"					110	
	3400	Transportation in 6900 gallon bulk truck				Mile					4.75	
	3410	In teflon lined truck				"					5.50	
	5000	Heavy sludge or dry vacuumable material				Hr.					110	
	6000	Dumpsite disposal charge, minimum				Ton					110	
	6020	Maximum				"					440	

02200 | Site Preparation

02225 | Selective Demolition

			CREW	DAILY OUTPUT	LABOR-HOURS	UNIT	2003 BARE COSTS				TOTAL INCL O&P	
							MAT.	LABOR	EQUIP.	TOTAL		
720	0010	DISPOSAL ONLY Urban buildings with salvage value allowed										720
	0020	Including loading and 5 mile haul to dump										
	0200	Steel frame	B-3	430	.112	C.Y.		2.97	3.90	6.87	8.85	
	0300	Concrete frame		365	.132			3.50	4.60	8.10	10.45	
	0400	Masonry construction		445	.108			2.87	3.77	6.64	8.60	
	0500	Wood frame		247	.194			5.20	6.80	12	15.45	
730	0010	RUBBISH HANDLING The following are to be added to the										730
	0020	demolition prices										
	0400	Chute, circular, prefabricated steel, 18" diameter	B-1	40	.600	L.F.	27	15.20		42.20	53	
	0440	30" diameter		30	.800		36	20.50		56.50	71	
	0460	36" diameter		28	.857		33.50	21.50		55	71	
	0600	Dumpster, weekly rental, 1 dump/week, 6 C.Y. capacity (2 Tons)				Week					315	
	0700	10 C.Y. capacity (4 Tons)									375	
	0725	Dumpster, weekly rental, 1 dump/week, 20 C.Y. capacity (8 Tons)									440	
	0750	20 C.Y. capacity	1 Trhv	8	1		320	25.50		345.50	390	
	0800	30 C.Y. capacity (10 Tons)									665	
	0840	40 C.Y. capacity (13 Tons)									805	
	0900	Alternate pricing for dumpsters										
	0910	Delivery, average for all sizes				Ea.					52	
	0920	Haul, average for all sizes									130	
	0930	Rent per day, average for all sizes									3.10	
	0940	Rent per month, average for all sizes									31	
	0950	Disposal fee per ton, average for all sizes				Ton					47	
	1000	Dust partition, 6 mil polyethylene, 4' x 8' panels, 1" x 3" frame	2 Carp	2,000	.008	S.F.	.16	.25		.41	.57	
	1080	2" x 4" frame	"	2,000	.008	"	.28	.25		.53	.69	
	1200	Handling in elevator, 10 floors, by material volume	B-1	280	.086	C.F.		2.17		2.17	3.39	

02200 | Site Preparation

		02225	Selective Demolition	CREW	DAILY OUTPUT	LABOR-HOURS	UNIT	2003 BARE COSTS MAT.	LABOR	EQUIP.	TOTAL	TOTAL INCL O&P	
730	2000		Load, haul to chute & dumping into chute, 50' haul	2 Clab	24	.667	C.Y.		16.45		16.45	25.50	730
	2040		100' haul		16.50	.970			24		24	37.50	
	2080		Over 100' haul, add per 100 L.F.		35.50	.451			11.10		11.10	17.35	
	2120		In elevators, per 10 floors, add		140	.114			2.82		2.82	4.40	
	3000		Loading & trucking, including 2 mile haul, chute loaded	B-16	45	.711			18.05	10	28.05	39	
	3040		Hand loading truck, 50' haul	"	48	.667			16.95	9.35	26.30	37	
	3080		Machine loading truck	B-17	120	.267			7.05	4.37	11.42	15.70	
	3090		Ramp loaded	B-16	40	.800			20.50	11.25	31.75	44	
	3120		Wheeled 50' and ramp dump loaded	2 Clab	24	.667			16.45		16.45	25.50	
	5000		Haul, per mile, up to 8 C.Y. truck	B-34B	1,165	.007			.18	.39	.57	.69	
	5100		Over 8 C.Y. truck	"	1,550	.005			.13	.29	.42	.52	
	5200		Minimum charge, chute load and up to 2 mile haul	B-16	2	16	Ton		405	225	630	875	
	5210		Debris hauling, per ton	"	15	2.133	"		54	30	84	117	
	5300		Minimum charge, haul pick-up truck load to dump	1 Clab	2	4	Ea.		98.50		98.50	154	
	9000		Minimum labor/equipment charge	B-16	2	16	Job		405	225	630	875	
740	0010		**DUMP CHARGES** Typical urban city, tipping fees only				Ton					70	740
	0100		Building construction materials									50	
	0200		Trees, brush, lumber									60	
	0300		Rubbish only									85	
	0500		Reclamation station, usual charge										

02800 | Site Improvements and Amenities

		02820	Fences & Gates	CREW	DAILY OUTPUT	LABOR-HOURS	UNIT	2003 BARE COSTS MAT.	LABOR	EQUIP.	TOTAL	TOTAL INCL O&P	
500	0011		**FENCE, METAL**										500
	4500		Security fence, prison grade, set in concrete, 12' high	B-80	25	1.280	L.F.	23	34.50	19.95	77.45	100	
	4600		16' high	"	20	1.600	"	27.50	43	25	95.50	124	
528	0010		**FENCE, CHAIN LINK INDUSTRIAL**, schedule 40										528
	0020		3 strands barb wire, 2" post @ 10' O.C., set in concrete, 6' H										
	0200		9 ga. wire, galv. steel	B-80	240	.133	L.F.	8.05	3.58	2.08	13.71	16.65	
	0300		Aluminized steel		240	.133		10.35	3.58	2.08	16.01	19.15	
	0500		6 ga. wire, galv. steel		240	.133		13.05	3.58	2.08	18.71	22	
	0600		Aluminized steel		240	.133		14.90	3.58	2.08	20.56	24	
	0800		6 ga. wire, 6' high but omit barbed wire, galv. steel		250	.128		12.60	3.43	2	18.03	21.50	
	0900		Aluminized steel		250	.128		17.65	3.43	2	23.08	27	
	0920		8' H, 6 ga. wire, 2-1/2" line post, galv. steel		180	.178		20.50	4.77	2.77	28.04	33	
	0940		Aluminized steel		180	.178		25.50	4.77	2.77	33.04	38.50	
	1100		Add for corner posts, 3" diam., galv. steel		40	.800	Ea.	61.50	21.50	12.50	95.50	114	
	1200		Aluminized steel		40	.800		73.50	21.50	12.50	107.50	128	
	1300		Add for braces, galv. steel		80	.400		16.70	10.75	6.25	33.70	42	
	1350		Aluminized steel		80	.400		22.50	10.75	6.25	39.50	48	
	1400		Gate for 6' high fence, 1-5/8" frame, 3' wide, galv. steel		10	3.200		98	86	50	234	295	
	1500		Aluminized steel		10	3.200		120	86	50	256	320	
	2000		5'-0" high fence, 9 ga., no barbed wire, 2" line post,										
	2010		10' O.C., 1-5/8" top rail										
	2100		Galvanized steel	B-80	300	.107	L.F.	6.70	2.86	1.66	11.22	13.60	
	2200		Aluminized steel		300	.107	"	8.10	2.86	1.66	12.62	15.15	

02820 | Fences & Gates

		CREW	DAILY OUTPUT	LABOR-HOURS	UNIT	2003 BARE COSTS MAT.	LABOR	EQUIP.	TOTAL	TOTAL INCL O&P
528	2400	Gate, 4' wide, 5' high, 2" frame, galv. steel	B-80	10	3.200	Ea.	111	86	50	247	310	**528**
	2500	Aluminized steel		10	3.200	"	123	86	50	259	320
	3100	Overhead slide gate, chain link, 6' high, to 18' wide		38	.842	L.F.	98	22.50	13.15	133.65	157
	3105	8' high		30	1.067		98.50	28.50	16.65	143.65	170
	3108	10' high		24	1.333		99.50	36	21	156.50	187
	3110	Cantilever type		48	.667		42.50	17.90	10.40	70.80	85.50
	3120	8' high		24	1.333		61.50	36	21	118.50	146
	3130	10' high		18	1.778		72.50	47.50	27.50	147.50	184
	3190	10' high, galvanized steel		190	.168		11.15	4.52	2.63	18.30	22
	3210	Vinyl covered 9 ga. wire		190	.168		12.25	4.52	2.63	19.40	23.50
	3240	Corner posts for above, 3" diameter, 10' high		30	1.067	Ea.	117	28.50	16.65	162.15	191
	5000	Double swing gates, incl. posts & hardware									
	5010	5' high, 12' opening	B-80	3.40	9.412	Opng.	299	253	147	699	880
	5020	20' opening		2.80	11.429		405	305	178	888	1,125
	5060	6' high, 12' opening		3.20	10		505	268	156	929	1,150
	5070	20' opening		2.60	12.308		695	330	192	1,217	1,475
	5080	8' high, 12' opening		2.13	15.002		785	405	234	1,424	1,750
	5090	20' opening		1.45	22.069		1,025	590	345	1,960	2,425
	5100	10' high, 12' opening		1.31	24.427		890	655	380	1,925	2,400
	5110	20' opening		1.03	31.068		1,350	835	485	2,670	3,275
	5120	12' high, 12' opening		1.05	30.476		1,300	820	475	2,595	3,200
	5130	20' opening		.85	37.647		1,675	1,000	585	3,260	4,050
	5190	For aluminized steel add					20%				
535	0010	**FENCE, CHAIN LINK, GATES & POSTS** (1/3 post length in ground)										**535**
	6580	Line posts, galvanized, 2-1/2" OD, set in conc., 4'	B-80	80	.400	Ea.	15.10	10.75	6.25	32.10	40
	6585	5'		76	.421		18.35	11.30	6.55	36.20	44.50
	6590	6'		74	.432		18.75	11.60	6.75	37.10	46
	6595	7'		72	.444		20.50	11.90	6.95	39.35	48.50
	6600	8'		69	.464		22.50	12.45	7.25	42.20	51.50
	6610	H-beam, 1-7/8", 4'		83	.386		17.25	10.35	6	33.60	41.50
	6615	5'		81	.395		19.75	10.60	6.15	36.50	45
	6620	6'		78	.410		23	11	6.40	40.40	49.50
	6625	7'		75	.427		25.50	11.45	6.65	43.60	53
	6630	8'		73	.438		27.50	11.75	6.85	46.10	56
	6635	Vinyl coated, 2-1/2" OD, set in conc., 4'		79	.405		30	10.85	6.30	47.15	56.50
	6640	5'		77	.416		34	11.15	6.50	51.65	62
	6645	6'		74	.432		43	11.60	6.75	61.35	73
	6650	7'		72	.444		46	11.90	6.95	64.85	76.50
	6655	8'		69	.464		50	12.45	7.25	69.70	82
	6657	For line posts with single barbed wire arm, add					4%				
	6658	For line posts with double barbed wire arm, add					10%				
	6659	For line posts with top rail fitting, add					9%				
	6660	End gate post, steel, 3" OD, set in conc.,4'	B-80	68	.471	Ea.	35	12.65	7.35	55	66
	6665	5'		65	.492		44.50	13.20	7.70	65.40	77.50
	6670	6'		63	.508		45	13.65	7.90	66.55	79
	6675	7'		61	.525		60	14.05	8.20	82.25	96.50
	6680	8'		59	.542		64.50	14.55	8.45	87.50	103
	6685	Vinyl, 4'		68	.471		58.50	12.65	7.35	78.50	92
	6690	5'		65	.492		64	13.20	7.70	84.90	99.50
	6695	6'		63	.508		79.50	13.65	7.90	101.05	117
	6700	7'		61	.525		77.50	14.05	8.20	99.75	116
	6705	8'		59	.542		95	14.55	8.45	118	137
	6708	For double gate posts greater than 24' wide, add					125%	30%			
	6709	For line posts with top rail fitting, add					9%				
	6710	Corner post, galv. steel, 4" OD, set in conc., 4'	B-80	65	.492	Ea.	58.50	13.20	7.70	79.40	93.50

02800 | Site Improvements and Amenities

02820 | Fences & Gates

		CREW	DAILY OUTPUT	LABOR-HOURS	UNIT	MAT.	LABOR	EQUIP.	TOTAL	TOTAL INCL O&P
						2003 BARE COSTS				
6715	6'	B-80	63	.508	Ea.	83	13.65	7.90	104.55	121
6720	7'		61	.525		93.50	14.05	8.20	115.75	134
6725	8'		65	.492		108	13.20	7.70	128.90	147
6730	Vinyl, 5'		65	.492		103	13.20	7.70	123.90	142
6735	6'		63	.508		136	13.65	7.90	157.55	180
6740	7'		61	.525		124	14.05	8.20	146.25	168
6745	8'		59	.542		162	14.55	8.45	185	211
6747	Corner, gate & end posts w/sgl barbed wire arm, add					8%				
6748	Corner, gate & end posts w/dbl barbed wire arm, add					13%				
6749	For line posts with top rail fitting, add					9%				
6750	Line post, galv., 2-1/2" OD, grouted in rock, 4'	B-80	76	.421	Ea.	15.10	11.30	6.55	32.95	41.50
6755	5'		74	.432		18.35	11.60	6.75	36.70	45.50
6760	6'		72	.444		18.75	11.90	6.95	37.60	46.50
6765	7'		70	.457		20.50	12.25	7.15	39.90	49.50
6770	8'		68	.471		22.50	12.65	7.35	42.50	52
6775	H-beams, galv, 2-1/4" OD, grouted in rock, 4'		76	.421		19.05	11.30	6.55	36.90	45.50
6780	5'		74	.432		22	11.60	6.75	40.35	49.50
6785	6'		72	.444		25	11.90	6.95	43.85	53.50
6790	7'		70	.457		27.50	12.25	7.15	46.90	57
6795	8'		68	.471		30	12.65	7.35	50	60.50
6800	Line post, vinyl, 2-1/2" OD, grouted in rock, 4'		76	.421		30	11.30	6.55	47.85	57.50
6805	5'		74	.432		34	11.60	6.75	52.35	63
6810	6'		72	.444		43	11.90	6.95	61.85	73.50
6815	7'		70	.457		46	12.25	7.15	65.40	77.50
6820	8'		68	.471		50	12.65	7.35	70	82.50
6823	For line posts with single barbed wire arm, add					4%				
6824	For line posts with double barbed wire arm, add					10%				
6825	End post, galv., 3" OD, grouted in rock, 4'	B-80	70	.457	Ea.	35	12.25	7.15	54.40	65.50
6830	5'		68	.471		44.50	12.65	7.35	64.50	76
6835	6'		64	.500		45	13.40	7.80	66.20	78.50
6840	7'		60	.533		60	14.30	8.30	82.60	97
6845	8'		58	.552		64.50	14.80	8.60	87.90	103
6850	Vinyl, 4'		68	.471		58.50	12.65	7.35	78.50	92
6855	5'		67	.478		64	12.80	7.45	84.25	98.50
6860	6'		65	.492		79.50	13.20	7.70	100.40	116
6865	7'		63	.508		77.50	13.65	7.90	99.05	115
6870	8'		61	.525		95	14.05	8.20	117.25	136
6873	For double gate posts greater than 24' wide, add					125%	30%			
6874	For line posts with top rail fitting, add					9%				
6875	Corner post, galv., 4" OD, grouted in rock, 4'	B-80	67	.478	Ea.	58.50	12.80	7.45	78.75	92.50
6880	6'		65	.492		83	13.20	7.70	103.90	120
6885	7'		63	.508		93.50	13.65	7.90	115.05	133
6890	8'		61	.525		108	14.05	8.20	130.25	149
6895	Vinyl, 4'		67	.478		103	12.80	7.45	123.25	141
6900	6'		65	.492		136	13.20	7.70	156.90	179
6905	7'		63	.508		124	13.65	7.90	145.55	167
6910	8'		61	.525		162	14.05	8.20	184.25	210
6912	Corner, gate & end posts w/sgl barbed wire arm, add					8%				
6913	Corner, gate & end posts w/ dbl barbed wire arm, add					13%				
6914	For line posts with top rail fitting, add					9%				
6915	Post w/fittings for fabric top rail, barb wire, galv.,corner, 4'				L.F.	19.20			19.20	21
6920	End post, 4'					19.15			19.15	21
6925	Corner post, 6'					24.50			24.50	27
6930	End post, 6'					24.50			24.50	27
6932	For barbed wire double arm, galvanized, add				Ea.	10.70				
6933	For barbed wire double arm, vinyl coated, add				"	19.25				

02800 | Site Improvements and Amenities

	02820	Fences & Gates	CREW	DAILY OUTPUT	LABOR-HOURS	UNIT	MAT.	LABOR	EQUIP.	TOTAL	TOTAL INCL O&P	
535	6934	For vinyl coated post, add					60%					535
	7075	Gates, swing, chain link, 4' high, sgle, 4' wide				Ea.	96.50			96.50	106	
	7080	Double, 12' wide					281			281	310	
	7085	Double, 24' wide					410			410	450	
	7090	6' high, single, 4' wide					137			137	151	
	7095	Double, 12' wide					400			400	440	
	7105	Double, 24' wide					450			450	495	
	7110	Without barbed wire, 4' high, single, 3' wide	B-80A	30	.800		99.50	19.70	4.60	123.80	145	
	7115	4' wide		30	.800		109	19.70	4.60	133.30	156	
	7120	Double, 10' wide		14	1.714		281	42.50	9.85	333.35	385	
	7125	Double, 12' wide		13	1.846		310	45.50	10.60	366.10	430	
	7130	Double, 14' wide	▼	12	2		315	49.50	11.50	376	435	
	7135	Double, 16' wide	B-80B	11	2.909		350	76.50	18.55	445.05	525	
	7140	Double, 18' wide		14	2.286		390	60	14.55	464.55	535	
	7145	Double, 20' wide		13	2.462		420	64.50	15.70	500.20	575	
	7150	Double, 22' wide		12	2.667		450	70	17	537	620	
	7155	Double, 24' wide		11	2.909		475	76.50	18.55	570.05	665	
	7160	Double, 26' wide		10	3.200		500	84	20.50	604.50	705	
	7165	Double, 28' wide		10	3.200		530	84	20.50	634.50	735	
	7170	Double, 30' wide	▼	9	3.556		560	93.50	22.50	676	785	
	7175	5' high, single, 3' wide	B-80A	29	.828		109	20.50	4.76	134.26	157	
	7180	4' wide		29	.828		121	20.50	4.76	146.26	170	
	7185	Double, 10' wide		13	1.846		284	45.50	10.60	340.10	400	
	7190	Double, 12' wide		12	2		315	49.50	11.50	376	435	
	7195	Double, 14' wide	▼	11	2.182		360	54	12.55	426.55	495	
	7205	Double, 16' wide	B-80B	14	2.286		390	60	14.55	464.55	540	
	7210	Double, 18' wide		13	2.462		415	64.50	15.70	495.20	570	
	7215	Double, 20' wide		12	2.667		445	70	17	532	615	
	7220	Double, 22' wide		11	2.909		475	76.50	18.55	570.05	660	
	7225	Double, 24' wide		10	3.200		505	84	20.50	609.50	715	
	7230	Double, 26' wide		10	3.200		535	84	20.50	639.50	745	
	7235	Double, 28' wide		9	3.556		565	93.50	22.50	681	790	
	7240	Double, 30' wide	▼	8	4		595	105	25.50	725.50	845	
	7245	6' high, single, 3' wide	B-80A	27	.889		109	22	5.10	136.10	160	
	7250	4' wide		27	.889		138	22	5.10	165.10	191	
	7255	Double, 10' wide		12	2		264	49.50	11.50	325	380	
	7260	Double, 12' wide	▼	11	2.182		287	54	12.55	353.55	415	
	7265	Double, 14' wide	B-80B	13	2.462		340	64.50	15.70	420.20	490	
	7270	Double, 16' wide		12	2.667		360	70	17	447	520	
	7272	Double, 18' wide		11	2.909		405	76.50	18.55	500.05	585	
	7275	Double, 20' wide		10	3.200		415	84	20.50	519.50	615	
	7280	Double, 22' wide		10	3.200		505	84	20.50	609.50	710	
	7285	Double, 24' wide		9	3.556		515	93.50	22.50	631	735	
	7290	Double, 26' wide		8	4		570	105	25.50	700.50	820	
	7295	Double, 28' wide		7	4.571		600	120	29	749	885	
	7305	Double, 30' wide	▼	6	5.333		630	140	34	804	950	
	7310	7' high, single, 3' wide	B-80A	25	.960		117	23.50	5.50	146	172	
	7315	4' wide		25	.960		128	23.50	5.50	157	184	
	7320	Double, 10' wide	▼	11	2.182		330	54	12.55	396.55	460	
	7325	Double, 12' wide	B-80B	13	2.462		390	64.50	15.70	470.20	545	
	7330	Double, 14' wide		12	2.667		425	70	17	512	595	
	7335	Double, 16' wide		11	2.909		460	76.50	18.55	555.05	650	
	7340	Double, 18' wide		10	3.200		480	84	20.50	584.50	685	
	7345	Double, 20' wide		10	3.200		505	84	20.50	609.50	715	
	7350	Double, 22' wide		9	3.556		545	93.50	22.50	661	770	
	7355	Double, 24' wide	▼	8	4		580	105	25.50	710.50	830	

SITE CONSTRUCTION 2

213

02800 | Site Improvements and Amenities

	02820	Fences & Gates	CREW	DAILY OUTPUT	LABOR-HOURS	UNIT	2003 BARE COSTS				TOTAL INCL O&P	
							MAT.	LABOR	EQUIP.	TOTAL		
535	7360	Double, 26' wide	B-80B	7	4.571	Ea.	615	120	29	764	895	535
	7365	Double, 28' wide		6	5.333		645	140	34	819	965	
	7370	Double, 30' wide	▼	5	6.400		675	168	41	884	1,050	
	7375	8' high, single, 3' wide	B-80A	23	1.043		138	25.50	6	169.50	198	
	7380	4' wide	"	23	1.043		153	25.50	6	184.50	216	
	7385	Double, 10' wide	B-80B	13	2.462		375	64.50	15.70	455.20	530	
	7390	Double, 12' wide		12	2.667		415	70	17	502	580	
	7395	Double, 14' wide		11	2.909		450	76.50	18.55	545.05	635	
	7400	Double, 16' wide		10	3.200		545	84	20.50	649.50	755	
	7405	Double, 18' wide		10	3.200		585	84	20.50	689.50	800	
	7410	Double, 20' wide		9	3.556		625	93.50	22.50	741	855	
	7415	Double, 22' wide		8	4		670	105	25.50	800.50	930	
	7420	Double, 24' wide		7	4.571		680	120	29	829	965	
	7425	Double, 26' wide		6	5.333		755	140	34	929	1,075	
	7430	Double, 28' wide		5	6.400		835	168	41	1,044	1,225	
	7435	Double, 30' wide	▼	4	8	▼	840	210	51	1,101	1,300	
	7436	For single gate with single barbed wire arm, add					5%					
	7437	For single gate with double barbed wire arm, add					10%					
	7438	For double gate with single barbed wire arm, add					5%					
	7439	For double gate with double barbed wire arm, add					10%					
	7440	Vinyl coated, 4' high, single, 3' wide	B-80A	30	.800	Ea.	194	19.70	4.60	218.30	250	
	7445	4' wide		30	.800		231	19.70	4.60	255.30	290	
	7450	Double, 10' wide		14	1.714		520	42.50	9.85	572.35	645	
	7455	Double, 12' wide		13	1.846		605	45.50	10.60	661.10	750	
	7460	Double, 14' wide		12	2		700	49.50	11.50	761	860	
	7465	Double, 16' wide	▼	11	2.182		775	54	12.55	841.55	950	
	7470	Double, 18' wide	B-80B	14	2.286		895	60	14.55	969.55	1,100	
	7475	Double, 20' wide		13	2.462		985	64.50	15.70	1,065.20	1,200	
	7480	Double, 22' wide		12	2.667		1,075	70	17	1,162	1,300	
	7485	Double, 24' wide		11	2.909		1,150	76.50	18.55	1,245.05	1,425	
	7490	Double, 26' wide		10	3.200		1,200	84	20.50	1,304.50	1,475	
	7500	Double, 28' wide		10	3.200		1,325	84	20.50	1,429.50	1,600	
	7505	Double, 30' wide	▼	9	3.556		1,500	93.50	22.50	1,616	1,825	
	7510	5' high, single, 3' wide	B-80A	29	.828		216	20.50	4.76	241.26	275	
	7515	4' wide		29	.828		250	20.50	4.76	275.26	310	
	7520	Double, 10' wide		13	1.846		555	45.50	10.60	611.10	695	
	7525	Double, 12' wide	▼	12	2		605	49.50	11.50	666	760	
	7530	Double, 14' wide	B-80B	11	2.909		670	76.50	18.55	765.05	875	
	7535	Double, 16' wide		14	2.286		730	60	14.55	804.55	915	
	7540	Double, 18' wide		13	2.462		795	64.50	15.70	875.20	990	
	7545	Double, 20' wide		12	2.667		855	70	17	942	1,075	
	7550	Double, 22' wide		11	2.909		905	76.50	18.55	1,000.05	1,125	
	7555	Double, 24' wide		10	3.200		1,000	84	20.50	1,104.50	1,250	
	7560	Double, 26' wide		10	3.200		1,050	84	20.50	1,154.50	1,325	
	7565	Double, 28' wide		9	3.556		1,125	93.50	22.50	1,241	1,400	
	7570	Double, 30' wide		8	4		1,175	105	25.50	1,305.50	1,500	
	7575	6' high, single, 3' wide	B-80A	27	.889		235	22	5.10	262.10	298	
	7580	4' wide		27	.889		265	22	5.10	292.10	330	
	7585	Double, 10' wide		12	2		600	49.50	11.50	661	750	
	7590	Double, 12' wide	▼	11	2.182		670	54	12.55	736.55	835	
	7595	Double, 14' wide	B-80B	13	2.462		750	64.50	15.70	830.20	940	
	7600	Double, 16' wide		12	2.667		835	70	17	922	1,050	
	7605	Double, 18' wide		11	2.909		880	76.50	18.55	975.05	1,100	
	7610	Double, 20' wide		10	3.200		935	84	20.50	1,039.50	1,175	
	7615	Double, 22' wide		10	3.200		1,000	84	20.50	1,104.50	1,250	
	7620	Double, 24, wide	▼	9	3.556	▼	1,075	93.50	22.50	1,191	1,375	

			DAILY	LABOR-		2003 BARE COSTS				TOTAL
02820	**Fences & Gates**	CREW	OUTPUT	HOURS	UNIT	MAT.	LABOR	EQUIP.	TOTAL	INCL O&P
7625	Double, 26' wide	B-80B	8	4	Ea.	1,150	105	25.50	1,280.50	1,475
7630	Double, 28' wide		7	4.571		1,225	120	29	1,374	1,575
7635	Double, 30' wide		6	5.333		1,300	140	34	1,474	1,675
7640	7' high, single, 3' wide	B-80A	25	.960		246	23.50	5.50	275	315
7645	4' wide		25	.960		273	23.50	5.50	302	345
7650	Double, 10' wide		11	2.182		660	54	12.55	726.55	825
7655	Double, 12' wide		13	1.846		725	45.50	10.60	781.10	885
7660	Double, 14' wide	B-80B	12	2.667		815	70	17	902	1,025
7665	Double, 16' wide		11	2.909		905	76.50	18.55	1,000.05	1,150
7670	Double, 18' wide		10	3.200		960	84	20.50	1,064.50	1,200
7675	Double, 20' wide		10	3.200		1,025	84	20.50	1,129.50	1,275
7680	Double, 22' wide		9	3.556		1,075	93.50	22.50	1,191	1,375
7685	Double, 24' wide		8	4		1,200	105	25.50	1,330.50	1,500
7690	Double, 26' wide		7	4.571		1,275	120	29	1,424	1,625
7695	Double, 28' wide		6	5.333		1,350	140	34	1,524	1,725
7700	Double, 30' wide		5	6.400		1,425	168	41	1,634	1,875
7705	8' high, single, 3' wide	B-80A	23	1.043		257	25.50	6	288.50	330
7710	4' wide	"	23	1.043		281	25.50	6	312.50	355
7715	Double, 10' wide	B-80B	13	2.462		725	64.50	15.70	805.20	910
7720	Double, 12' wide		12	2.667		785	70	17	872	990
7725	Double, 14' wide		11	2.909		885	76.50	18.55	980.05	1,100
7730	Double, 16' wide		10	3.200		980	84	20.50	1,084.50	1,225
7735	Double, 18' wide		10	3.200		1,025	84	20.50	1,129.50	1,300
7740	Double, 20' wide		9	3.556		1,125	93.50	22.50	1,241	1,400
7745	Double, 22' wide		8	4		1,175	105	25.50	1,305.50	1,500
7750	Double, 24' wide		7	4.571		1,300	120	29	1,449	1,650
7755	Double, 26' wide		6	5.333		1,375	140	34	1,549	1,775
7760	Double, 28' wide		5	6.400		1,475	168	41	1,684	1,925
7765	Double, 30' wide		4	8		1,575	210	51	1,836	2,100
7766	For single gate with single barbed wire arm, add					5%				
7767	For single gate with double barbed wire arm, add					10%				
7768	For double gate with single barbed wire arm, add					5%				
7769	For double gate with double barbed wire arm, add					10%				
7770	Gates, sliding w/overhead support, 4' high	B-80B	35	.914	L.F.	31.50	24	5.80	61.30	78
7775	5' high		32	1		34	26.50	6.35	66.85	85
7780	6' high		28	1.143		37	30	7.30	74.30	95
7785	7' high		25	1.280		48.50	33.50	8.15	90.15	114
7790	8' high		23	1.391		60	36.50	8.85	105.35	132
7795	Cantilever, manual, exp. roller, (pr), 40' wide x 8' high	B-22	1	30	Ea.	2,475	870	245	3,590	4,350
7800	30' wide x 8' high		1	30		2,075	870	245	3,190	3,900
7805	24' wide x 8' high		1	30		1,550	870	245	2,665	3,325
7810	Motor operators for gates, (no elec wiring), 3' wide swing	2 Skwk	.50	32		840	1,025		1,865	2,550
7815	Up to 20' wide swing		.50	32		2,850	1,025		3,875	4,775
7820	Up to 45' sliding		.50	32		2,900	1,025		3,925	4,825
7825	Overhead gate, 6' to 18' wide, sliding/cantilever		45	.356	L.F.	101	11.45		112.45	129
7830	Gate operators, digital receiver		7	2.286	Ea.	305	73.50		378.50	450
7835	Two button transmitter		24	.667		39	21.50		60.50	76.50
7840	3 button station		14	1.143		48.50	37		85.50	111
7845	Master slave system		4	4		172	129		301	390

890	0010	**WIRE FENCING**									
	0015	Barbed wire, galvanized, domestic steel, hi-tensile 15-1/2 ga.			M.L.F.	26			26	28.50
	0020	Standard, 12-3/4 ga.				34.50			34.50	38
	0210	Barbless wire, 2-strand galvanized, 12-1/2 ga.				34.50			34.50	38
	0500	Helical razor ribbon, stainless steel, 18" dia x 18" spacing			C.L.F.	100			100	111
	0600	Hardware cloth galv., 1/4" mesh, 23 ga., 2' wide			C.S.F.	45			45	49.50

2 SITE CONSTRUCTION

02800 | Site Improvements and Amenities

02820 | Fences & Gates

		CREW	DAILY OUTPUT	LABOR-HOURS	UNIT	2003 BARE COSTS MAT.	LABOR	EQUIP.	TOTAL	TOTAL INCL O&P	
890											890
0700	3' wide				C.S.F.	44			44	48	
0900	1/2" mesh, 19 ga., 2' wide					40			40	44	
1000	4' wide					39			39	43	
1200	Chain link fabric, steel, 2" mesh, 6 ga, galvanized					115			115	127	
1300	9 ga, galvanized					57			57	62.50	
1310	Steel gate fencing, 6' high				L.F.	3.42			3.42	3.76	
1350	Vinyl coated				C.S.F.	47.50			47.50	52.50	
1360	Aluminized				"	74			74	81.50	
1370	Aluminum gate fencing				S.F.	.74			.74	.81	
1400	2-1/4" mesh, 11.5 ga, galvanized				C.S.F.	38.50			38.50	42.50	
1600	1-3/4" mesh (tennis courts), 11.5 ga (core), vinyl coated					54.50			54.50	60	
1700	9 ga, galvanized					49			49	54	
2100	Welded wire fabric, galvanized, 1" x 2", 14 ga.					32.50			32.50	36	
2200	2" x 4", 12-1/2 ga.					21.50			21.50	24	
2300	Fence, anti-cut/climb, 8 ga, 1/2" x 3" ww mesh, galv, 8' H, incl posts	B-1	1,300	.018	S.F.	2.55	.47		3.02	3.54	

02840 | Walk/Road/Parking Appurtenances

		CREW	DAILY OUTPUT	LABOR-HOURS	UNIT	MAT.	LABOR	EQUIP.	TOTAL	TOTAL INCL O&P	
700											700
0010	**PARKING BARRIERS** Timber with saddles, treated type										
0100	4" x 4" for cars	B-2	520	.077	L.F.	2.76	1.93		4.69	6.05	
0200	6" x 6" for trucks		520	.077	"	5.95	1.93		7.88	9.55	
0400	Folding with individual padlocks		50	.800	Ea.	350	20		370	415	
0600	Flexible fixed stanchion, 2' high, 3" diameter		100	.400	"	17.75	10		27.75	35	
0700	Barrier, precast concrete w/dowels, 12" x 6"		480	.083	L.F.	21.50	2.09		23.59	27	
1000	Wheel stops, precast concrete incl. dowels, 6" x 10" x 6'-0"		120	.333	Ea.	31.50	8.35		39.85	47.50	
1100	8" x 13" x 6'-0"		120	.333		36.50	8.35		44.85	53	
1200	Thermoplastic, 6" x 10" x 6'-0"		120	.333		57	8.35		65.35	75.50	
1300	Pipe bollards, conc filled/paint, 8' L x 4' D hole, 6" diam.	B-6	20	1.200		189	32	10.95	231.95	270	
1400	8" diam.		15	1.600		287	43	14.60	344.60	395	
1500	12" diam.		12	2		375	53.50	18.25	446.75	515	
1540	Bollards, precast concrete, free standing, round, 15" Dia x 36" H		14	1.714		100	46	15.65	161.65	198	
1550	16" Dia x 30" H		14	1.714		100	46	15.65	161.65	198	
1560	18" Dia x 34" H		14	1.714		205	46	15.65	266.65	315	
1570	18" Dia x 72" H		14	1.714		250	46	15.65	311.65	365	
1572	26" Dia x 18" H		12	2		250	53.50	18.25	321.75	380	
1574	26" Dia x 30" H		12	2		370	53.50	18.25	441.75	510	
1578	26" Dia x 50" H		12	2		500	53.50	18.25	571.75	655	
1580	Square, 22" x 32" H		12	2		265	53.50	18.25	336.75	395	
1585	22" x 41" H		12	2		470	53.50	18.25	541.75	620	
1590	Hexagon, 26" x 41" H		10	2.400		490	64.50	22	576.50	665	
1592	Bollards, steel, 3' H, retractable, incl hydraulic controls, min		4	6		17,500	161	54.50	17,715.50	19,600	
1594	Max		2	12		19,500	320	109	19,929	22,100	

02870 | Site Furnishings

		CREW	DAILY OUTPUT	LABOR-HOURS	UNIT	MAT.	LABOR	EQUIP.	TOTAL	TOTAL INCL O&P	
800											800
0010	**TRASH RECEPTACLE** Fiberglass, 2' square, 18" high	2 Clab	30	.533	Ea.	214	13.15		227.15	257	
0420	Waste receptacles, bomb-resistant, 30 gal, min		15	1.067		2,000	26.50		2,026.50	2,250	
0430	Max		15	1.067		5,000	26.50		5,026.50	5,550	

02930 | Exterior Plants

		CREW	DAILY OUTPUT	LABOR-HOURS	UNIT	MAT.	LABOR	EQUIP.	TOTAL	TOTAL INCL O&P	
050	**0010** **SHRUBS AND TREES** Evergreen, in prepared beds, B & B										**050**
	0100 Arborvitae pyramidal, 4'-5'	B-17	30	1.067	Ea.	42.50	28.50	17.50	88.50	110	
	0150 Globe, 12"-15"	B-1	96	.250		10.40	6.35		16.75	21.50	
	0200 Balsam, fraser, 6' - 7'	B-17	30	1.067		103	28.50	17.50	149	176	
	0300 Cedar, blue, 8'-10'		18	1.778		113	47	29	189	229	
	0350 Japanese, 4' - 5'	↓	55	.582		79	15.40	9.55	103.95	121	
	0400 Cypress, hinoki, 15" - 18"	B-1	80	.300		54	7.60		61.60	71.50	
	0500 Hemlock, canadian, 2-1/2'-3'		36	.667		16.75	16.90		33.65	45	
	0550 Holly, Savannah, 8' - 10' H	↓	9.68	2.479		515	63		578	665	
	0560 Yaupon, 6' - 7'	B-17	10	3.200		11.75	85	52.50	149.25	201	
	0570 Burford, 3' - 4'		37	.865		12.55	23	14.20	49.75	65	
	0580 Dwarf Burford, 2' - 3'		21	1.524		14.75	40.50	25	80.25	106	
	0590 Dwarf Chinese, 2' - 3'	↓	40	.800		13.15	21	13.10	47.25	61.50	
	0600 Juniper, andorra, 18"-24"	B-1	80	.300		15	7.60		22.60	28.50	
	0620 Wiltoni, 15"-18"	"	80	.300		11.65	7.60		19.25	24.50	
	0640 Skyrocket, 4-1/2'-5'	B-17	55	.582		45.50	15.40	9.55	70.45	84	
	0660 Blue pfitzer, 2'-2-1/2'	B-1	44	.545		20	13.80		33.80	43.50	
	0670 Repandens holly, 15" to 18" high, in place		37	.649		18.15	16.40		34.55	45.50	
	0675 Pfitzer juniper, 18" - 24"		26	.923		24	23.50		47.50	62.50	
	0680 Ketleerie, 2-1/2'-3'		50	.480		30	12.15		42.15	52	
	0700 Pine, black, 2-1/2'-3'		50	.480		31.50	12.15		43.65	53.50	
	0720 Mugo, 18"-24"	↓	60	.400		32	10.15		42.15	51.50	
	0740 White, 4'-5'	B-17	75	.427		47	11.30	7	65.30	76.50	
	0750 5' - 6'	B-1	22	1.091		52	27.50		79.50	101	
	0760 Jack, 5' - 6'	B-17	22	1.455		86	38.50	24	148.50	180	
	0800 Spruce, blue, 18"-24"	B-1	60	.400		31	10.15		41.15	50	
	0820 Dwarf alberta, 18" - 24"	"	60	.400		26	10.15		36.15	44.50	
	0840 Norway, 4'-5'	B-17	75	.427		58.50	11.30	7	76.80	89.50	
	0900 Yew, denisforma, 12"-15"	B-1	60	.400		22	10.15		32.15	40.50	
	1000 Capitata, 18"-24"		30	.800		18.80	20.50		39.30	52	
	1100 Hicksi, 2'-2-1/2'	↓	30	.800	↓	27	20.50		47.50	61.50	
410	**0010** **SHRUBS** Broadleaf evergreen, planted in prepared beds										**410**
	0100 Andromeda, 15"-18", container	B-1	96	.250	Ea.	16.50	6.35		22.85	28	
	0150 Aucuba, 3' - 4'		32	.750		15.60	19		34.60	46.50	
	0200 Azalea, 15" - 18", container		96	.250		21	6.35		27.35	33.50	
	0300 Barberry, 9"-12", container		130	.185		9.75	4.67		14.42	18.05	
	0400 Boxwood, 15"-18", B & B		96	.250		20	6.35		26.35	32	
	0450 Cast Iron Plant, 12" - 15" H		41.92	.573		13.55	14.50		28.05	37.50	
	0470 Cleyera, 3' - 4' H, B & B		32.48	.739		25	18.70		43.70	56.50	
	0480 Creeping gardenia, 2 gal. cont.		98.48	.244		10.05	6.15		16.20	20.50	
	0500 Euonymus, emerald gaiety, 12" to 15", container		115	.209		13.75	5.30		19.05	23.50	
	0520 Glossy Abelia, 2' - 3'		33	.727		14.40	18.40		32.80	45	
	0600 Holly, 15"-18", B & B		96	.250		15	6.35		21.35	26.50	
	0650 Indian Hawthorn, 18" - 24"		29.40	.816		15.30	20.50		35.80	49.50	
	0700 Leucothoe, 15" - 18", container		96	.250		13.40	6.35		19.75	24.50	
	0800 Mahonia, 18" - 24", container		80	.300		23	7.60		30.60	37.50	
	0900 Mount laurel, 18" - 24", B & B		80	.300		69.50	7.60		77.10	88.50	
	1000 Paxistema, 9 - 12" high		130	.185		14.65	4.67		19.32	23.50	
	1100 Rhododendron, 18"-24", container		48	.500		33.50	12.65		46.15	56.50	
	1200 Rosemary, 1 gal container		600	.040		57.50	1.01		58.51	65	
	1300 Wax Myrtle, 3' - 4'		32	.750		23.50	19		42.50	55.50	
	2000 Deciduous, amelanchier, 2'-3', B & B		57	.421		83	10.65		93.65	108	
	2100 Azalea, 15"-18", B & B		96	.250		19.15	6.35		25.50	31	
	2120 Kurume, 18" - 24"		29.80	.805		15.55	20.50		36.05	49	
	2200 Barberry, 2' - 3', B & B	↓	57	.421	↓	19.95	10.65		30.60	38.50	

02900 | Planting

02930 | Exterior Plants

		CREW	DAILY OUTPUT	LABOR-HOURS	UNIT	2003 BARE COSTS				TOTAL INCL O&P
						MAT.	LABOR	EQUIP.	TOTAL	
2300	Bayberry, 2'-3', B & B	B-1	57	.421	Ea.	24	10.65		34.65	43
2400	Boston ivy, 2 year, container	↓	600	.040		15.10	1.01		16.11	18.20
2500	Corylus, 3'-4', B & B	B-17	75	.427		29	11.30	7	47.30	57
2600	Cotoneaster, 15"-18", B & B	B-1	80	.300		12.90	7.60		20.50	26
2650	Crape Myrtle, 8'-9'	B-17	10.50	3.048		44	81	50	175	227
2700	Deutzia, 12"-15", B & B	B-1	96	.250		7.90	6.35		14.25	18.55
2800	Dogwood, 3'-4', B & B	B-17	40	.800		21	21	13.10	55.10	70.50
2900	Euonymus, alatus compacta, 15"-18", container	B-1	80	.300		21	7.60		28.60	35.50
3000	Flowering almond, 2'-3', container	"	36	.667		16.50	16.90		33.40	44.50
3100	Flowering currant, 3'-4', container	B-17	75	.427		18.95	11.30	7	37.25	46
3200	Forsythia, 2'-3', container	B-1	60	.400		13.95	10.15		24.10	31
3300	Hibiscus, 3'-4', B & B	B-17	75	.427		12.90	11.30	7	31.20	39.50
3400	Honeysuckle, 3'-4', B & B	B-1	60	.400		16.75	10.15		26.90	34
3500	Hydrangea, 2'-3', B & B	"	57	.421		19.50	10.65		30.15	38
3550	Ligustrum, 2'-3'	B-17	10.50	3.048		12.15	81	50	143.15	192
3600	Lilac, 3'-4', B & B	"	40	.800		24.50	21	13.10	58.60	73.50
3700	Mockorange, 3'-4', B & B	B-1	36	.667		14.25	16.90		31.15	42
3800	Osier willow, 2'-3', B & B		57	.421		16.25	10.65		26.90	34.50
3850	Pampas Grass, 3'-4'		58	.414		14.65	10.50		25.15	32.50
3900	Privet, bare root, 18"-24"		80	.300		9.85	7.60		17.45	22.50
4000	Pyracantha, 2'-3', container		80	.300		34	7.60		41.60	49.50
4100	Quince, 2'-3', B & B	↓	57	.421		18.95	10.65		29.60	37.50
4200	Russian olive, 3'-4', B & B	B-17	75	.427		20.50	11.30	7	38.80	47.50
4300	Snowberry, 2'-3', B & B	B-1	57	.421		11.25	10.65		21.90	29
4400	Spirea, 3'-4', B & B	"	70	.343		26	8.70		34.70	42.50
4500	Viburnum, 3'-4', B & B	B-17	40	.800		19.30	21	13.10	53.40	68
4510	12"-15"	"	62	.516		19.30	13.70	8.45	41.45	51.50
4600	Weigela, 3'-4', B & B	B-1	70	.343		17.25	8.70		25.95	32.50

02945 | Planting Accessories

		CREW	DAILY OUTPUT	LABOR-HOURS	UNIT	MAT.	LABOR	EQUIP.	TOTAL	TOTAL INCL O&P
0010	**PLANTERS** Concrete, sandblasted, precast, 48" diameter, 24" high	2 Clab	15	1.067	Ea.	515	26.50		541.50	610
0020	24" diameter, 18" high		12	1.333		232	33		265	305
0040	42" diameter, 30" high		15	1.067		535	26.50		561.50	630
0080	Fluted, precast, 72" diameter, 36" high		12	1.333		1,050	33		1,083	1,200
0100	Fluted, precast, 7' diameter, 36" high		10	1.600		870	39.50		909.50	1,025
0120	Planters, precast concrete, used as security barriers, round, 3' x 3' H		10	1.600		515	39.50		554.50	625
0130	4' x 3' H		10	1.600		730	39.50		769.50	865
0140	5' x 2' H		9	1.778		700	44		744	840
0150	5' x 3' H		9	1.778		970	44		1,014	1,150
0160	5' x 3-1/2' H		8	2		1,100	49.50		1,149.50	1,275
0170	6' x 3' H		8	2		1,300	49.50		1,349.50	1,500
0180	6' x 3-1/2' H		8	2		1,375	49.50		1,424.50	1,600
0190	6' x 4' H		8	2		1,500	49.50		1,549.50	1,725
0200	Square, 3' x 3' H		10	1.600		560	39.50		599.50	675
0210	4' x 3' H		10	1.600		770	39.50		809.50	905
0220	5' x 3' H		10	1.600		930	39.50		969.50	1,075
0230	Rectangular, 2' x 6' x 3' H		10	1.600		790	39.50		829.50	930
0240	4' x 6' x 3' H		8	2		930	49.50		979.50	1,100
0260	Boulders, for bldg perimeter security, excl freight & setup, per ton, min								110	130
0270	Max				↓				150	170
0280	Jersey barriers, concrete, 42"H, for bldg perimeter security, excl freight	B-29	350	.160	L.F.	37	4.28	2.42	43.70	50
0282	Plastic, water-filled, 42"H x 8'L x 24" W base, incl conn	2 Clab	40	.400	Ea.	450	9.85		459.85	510
0300	Fiberglass, circular, 36" diameter, 24" high		15	1.067		365	26.50		391.50	445
0320	36" diameter, 27" high		12	1.333		292	33		325	370
0330	33" high		15	1.067		380	26.50		406.50	460
0335	24" diameter, 36" high		15	1.067		340	26.50		366.50	410

02945 | Planting Accessories

SITE CONSTRUCTION 2

		CREW	DAILY OUTPUT	LABOR-HOURS	UNIT	2003 BARE COSTS MAT.	LABOR	EQUIP.	TOTAL	TOTAL INCL O&P	
500	0340	2 Clab	8	2	Ea.	875	49.50		924.50	1,025	500
	0400		10	1.600		620	39.50		659.50	740	
	0600		15	1.067		355	26.50		381.50	430	
	0610		12	1.333		233	33		266	310	
	0620		20	.800		258	19.70		277.70	315	
	0700		15	1.067		795	26.50		821.50	915	
	0740		15	1.067		770	26.50		796.50	885	
	0800		12	1.333		299	33		332	380	
	0820		12	1.333		385	33		418	475	
	0900		5	3.200		990	79		1,069	1,225	
	1000		5	3.200		1,550	79		1,629	1,850	
	1100		18	.889		325	22		347	395	
	1110		16	1		385	24.50		409.50	460	
	1140		16	1		530	24.50		554.50	625	
	1150		14	1.143		615	28		643	725	
	1160		15	1.067		605	26.50		631.50	705	
	1170		14	1.143		695	28		723	810	
	1180		12	1.333		805	33		838	935	
	1200		15	1.067		820	26.50		846.50	945	
	1210		12	1.333		605	33		638	715	
	1220		10	1.600		840	39.50		879.50	985	
	1230		8	2		1,075	49.50		1,124.50	1,250	
	1240		8	2		1,375	49.50		1,424.50	1,600	
	1245		15	1.067		355	26.50		381.50	430	
	1250		14	1.143		350	28		378	435	
	1260		12	1.333		370	33		403	455	
	1270		12	1.333		430	33		463	525	
	1280		10	1.600		520	39.50		559.50	635	
	1290		10	1.600		575	39.50		614.50	695	
	1300		10	1.600		675	39.50		714.50	805	
	1310		8	2		840	49.50		889.50	1,000	
	1320		8	2		1,025	49.50		1,074.50	1,200	
	1500		10	1.600		1,200	39.50		1,239.50	1,375	
	1600		5	3.200		2,650	79		2,729	3,025	

Line descriptions:
- 0340 — 60" diameter, 39" high
- 0400 — 60" diameter, 24" high
- 0600 — Square, 24" side, 36" high
- 0610 — 24" side, 27" high
- 0620 — 24" side, 16" high
- 0700 — 48" side, 36" high
- 0740 — 48" side, 39" high
- 0800 — Rectangular, 48" x 12" sides, 18" high
- 0820 — 48" x 24" sides, 21" high
- 0900 — Planter/bench, 72" square, 36" high
- 1000 — 96" square, 27" high
- 1100 — Wood, square, 18" side, 18" high
- 1110 — 24" side, 18" high
- 1140 — 30" high
- 1150 — 30" side, 18" high
- 1160 — 24" high
- 1170 — 36" side, 18" high
- 1180 — 24" high
- 1200 — Wood, square, 48" side, 24" high
- 1210 — Rectangular, 18" x 36" sides, 24" high
- 1220 — 18" x 72" sides, 24" high
- 1230 — 36" x 72" sides, 24" high
- 1240 — 48" x 72" sides, 30" high
- 1245 — Circular, 18" diameter, 18" high
- 1250 — 24" diameter, 18" high
- 1260 — 24" high
- 1270 — 30" diameter, 24" high
- 1280 — 36" diameter, 24" high
- 1290 — 30" high
- 1300 — Circular, 48" diameter, 30" high
- 1310 — 60" diameter, 24" high
- 1320 — 72" diameter, 24" high
- 1500 — 72" diameter, 30" high
- 1600 — Planter/bench, 72"

03200 | Concrete Reinforcement

			DAILY	LABOR-			2003 BARE COSTS			TOTAL	
03210		**Reinforcing Steel**									
			CREW	OUTPUT	HOURS	UNIT	MAT.	LABOR	EQUIP.	TOTAL	INCL O&P
600	0010	**REINFORCING IN PLACE** A615 Grade 60										**600**
	0100	Beams & Girders, #3 to #7	4 Rodm	1.60	20	Ton	560	710		1,270	1,825
	0150	#8 to #18		2.70	11.852		550	420		970	1,325
	0200	Columns, #3 to #7		1.50	21.333		560	760		1,320	1,900
	0250	#8 to #18		2.30	13.913		550	495		1,045	1,425
	0300	Spirals, hot rolled, 8" to 15" diameter		2.20	14.545		945	515		1,460	1,925
	0400	Elevated slabs, #4 to #7		2.90	11.034		595	390		985	1,325
	0500	Footings, #4 to #7		2.10	15.238		535	540		1,075	1,500
	0550	#8 to #18		3.60	8.889		505	315		820	1,075
	0600	Slab on grade, #3 to #7		2.30	13.913		535	495		1,030	1,425
	0700	Walls, #3 to #7		3	10.667		535	380		915	1,225
	0750	#8 to #18		4	8		535	284		819	1,075

04050 | Basic Masonry Materials & Methods

04080 | Masonry Anchor & Reinforcement

			CREW	DAILY OUTPUT	LABOR-HOURS	UNIT	2003 BARE COSTS				TOTAL INCL O&P	
							MAT.	LABOR	EQUIP.	TOTAL		
070	0010	ANCHOR BOLTS Hooked type with nut and washer, 1/2" diam., 8" long	1 Bric	200	.040	Ea.	.52	1.30		1.82	2.56	070
	0030	12" long		190	.042		.97	1.36		2.33	3.17	
	0040	5/8" diameter, 8" long		180	.044		.80	1.44		2.24	3.09	
	0050	12" long		170	.047		.88	1.52		2.40	3.31	
	0060	3/4" diameter, 8" long		160	.050		1.15	1.62		2.77	3.76	
	0070	12" long		150	.053		1.44	1.73		3.17	4.24	
200	0010	REINFORCING Steel bars A615, placed horiz., #3 & #4 bars	1 Bric	450	.018	Lb.	.28	.58		.86	1.20	200
	0020	#5 & #6 bars		800	.010		.28	.32		.60	.81	
	0050	Placed vertical, #3 & #4 bars		350	.023		.28	.74		1.02	1.45	
	0060	#5 & #6 bars		650	.012		.28	.40		.68	.92	

04200 | Masonry Units

04210 | Clay Masonry Units

			CREW	DAILY OUTPUT	LABOR-HOURS	UNIT	2003 BARE COSTS				TOTAL INCL O&P	
							MAT.	LABOR	EQUIP.	TOTAL		
120	0010	BRICK VENEER Scaffolding not included, truck load lots										120
	0015	Material costs incl. 3% brick and 25% mortar waste										
	0020	Standard, select common, 4" x 2-2/3" x 8" (6.75/S.F.)	D-8	1.50	26.667	M	370	780		1,150	1,600	
	0050	Red, 4" x 2-2/3" x 8", running bond		1.50	26.667		410	780		1,190	1,650	
	0100	Full header every 6th course (7.88/S.F.)		1.45	27.586		410	810		1,220	1,700	
	0150	English, full header every 2nd course (10.13/S.F.)		1.40	28.571		405	835		1,240	1,725	
	0200	Flemish, alternate header every course (9.00/S.F.)		1.40	28.571		405	835		1,240	1,725	
	0250	Flemish, alt. header every 6th course (7.13/S.F.)		1.45	27.586		410	810		1,220	1,700	
	0300	Full headers throughout (13.50/S.F.)		1.40	28.571		405	835		1,240	1,725	
	0350	Rowlock course (13.50/S.F.)		1.35	29.630		405	870		1,275	1,775	
	0400	Rowlock stretcher (4.50/S.F.)		1.40	28.571		410	835		1,245	1,725	
	0450	Soldier course (6.75/S.F.)		1.40	28.571		410	835		1,245	1,725	
	0500	Sailor course (4.50/S.F.)		1.30	30.769		410	900		1,310	1,825	
	0601	Buff or gray face, running bond, (6.75/S.F.)		1.50	26.667		410	780		1,190	1,650	
	0609	Running bond, buff or gray face, (6.75/S.F.)		1.50	27.567		520	755		1,275	1,750	
	0700	Glazed face, 4" x 2-2/3" x 8", running bond		1.40	28.571		1,050	835		1,885	2,425	
	0750	Full header every 6th course (7.88/S.F.)		1.35	29.630		1,000	870		1,870	2,425	
	1000	Jumbo, 6" x 4" x 12",(3.00/S.F.)		1.30	30.769		1,275	900		2,175	2,800	
	1051	Norman, 4" x 2-2/3" x 12" (4.50/S.F.)		1.45	27.586		755	810		1,565	2,075	
	1100	Norwegian, 4" x 3-1/5" x 12" (3.75/S.F.)		1.40	28.571		590	835		1,425	1,925	
	1150	Economy, 4" x 4" x 8" (4.50 per S.F.)		1.40	28.571		575	835		1,410	1,900	
	1201	Engineer, 4" x 3-1/5" x 8", (5.63/S.F.)		1.45	27.586		375	810		1,185	1,650	
	1251	Roman, 4" x 2" x 12", (6.00/S.F.)		1.50	26.667		780	780		1,560	2,050	
	1300	S.C.R. 6" x 2-2/3" x 12" (4.50/S.F.)		1.40	28.571		925	835		1,760	2,300	
	1350	Utility, 4" x 4" x 12" (3.00/S.F.)		1.35	29.630		1,100	870		1,970	2,550	
	1360	For less than truck load lots, add					10			10	11	
	1400	For battered walls, add						30%				
	1450	For corbels, add						75%				
	1500	For curved walls, add						30%				
	1550	For pits and trenches, deduct						20%				
	1999	Alternate method of figuring by square foot										
	2000	Standard, sel. common, 4" x 2-2/3" x 8", (6.75/S.F.)	D-8	230	.174	S.F.	2.76	5.10		7.86	10.90	
	2020	Standard, red, 4" x 2-2/3" x 8", running bond (6.75/SF)		220	.182		2.76	5.30		8.06	11.25	
	2030	Replace interior face brick		187	.214		2.48	6.25		8.73	12.40	
	2033	Replace w/new masonry		169.23	.236		2.48	6.90		9.38	13.40	
	2050	Full header every 6th course (7.88/S.F.)		185	.216		3.21	6.35		9.56	13.30	

MASONRY 4

04200 | Masonry Units

		04210	Clay Masonry Units	CREW	DAILY OUTPUT	LABOR-HOURS	UNIT	2003 BARE COSTS MAT.	LABOR	EQUIP.	TOTAL	TOTAL INCL O&P	
120	2100		English, full header every 2nd course (10.13/S.F.)	D-8	140	.286	S.F.	4.12	8.35		12.47	17.40	120
	2150		Flemish, alternate header every course (9.00/S.F.)		150	.267		3.67	7.80		11.47	16.05	
	2200		Flemish, alt. header every 6th course (7.13/S.F.)		205	.195		2.91	5.70		8.61	12	
	2250		Full headers throughout (13.50/S.F.)		105	.381		5.50	11.15		16.65	23	
	2300		Rowlock course (13.50/S.F.)		100	.400		5.50	11.70		17.20	24	
	2350		Rowlock stretcher (4.50/S.F.)		310	.129		1.85	3.78		5.63	7.85	
	2400		Soldier course (6.75/S.F.)		200	.200		2.76	5.85		8.61	12.05	
	2450		Sailor course (4.50/S.F.)		290	.138		1.85	4.04		5.89	8.25	
	2600		Buff or gray face, running bond, (6.75/S.F.)		220	.182		2.93	5.30		8.23	11.40	
	2603		Install brick		169.23	.236		2.48	6.90		9.38	13.40	
	2700		Glazed face brick, running bond		210	.190		6.80	5.60		12.40	16.05	
	2750		Full header every 6th course (7.88/S.F.)		170	.235		7.95	6.90		14.85	19.35	
	3000	Jumbo, 6" x 4" x 12" running bond (3.00/S.F.)			435	.092		3.61	2.69		6.30	8.10	
	3050	Norman, 4" x 2-2/3" x 12" running bond, (4.5/S.F.)			320	.125		3.58	3.66		7.24	9.60	
	3100	Norwegian, 4" x 3-1/5" x 12" (3.75/S.F.)			375	.107		2.16	3.12		5.28	7.15	
	3150	Economy, 4" x 4" x 8" (4.50/S.F.)			310	.129		2.56	3.78		6.34	8.60	
	3200	Engineer, 4" x 3-1/5" x 8" (5.63/S.F.)			260	.154		2.10	4.50		6.60	9.20	
	3250	Roman, 4" x 2" x 12" (6.00/S.F.)			250	.160		4.62	4.68		9.30	12.30	
	3300	SCR, 6" x 2-2/3" x 12" (4.50/S.F.)			310	.129		4.23	3.78		8.01	10.45	
	3350	Utility, 4" x 4" x 12" (3.00/S.F.)			450	.089		3.27	2.60		5.87	7.60	
	3375		Buff face brick, (6.4/S.F.)	▼	215	.186	▼	2.82	5.45		8.27	11.45	
	3385		For marble chip, add					15%					
	3400	For cavity wall construction, add							15%				
	3450	For stacked bond, add							10%				
	3500	For interior veneer construction, add							15%				
	3550	For curved walls, add							30%				

05500 | Metal Fabrications

05580 | Formed Metal Fabrications

			CREW	DAILY OUTPUT	LABOR-HOURS	UNIT	2003 BARE COSTS MAT.	LABOR	EQUIP.	TOTAL	TOTAL INCL O&P	
900	0010	**WINDOW GUARDS**										900
	0015	Expanded metal, steel angle frame, permanent	E-4	350	.091	S.F.	15.95	3.31	.22	19.48	24	
	0025	Steel bars, 1/2" x 1/2", spaced 5" O.C.	"	290	.110	"	11.05	3.99	.27	15.31	19.70	
	0030	Hinge mounted, add				Opng.	32			32	35	
	0040	Removable type, add				"	20.50			20.50	22.50	
	0050	For galvanized guards, add				S.F.	35%					
	0070	For pivoted or projected type, add					105%	40%				
	0100	Mild steel, stock units, economy	E-4	405	.079		4.33	2.86	.19	7.38	10.15	
	0200	Deluxe		405	.079	↓	8.90	2.86	.19	11.95	15.20	
	0400	Woven wire, stock units, 3/8" channel frame, 3' x 5' opening		40	.800	Opng.	117	29	1.97	147.97	184	
	0500	4' x 6' opening	↓	38	.842		187	30.50	2.07	219.57	264	
	0800	Basket guards for above, add					160			160	176	
	1000	Swinging guards for above, add				↓	55			55	60.50	

METALS 5

223

07800 | Fire & Smoke Protection

07812 | Cementitious Fireproofing

		Description	CREW	DAILY OUTPUT	LABOR-HOURS	UNIT	MAT.	LABOR	EQUIP.	TOTAL	TOTAL INCL O&P
600	0010	**SPRAYED** Mineral fiber or cementitious for fireproofing,									600
	0050	not incl tamping or canvas protection									
	0100	1" thick, on flat plate steel	G-2	3,000	.008	S.F.	.42	.21	.04	.67	.83
	0200	Flat decking		2,400	.010		.42	.26	.05	.73	.93
	0300	Ceiling/decking fireproofing, 1 hr rated, 1/2" thick		2,400	.010		.21	.26	.05	.52	.69
	0310	2 hr rated, 7/8" thick		2,400	.010		.37	.26	.05	.68	.87
	0320	Beam and deck fireproofing, 1 hr rated, 1-3/8" thick		1,200	.020		.87	.52	.10	1.49	1.88
	0330	2 hr rated, 1-1/2" thick		1,200	.020		.95	.52	.10	1.57	1.97
	0340	1-5/8" thick		1,200	.020		1.03	.52	.10	1.65	2.06
	0400	Beams		1,500	.016		.42	.42	.08	.92	1.21
	0440	Beam fireproofing, 1 hr rated, 7/16" thick (min W8 x 24)		2,400	.010		.19	.26	.05	.50	.66
	0450	2 hr rated, 1/2" thick, (min W 8 x 24)		2,400	.010		.21	.26	.05	.52	.69
	0460	3 hr rated, 7/8" thick, (min W 8 x 24)		2,400	.010		.37	.26	.05	.68	.87
	0470	4 hr rated, 1-1/4" thick, (min W 8 x 24)		1,200	.020		.53	.52	.10	1.15	1.50
	0500	Corrugated or fluted decks		1,250	.019		.64	.50	.10	1.24	1.59
	0700	Columns, 1-1/8" thick		1,100	.022		.48	.57	.11	1.16	1.52
	0710	Column fireproofing, 1 hr rated, 1-3/16" thick, (W 10 x 49)		1,200	.020		.50	.52	.10	1.12	1.47
	0720	2 hr rated, 5/8" thick, (W 14 x 228)		1,200	.020		.26	.52	.10	.88	1.21
	0730	1-1/4" thick, (W 10 x 49)		1,200	.020		.53	.52	.10	1.15	1.50
	0740	3 hr rated, 7/8" thick, (W 14 x 228)		1,200	.020		.37	.52	.10	.99	1.33
	0750	1-7/8" thick, (W 10 x 49)		2,400	.010		.79	.26	.05	1.10	1.33
	0760	4 hr rated, 1-1/4" thick, (W 14 x 228)		2,400	.010		.53	.26	.05	.84	1.04
	0770	2-1/2" thick, (W 10 x 49)		1,200	.020		1.06	.52	.10	1.68	2.08
	0800	2-3/16" thick	▼	700	.034	▼	.88	.90	.17	1.95	2.55
	0850	For tamping, add						10%			
	0900	For canvas protection, add	G-2	5,000	.005	S.F.	.06	.13	.02	.21	.29
	1000	Acoustical sprayed, 1" thick, finished, straight work, minimum		520	.046		.44	1.21	.23	1.88	2.59
	1100	Maximum		200	.120		.47	3.14	.60	4.21	6.05
	1300	Difficult access, minimum		225	.107		.47	2.79	.53	3.79	5.40
	1400	Maximum	▼	130	.185	▼	.51	4.83	.92	6.26	9.05
	1500	Intumescent epoxy fireproofing on wire mesh, 3/16" thick									
	1550	1 hour rating, exterior use	G-2	136	.176	S.F.	5.40	4.62	.88	10.90	14.05
	1600	Magnesium oxychloride, 35# to 40# density, 1/4" thick		3,000	.008		1.14	.21	.04	1.39	1.61
	1650	1/2" thick		2,000	.012		2.28	.31	.06	2.65	3.06
	1700	60# to 70# density, 1/4" thick		3,000	.008		1.50	.21	.04	1.75	2.01
	1750	1/2" thick		2,000	.012		3.03	.31	.06	3.40	3.88
	2000	Vermiculite cement, troweled or sprayed, 1/4" thick		3,000	.008		1.03	.21	.04	1.28	1.49
	2050	1/2" thick	▼	2,000	.012	▼	2.04	.31	.06	2.41	2.79
	9000	Minimum labor/equipment charge	▼	3	8	Job		209	40	249	370

07840 | Firestopping

		Description	CREW	DAILY OUTPUT	LABOR-HOURS	UNIT	MAT.	LABOR	EQUIP.	TOTAL	TOTAL INCL O&P
100	0010	**FIRESTOPPING**									100
	0100	Metallic piping, non insulated									
	0110	Through walls, 2" diameter	1 Carp	16	.500	Ea.	9.60	15.80		25.40	35
	0120	4" diameter		14	.571		14.65	18.05		32.70	44
	0130	6" diameter		12	.667		19.70	21		40.70	54.50
	0140	12" diameter		10	.800		35	25		60	78
	0150	Through floors, 2" diameter		32	.250		5.80	7.90		13.70	18.75
	0160	4" diameter		28	.286		8.35	9		17.35	23.50
	0170	6" diameter		24	.333		11	10.50		21.50	28.50
	0180	12" diameter	▼	20	.400	▼	18.50	12.60		31.10	40
	0190	Metallic piping, insulated									
	0200	Through walls, 2" diameter	1 Carp	16	.500	Ea.	13.60	15.80		29.40	39.50
	0210	4" diameter		14	.571		18.65	18.05		36.70	48.50
	0220	6" diameter	▼	12	.667		23.50	21		44.50	59

			DAILY	LABOR-		2003 BARE COSTS				TOTAL
07840	**Firestopping**	CREW	OUTPUT	HOURS	UNIT	MAT.	LABOR	EQUIP.	TOTAL	INCL O&P
100 0230	12" diameter	1 Carp	10	.800	Ea.	39	25		64	82	100
0240	Through floors, 2" diameter	↓	32	.250	↓	9.80	7.90		17.70	23
0280	Non metallic piping, non insulated									
0290	Through walls, 2" diameter	1 Carp	12	.667	Ea.	39.50	21		60.50	76.50
0300	4" diameter		10	.800		49.50	25		74.50	94
0310	6" diameter		8	1		69	31.50		100.50	126
0330	Through floors, 2" diameter		16	.500		31	15.80		46.80	58.50
0340	4" diameter		6	1.333		38.50	42		80.50	108
0350	6" diameter	↓	6	1.333	↓	46	42		88	116
0370	Ductwork, insulated & non insulated, round									
0380	Through walls, 6" diameter	1 Carp	12	.667	Ea.	20	21		41	55
0390	12" diameter		10	.800		40	25		65	83.50
0400	18" diameter		8	1		65	31.50		96.50	121
0410	Through floors, 6" diameter		16	.500		11	15.80		26.80	36.50
0420	12" diameter		14	.571		20	18.05		38.05	50
0430	18" diameter	↓	12	.667	↓	35	21		56	71.50
0440	Ductwork, insulated & non insulated, rectangular									
0450	With stiffener/closure angle, through walls, 6" x 12"	1 Carp	8	1	Ea.	16.65	31.50		48.15	68
0460	12" x 24"		6	1.333		22	42		64	90
0470	24" x 48"		4	2		63	63		126	168
0480	With stiffener/closure angle, through floors, 6" x 12"		10	.800		9	25		34	49.50
0490	12" x 24"		8	1		16.20	31.50		47.70	67.50
0500	24" x 48"		6	1.333		32	42		74	101
0520	Through walls, 6" x 12"		2	4		35	126		161	236
0530	12" x 24"	↓	1	8		141	252		393	550
0540	24" x 48"	2 Carp	1	16		565	505		1,070	1,400
0550	48" x 96"	"	.75	21.333		2,275	675		2,950	3,550
0560	Through floors, 6" x 12"	1 Carp	2	4		35	126		161	236
0570	12" x 24"	"	1	8		141	252		393	550
0580	24" x 48"	2 Carp	.75	21.333		565	675		1,240	1,675
0590	48" x 96"	"	.50	32	↓	2,275	1,000		3,275	4,075
0600	Structural penetrations, through walls									
0610	Steel beams, W8 x 10	1 Carp	8	1	Ea.	22	31.50		53.50	73.50
0620	W12 x 14		6	1.333		35	42		77	104
0630	W21 x 44		5	1.600		70	50.50		120.50	156
0640	W36 x 135		3	2.667		170	84		254	320
0650	Bar joists, 18" deep		6	1.333		32	42		74	101
0660	24" deep		6	1.333		40	42		82	110
0670	36" deep		5	1.600		60	50.50		110.50	145
0680	48" deep	↓	4	2	↓	70	63		133	176
0690	Construction joints, floor slab at exterior wall									
0700	Precast, brick, block or drywall exterior									
0710	2" wide joint	1 Carp	125	.064	L.F.	5	2.02		7.02	8.65
0720	4" wide joint	"	75	.107	"	10	3.37		13.37	16.25
0730	Metal panel, glass or curtain wall exterior									
0740	2" wide joint	1 Carp	40	.200	L.F.	11.85	6.30		18.15	23
0750	4" wide joint	"	25	.320	"	16.15	10.10		26.25	33.50
0760	Floor slab to drywall partition									
0770	Flat joint	1 Carp	100	.080	L.F.	4.90	2.52		7.42	9.35
0780	Fluted joint		50	.160		10	5.05		15.05	18.90
0790	Etched fluted joint	↓	75	.107	↓	6.50	3.37		9.87	12.40
0800	Floor slab to concrete/masonry partition									
0810	Flat joint	1 Carp	75	.107	L.F.	11	3.37		14.37	17.35
0820	Fluted joint	"	50	.160	"	13	5.05		18.05	22
0830	Concrete/CMU wall joints									
0840	1" wide	1 Carp	100	.080	L.F.	6	2.52		8.52	10.55

THERMAL & MOISTURE PROTECTION 7

07800 | Fire & Smoke Protection

			DAILY	LABOR-			2003 BARE COSTS			TOTAL	
	07840	**Firestopping**	CREW	OUTPUT	HOURS	UNIT	MAT.	LABOR	EQUIP.	TOTAL	INCL O&P
100	0850	2" wide	1 Carp	75	.107	L.F.	11	3.37		14.37	17.35	100
	0860	4" wide	↓	50	.160	↓	21	5.05		26.05	31
	0870	Concrete/CMU floor joints	1 Carp	200	.040	L.F.	3	1.26		4.26	5.25
	0880	1" wide		150	.053		5.50	1.68		7.18	8.70
	0890	2" wide		100	.080		10.50	2.52		13.02	15.50
	0900	4" wide	↓			↓					

08100 | Metal Doors & Frames

08110 | Steel Doors & Frames

			CREW	DAILY OUTPUT	LABOR-HOURS	UNIT	MAT.	LABOR	EQUIP.	TOTAL	TOTAL INCL O&P	
300	0010	**FIRE DOOR**										300
	0015	Steel, flush, "B" label, 90 minute										
	0020	Full panel, 20 ga., 2'-0" x 6'-8"	2 Carp	20	.800	Ea.	176	25		201	233	
	0040	2'-8" x 6'-8"		18	.889		183	28		211	245	
	0060	3'-0" x 6'-8"		17	.941		183	29.50		212.50	248	
	0080	3'-0" x 7'-0"		17	.941		191	29.50		220.50	257	
	0140	18 ga., 3'-0" x 6'-8"		16	1		203	31.50		234.50	274	
	0160	2'-8" x 7'-0"		17	.941		216	29.50		245.50	285	
	0180	3'-0" x 7'-0"		16	1		211	31.50		242.50	282	
	0200	4'-0" x 7'-0"		15	1.067		279	33.50		312.50	360	
	0210											
	0220	For "A" label, 3 hour, 18 ga., use same price as "B" label										
	0240	For vision lite, add				Ea.	19.10			19.10	21	
	0245	Fire door, steel, flush, for narrow lite, add					47			47	51.50	
	0520	Flush, "B" label 90 min., composite, 20 ga., 2'-0" x 6'-8"	2 Carp	18	.889		238	28		266	305	
	0540	2'-8" x 6'-8"		17	.941		242	29.50		271.50	315	
	0560	3'-0" x 6'-8"		16	1		245	31.50		276.50	320	
	0580	3'-0" x 7'-0"		16	1		253	31.50		284.50	330	
	0600	Fire door, st, fl, "A" lbl, 3 hr, full pnl, 18 Ga., 3'-0" x 6'-8"		16	1		203	31.50		234.50	274	
	0605	Fire door, st, fl, "A" lbl, 3 hr, full pnl, 18 Ga., 2'-8" x 7'-0"		17	.941		216	29.50		245.50	285	
	0610	Fire door, st, fl, "A" lbl, 3 hr, full pnl, 18 Ga., 3'-0" x 7'-0"		16	1		211	31.50		242.50	282	
	0615	Fire door, st, fl, "A" lbl, 3 hr, full pnl, 18 Ga., 4'-0" x 7'-0"		15	1.067		279	33.50		312.50	360	
	0640	Flush, "A" label 3 hour, composite, 18 ga., 3'-0" x 6'-8"		15	1.067		266	33.50		299.50	345	
	0660	2'-8" x 7'-0"		16	1		276	31.50		307.50	355	
	0680	3'-0" x 7'-0"		15	1.067		273	33.50		306.50	355	
	0700	4'-0" x 7'-0"		14	1.143		330	36		366	420	

08200 | Wood & Plastic Doors

08210 | Wood Doors

			CREW	DAILY OUTPUT	LABOR-HOURS	UNIT	MAT.	LABOR	EQUIP.	TOTAL	TOTAL INCL O&P	
950	0010	**WOOD FIRE DOORS**										950
	0020	Particle core, 7 face plys, "B" label,										
	0040	1 hour, birch face, 1-3/4" x 2'-6" x 6'-8"	2 Carp	14	1.143	Ea.	219	36		255	298	
	0080	3'-0" x 6'-8"		13	1.231		226	39		265	310	
	0090	3'-0" x 7'-0"		12	1.333		236	42		278	325	
	0100	4'-0" x 7'-0"		12	1.333		315	42		357	410	
	0140	Oak face, 2'-6" x 6'-8"		14	1.143		219	36		255	298	
	0180	3'-0" x 6'-8"		13	1.231		227	39		266	310	
	0190	3'-0" x 7'-0"		12	1.333		237	42		279	325	
	0200	4'-0" x 7'-0"		12	1.333		310	42		352	405	
	0240	Walnut face, 2'-6" x 6'-8"		14	1.143		288	36		324	370	
	0280	3'-0" x 6'-8"		13	1.231		294	39		333	385	
	0290	3'-0" x 7'-0"		12	1.333		305	42		347	405	
	0300	4'-0" x 7'-0"		12	1.333		415	42		457	520	
	0440	M.D. overlay on hardboard, 2'-6" x 6'-8"		15	1.067		192	33.50		225.50	264	
	0480	3'-0" x 6'-8"		14	1.143		200	36		236	277	
	0490	3'-0" x 7'-0"		13	1.231		211	39		250	293	
	0500	4'-0" x 7'-0"		12	1.333		258	42		300	350	
	0540	H.P. plastic laminate, 2'-6" x 6'-8"		13	1.231		257	39		296	345	
	0580	3'-0" x 6'-8"		12	1.333		270	42		312	365	

08200 | Wood & Plastic Doors

08210 | Wood Doors

			CREW	DAILY OUTPUT	LABOR-HOURS	UNIT	2003 BARE COSTS				TOTAL INCL O&P	
							MAT.	LABOR	EQUIP.	TOTAL		
950	0590	3'-0" x 7'-0"	2 Carp	11	1.455	Ea.	273	46		319	370	950
	0600	4'-0" x 7'-0"		10	1.600		350	50.50		400.50	460	
	0740	90 minutes, birch face, 1-3/4" x 2'-6" x 6'-8"		14	1.143		217	36		253	296	
	0780	3'-0" x 6'-8"		13	1.231		229	39		268	315	
	0790	3'-0" x 7'-0"		12	1.333		237	42		279	325	
	0800	4'-0" x 7'-0"		12	1.333		325	42		367	425	
	0810	For additional 12" of height, add					30%					
	0840	Oak face, 2'-6" x 6'-8"	2 Carp	14	1.143	Ea.	205	36		241	283	
	0880	3'-0" x 6'-8"		13	1.231		213	39		252	296	
	0890	3'-0" x 7'-0"		12	1.333		224	42		266	310	
	0900	4'-0" x 7'-0"		12	1.333		310	42		352	405	
	0940	Walnut face, 2'-6" x 6'-8"		14	1.143		282	36		318	365	
	0980	3'-0" x 6'-8"		13	1.231		289	39		328	380	
	0990	3'-0" x 7'-0"		12	1.333		300	42		342	400	
	1000	4'-0" x 7'-0"		12	1.333		435	42		477	545	
	1140	M.D. overlay on hardboard, 2'-6" x 6'-8"		15	1.067		223	33.50		256.50	299	
	1180	3'-0" x 6'-8"		14	1.143		229	36		265	310	
	1190	3'-0" x 7'-0"		13	1.231		238	39		277	325	
	1200	4'-0" x 7'-0"		12	1.333		325	42		367	420	
	1240	For 8'-0" height, add					41			41	45	
	1260	For 8'-0" height walnut, add					54			54	59.50	
	1340	H.P. plastic laminate, 2'-6" x 6'-8"	2 Carp	13	1.231		278	39		317	365	
	1380	3'-0" x 6'-8"		12	1.333		292	42		334	385	
	1390	3'-0" x 7'-0"		11	1.455		295	46		341	395	
	1400	4'-0" x 7'-0"		10	1.600		385	50.50		435.50	500	

08300 | Specialty Doors

08320 | Detention Doors & Frames

			CREW	DAILY OUTPUT	LABOR-HOURS	UNIT	2003 BARE COSTS				TOTAL INCL O&P	
							MAT.	LABOR	EQUIP.	TOTAL		
950	0010	**VAULT FRONT**										950
	0020	Door and frame, 32" x 78", clear opening										
	0100	1 hour test, 32" door, weighs 750 lbs.	2 Sswk	1.50	10.667	Opng.	2,675	380		3,055	3,650	
	0150	40" door, weighs 995 lbs.		1.10	14.545	Ea.	2,950	520		3,470	4,200	
	0200	2 hour test, 32" door, weighs 950 lbs.		1.30	12.308	Opng.	3,200	440		3,640	4,325	
	0250	40" door, weighs 1130 lbs.		1	16		3,350	570		3,920	4,725	
	0300	4 hour test, 32" door, weighs 1025 lbs.		1.20	13.333		3,225	475		3,700	4,425	
	0350	40" door, weighs 1140 lbs.		.90	17.778		3,750	635		4,385	5,275	
	0400	6 hour test, 32" door, weighs 875		1.30	12.308	Ea.	3,900	440		4,340	5,100	
	0420	40" door, weighs 1075 lbs.		1.10	14.545	"	4,225	520		4,745	5,600	
	0500	For stainless steel front, including frame, add to above				Opng.	1,650			1,650	1,825	
	0550	Back, add				"	1,650			1,650	1,825	
	0600	For time lock, two movement, add	1 Elec	2	4	Ea.	1,350	150		1,500	1,700	
	0605	Timelock, two movement for vault door					1,350			1,350	1,475	
	0650	Three movement, add	1 Elec	2	4		1,725	150		1,875	2,125	
	0800	Day gate, painted, steel, 32" wide	2 Sswk	1.50	10.667		1,500	380		1,880	2,350	
	0850	40" wide		1.40	11.429		1,650	405		2,055	2,575	
	0900	Aluminum, 32" wide		1.50	10.667		2,275	380		2,655	3,200	
	0950	40" wide		1.40	11.429		2,525	405		2,930	3,525	
	2050	Security vault door, class I, 3' wide, 3 1/2" thick	E-24	.19	166	Opng.	13,700	5,825	3,400	22,925	29,100	

8 DOORS & WINDOWS

		08320	Detention Doors & Frames	CREW	DAILY OUTPUT	LABOR-HOURS	UNIT	2003 BARE COSTS				TOTAL INCL O&P	
								MAT.	LABOR	EQUIP.	TOTAL		
950	2100		Class II, 3' wide, 7" thick	E-24	.19	166	Opng.	16,300	5,825	3,400	25,525	32,000	950
	2150		Class III, 9R, 3' wide, 10" thick, minimum	↓	.13	250	↓	22,300	8,725	5,125	36,150	45,400	
	2155		Vault door, Class III, 9R, 3' wide, 10" thick				Ea.	22,300			22,300	24,600	
	2160		Class V, type 1, 40" door	E-24	2.48	12.903		4,950	450	264	5,664	6,525	
	2170		Class V, type 2, 40" door	"	2.48	12.903		4,975	450	264	5,689	6,550	
	2180		Day gate for class V vault	2 Sswk	2	8	↓	970	285		1,255	1,600	

		08330	Coiling Doors & Grilles										
720	0010		ROLLING SERVICE DOORS Steel, manual, 20 ga., incl. hardware										720
	0050		8' x 8' high	2 Sswk	1.60	10	Ea.	720	355		1,075	1,450	
	0100		10' x 10' high		1.40	11.429		945	405		1,350	1,800	
	0120		8' x 8' high, class A fire door		1.40	11.429		940	405		1,345	1,775	
	0130		12' x 12' high, standard		1.20	13.333		1,175	475		1,650	2,175	
	0140		12' x 12' high, class A fire door		1	16		1,675	570		2,245	2,850	
	0160		10' x 20' high, standard		.50	32		1,400	1,150		2,550	3,625	
	0180		10' x 20' high, class A fire door		.40	40		2,500	1,425		3,925	5,350	
	0200		20' x 10' high		1	16		1,950	570		2,520	3,150	
	0300		12' x 12' high		1.20	13.333		1,225	475		1,700	2,225	
	0400		20' x 12' high		.90	17.778		2,000	635		2,635	3,350	
	0420		14' x 12' high		.80	20		1,375	715		2,090	2,825	
	0430		14' x 13' high		.80	20		1,500	715		2,215	2,950	
	0500		14' x 14' high		.80	20		1,625	715		2,340	3,100	
	0520		14' x 16' high		.80	20	Opng.	1,950	715		2,665	3,450	
	0540		14' x 20' high		.56	28.571		2,975	1,025		4,000	5,125	
	0550		18' x 18' high		.60	26.667	↓	2,125	950		3,075	4,075	
	0600		20' x 16' high		.60	26.667	Ea.	2,325	950		3,275	4,275	
	0700		10' x 20' high		.50	32	"	1,400	1,150		2,550	3,625	
	0750		16' x 24' high		.48	33.333	Opng.	3,600	1,200		4,800	6,100	
	1000		12' x 12', crank operated, crank on door side		.80	20	Ea.	1,100	715		1,815	2,500	
	1100		Crank thru wall	↓	.70	22.857	↓	1,225	815		2,040	2,825	
	1300		For vision panel, add				↓	200			200	219	
	1400		For 22 ga., deduct				S.F.	.68			.68	.75	
	1600		3' x 7' pass door within rolling steel door, new construction				Ea.	1,075			1,075	1,200	
	1700		Existing construction	2 Sswk	2	8		1,075	285		1,360	1,725	
	2000		Class A fire doors, manual, 20 ga., 8' x 8' high		1.40	11.429		940	405		1,345	1,775	
	2100		10' x 10' high		1.10	14.545		1,250	520		1,770	2,325	
	2200		20' x 10' high		.80	20		2,500	715		3,215	4,050	
	2300		12' x 12' high		1	16		1,675	570		2,245	2,850	
	2400		20' x 12' high		.80	20		2,875	715		3,590	4,450	
	2500		14' x 14' high		.60	26.667		2,150	950		3,100	4,100	
	2600		20' x 16' high		.50	32		3,600	1,150		4,750	6,025	
	2700		10' x 20' high		.40	40	↓	2,275	1,425		3,700	5,100	
	2730		Manual steel rollup fire doors		160	.100	S.F.	14.05	3.57		17.62	22	
	2740		For motor operated, add	↓	1	16	Ea.	775	570		1,345	1,875	
	3000		For 18 ga. doors, add				S.F.	.71			.71	.78	
	3300		For enamel finish, add				"	.84			.84	.92	
	3600		For safety edge bottom bar, pneumatic, add				L.F.	11.05			11.05	12.20	
	3700		Electric, add				"	21			21	23	
	3900		Fire doors, overhead, annually	1 Sswk	6.02	1.329	Ea.	3.15	47.50		50.65	89.50	
	3950		Fire doors, overhead, annualized	"	2.80	2.856	"	12.60	102		114.60	199	
	4000		For weatherstripping, extruded rubber, jambs, add				L.F.	7.15			7.15	7.90	
	4100		Hood, add				↓	4.56			4.56	5	
	4200		Sill, add				↓	2.60			2.60	2.86	
	4500		Motor operators, to 14' x 14' opening	2 Sswk	5	3.200	Ea.	690	114		804	965	
	4600		Over 14' x 14', jack shaft type	"	5	3.200		675	114		789	950	
	4700		For fire door, additional fusible link, add				↓	13			13	14.30	

08400 | **Entrances & Storefronts**

08470	**Revolving Entrance Doors**	CREW	DAILY OUTPUT	LABOR-HOURS	UNIT	2003 BARE COSTS				TOTAL INCL O&P	
						MAT.	LABOR	EQUIP.	TOTAL		
600	0010	**REVOLVING DOORS** Aluminum, 6'-6" to 7'-0" diameter,	4 Sswk	.75	42.667	Opng.	15,400	1,525		16,925	19,700	600
	0020	6'-10" to 7' high, stock units, minimum		.60	53.333		19,000	1,900		20,900	24,400	
	0050	Average		.60	53.333		19,000	1,900		20,900	24,400	
	0100	Maximum		.45	71.111		25,000	2,525		27,525	32,100	
	1000	Stainless steel		.30	105		28,800	3,775		32,575	38,600	
	1100	Solid bronze		.15	213		33,600	7,600		41,200	50,500	
	1500	For automatic controls, add	2 Elec	2	8		11,600	300		11,900	13,200	
	1600	Revolving doors, security type, 7' H x 6'-6" W, excl controller, min	4 Sswk	.40	80		38,500	2,850		41,350	47,600	
	1610	Max	"	.40	80		66,000	2,850		68,850	77,500	

08500 | **Windows**

08510	**Steel Windows**	CREW	DAILY OUTPUT	LABOR-HOURS	UNIT	2003 BARE COSTS				TOTAL INCL O&P	
						MAT.	LABOR	EQUIP.	TOTAL		
700	0010	**SCREENS**										700
	0800	Security screen, aluminum frame with stainless steel cloth	2 Sswk	1,200	.013	S.F.	16.95	.48		17.43	19.50	
	0900	Steel grate, painted, on steel frame	"	1,600	.010	"	9.10	.36		9.46	10.65	
750	0010	**STEEL SASH** Custom units, glazing and trim not included										750
	0100	Casement, 100% vented	2 Sswk	200	.080	S.F.	37	2.85		39.85	46	
	0200	50% vented		200	.080		34	2.85		36.85	42.50	
	0300	Fixed		200	.080		23.50	2.85		26.35	30.50	
	0306	Steel window, fixed, no glazing, 3'x4'				Ea.	23.50			23.50	25.50	
	1000	Projected, commercial, 40% vented	2 Sswk	200	.080	S.F.	38.50	2.85		41.35	47.50	
	1005	Steel window, venting, no glazing					38.50			38.50	42.50	
	1100	Intermediate, 50% vented	2 Sswk	200	.080		42	2.85		44.85	51	
	1500	Industrial, horizontally pivoted		200	.080		41	2.85		43.85	50	
	1600	Fixed		200	.080		22.50	2.85		25.35	30	
	2000	Industrial security sash, 50% vented		200	.080		43	2.85		45.85	52	
	2100	Fixed		200	.080		36	2.85		38.85	44.50	

08700 | **Hardware**

08710	**Door Hardware**	CREW	DAILY OUTPUT	LABOR-HOURS	UNIT	2003 BARE COSTS				TOTAL INCL O&P	
						MAT.	LABOR	EQUIP.	TOTAL		
300	0010	**DOOR CLOSER** Rack and pinion	1 Carp	6.50	1.231	Ea.	121	39		160	194	300
	0020	Adjustable backcheck, 3 way mount, all sizes, regular arm	"	6	1.333		125	42		167	203	
	0025	Door closer, adjustable backset, 3-way mount					125			125	137	
	0040	Hold open arm	1 Carp	6	1.333		137	42		179	217	
	0100	Fusible link		6.50	1.231		107	39		146	178	
	0200	Non sized, regular arm		6	1.333		119	42		161	197	
	0240	Hold open arm		6	1.333		148	42		190	229	
	0400	4 way mount, non sized, regular arm		6	1.333		163	42		205	246	
	0440	Hold open arm		6	1.333		176	42		218	259	
	0500	Int. doors to 4' wide or ext. to 3'-4" wide, regular		6.50	1.231		78.50	39		117.50	147	

8 DOORS & WINDOWS

08710 | Door Hardware

		CREW	DAILY OUTPUT	LABOR-HOURS	UNIT	MAT.	LABOR	EQUIP.	TOTAL	TOTAL INCL O&P	
300	0550	Fusible link	1 Carp	6.50	1.231	Ea.	91	39		130	161	**300**
	1000	3'-8" wide					101			101	111	
	1500	Concealed closers, normal use, head, pivot hung, interior	1 Carp	5.50	1.455		284	46		330	380	
	1510	Exterior		5.50	1.455		284	46		330	380	
	1550	Floor		2.20	3.636		158	115		273	355	
	1570	Interior, floor, offset pivot, single acting		3.50	2.286		475	72		547	640	
	1590	Exterior		3.50	2.286		480	72		552	640	
	2000	Backcheck and adjustable power, hinge face mount										
	2010	All sizes, regular arm	1 Carp	6.50	1.231	Ea.	150	39		189	226	
	2040	Hold open arm		6.50	1.231		162	39		201	239	
	2400	Top jamb mount, all sizes, regular arm		6	1.333		150	42		192	231	
	2440	Hold open arm		6	1.333		162	42		204	244	
	2800	Top face mount, all sizes, regular arm		6.50	1.231		150	39		189	226	
	2840	Hold open arm		6.50	1.231		161	39		200	239	
	4000	Backcheck, overhead concealed, all sizes, regular arm		5.50	1.455		159	46		205	247	
	4040	Concealed arm		5	1.600		170	50.50		220.50	266	
	4400	Compact overhead, concealed, all sizes, regular arm		5.50	1.455		290	46		336	390	
	4440	Concealed arm		5	1.600		300	50.50		350.50	410	
	4800	Concealed in door, all sizes, regular arm		5.50	1.455		107	46		153	190	
	4840	Concealed arm		5	1.600		116	50.50		166.50	206	
	4900	Floor concealed, all sizes, single acting		2.20	3.636		136	115		251	330	
	4940	Double acting		2.20	3.636		175	115		290	370	
	5000	For cast aluminum cylinder, deduct					14.45			14.45	15.85	
	5040	For delayed action, add					25.50			25.50	28	
	5080	For fusible link arm, add					10.45			10.45	11.50	
	5120	For shock absorbing arm, add					31.50			31.50	34.50	
	5160	For spring power adjustment, add					24			24	26.50	
	6000	Closer-holder, hinge face mount, all sizes, exposed arm	1 Carp	6.50	1.231		111	39		150	183	
	7000	Electronic closer-holder, hinge facemount, concealed arm		5	1.600		168	50.50		218.50	264	
	7400	With built-in detector		5	1.600		505	50.50		555.50	640	
320	0010	**DEADLOCKS** Mortise, heavy duty, outside key	1 Carp	9	.889	Ea.	114	28		142	170	**320**
	0013	Replace deadbolt		6.92	1.156		114	36.50		150.50	183	
	0020	Double cylinder		9	.889		127	28		155	183	
	0030	Brass		7	1.143		74.50	36		110.50	138	
	0100	Medium duty, outside key		10	.800		88.50	25		113.50	137	
	0110	Double cylinder		10	.800		111	25		136	162	
	1000	Tubular, standard duty, outside key		10	.800		48	25		73	92	
	1010	Double cylinder		10	.800		61.50	25		86.50	107	
	1050	Bored, double cylinder, brass		7	1.143		57.50	36		93.50	120	
	1200	Night latch, outside key		10	.800		60.50	25		85.50	106	
750	0010	**PANIC DEVICE** For rim locks, single door, exit only	1 Carp	6	1.333	Ea.	335	42		377	435	**750**
	0020	Outside key and pull		5	1.600		380	50.50		430.50	500	
	0200	Bar and vertical rod, exit only		5	1.600		485	50.50		535.50	615	
	0203	Install panic bar		3.85	2.080		485	65.50		550.50	640	
	0205	Panic device for exit door					485			485	535	
	0210	Outside key and pull	1 Carp	4	2		580	63		643	740	
	0220	Surface vertical rod w/thumb piece, brass, US26D		4	2		755	63		818	930	
	0400	Bar and concealed rod		4	2		495	63		558	645	
	0500	Concealed vertical rod w/lever handle, brass, US26D		4	2		725	63		788	900	
	0600	Touch bar, exit only		6	1.333		390	42		432	495	
	0610	Outside key and pull		5	1.600		470	50.50		520.50	600	
	0700	Touch bar and vertical rod, exit only		5	1.600		535	50.50		585.50	665	
	0710	Outside key and pull		4	2		620	63		683	785	
	0800	Touch bar, low profile, exit only		6	1.333		290	42		332	385	
	0810	Outside key and pull		5	1.600		340	50.50		390.50	455	
	0900	Touch bar and vertical rod, low profile, exit only		5	1.600		420	50.50		470.50	540	

DOORS & WINDOWS 8

08700 | Hardware

08710 | Door Hardware

		CREW	DAILY OUTPUT	LABOR-HOURS	UNIT	2003 BARE COSTS MAT.	LABOR	EQUIP.	TOTAL	TOTAL INCL O&P	
750	0910	Outside key and pull	1 Carp	4	2	Ea.	455	63		518	600	**750**
	1000	Mortise, bar, exit only		4	2		440	63		503	580	
	1100	Mortise bar, with thumb piece, brass, US26D		4	2		855	63		918	1,050	
	1600	Touch bar, exit only		4	2		500	63		563	650	
	2000	Narrow stile, rim mounted, bar, exit only		6	1.333		525	42		567	645	
	2010	Outside key and pull		5	1.600		570	50.50		620.50	710	
	2020	Rim type with thumb piece, brass, US26D	↓	5	1.600	↓	640	50.50		690.50	785	
	2030	For satin brass finish, add					3%					
	2200	Bar and vertical rod, exit only	1 Carp	5	1.600	Ea.	545	50.50		595.50	675	
	2210	Outside key and pull		4	2		545	63		608	695	
	2400	Bar and concealed rod, exit only		3	2.667		630	84		714	825	
	3000	Mortise, bar, exit only		4	2		440	63		503	585	
	3600	Touch bar, exit only	↓	4	2	↓	645	63		708	805	
800	0010	**SPECIAL HINGES**										**800**
	0015	Paumelle, high frequency										
	0020	Steel base, 6" x 4-1/2", US10				Pr.	111			111	122	
	0040	US26D					138			138	152	
	0080	US10A					145			145	160	
	0100	Bronze base, 5" x 4-1/2", US10					150			150	165	
	0140	US26D					166			166	182	
	0180	US3					175			175	192	
	0200	Paumelle, average frequency, steel base, 4-1/2" x 3-1/2", US10					75.50			75.50	83	
	0240	US26D					78.50			78.50	86.50	
	0280	US10A					81			81	89	
	0400	Olive knuckle, low frequency, brass base, 6" x 4-1/2", US10					137			137	151	
	0440	US26D					154			154	170	
	0480	US3				↓	155			155	171	
	0800	Emergency door pivot, average frequency										
	0810	Brass base, 4-7/8" jamb plate, USP				Pr.	52			52	57	
	0840	US26D					57.50			57.50	63.50	
	0880	For emergency door stop and hold back, add				↓	49			49	54	
	1000	Electric hinge with concealed conductor, average frequency										
	1010	Steel base, 4-1/2" x 4-1/2", US26D				Pr.	250			250	275	
	1100	Bronze base, 4-1/2" x 4-1/2", US26D				"	263			263	289	
	1200	Electric hinge with concealed conductor, high frequency										
	1210	Steel base, 4-1/2" x 4-1/2", US26D				Pr.	186			186	205	
	1400	Non template, full mortise, low frequency										
	1410	Steel base, 4" x 4", USP				Pr.	13.35			13.35	14.70	
	1440	US26D					15.05			15.05	16.55	
	1480	US10A				↓	17.80			17.80	19.60	
	1500	Non template, full mortise, average frequency										
	1510	Steel base, 4" x 4", USP				Pr.	28			28	30.50	
	1540	US26D					26.50			26.50	29.50	
	1580	US10A					34.50			34.50	38	
	1600	Double weight, 800 lb., steel base, removable pin, 5" x 6", USP					117			117	129	
	1700	Steel base-welded pin, 5" x 6", USP					129			129	142	
	1800	Triple weight, 2000 lb., steel base, welded pin, 5" x 6", USP					135			135	148	
	2000	Pivot reinf., high frequency, steel base, 7-3/4" door plate, USP					150			150	165	
	2040	US26D					130			130	143	
	2080	US10A					158			158	174	
	2200	Bronze base, 7-3/4" door plate, US10					181			181	200	
	2240	US26D					189			189	208	
	2280	US10A				↓	217			217	239	
	3000	Swing clear, full mortise, full or half surface, high frequency,										
	3010	Steel base, 5" high, USP				Pr.	126			126	139	

08700 | Hardware

08710 | Door Hardware

			CREW	DAILY OUTPUT	LABOR-HOURS	UNIT	2003 BARE COSTS				TOTAL INCL O&P	
							MAT.	LABOR	EQUIP.	TOTAL		
800	3040	US26D				Pr.	121			121	134	800
	3080	US10A				↓	153			153	168	
	3200	Swing clear, full mortise, average frequency										
	3210	Steel base, 4-1/2" high, USP				Pr.	100			100	110	
	3280	US10A				"	123			123	135	
	3400	Swing clear, half mortise, high frequency										
	3410	Steel base, 4-1/2" high, USP				Pr.	126			126	139	
	3440	US26D					130			130	143	
	3480	US10A					154			154	169	
	4000	Wide throw, average frequency, steel base, 4-1/2" x 6", USP					76.50			76.50	84	
	4040	US26D					81.50			81.50	89.50	
	4080	US10A					88			88	97	
	4100	5" x 7", USP					93.50			93.50	103	
	4200	High frequency, steel base, 4-1/2" x 6", USP					117			117	129	
	4240	US26D					128			128	141	
	4280	US10A					150			150	165	
	4300	5" x 7", USP					119			119	131	
	4400	Wide throw, low frequency, steel base, 4-1/2" x 6", USP					57.50			57.50	63	
	4440	US26D					70.50			70.50	77.50	
	4480	US10A					75.50			75.50	83	
	4500	5" x 7", USP				↓	81.50			81.50	89.50	
	4600	Spring hinge, single acting, 6" flange, steel				Ea.	43			43	47.50	
	4700	Brass					76			76	83.50	
	4900	Double acting, 6" flange, steel					78.50			78.50	86	
	4950	Brass				↓	128			128	141	
	5000	T-strap, galvanized, 4"				Pr.	15.20			15.20	16.75	
	5010	6"					24			24	26.50	
	5020	8"				↓	36.50			36.50	40.50	
	6000	Offset pivot hinge, top pivot, mortise	1 Carp	4	2	Ea.	63	63		126	168	
	6050	Intermediate, surface mounted		5	1.600		91	50.50		141.50	179	
	7000	Bottom pivot, cement mounted		2	4		122	126		248	330	
	7600	Door coordinator, UL rated, brass, US26D	↓	8	1	↓	77	31.50		108.50	135	
	7610	For satin brass finish, add					3%					
	9000	Continuous hinge, steel, full mortise, heavy duty	2 Carp	64	.250	L.F.	10.80	7.90		18.70	24.50	

08720 | Weatherstripping & Seals

			CREW	DAILY OUTPUT	LABOR-HOURS	UNIT	MAT.	LABOR	EQUIP.	TOTAL	TOTAL INCL O&P	
100	0010	ASTRAGALS One piece overlapping										100
	2400	Spring hinged security seal, with cam	1 Carp	75	.107	L.F.	4.76	3.37		8.13	10.50	
	2600	Spring loaded locking bolt, vinyl insert	"	45	.178	"	6.50	5.60		12.10	15.90	

08800 | Glazing

08810 | Glass

			CREW	DAILY OUTPUT	LABOR-HOURS	UNIT	2003 BARE COSTS				TOTAL INCL O&P	
							MAT.	LABOR	EQUIP.	TOTAL		
500	0010	LAMINATED GLASS Clear float, .03" vinyl, 1/4" thick	2 Glaz	90	.178	S.F.	7.70	5.50		13.20	16.80	500
	0020	Tempered, double coated		100	.160		32	4.95		36.95	42.50	
	0100	3/8" thick		78	.205		12.50	6.35		18.85	23.50	
	0200	.06" vinyl, 1/2" thick		65	.246		14.65	7.60		22.25	27.50	
	1000	5/8" thick		90	.178		17.15	5.50		22.65	27.50	
	2000	Bullet-resisting, 1-3/16" thick, to 15 S.F.	↓	16	1	↓	45	31		76	96.50	

233

08800 | Glazing

		08810	Glass	CREW	DAILY OUTPUT	LABOR-HOURS	UNIT	2003 BARE COSTS				TOTAL INCL O&P	
								MAT.	LABOR	EQUIP.	TOTAL		
500	2100		Over 15 S.F.	2 Glaz	16	1	S.F.	40.50	31		71.50	91.50	500
	2200		2" thick, to 15 S.F.		10	1.600		81.50	49.50		131	165	
	2300		Over 15 S.F.		10	1.600		74.50	49.50		124	157	
	2500		2-1/4" thick, to 15 S.F.		12	1.333		56.50	41.50		98	125	
	2600		Over 15 S.F.	▼	12	1.333	▼	50	41.50		91.50	118	

		08830	Mirrors										
100	0011	**MIRRORS**											100
	2600		Glass, convex, security type, indoor/outdoor, 30" dia.	1 Carp	8	1	Ea.	165	31.50		196.50	232	
	2610		36" dia.		8	1		165	31.50		196.50	232	
	2615		Indoor, 180 dome, 36" dia.		8	1		143	31.50		174.50	207	
	2620		360 dome, 36" dia.		8	1		231	31.50		262.50	305	
	2630		48" dia.	▼	8	1	▼	425	31.50		456.50	515	

8

DOORS & WINDOWS

09800 | Acoustical Treatment

09820 | Acoustical Insul/Sealants

			CREW	DAILY OUTPUT	LABOR-HOURS	UNIT	2003 BARE COSTS				TOTAL INCL O&P	
							MAT.	LABOR	EQUIP.	TOTAL		
500	0010	**SOUND ATTENUATION** Blanket, 1" thick	1 Carp	925	.009	S.F.	.24	.27		.51	.69	500
	0500	1-1/2" thick		920	.009		.23	.27		.50	.68	
	1000	2" thick		915	.009		.29	.28		.57	.75	
	1500	3" thick		910	.009		.39	.28		.67	.86	
	3000	Thermal or acoustical batt above ceiling, 2" thick		900	.009		.42	.28		.70	.90	
	3100	3" thick		900	.009		.63	.28		.91	1.13	
	3200	4" thick		900	.009		.77	.28		1.05	1.29	
	3400	Urethane plastic foam, open cell, on wall, 2" thick	2 Carp	2,050	.008		2.56	.25		2.81	3.20	
	3500	3" thick		1,550	.010		3.40	.33		3.73	4.25	
	3600	4" thick		1,050	.015		4.77	.48		5.25	6	
	3700	On ceiling, 2" thick		1,700	.009		2.55	.30		2.85	3.27	
	3800	3" thick		1,300	.012		3.40	.39		3.79	4.35	
	3900	4" thick		900	.018		4.77	.56		5.33	6.15	
	4000	Nylon matting 0.4" thick, with carbon black spinerette										
	4010	plus polyester fabric, on floor	J-4	4,000	.004	S.F.	1.90	.11		2.01	2.25	
	4200	Fiberglass reinf. backer board underlayment, 7/16" thick, on floor	"	800	.020		1.59	.54		2.13	2.55	
	5000	Sound control matting/underlayment to 1/4"	D-1	600	.027		1.78	.76		2.54	3.13	
	9000	Minimum labor/equipment charge	1 Carp	5	1.600	Job		50.50		50.50	79	

09830 | Acoustical Barriers

			CREW	DAILY OUTPUT	LABOR-HOURS	UNIT	MAT.	LABOR	EQUIP.	TOTAL	TOTAL INCL O&P	
100	0011	**BARRIERS** Plenum										100
	0600	Aluminum foil, fiberglass reinf., parallel with joists	1 Carp	275	.029	S.F.	.72	.92		1.64	2.22	
	0700	Perpendicular to joists		180	.044		.73	1.40		2.13	2.99	
	0900	Aluminum mesh, kraft paperbacked		275	.029		.69	.92		1.61	2.19	
	0970	Fiberglass batts, kraft faced, 3-1/2" thick		1,400	.006		.25	.18		.43	.56	
	0980	6" thick		1,300	.006		.42	.19		.61	.76	
	1000	Sheet lead, 1 lb., 1/64" thick, perpendicular to joists		150	.053		1.97	1.68		3.65	4.80	
	1100	Vinyl foam reinforced, 1/8" thick, 1.0 lb. per S.F.		150	.053		2.84	1.68		4.52	5.75	

09840 | Acoustical Wall Treatment

			CREW	DAILY OUTPUT	LABOR-HOURS	UNIT	MAT.	LABOR	EQUIP.	TOTAL	TOTAL INCL O&P	
100	0010	**SOUND ABSORBING PANELS** Perforated steel facing, painted with										100
	0100	fiberglass or mineral filler, no backs, 2-1/4" thick, modular										
	0200	space units, ceiling or wall hung, white or colored	1 Carp	100	.080	S.F.	8.90	2.52		11.42	13.75	
	0300	Fiberboard sound deadening panels, 1/2" thick	"	600	.013	"	.29	.42		.71	.98	
	0500	Fiberglass panels, 4' x 8' x 1" thick, with										
	0600	glass cloth face for walls, cemented	1 Carp	155	.052	S.F.	5.60	1.63		7.23	8.70	
	0700	1-1/2" thick, dacron covered, inner aluminum frame,										
	0710	wall mounted	1 Carp	300	.027	S.F.	7.35	.84		8.19	9.40	
	0900	Mineral fiberboard panels, fabric covered, 30"x 108",										
	1000	3/4" thick, concealed spline, wall mounted	1 Carp	150	.053	S.F.	5.30	1.68		6.98	8.50	
	9000	Minimum labor/equipment charge	"	4	2	Job		63		63	98.50	

FINISHES **9**

235

10450 | Pedestrian Control Devices

			CREW	DAILY OUTPUT	LABOR-HOURS	UNIT	2003 BARE COSTS MAT.	LABOR	EQUIP.	TOTAL	TOTAL INCL O&P	
		10455 | **Turnstiles**										
900	0010	**TURNSTILES** One way, 4 arm, 46" diameter, economy, manual	2 Carp	5	3.200	Ea.	261	101		362	445	900
	0100	Electric		1.20	13.333		870	420		1,290	1,625	
	0300	High security, galv., 5'-5" diameter, 7' high, manual		1	16		2,275	505		2,780	3,300	
	0350	Electric		.60	26.667		2,925	840		3,765	4,550	
	0420	Three arm, 24" opening, light duty, manual		2	8		840	252		1,092	1,325	
	0450	Heavy duty		1.50	10.667		2,300	335		2,635	3,050	
	0460	Manual, with registering & controls, light duty		2	8		1,825	252		2,077	2,400	
	0470	Heavy duty		1.50	10.667		2,225	335		2,560	2,975	
	0480	Electric, heavy duty	▼	1.10	14.545		2,600	460		3,060	3,600	
	0500	For coin or token operating, add				▼	345			345	380	
	1200	One way gate with horizontal bars, 5'-5" diameter										
	1300	7' high, recreation or transit type	2 Carp	.80	20	Ea.	2,925	630		3,555	4,200	
	1400	7' security turnstile w/auto control free turning 1 direction, type "B"		.72	22.222		3,975	700		4,675	5,475	
	1420	Free turning in both directions		.72	22.222		4,000	700		4,700	5,500	
	1440	Type "AA", w/auto control free turning 1 direction		.72	22.222		4,300	700		5,000	5,825	
	1460	Free turning in both directions	▼	.72	22.222	▼	4,750	700		5,450	6,325	
	1500	For electronic counter, add					171			171	188	

10520 | Fire Protection Specialties

			CREW	DAILY OUTPUT	LABOR-HOURS	UNIT	2003 BARE COSTS MAT.	LABOR	EQUIP.	TOTAL	TOTAL INCL O&P	
		10525 | **Fire Prot. Specialties**										
200	0010	**FIRE EQUIPMENT CABINETS** Not equipped, 20 ga. steel box,										200
	0040	recessed, D.S. glass in door, box size given										
	1000	Portable extinguisher, single, 8" x 12" x 27", alum. door & frame	Q-12	8	2	Ea.	76	67.50		143.50	187	
	1100	Steel door and frame		8	2		56.50	67.50		124	165	
	1200	Stainless steel door and frame		8	2		117	67.50		184.50	231	
	2000	Portable extinguisher, large, 8" x 12" x 36", alum. door & frame		8	2		130	67.50		197.50	246	
	2100	Steel door and frame		8	2		84.50	67.50		152	196	
	2200	Stainless steel door and frame		8	2		133	67.50		200.50	249	
	2500	8" x 16" x 38", aluminum door & frame		8	2		138	67.50		205.50	254	
	2600	Steel door and frame	▼	8	2	▼	126	67.50		193.50	242	
	3000	Hose rack assy., 1-1/2" valve & 100' hose, 24" x 40" x 5-1/2"										
	3100	Aluminum door and frame	Q-12	6	2.667	Ea.	186	90		276	340	
	3200	Steel door and frame		6	2.667		122	90		212	271	
	3300	Stainless steel door and frame	▼	6	2.667	▼	243	90		333	405	
	4000	Hose rack assy., 2-1/2" x 1-1/2" valve, 100' hose, 24" x 40" x 8"										
	4100	Aluminum door and frame	Q-12	6	2.667	Ea.	188	90		278	345	
	4200	Steel door and frame		6	2.667		127	90		217	277	
	4300	Stainless steel door and frame	▼	6	2.667	▼	245	90		335	405	
	5000	Hose rack assy., 2-1/2" x 1-1/2" valve, 100' hose										
	5010	and extinguisher, 30" x 40" x 8"										
	5100	Aluminum door and frame	Q-12	5	3.200	Ea.	240	108		348	430	
	5200	Steel door and frame		5	3.200		140	108		248	315	
	5300	Stainless steel door and frame	▼	5	3.200	▼	263	108		371	455	
	6000	Hose rack assy., 1-1/2" valve, 100' hose										
	6010	and 2-1/2" FD valve, 24" x 44" x 8"										
	6100	Aluminum door and frame	Q-12	5	3.200	Ea.	213	108		321	400	
	6200	Steel door and frame		5	3.200		136	108		244	315	
	6300	Stainless steel door and frame	▼	5	3.200	▼	276	108		384	470	

10 SPECIALTIES

236

10520 | Fire Protection Specialties

10525 | Fire Prot. Specialties

		CREW	DAILY OUTPUT	LABOR-HOURS	UNIT	2003 BARE COSTS				TOTAL INCL O&P
						MAT.	LABOR	EQUIP.	TOTAL	
200	**7000** Hose rack assy., 1-1/2" valve & 100' hose, 2-1/2" FD valve										**200**
	7010 and extinguisher, 30" x 44" x 8"									
	7100 Aluminum door and frame	Q-12	5	3.200	Ea.	252	108		360	440
	7200 Steel door and frame		5	3.200		257	108		365	445
	7300 Stainless steel door and frame	↓	5	3.200	↓	335	108		443	535
	8000 Valve cabinet for 2-1/2" FD angle valve, 18" x 18" x 8"									
	8100 Aluminum door and frame	Q-12	12	1.333	Ea.	83	45		128	160
	8200 Steel door and frame		12	1.333		62.50	45		107.50	138
	8300 Stainless steel door and frame	↓	12	1.333	↓	109	45		154	189
300	**0010 FIRE EXTINGUISHERS**										**300**
	0120 CO2, portable with swivel horn, 5 lb.				Ea.	101			101	111
	0140 With hose and "H" horn, 10 lb.					150			150	165
	0160 15 lb.					172			172	189
	0180 20 lb.					207			207	228
	0360 Wheeled type, cart mounted, 50 lb.					1,200			1,200	1,325
	0400 100 lb.				↓	1,525			1,525	1,675
	1000 Dry chemical, pressurized									
	1040 Standard type, portable, painted, 2-1/2 lb.				Ea.	27.50			27.50	30.50
	1060 5 lb.					40			40	44
	1080 10 lb.					67			67	73.50
	1100 20 lb.					90			90	99
	1120 30 lb.					157			157	173
	1200 Chrome plated, 2-1/2 lb.					23.50			23.50	26
	1300 Standard type, wheeled, 150 lb.					1,400			1,400	1,550
	1400 250 lb.					1,575			1,575	1,725
	2000 ABC all purpose type, portable, 2-1/2 lb.					27.50			27.50	30.50
	2060 5 lb.					40			40	44
	2080 9-1/2 lb.					60			60	66
	2100 20 lb.					85			85	93.50
	2300 Wheeled, 45 lb.					650			650	715
	2360 150 lb.					1,450			1,450	1,600
	3000 Dry chemical, outside cartridge to -65°F, painted, 9 lb.					200			200	220
	3060 26 lb.					250			250	275
	3100 Foam type, stainless steel, 2-1/2 gallon					213			213	235
	3150 Wheeled type, cart mounted, 30 gallon					4,825			4,825	5,300
	5000 Pressurized water, 2-1/2 gallon, stainless steel					75			75	82.50
	5060 With anti-freeze					110			110	121
	6000 Soda & acid, 2-1/2 gallon, stainless steel					75			75	82.50
	9400 Installation of extinguishers, 12 or more, on wood	1 Carp	30	.267			8.40		8.40	13.15
	9420 On masonry or concrete	"	15	.533	↓		16.85		16.85	26.50

10600 | Partitions

10610 | Folding Gates

		CREW	DAILY OUTPUT	LABOR-HOURS	UNIT	2003 BARE COSTS				TOTAL INCL O&P
						MAT.	LABOR	EQUIP.	TOTAL	
100	**0010 SECURITY GATES** For roll up type, see division 08330-130										**100**
	0300 Scissors type folding gate, ptd. steel, single, 6' high, 5-1/2'wide	2 Sswk	4	4	Opng.	123	143		266	395
	0350 6-1/2' wide		4	4		132	143		275	405
	0400 7-1/2' wide	↓	4	4	↓	163	143		306	440

10600 | Partitions

		10610	**Folding Gates**	CREW	DAILY OUTPUT	LABOR-HOURS	UNIT	\multicolumn{4}{c}{2003 BARE COSTS}				TOTAL INCL O&P	
								MAT.	LABOR	EQUIP.	TOTAL		
100	0600		Double gate, 7-1/2' high, 8' wide	2 Sswk	2.50	6.400	Opng.	209	228		437	645	100
	0650		10' wide		2.50	6.400		241	228		469	680	
	0700		12' wide		2	8		320	285		605	875	
	0750		14' wide		2	8		370	285		655	930	
	0900		Door gate, folding steel, 4' wide, 61" high		4	4		59.50	143		202.50	325	
	1000		71" high		4	4		62	143		205	325	
	1200		81" high		4	4		67	143		210	335	
	1300		Window gates, 2' to 4' wide, 31" high		4	4		34	143		177	297	
	1500		55" high		3.75	4.267		48	152		200	330	
	1600		79" high		3.50	4.571		62	163		225	365	

10 SPECIALTIES

11020 | Security & Vault Equipment

		11021	Safes	CREW	DAILY OUTPUT	LABOR-HOURS	UNIT	2003 BARE COSTS				TOTAL INCL O&P	
								MAT.	LABOR	EQUIP.	TOTAL		
600	0010	SAFE											600
	0015	Office, 4 hr. rating, 30" x 18" x 18" inside				Ea.	2,925			2,925	3,200	
	0060	48" x 20" x 20"	2 Clab	3	5.333		2,825	131		2,956	3,300	
	0080	60" x 33" x 20"	"	1.60	10		4,825	247		5,072	5,700	
	0100	60" x 36" x 18"					6,325			6,325	6,975	
	0110	2 hr. rating, 30" x 16" x 15"	2 Clab	4	4		1,925	98.50		2,023.50	2,275	
	0150	30" x 20" x 20"	"	4	4		2,275	98.50		2,373.50	2,675	
	0200	1 hr. rating, 30" x 18" x 18"					1,500			1,500	1,650	
	0220	1 hr. rating, 30" x 20" x 20"	2 Clab	4	4		1,675	98.50		1,773.50	2,000	
	0250	40" x 18" x 18"					1,675			1,675	1,850	
	0300	60" x 36" x 18", double door					4,175			4,175	4,575	
	0400	Data, 4 hr. rating, 23-1/2" x 19-1/2" x 17" inside					2,250			2,250	2,475	
	0450	52" x 19" x 17"					5,500			5,500	6,050	
	0500	63" x 34" x 16", double door					8,525			8,525	9,375	
	0550	52" x 34" x 16", inside					8,000			8,000	8,800	
	0600	1 hr. rating, 27" x 19" x 16"					4,200			4,200	4,625	
	0700	63" x 34" x 16"					7,250			7,250	7,975	
	0750	Diskette, 1 hr., 14" x 12" x 11", inside					2,175			2,175	2,375	
	0800	Money, "B" label, 9" x 14" x 14"					450			450	495	
	0900	Tool resistive, 24" x 24" x 20"					2,525			2,525	2,775	
	1050	Tool and torch resistive, 24" x 24" x 20"					6,400			6,400	7,050	
	1150	Jewelers, 23" x 20" x 18"					8,200			8,200	9,000	
	1200	63" x 25" x 18"					14,600			14,600	16,000	
	1300	For handling into building, add, minimum	A-2	8.50	2.824			70	14.15	84.15	124	
	1400	Maximum	"	.78	30.769			760	154	914	1,350	

11030 | Teller & Service Equipment

		11038	Bank Equipment	CREW	DAILY OUTPUT	LABOR-HOURS	UNIT	2003 BARE COSTS				TOTAL INCL O&P	
								MAT.	LABOR	EQUIP.	TOTAL		
150	0010	BANK EQUIPMENT											150
	0020	Alarm system, police	2 Elec	1.60	10	Ea.	3,650	375		4,025	4,575	
	0100	With vault alarm	"	.40	40		14,500	1,500		16,000	18,300	
	0400	Bullet resistant teller window, 44" x 60"	1 Glaz	.60	13.333		2,600	415		3,015	3,475	
	0450	44" x 48"		.60	13.333		1,850	415		2,265	2,675	
	0500	48" x 60"		.60	13.333		3,275	415		3,690	4,225	
	3000	Counters for banks, frontal only	2 Carp	1	16	Station	1,375	505		1,880	2,300	
	3010	Counters for banks, frontal only		4	4	L.F.	340	126		466	570	
	3100	Complete with steel undercounter		.50	32	Station	2,675	1,000		3,675	4,500	
	3110	Complete with steel undercounter		2	8	L.F.	665	252		917	1,125	
	4600	Door and frame, bullet-resistant, with vision panel, minimum	2 Sswk	1.10	14.545	Ea.	2,750	520		3,270	3,975	
	4700	Maximum		1.10	14.545		3,750	520		4,270	5,075	
	4750	Door and frame, bullet resistant, 3' x 7'		1.10	14.545		3,300	520		3,820	4,575	
	4800	Drive-up window, drawer & mike, not incl. glass, minimum		1	16		3,675	570		4,245	5,050	
	4900	Maximum		.50	32		7,200	1,150		8,350	10,000	
	5000	Night depository, with chest, minimum		1	16		5,350	570		5,920	6,900	
	5100	Maximum		.50	32		7,700	1,150		8,850	10,600	
	5200	Package receiver, painted		3.20	5		1,025	178		1,203	1,450	
	5210	Package receiver										
	5240	Bullet resistant, 13" deep	2 Sswk	3.20	5	Ea.	2,025	178		2,203	2,550	

11030 | Teller & Service Equipment

11038	Bank Equipment	CREW	DAILY OUTPUT	LABOR-HOURS	UNIT	2003 BARE COSTS MAT.	LABOR	EQUIP.	TOTAL	TOTAL INCL O&P	
150	5260	24" deep	2 Sswk	3.20	5	Ea.	2,975	178		3,153	3,600	150
	5300	Stainless steel	↓	3.20	5	↓	1,725	178		1,903	2,225	
	5400	Partitions, bullet-resistant, 1-3/16" glass, 8' high	2 Carp	10	1.600	L.F.	148	50.50		198.50	242	
	5450	Acrylic		10	1.600	"	281	50.50		331.50	390	
	5460	Partition, bullet resistant, 2-1/2" thick, 1' to 12' high, level 4	↓	80	.200	S.F.	315	6.30		321.30	355	
	5500	Pneumatic tube systems, 2 lane drive-up, complete	L-3	.25	64	Total	19,300	2,200		21,500	24,600	
	5550	With T.V. viewer	"	.20	80	"	37,300	2,750		40,050	45,400	
	5570	Safety deposit boxes, minimum	1 Sswk	44	.182	Opng.	43	6.50		49.50	59	
	5580	Maximum, 10" x 15" opening		19	.421		91	15		106	128	
	5590	Teller locker, average	↓	15	.533	↓	1,175	19		1,194	1,325	
	5600	Pass thru, bullet-res. window, painted steel, 24" x 36"	2 Sswk	1.60	10	Ea.	1,575	355		1,930	2,375	
	5650	48" x 40"		1.30	12.308		2,175	440		2,615	3,200	
	5700	48" x 48"		1.20	13.333		2,000	475		2,475	3,075	
	5800	72" x 40"	↓	.80	20	↓	2,775	715		3,490	4,350	
	5900	For stainless steel frames, add					20%					
	6000	Surveillance system, 16 mm film camera, complete	2 Elec	1	16	Ea.	3,750	600		4,350	5,000	
	6010	For each additional camera, add					1,600			1,600	1,775	
	6100	Surveillance system, video camera, complete	2 Elec	1	16		11,800	600		12,400	13,900	
	6110	For each additional camera, add				↓	740			740	815	
	6120	CCTV system, see Div. 16850-600										
	6200	Twenty-four hour teller, single unit,										
	6300	automated deposit, cash and memo	L-3	.25	64	Ea.	35,700	2,200		37,900	42,600	
	7000	Vault front, see Div. 08320-950										

11150 | Parking Control Equipment

11156	Parking Equipment	CREW	DAILY OUTPUT	LABOR-HOURS	UNIT	2003 BARE COSTS MAT.	LABOR	EQUIP.	TOTAL	TOTAL INCL O&P	
600	0010	**PARKING EQUIPMENT**										600
	0020	Traffic detectors, magnetic	2 Elec	2.70	5.926	Ea.	485	223		708	870	
	0200	Single treadle		2.40	6.667		2,075	251		2,326	2,650	
	0500	Automatic gates, 8' arm, one way		1.10	14.545		3,100	545		3,645	4,250	
	0650	Two way	↓	1.10	14.545		3,250	545		3,795	4,425	
	1000	Booth for attendant, minimum					4,875			4,875	5,375	
	1050	Average					7,500			7,500	8,250	
	1150	Maximum					21,800			21,800	24,000	
	1400	Fee indicator, 1" display	2 Elec	4.10	3.902		1,625	147		1,772	2,025	
	2400	Vehicle stop stick, nail embedded, roll-out type, 16'	1 Clab	10	.800		325	19.70		344.70	390	
	2410	25'	"	10	.800		435	19.70		454.70	510	
	3500	Ticket printer and dispenser, standard	2 Elec	1.40	11.429		5,225	430		5,655	6,400	
	3600	Ticket printer and dispenser, standard tickets		1.40	11.429		2,725	430		3,155	3,650	
	3700	Rate computing		1.40	11.429		6,925	430		7,355	8,275	
	3800	Machine readable tickets		1.40	11.429		8,025	430		8,455	9,500	
	4000	Card control station, single period		4.10	3.902		835	147		982	1,125	
	4200	4 period		4.10	3.902		945	147		1,092	1,275	
	4500	Key station on pedestal		4.10	3.902		635	147		782	915	
	4750	Coin station, multiple coins		4.10	3.902		4,000	147		4,147	4,625	
	5000	Barrier gate with programmable controller		3	5.333		2,975	201		3,176	3,575	
	5020	Industrial	↓	3	5.333		4,075	201		4,276	4,775	
	5100	Card reader	1 Elec	2	4	↓	1,650	150		1,800	2,025	

11150 | Parking Control Equipment

11156	Parking Equipment	CREW	DAILY OUTPUT	LABOR-HOURS	UNIT	2003 BARE COSTS				TOTAL INCL O&P	
						MAT.	LABOR	EQUIP.	TOTAL		
600	5120	Proximity with customer display	2 Elec	1	16	Ea.	5,050	600		5,650	6,450	600
	5200	Cashier booth, average	B-22	1	30		8,675	870	245	9,790	11,200	
	5300	Collector station, pay on foot	2 Elec	.20	80		100,500	3,000		103,500	115,000	
	5320	Credit card only		.50	32		18,500	1,200		19,700	22,200	
	5500	Exit verifier		1	16		16,000	600		16,600	18,500	
	5600	Fee computer	1 Elec	1.50	5.333		12,100	201		12,301	13,600	
	5700	Full sign, 4" letters	"	2	4		1,100	150		1,250	1,450	
	5800	Inductive loop	2 Elec	4	4		155	150		305	395	
	5900	Ticket spitter with time/date stamp, standard		2	8		5,675	300		5,975	6,675	
	5920	Mag stripe encoding		2	8		17,000	300		17,300	19,200	
	5950	Vehicle detector, microprocessor based	1 Elec	3	2.667		350	100		450	530	
	6000	Parking control software, minimum		.50	16		20,100	600		20,700	23,000	
	6020	Maximum		.20	40		83,500	1,500		85,000	94,500	

11700 | Medical Equipment

11710	Medical Equipment	CREW	DAILY OUTPUT	LABOR-HOURS	UNIT	2003 BARE COSTS				TOTAL INCL O&P	
						MAT.	LABOR	EQUIP.	TOTAL		
500	0010	**MEDICAL EQUIPMENT**										500
	0390	Defibrillator, portable				Ea.				3,000	3,300	

12400 | Furnishings & Accessories

		12493	Curtains and Drapes	CREW	DAILY OUTPUT	LABOR-HOURS	UNIT	2003 BARE COSTS				TOTAL INCL O&P	
								MAT.	LABOR	EQUIP.	TOTAL		
200	0010		**DRAPERY HARDWARE**				S.F.						200
	6000		Drapes, safety, poly fabric, control bomb blast damage, installed, min				"					12	
	6010		Maximum									20	

13070 | Bullet Resistant Protection

		13071	Wallboard, Doors, Frames, Etc.	CREW	DAILY OUTPUT	LABOR-HOURS	UNIT	2003 BARE COSTS				TOTAL INCL O&P	
								MAT.	LABOR	EQUIP.	TOTAL		
100	0010		**WALLBOARD**, 7/16" T, mat only, per SF, Level 1				S.F.	7.50			7.50	8.25	100
	0020		Level 2					11.50			11.50	12.65	
	0030		Level 3					12.50			12.50	13.75	
	0040		Level 4-7					34			34	37.50	
	0050		Level 8					36			36	39.50	
	0060		Door, 3' x 7' x 1-3/4", 6 panel pine, excl frame, Level 3					2,000			2,000	2,200	
	0070		Door frame, 3' x 7', excl lock, casing & hinges, Level 3					500			500	550	
	0080		For Windows and Glazings, See Div. 08810 and 11038										

13080 | Sound, Vibration & Seismic Control

		13081	Sound Control	CREW	DAILY OUTPUT	LABOR-HOURS	UNIT	2003 BARE COSTS				TOTAL INCL O&P	
								MAT.	LABOR	EQUIP.	TOTAL		
100	0010		**ACOUSTICAL** Enclosure, 4" thick wall and ceiling panels										100
	0020		8# per S.F., up to 12' span	3 Carp	72	.333	SF Surf	25	10.50		35.50	43.50	
	0300		Better quality panels, 10.5# per S.F.		64	.375		28	11.85		39.85	49.50	
	0400		Reverb-chamber, 4" thick, parallel walls		60	.400		35	12.60		47.60	58	
	0600		Skewed wall, parallel roof, 4" thick panels		55	.436		40	13.75		53.75	65.50	
	0700		Skewed walls, skewed roof, 4" layers, 4" air space		48	.500		45	15.80		60.80	74	
	0900		Sound-absorbing panels, pntd mtl, 2'-6" x 8', under 1,000 S.F.		215	.112		9.30	3.52		12.82	15.75	
	1100		Over 1000 S.F.		240	.100		8.95	3.16		12.11	14.80	
	1200		Fabric faced		240	.100		7.25	3.16		10.41	12.95	
	1600		50% foam	3 Shee	215	.112		7.85	4.13		11.98	15	
	1700		75% foam		215	.112		7.85	4.13		11.98	15	
	1800		100% foam		215	.112		7.85	4.13		11.98	15	
	3100		Audio masking system, including speakers, amplification										
	3110		and signal generator										
	3200		Ceiling mounted, 5,000 S.F.	2 Elec	2,400	.007	S.F.	1.09	.25		1.34	1.57	
	3300		10,000 S.F.		2,800	.006		1	.21		1.21	1.42	
	3400		Plenum mounted, 5,000 S.F.		3,800	.004		.81	.16		.97	1.13	
	3500		10,000 S.F.		4,400	.004		.54	.14		.68	.79	

13120 | Pre-Engineered Structures

		13128	Pre-Engineered Structures	CREW	DAILY OUTPUT	LABOR-HOURS	UNIT	2003 BARE COSTS				TOTAL INCL O&P	
								MAT.	LABOR	EQUIP.	TOTAL		
060	0010		**PORTABLE BOOTHS** Prefab aluminum with doors, windows, ext. roof										060
	0100		lights wiring & insulation, 15 S.F. building, O.D., painted, minimum				S.F.	268			268	295	
	1400		Prefab guard shack, incl heat/lights/AC/door/glaz, excl slab, 4'x6'	2 Carp	1.50	10.667	Ea.	3,800	335		4,135	4,700	
	1410		6' x 8'		1	16		7,700	505		8,205	9,275	
	1420		8' x 8'		1	16		8,000	505		8,505	9,600	
	1430		Add for bullet-resistant glass, 1-3/16" T, per SF				S.F.	105			105	116	

13200 | Storage Tanks

13201 | Storage Tanks

			CREW	DAILY OUTPUT	LABOR-HOURS	UNIT	MAT.	LABOR	EQUIP.	TOTAL	TOTAL INCL O&P	
300	0010	**GROUND TANKS** Not incl. pipe or pumps, prestress conc., 250,000 gal.				Ea.					280,000	300
	0100	500,000 gallons									380,000	
	0300	1,000,000 gallons									540,000	
	0400	2,000,000 gallons									816,000	
	0600	4,000,000 gallons									1,290,000	
	0700	6,000,000 gallons									1,760,000	
	0750	8,000,000 gallons									2,240,000	
	0800	10,000,000 gallons									2,700,000	

13700 | Security Access and Surveillance

13710 | Security Access

			CREW	DAILY OUTPUT	LABOR-HOURS	UNIT	MAT.	LABOR	EQUIP.	TOTAL	TOTAL INCL O&P	
300	0010	**ACCESS CONTROL**				Ea.	300			300	330	300
	0020	Card type, 1 time zone, minimum					1,025			1,025	1,125	
	0040	Maximum					740			740	815	
	0060	3 time zones, minimum					1,700			1,700	1,875	
	0080	Maximum				Total	8,300			8,300	9,125	
	0100	System with printer, and control console, 3 zones				"	10,900			10,900	12,000	
	0120	6 zones				Ea.	1,225			1,225	1,350	
	0140	For each door, minimum, add					1,800			1,800	2,000	
	0160	Maximum, add	1 Elec	4	2		5,000	75		5,075	5,600	
	0200	Fingerprint scanner unit, excl striker/power supply		8	1		120	37.50		157.50	188	
	0210	Fingerprint scanner unit, for computer keyboard access		3	2.667		1,600	100		1,700	1,900	
	0220	Hand geometry scanner, mem of 512 users, excl striker/powr		8	1		225	37.50		262.50	305	
	0230	Memory upgrade for, adds 9,700 user profiles		8	1		450	37.50		487.50	550	
	0240	Adds 32,500 user profiles		3	2.667		2,150	100		2,250	2,525	
	0250	Prison type, memory of 256 users, excl striker, power		8	1		160	37.50		197.50	232	
	0260	Memory upgrade for, adds 3,300 user profiles		8	1		350	37.50		387.50	440	
	0270	Adds 9,700 user profiles		8	1		450	37.50		487.50	550	
	0280	Adds 27,900 user profiles		3	2.667		3,225	100		3,325	3,700	
	0290	All weather, mem of 512 users, excl striker/pwr		3	2.667		4,200	100		4,300	4,775	
	0300	Facial & fingerprint scanner, combination unit, excl striker/power		3	2.667		100	100		200	260	
	0310	Access for, for initial setup, excl striker/power		3	2.667		200	100		300	370	
	0320	Card reader, int/ext, basic, excl striker/power/wiring		3	2.667		200	100		300	370	
	0330	Tag reader, int/ext, basic, excl striker/power/wiring		3	2.667		150	100		250	315	
	0340	Digital keypad, int/ext, basic, excl striker/power/wiring	1 Carp	4	2		360	63		423	495	
	0350	Lockset, mechanical push-button type, complete, incl hardware	1 Elec	4	2		250	75		325	385	
	0360	Scanner/reader access, power supply/transf, 110V to 12/24V		4	2		300	75		375	440	
	0370	Elec/mag strikers, 12/24V		4	2		85	75		160	206	
	0380	1 hour battery backup power supply		4	2		150	63		213	264	
	0390	Deadbolt, digital, batt-operated, indoor/outdoor, complete, incl hardware	1 Carp	4	2							
400	0010	**ACCESS CONTROL**	1 Elec	3	2.667	Ea.	300	100		400	480	400
	0200	Video cameras, wireless, hidden in exit signs, clocks, etc, incl receiver		3	2.667		500	100		600	700	
	0210	Accessories for, VCR, single camera		3	2.667		1,500	100		1,600	1,800	
	0220	For multiple cameras		2	4		3,500	150		3,650	4,075	
	0230	Video cameras, wireless, for under vehicle searching, complete									90	
	0240	Metal detector, hand-held, wand type, unit only	1 Elec	2	4		4,000	150		4,150	4,625	
	0250	Metal detector, walk through portal type, single zone		2	4		5,000	150		5,150	5,725	
	0260	Multi zone										

13 SPECIAL CONSTRUCTION

13700 | Security Access and Surveillance

13710 | Security Access

			CREW	DAILY OUTPUT	LABOR-HOURS	UNIT	2003 BARE COSTS				TOTAL INCL O&P	
							MAT.	LABOR	EQUIP.	TOTAL		
400	0270	Explosives detector, walk through portal type	1 Elec	2	4	Ea.	3,500	150		3,650	4,075	400
	0280	Explosives detector, hand-held, battery operated									28,000	
	0290	X-ray machine, desk top, for mail/small packages/letters	1 Elec	4	2		3,000	75		3,075	3,400	
	0300	Conveyor type, incl monitor, min		2	4		14,000	150		14,150	15,600	
	0310	Maximum	↓	2	4		25,000	150		25,150	27,700	
	0320	X-ray machine, large unit, for airports, incl monitor, min	2 Elec	1	16		35,000	600		35,600	39,400	
	0330	Maximum	"	.50	32		60,000	1,200		61,200	68,000	
	0340	Counterfeit money detector									250	
	0350	Debugging kit, incl probe, headphones & monitor, complete									3,500	
	0360	Mail scanners, x-ray type, small, desk top	2 Elec	4	4		3,200	150		3,350	3,750	
	0370	Mid size, incl monitor		3	5.333		15,000	201		15,201	16,800	
	0380	Large size, incl monitor		2	8		25,000	300		25,300	28,000	
	1000	Full body imaging machine, detects metals & non-metals	↓	2	8		120,000	300		120,300	132,500	
	5000	Vehicle barriers, pop-up wedge-type, 10' W x 28" H, incl installation, min									35,000	
	5010	Maximum									47,000	
	6000	Vehicle barriers, crash beam gate, 7 ton veh cap, drop arm, min	2 Carp	1	16		45,000	505		45,505	50,500	
	6010	Maximum	"	.50	32		55,000	1,000		56,000	62,000	
	7000	Vehicle & cargo insp syst, x-ray imaging, truck-mounted, min									2,500,000	
	7010	Maximum									9,900,000	
	7020	Vehicle & cargo inspection system, x-ray imaging type, fixed, min									2,230,000	
	7030	Maximum				↓					5,500,000	

13850 | Detection & Alarm

13851 | Detection & Alarm

			CREW	DAILY OUTPUT	LABOR-HOURS	UNIT	2003 BARE COSTS				TOTAL INCL O&P	
							MAT.	LABOR	EQUIP.	TOTAL		
065	0010	**DETECTION SYSTEMS**, not including wires & conduits										065
	0100	Burglar alarm, battery operated, mechanical trigger	1 Elec	4	2	Ea.	249	75		324	385	
	0200	Electrical trigger		4	2		297	75		372	435	
	0400	For outside key control, add		8	1		70.50	37.50		108	134	
	0600	For remote signaling circuitry, add		8	1		112	37.50		149.50	179	
	0800	Card reader, flush type, standard		2.70	2.963		835	111		946	1,075	
	1000	Multi-code		2.70	2.963		1,075	111		1,186	1,350	
	1010	Card reader, proximity type		2.70	2.963		460	111		571	670	
	1200	Door switches, hinge switch		5.30	1.509		52.50	57		109.50	143	
	1400	Magnetic switch		5.30	1.509		62	57		119	153	
	1500	Door/window contact, biased		5.30	1.509		31.50	57		88.50	120	
	1510	Balance		5.30	1.509		31.50	57		88.50	120	
	1600	Exit control locks, horn alarm		4	2		310	75		385	450	
	1800	Flashing light alarm		4	2		350	75		425	495	
	2000	Indicating panels, 1 channel	↓	2.70	2.963		330	111		441	530	
	2200	10 channel	2 Elec	3.20	5		1,125	188		1,313	1,525	
	2400	20 channel		2	8		2,200	300		2,500	2,875	
	2600	40 channel	↓	1.14	14.035		4,000	530		4,530	5,200	
	2650	Residential panel, 6 zone	1 Elec	2	4		150	150		300	390	
	2700	Security system head end equip, incl switcher & control	2 Elec	.30	53.333		24,100	2,000		26,100	29,500	
	2800	Ultrasonic motion detector, 12 volt	1 Elec	2.30	3.478		206	131		337	420	
	3000	Infrared photoelectric detector		2.30	3.478		170	131		301	380	
	3200	Passive infrared detector		2.30	3.478		254	131		385	475	
	3400	Glass break alarm switch	↓	8	1	↓	42.50	37.50		80	103	

13850 | Detection & Alarm

13851	Detection & Alarm	CREW	DAILY OUTPUT	LABOR-HOURS	UNIT	2003 BARE COSTS				TOTAL INCL O&P	
						MAT.	LABOR	EQUIP.	TOTAL		
065											065
3420	Switchmats, 30" x 5'	1 Elec	5.30	1.509	Ea.	76	57		133	169	
3440	30" x 25'		4	2		182	75		257	310	
3460	Police connect panel		4	2		219	75		294	355	
3480	Telephone dialer		5.30	1.509		345	57		402	465	
3500	Alarm bell		4	2		69.50	75		144.50	189	
3520	Siren		4	2		131	75		206	256	
3540	Microwave detector, 10' to 200'		2	4		600	150		750	885	
3560	10' to 350'		2	4		1,750	150		1,900	2,150	
3570	Limit switch, HD, lever arm, weatherproof, 10 amp rated	R-19	16	1.250		65.50	47		112.50	143	
3572	Ultrasonic level sensing xmitter, sensing range: 4-20 mA output	"	4	5		2,550	189		2,739	3,100	
3574	Water level sensor, float switch, w/50' cable					430			430	475	
3590	Signal device, beacon	1 Elec	8	1		152	37.50		189.50	223	
3594	Fire, alarm control panel										
3600	4 zone	2 Elec	2	8	Ea.	920	300		1,220	1,450	
3800	8 zone		1	16		1,400	600		2,000	2,450	
4000	12 zone		.67	23.988		1,825	900		2,725	3,350	
4005	Fire alarm control panel, 12-zone					1,825			1,825	2,000	
4020	Alarm device	1 Elec	8	1		122	37.50		159.50	190	
4050	Actuating device	"	8	1		292	37.50		329.50	375	
4160	Alarm command center multiplex, addressable w/o voice large	2 Elec	.33	48.048		31,500	1,800		33,300	37,400	
4170	addressable w/ voice large	"	.30	53.333		49,900	2,000		51,900	58,000	
4175	Addressable interface device	1 Elec	7.25	1.103		205	41.50		246.50	288	
4200	Battery and rack		4	2		690	75		765	870	
4400	Automatic charger		8	1		445	37.50		482.50	545	
4405	UPS battery charger					445			445	490	
4600	Signal bell	1 Elec	8	1		49.50	37.50		87	111	
4605	Signal bell for fire alarm					49.50			49.50	54.50	
4800	Trouble buzzer or manual station	1 Elec	8	1		37	37.50		74.50	96.50	
5000	Detector, rate of rise		8	1		33.50	37.50		71	93	
5010	Detector, heat (addressable type)		7.25	1.103		150	41.50		191.50	227	
5100	Fixed temperature		8	1		28	37.50		65.50	87	
5200	Smoke detector, ceiling type		6.20	1.290		75	48.50		123.50	155	
5240	Smoke detector (addressable type)		6	1.333		150	50		200	240	
5400	Duct type		3.20	2.500		250	94		344	415	
5420	Duct (addressable type)		3.20	2.500		285	94		379	455	
5600	Strobe and horn		5.30	1.509		95	57		152	190	
5610	Strobe and horn (ADA type)		5.30	1.509		95	57		152	190	
5620	Visual alarm (ADA type)		6.70	1.194		47.50	45		92.50	120	
5800	Fire alarm horn		6.70	1.194		36.50	45		81.50	107	
6000	Door holder, electro-magnetic		4	2		77.50	75		152.50	198	
6004	Electric strike lock		5.33	1.501		90	56.50		146.50	184	
6200	Combination holder and closer		3.20	2.500		430	94		524	615	
6400	Code transmitter		4	2		690	75		765	870	
6600	Drill switch		8	1		86.50	37.50		124	151	
6800	Master box		2.70	2.963		3,100	111		3,211	3,575	
7000	Break glass station		8	1		50	37.50		87.50	111	
7005	Fire alarm break glass station					50			50	55	
7010	Break glass station, addressable	1 Elec	7.25	1.103		68	41.50		109.50	137	
7800	Remote annunciator, 8 zone lamp	"	1.80	4.444		175	167		342	445	
8000	12 zone lamp	2 Elec	2.60	6.154		300	231		531	675	
8005	Annunciator panel, 12-zone					300			300	330	
8200	16 zone lamp	2 Elec	2.20	7.273		300	273		573	740	
8400	Standpipe or sprinkler alarm, alarm device	1 Elec	8	1		125	37.50		162.50	194	
8600	Actuating device		8	1		290	37.50		327.50	375	
8700	Carbon monoxide detector, battery operated, wall mounted		16	.500		35	18.80		53.80	66.50	
8710	Carbon dioxide detector, hard wired, wall mounted		8	1		120	37.50		157.50	188	

13850 | Detection & Alarm

	13851	Detection & Alarm	CREW	DAILY OUTPUT	LABOR-HOURS	UNIT	2003 BARE COSTS				TOTAL INCL O&P	
							MAT.	LABOR	EQUIP.	TOTAL		
065	8720	Duct mounted	1 Elec	8	1	Ea.	140	37.50		177.50	210	065
	8730	Continuous air monitoring system, PC based, incl remote sensors, min	2 Elec	.25	64		40,000	2,400		42,400	47,600	
	8740	Maximum	"	.10	160	↓	200,000	6,025		206,025	229,000	
	9410	Minimum labor/equipment charge	1 Elec	4	2	Job		75		75	112	

13900 | Fire Suppression

	13910	Basic Fire Protection Matl/Methd	CREW	DAILY OUTPUT	LABOR-HOURS	UNIT	2003 BARE COSTS				TOTAL INCL O&P	
							MAT.	LABOR	EQUIP.	TOTAL		
400	0010	**FIRE HOSE AND EQUIPMENT**										400
	0200	Adapters, rough brass, straight hose threads										
	0220	One piece, female to male, rocker lugs										
	0240	1" x 1"				Ea.	21			21	23	
	0260	1-1/2" x 1"					9			9	9.90	
	0280	1-1/2" x 1-1/2"					6.75			6.75	7.45	
	0300	2" x 1-1/2"					42.50			42.50	46.50	
	0320	2" x 2"					38.50			38.50	42.50	
	0340	2-1/2" x 1-1/2"					28			28	31	
	0360	2-1/2" x 2"					18.75			18.75	20.50	
	0380	2-1/2" x 2-1/2"					13.10			13.10	14.45	
	0400	3" x 2-1/2"					35.50			35.50	39	
	0420	3" x 3"					94			94	104	
	0500	For polished brass, add					50%					
	0520	For polished chrome, add				↓	75%					
	0700	One piece, female to male, hexagon										
	0740	1-1/2" x 3/4"				Ea.	19.85			19.85	22	
	0760	2" x 1-1/2"					30.50			30.50	33.50	
	0780	2-1/2" x 1"					37.50			37.50	41.50	
	0800	2-1/2" x 1-1/2"					28.50			28.50	31.50	
	0820	2-1/2" x 2"					29.50			29.50	32	
	0840	3" x 2-1/2"					33.50			33.50	36.50	
	0900	For polished chrome, add				↓	75%					
	1100	Swivel, female to female, pin lugs										
	1120	1-1/2" x 1-1/2"				Ea.	31			31	34	
	1200	2-1/2" x 2-1/2"					60.50			60.50	67	
	1260	For polished brass, add					50%					
	1280	For polished chrome, add				↓	75%					
	1400	Couplings, sngl & dbl jacket, pin lug or rocker lug, cast brass										
	1410	1-1/2"				Ea.	26.50			26.50	29	
	1420	2-1/2"				"	35			35	38.50	
	1500	For polished brass, add					20%					
	1520	For polished chrome, add					40%					
	1580	Reducing, F x M, interior installation, cast brass										
	1590	2" x 1-1/2"				Ea.	33.50			33.50	36.50	
	1600	2-1/2" x 1-1/2"					7.50			7.50	8.25	
	1680	For polished brass, add					50%					
	1720	For polished chrome, add					75%					
	1900	Escutcheon plate, for angle valves, polished brass, 1-1/2"					10.50			10.50	11.55	
	1920	2-1/2"					25			25	27.50	
	1940	3"					23.50			23.50	25.50	
	1980	For polished chrome, add				↓	15%					

SPECIAL CONSTRUCTION **13**

13900 | Fire Suppression

			DAILY OUTPUT	LABOR-HOURS	UNIT	2003 BARE COSTS				TOTAL INCL O&P
13910		**Basic Fire Protection Matl/Methd**	CREW			MAT.	LABOR	EQUIP.	TOTAL	
400	2200	Hose, less couplings									**400**
	2260	Synthetic jacket, lined, 300 lb. test, 1-1/2" diameter	Q-12	2,600	.006	L.F.	1.47	.21		1.68	1.94
	2280	2-1/2" diameter		2,200	.007		2.45	.25		2.70	3.07
	2360	High strength, 500 lb. test, 1-1/2" diameter		2,600	.006		1.52	.21		1.73	1.99
	2380	2-1/2" diameter		2,200	.007		2.64	.25		2.89	3.27
	2600	Hose rack, swinging, for 1-1/2" diameter hose,									
	2620	Enameled steel, 50' & 75' lengths of hose	Q-12	20	.800	Ea.	32.50	27		59.50	76.50
	2640	100' and 125' lengths of hose		20	.800		32.50	27		59.50	76.50
	2680	Chrome plated, 50' and 75' lengths of hose		20	.800		50	27		77	96
	2700	100' and 125' lengths of hose		20	.800		50	27		77	96
	2780	For hose rack nipple, 1-1/2" polished brass, add					15.60			15.60	17.15
	2820	2-1/2" polished brass, add					26			26	28.50
	2840	1-1/2" polished chrome, add					16.20			16.20	17.80
	2860	2-1/2" polished chrome, add					28			28	31
	2990	Hose reel, swinging, for 1-1/2" polyester neoprene lined hose									
	3000	50' long	Q-12	14	1.143	Ea.	68.50	38.50		107	134
	3020	100' long		14	1.143		93	38.50		131.50	161
	3060	For 2-1/2" cotton rubber hose, 75' long		14	1.143		111	38.50		149.50	181
	3100	150' long		14	1.143		126	38.50		164.50	197
	3750	Hydrants, wall, w/caps, single, flush, polished brass									
	3800	2-1/2" x 2-1/2"	Q-12	5	3.200	Ea.	105	108		213	280
	3840	2-1/2" x 3"		5	3.200		141	108		249	320
	3860	3" x 3"		4.80	3.333		172	113		285	360
	3900	For polished chrome, add					20%				
	3950	Double, flush, polished brass									
	4000	2-1/2" x 2-1/2" x 4"	Q-12	5	3.200	Ea.	282	108		390	475
	4040	2-1/2" x 2-1/2" x 6"		4.60	3.478		405	118		523	630
	4080	3" x 3" x 4"		4.90	3.265		615	110		725	845
	4120	3" x 3" x 6"		4.50	3.556		635	120		755	880
	4200	For polished chrome, add					10%				
	4350	Double, projecting, polished brass									
	4400	2-1/2" x 2-1/2" x 4"	Q-12	5	3.200	Ea.	130	108		238	305
	4450	2-1/2" x 2-1/2" x 6"	"	4.60	3.478	"	251	118		369	455
	4460	Valve control, dbl. flush/projecting hydrant, cap &									
	4470	chain, ext. rod & cplg., escutcheon, polished brass	Q-12	8	2	Ea.	157	67.50		224.50	275
	4480	Four-way square, flush, polished brass									
	4540	2-1/2"(4) x 6"	Q-12	3.60	4.444	Ea.	1,550	150		1,700	1,925
	5000	Nipples, straight hose to tapered iron pipe, brass									
	5060	Female to female, 1-1/2" x 1-1/2"				Ea.	13.20			13.20	14.50
	5080	2" x 2"					14.60			14.60	16.10
	5100	2-1/2" x 2-1/2"					17.25			17.25	19
	5200	Double male or male to female, 1" x 1"					21			21	23
	5220	1-1/2" x 1"					31			31	34
	5230	1-1/2" x 1-1/2"					6.75			6.75	7.45
	5260	2" x 1-1/2"					34			34	37
	5270	2" x 2"					42.50			42.50	46.50
	5280	2-1/2" x 1-1/2"					28			28	31
	5300	2-1/2" x 2"					23			23	25
	5310	2-1/2" x 2-1/2"					13.10			13.10	14.45
	5340	For polished chrome, add					75%				
	5600	Nozzles, brass									
	5620	Adjustable fog, 3/4" booster line				Ea.	69			69	76
	5630	1" booster line					80.50			80.50	88.50
	5640	1-1/2" leader line					84.50			84.50	93
	5660	2-1/2" direct connection					165			165	182
	5680	2-1/2" playpipe nozzle					136			136	150

13910	Basic Fire Protection Matl/Methd	CREW	DAILY OUTPUT	LABOR-HOURS	UNIT	2003 BARE COSTS				TOTAL INCL O&P
						MAT.	LABOR	EQUIP.	TOTAL	
400	5780	For chrome plated, add					8%					400
5850	Electrical fire, adjustable fog, no shock									
5900	1-1/2"				Ea.	263			263	289
5920	2-1/2"					360			360	395
5980	For polished chrome, add				↓	6%				
6200	Heavy duty, comb. adj. fog and str. stream, with handle									
6210	1" booster line				Ea.	251			251	277
6240	1-1/2"					248			248	273
6260	2-1/2", for playpipe					284			284	315
6280	2-1/2" direct connection					355			355	390
6300	2-1/2" playpipe combination					510			510	560
6480	For polished chrome, add					7%				
6500	Plain fog, polished brass, 1-1/2"					43.50			43.50	48
6540	Chrome plated, 1-1/2"					44			44	48.50
6700	Plain stream, polished brass, 1-1/2" x 10"					22			22	24
6760	2-1/2" x 15" x 7/8" or 1-1/2"				↓	44			44	48.50
6860	For polished chrome, add					20%				
7000	Underwriters playpipe, 2-1/2" x 30" with 1-1/8" tip				Ea.	179			179	197
7040	Less tip				"	142			142	156
7140	Standpipe connections, wall, w/plugs & chains									
7160	Single, flush, brass, 2-1/2" x 2-1/2"	Q-12	5	3.200	Ea.	80	108		188	253
7180	2-1/2" x 3"	"	5	3.200	"	83.50	108		191.50	256
7240	For polished chrome, add					15%				
7280	Double, flush, polished brass									
7300	2-1/2" x 2-1/2" x 4"	Q-12	5	3.200	Ea.	270	108		378	460
7330	2-1/2" x 2-1/2" x 6"		4.60	3.478		365	118		483	585
7340	3" x 3" x 4"		4.90	3.265		480	110		590	695
7370	3" x 3" x 6"	↓	4.50	3.556	↓	575	120		695	810
7400	For polished chrome, add					15%				
7440	For sill cock combination, add				Ea.	45.50			45.50	50.50
7580	Double projecting, polished brass									
7600	2-1/2" x 2-1/2" x 4"	Q-12	5	3.200	Ea.	246	108		354	435
7630	2-1/2" x 2-1/2" x 6"	"	4.60	3.478	"	405	118		523	625
7680	For polished chrome, add					15%				
7900	Three way, flush, polished brass									
7920	2-1/2" (3) x 4"	Q-12	4.80	3.333	Ea.	845	113		958	1,100
7930	2-1/2" (3) x 6"	"	4.80	3.333		850	113		963	1,100
8000	For polished chrome, add				↓	9%				
8020	Three way, projecting, polished brass									
8040	2-1/2" (3) x 4"	Q-12	4.80	3.333	Ea.	595	113		708	820
8070	2-1/2" (3) x 6"	"	4.60	3.478		595	118		713	835
8100	For polished chrome, add				↓	12%				
8200	Four way, square, flush, polished brass,									
8240	2-1/2" (4) x 6"	Q-12	3.60	4.444	Ea.	1,475	150		1,625	1,850
8300	For polished chrome, add				"	10%				
8550	Wall, vertical, flush, cast brass									
8600	Two way, 2-1/2" x 2-1/2" x 4"	Q-12	5	3.200	Ea.	600	108		708	825
8660	Four way, 2-1/2" (4) x 6"		3.80	4.211		1,325	142		1,467	1,675
8680	Six way, 2-1/2" (6) x 6"	↓	3.40	4.706		1,775	159		1,934	2,200
8700	For polished chrome, add				↓	10%				
8800	Sidewalk siamese unit, polished brass, two way									
8820	2-1/2" x 2-1/2" x 4"	Q-12	2.50	6.400	Ea.	310	216		526	670
8850	2-1/2" x 2-1/2" x 6"		2	8		515	270		785	975
8860	3" x 3" x 4"		2.50	6.400		445	216		661	820
8890	3" x 3" x 6"	↓	2	8	↓	605	270		875	1,075
8940	For polished chrome, add					12%				

13900 | Fire Suppression

			CREW	DAILY OUTPUT	LABOR-HOURS	UNIT	2003 BARE COSTS				TOTAL INCL O&P
	13910	**Basic Fire Protection Matl/Methd**					MAT.	LABOR	EQUIP.	TOTAL	
400	9100	Sidewalk siamese unit, polished brass, three way										**400**
	9120	2-1/2" x 2-1/2" x 2-1/2" x 6"	Q-12	2	8	Ea.	685	270		955	1,150
	9160	For polished chrome, add					15%				
	9200	Storage house, hose only, primed steel					430			430	475
	9220	Aluminum					945			945	1,050
	9280	Hose and hydrant house, primed steel					580			580	640
	9300	Aluminum					845			845	925
	9340	Tools, crowbar and brackets	1 Carp	12	.667		58	21		79	97
	9360	Combination hydrant wrench and spanner					15.80			15.80	17.40
	9380	Fire axe and brackets									
	9400	6 lb.	1 Carp	12	.667	Ea.	60.50	21		81.50	99.50

13920 | Fire Pumps

			CREW	DAILY OUTPUT	LABOR-HOURS	UNIT	MAT.	LABOR	EQUIP.	TOTAL	TOTAL INCL O&P
400	0010	**FIRE PUMPS** Including controller, fittings and relief valve										**400**
	0030	Diesel									
	0050	500 GPM, 50 psi, 27 HP, 4" pump	Q-13	.64	50	Ea.	46,600	1,800		48,400	54,000
	0100	500 GPM, 100 psi, 62 HP, 4" pump		.60	53.333		49,300	1,900		51,200	57,000
	0150	500 GPM, 125 psi, 78 HP, 4" pump		.56	57.143		49,900	2,050		51,950	58,000
	0200	750 GPM, 50 psi, 44 HP, 5" pump		.60	53.333		49,700	1,900		51,600	57,500
	0250	750 GPM, 100 psi, 80 HP, 4" pump		.56	57.143		52,000	2,050		54,050	60,000
	0300	750 GPM, 165 psi, 203 HP, 5" pump		.52	61.538		53,500	2,200		55,700	62,500
	0350	1000 GPM, 50 psi, 48 HP, 5" pump		.58	55.172		50,000	1,975		51,975	58,000
	0400	1000 GPM, 100 psi, 89 HP, 4" pump		.56	57.143		53,500	2,050		55,550	61,500
	0450	1000 GPM, 150 psi, 148 HP, 4" pump		.48	66.667		52,500	2,375		54,875	61,000
	0470	1000 GPM, 200 psi, 280 HP, 5" pump		.40	80		66,000	2,875		68,875	77,000
	0480	1250 GPM, 75 psi, 75 HP, 5" pump		.54	59.259		50,500	2,125		52,625	58,500
	0500	1500 GPM, 50 psi, 66 HP, 6" pump		.50	64		54,000	2,300		56,300	62,500
	0550	1500 GPM, 100 psi, 140 HP, 6" pump		.46	69.565		55,000	2,500		57,500	64,500
	0600	1500 GPM, 150 psi, 228 HP, 6" pump		.42	76.190		62,000	2,725		64,725	72,500
	0650	1500 GPM, 200 psi, 279 HP, 6" pump		.38	84.211		97,500	3,025		100,525	112,000
	0700	2,000 GPM, 100 psi, 167 HP, 6" pump		.34	94.118		56,500	3,375		59,875	67,000
	0750	2000 GPM, 150 psi, 284 HP, 6"pump		.30	106		76,500	3,825		80,325	90,000
	0800	2500 GPM, 100 psi, 213 HP, 8" pump		.32	100		72,000	3,575		75,575	85,000
	0820	2500 GPM, 150 psi, 365 HP, 8" pump		.26	123		84,500	4,400		88,900	99,500
	0850	3000 GPM, 100 psi, 250 HP, 8" pump		.28	114		83,000	4,100		87,100	97,500
	0900	3000 GPM, 150 psi, 384 HP, 10" pump		.20	160		97,000	5,725		102,725	115,000
	0950	3500 GPM, 100 psi, 300 HP, 10" pump		.24	133		99,500	4,775		104,275	117,000
	1000	3500 GPM, 150 psi, 518 HP, 10" pump		.20	160		140,500	5,725		146,225	163,000
	1010	4000 GPM, 125 psi, 410 HP, 8" pump		.18	177		126,000	6,375		132,375	148,500
	1020	5000 GPM, 125 psi, 540 HP, 8" pump		.16	200		132,500	7,150		139,650	156,500
	3000	Electric									
	3100	250 GPM, 55 psi, 15 HP, 3,550 RPM, 2" pump	Q-13	.70	45.714	Ea.	10,900	1,625		12,525	14,500
	3200	500 GPM, 50 psi, 27 HP, 1770 RPM, 4" pump		.68	47.059		13,500	1,675		15,175	17,500
	3250	500 GPM, 100 psi, 47 HP, 3550 RPM, 3" pump		.66	48.485		16,500	1,725		18,225	20,700
	3300	500 GPM, 125 psi, 64 HP, 3550 RPM, 3" pump		.62	51.613		18,000	1,850		19,850	22,600
	3350	750 GPM, 50 psi, 44 HP, 1,770 RPM, 5" pump		.64	50		19,800	1,800		21,600	24,500
	3400	750 GPM, 100 psi, 66 HP, 3550 RPM, 4" pump		.58	55.172		17,500	1,975		19,475	22,300
	3450	750 GPM, 165 psi, 120 HP, 3550 RPM, 4" pump		.56	57.143		22,900	2,050		24,950	28,200
	3500	1000 GPM, 50 psi, 48 HP 1770 RPM, 5" pump		.60	53.333		19,800	1,900		21,700	24,700
	3550	1000 GPM, 100 psi, 86 HP, 3550 RPM, 5" pump		.54	59.259		22,200	2,125		24,325	27,600
	3600	1000 GPM, 150 psi, 142 HP, 3550 RPM, 5" pump		.50	64		25,200	2,300		27,500	31,200
	3650	1000 GPM, 200 psi, 245 HP, 1770 RPM, 6" pump		.36	88.889		54,500	3,175		57,675	65,000
	3660	1250 GPM, 75 psi, 75 HP, 1770 RPM, 5" pump		.55	58.182		20,300	2,075		22,375	25,600
	3700	1500 GPM, 50 psi, 66 HP, 1770 RPM, 6" pump		.50	64		21,300	2,300		23,600	27,000
	3750	1500 GPM, 100 psi, 139 HP, 1770 RPM, 6" pump		.46	69.565		24,100	2,500		26,600	30,300

13920 | Fire Pumps

		CREW	DAILY OUTPUT	LABOR-HOURS	UNIT	2003 BARE COSTS MAT.	LABOR	EQUIP.	TOTAL	TOTAL INCL O&P	
400	3800	1500 GPM, 150 psi, 200 HP, 1770 RPM, 6" pump	Q-13	.36	88.889	Ea.	51,000	3,175		54,175	61,500	400
	3850	1500 GPM, 200 psi, 279 HP, 1770 RPM, 6" pump		.32	100		56,000	3,575		59,575	67,500	
	3900	2000 GPM, 100 psi, 167 HP, 1770 RPM, 6" pump		.34	94.118		30,800	3,375		34,175	39,000	
	3950	2000 GPM, 150 psi, 292 HP, 1770 RPM, 6" pump		.28	114		41,300	4,100		45,400	51,500	
	4000	2500 GPM, 100 psi, 213 HP, 1770 RPM, 8" pump		.30	106		33,700	3,825		37,525	42,900	
	4040	2500 GPM, 135 psi, 339 HP, 1770 RPM, 8" pump		.26	123		48,200	4,400		52,600	59,500	
	4100	3000 GPM, 100 psi, 250 HP, 1770 RPM, 8" pump		.28	114		40,400	4,100		44,500	50,500	
	4150	3000 GPM, 140 psi, 428 HP, 1770 RPM, 10" pump		.24	133		64,000	4,775		68,775	78,000	
	4200	3500 GPM, 100 psi, 300 HP, 1770 RPM, 10" pump		.26	123		50,000	4,400		54,400	61,500	
	4250	3500 GPM, 140 psi, 450 HP, 1770 RPM, 10" pump		.24	133		64,000	4,775		68,775	78,000	
	5000	For jockey pump 1", 3 HP, with control, add	Q-12	2	8		2,425	270		2,695	3,075	

13930 | Wet-Pipe Fire Supp. Sprinklers

			CREW	DAILY OUTPUT	LABOR-HOURS	UNIT	MAT.	LABOR	EQUIP.	TOTAL	TOTAL INCL O&P	
400	0010	SPRINKLER SYSTEM COMPONENTS										400
	0600	Accelerator	1 Spri	8	1	Ea.	335	37.50		372.50	425	
	0800	Air compressor for dry pipe system, automatic, complete										
	0820	280 gal. system capacity, 3/4 HP	1 Spri	1.30	6.154	Ea.	720	231		951	1,150	
	0860	520 gal. system capacity, 1 HP		1.30	6.154		750	231		981	1,175	
	0910	650 gal. system capacity, 1-1/2 HP		1.30	6.154		780	231		1,011	1,200	
	0920	790 gal. system capacity, 2 HP		1.30	6.154		880	231		1,111	1,325	
	0960	Air pressure maintenance control		24	.333		139	12.50		151.50	172	
	1100	Alarm, electric pressure switch (circuit closer)		26	.308		131	11.55		142.55	162	
	1140	For explosion proof, max 20 PSI, contacts close or open		26	.308		261	11.55		272.55	305	
	1220	Water motor, complete with gong		4	2		166	75		241	297	
	1400	Deluge system, pressured monitoring panel, 120V		18	.444		785	16.70		801.70	890	
	1600	Dehydrator package, incl. valves and nipples		12	.667		286	25		311	355	
	1800	Firecycle system, controls, includes panel,										
	1820	batteries, solenoid valves and pressure switches	Q-13	1	32	Ea.	7,775	1,150		8,925	10,300	
	1980	Detector	1 Spri	16	.500		285	18.80		303.80	345	
	2000	Release, emergency, manual, for hydraulic or pneumatic system		12	.667		87.50	25		112.50	134	
	2060	Release, thermostatic, for hydraulic or pneumatic release line		20	.400		266	15		281	315	
	2200	Sprinkler cabinets, 6 head capacity		16	.500		31	18.80		49.80	62.50	
	2260	12 head capacity		16	.500		33	18.80		51.80	64.50	
	2340	Sprinkler head escutcheons, standard, brass tone, 1" size		40	.200		3.07	7.50		10.57	14.80	
	2360	Chrome, 1" size		40	.200		1.59	7.50		9.09	13.15	
	2365	Sprinkler head escutcheon					1.59			1.59	1.75	
	2400	Recessed type, brass tone	1 Spri	40	.200		3.96	7.50		11.46	15.75	
	2440	Chrome or white enamel	"	40	.200		1.78	7.50		9.28	13.35	
	2600	Sprinkler heads, not including supply piping										
	2610	Deluge sprinkler head										
	2612	3/8" automatic	1 Spri	16	.500	Ea.	9.90	18.80		28.70	39.50	
	2614	1/2" pendant, with open head		16	.500		10.80	18.80		29.60	40.50	
	2616	1/2" pendant, open head with canopy		16	.500		10.80	18.80		29.60	40.50	
	2640	Dry, pendent, 1/2" orifice, 3/4" or 1" NPT										
	2660	1/2" to 6" length	1 Spri	14	.571	Ea.	34.50	21.50		56	70.50	
	2670	6-1/4" to 9" length		14	.571		37	21.50		58.50	73	
	2680	9-1/4" to 12" length		14	.571		39.50	21.50		61	76	
	2690	12-1/4" to 15" length		14	.571		42	21.50		63.50	78.50	
	2700	15-1/4" to 18" length		14	.571		44.50	21.50		66	81.50	
	2710	18-1/4" to 21" length		13	.615		47	23		70	86.50	
	2720	21-1/4" to 24" length		13	.615		49.50	23		72.50	89.50	
	2730	24-1/4" to 27" length		13	.615		52	23		75	92	
	2740	27-1/4" to 30" length		13	.615		53.50	23		76.50	94	
	2750	30-1/4" to 33" length		13	.615		57	23		80	97.50	
	2760	33-1/4" to 36" length		13	.615		59.50	23		82.50	101	

SPECIAL CONSTRUCTION 13

13900 | Fire Suppression

	13930	Wet-Pipe Fire Supp. Sprinklers	CREW	DAILY OUTPUT	LABOR-HOURS	UNIT	MAT.	2003 BARE COSTS LABOR	EQUIP.	TOTAL	TOTAL INCL O&P	
400	2780	36-1/4" to 39" length	1 Spri	12	.667	Ea.	62	25		87	106	400
	2790	39-1/4" to 42" length	↓	12	.667		64.50	25		89.50	109	
	2800	For each inch or fraction, add					.84			.84	.92	
	3600	Foam-water, pendent or upright, 1/2" NPT	1 Spri	12	.667	↓	50	25		75	93	
	3700	Standard spray, pendent or upright, brass, 135° to 286°F										
	3720	1/2" NPT, 3/8" orifice	1 Spri	16	.500	Ea.	6	18.80		24.80	35	
	3730	1/2" NPT, 7/16" orifice		16	.500		6	18.80		24.80	35	
	3732	1/2" NPT, 7/16" orifice, chrome		16	.500		6.30	18.80		25.10	35.50	
	3740	1/2" NPT, 1/2" orifice		16	.500		4.55	18.80		23.35	33.50	
	3760	1/2" NPT, 17/32" orifice		16	.500		5.20	18.80		24	34.50	
	3780	3/4" NPT, 17/32" orifice	↓	16	.500	↓	4.95	18.80		23.75	34	
	3800	For open sprinklers, deduct					15%					
	3840	For chrome, add				Ea.	1.13			1.13	1.24	
	3860	For wax and lead coating, add					5.50			5.50	6.05	
	3880	For wax coating, add					2.50			2.50	2.75	
	3900	For lead coating, add				↓	3			3	3.30	
	3920	For 360°F, same cost										
	3930	For 400°F, add				Ea.	5.50			5.50	6.05	
	3940	For 500°F, add				"	5.50			5.50	6.05	
	4200	Sidewall, vertical brass, 135 -286°F										
	4240	1/2" NPT, 1/2" orifice	1 Spri	16	.500	Ea.	7	18.80		25.80	36	
	4280	3/4" NPT, 17/32" orifice	"	16	.500		7.50	18.80		26.30	37	
	4360	For satin chrome, add				↓	1			1	1.10	
	4400	For 360°F, same cost										
	4410	For 400°F, add				Ea.	5.50			5.50	6.05	
	4420	For 500°F, add				"	7			7	7.70	
	4500	Sidewall, horizontal, brass, 135° to 286°F										
	4520	1/2" NPT, 1/2" orifice	1 Spri	16	.500	Ea.	6	18.80		24.80	35	
	4540	For 360°F, same cost										
	4800	Recessed pendent, brass, 135° to 286°F										
	4820	1/2" NPT, 3/8" orifice	1 Spri	10	.800	Ea.	14.50	30		44.50	61.50	
	4830	1/2" NPT, 7/16" orifice		10	.800		10.25	30		40.25	57	
	4840	1/2" NPT, 1/2" orifice		10	.800		12	30		42	58.50	
	4860	1/2" NPT, 17/32" orifice	↓	10	.800		9.55	30		39.55	56	
	4900	For satin chrome, add				↓	.75			.75	.83	
	5000	Recessed-vertical sidewall, brass, 135°-286°F										
	5020	1/2" NPT, 3/8" orifice	1 Spri	10	.800	Ea.	11.25	30		41.25	58	
	5030	1/2" NPT, 7/16" orifice		10	.800		11	30		41	57.50	
	5040	1/2" NPT, 1/2" orifice	↓	10	.800	↓	10.25	30		40.25	57	
	5100	For bright nickel, same cost										
	5600	Concealed, complete with cover plate										
	5620	1/2" NPT, 1/2" orifice, 135°F to 212°F	1 Spri	9	.889	Ea.	14	33.50		47.50	66	
	5800	Window, brass, 1/2" NPT, 1/4" orifice		16	.500		13.25	18.80		32.05	43	
	5810	1/2" NPT, 5/16" orifice		16	.500		13.25	18.80		32.05	43	
	5820	1/2" NPT, 3/8" orifice		16	.500		13.25	18.80		32.05	43	
	5830	1/2" NPT, 7/16" orifice		16	.500		13.25	18.80		32.05	43	
	5840	1/2" NPT, 1/2" orifice	↓	16	.500		14.05	18.80		32.85	44	
	5860	For polished chrome, add					1.95			1.95	2.15	
	5880	3/4" NPT, 5/8" orifice	1 Spri	16	.500		14.65	18.80		33.45	44.50	
	5890	3/4 NPT, 3/4" orifice	"	16	.500		14.65	18.80		33.45	44.50	
	6000	Sprinkler head guards, bright zinc, 1/2" NPT					2.37			2.37	2.61	
	6020	Bright zinc, 3/4" NPT				↓	2.37			2.37	2.61	
	6025	Residential sprinkler components, (one and two family)										
	6026	Water motor alarm, with strainer	1 Spri	4	2	Ea.	166	75		241	297	
	6027	Fast response, glass bulb, 135° to 155° f.										
	6028	1/2" NPT, pendent, brass	1 Spri	16	.500	Ea.	9.05	18.80		27.85	38.50	

13930 | Wet-Pipe Fire Supp. Sprinklers

		CREW	DAILY OUTPUT	LABOR-HOURS	UNIT	2003 BARE COSTS				TOTAL INCL O&P
						MAT.	LABOR	EQUIP.	TOTAL	
400	6029	1/2" NPT, sidewall, brass	1 Spri	16	.500	Ea.	9.45	18.80		28.25	39	400
6030	1/2" NPT, pendent, brass, extended coverage		16	.500		9.45	18.80		28.25	39
6031	1/2" NPT, sidewall, brass, extended coverage		16	.500		9	18.80		27.80	38.50
6032	3/4" NPT sidewall, brass, extended coverage		16	.500		9.45	18.80		28.25	39
6033	For chrome, add					15%				
6034	For polyester/teflon coating add					20%				
6100	Sprinkler head wrenches, standard head				Ea.	14			14	15.40
6120	Recessed head					14.50			14.50	15.95
6160	Tamper switch, (valve supervisory switch)	1 Spri	16	.500		54.50	18.80		73.30	88.50
6200	Valves									
6210	Alarm, includes									
6220	retard chamber, trim, gauges, alarm line strainer									
6260	3" size	Q-12	3	5.333	Ea.	745	180		925	1,100
6280	4" size	"	2	8		755	270		1,025	1,250
6300	6" size	Q-13	4	8		840	286		1,126	1,350
6320	8" size	"	3	10.667		995	380		1,375	1,675
6330	Alarm, dry system									
6340	4"	Q-12	3	5.333	Ea.	2,100	180		2,280	2,575
6350	6"	"	2	8	"	2,700	270		2,970	3,375
6500	Check, swing, C.I. body, brass fittings, auto. ball drip									
6520	4" size	Q-12	3	5.333	Ea.	141	180		321	430
6540	6" size	Q-13	4	8		261	286		547	720
6580	8" size	"	3	10.667		490	380		870	1,125
6800	Check, wafer, butterfly type, C.I. body, bronze fittings									
6820	4" size	Q-12	4	4	Ea.	152	135		287	370
6840	6" size	Q-13	5.50	5.818		261	208		469	600
6860	8" size		5	6.400		470	229		699	865
6880	10" size		4.50	7.111		710	255		965	1,175
7000	Deluge, assembly, incl. trim, pressure									
7020	operated relief, emergency release, gauges									
7040	2" size	Q-12	2	8	Ea.	1,000	270		1,270	1,500
7060	3" size		1.50	10.667		1,175	360		1,535	1,850
7080	4" size		1	16		1,425	540		1,965	2,375
7100	6" size	Q-13	1.80	17.778		1,750	635		2,385	2,900
7800	Pneumatic actuator, bronze, required on all									
7820	pneumatic release systems, any size deluge	1 Spri	18	.444	Ea.	166	16.70		182.70	209
8000	Dry pipe air check valve, 3" size	Q-12	2	8		990	270		1,260	1,500
8200	Dry pipe valve, incl. trim and gauges, 3" size		2	8		1,050	270		1,320	1,550
8220	4" size		1	16		1,175	540		1,715	2,125
8240	6" size	Q-13	2	16		1,350	575		1,925	2,350
8280	For accelerator trim with gauges, add	1 Spri	8	1		360	37.50		397.50	450
8400	Firecycle package, includes swing check									
8420	and flow control valves with required trim									
8440	2" size	Q-12	2	8	Ea.	1,225	270		1,495	1,750
8460	3" size		1.50	10.667		1,900	360		2,260	2,625
8480	4" size		1	16		2,125	540		2,665	3,150
8500	6" size	Q-13	1.40	22.857		2,875	820		3,695	4,400
8800	Flow control valve, includes trim and gauges, 2" size	Q-12	2	8		1,075	270		1,345	1,575
8820	3" size	"	1.50	10.667		1,275	360		1,635	1,950
8840	4" size	Q-13	2.80	11.429		1,500	410		1,910	2,275
8860	6" size	"	2	16		1,600	575		2,175	2,625
9200	Pressure operated relief valve, brass body	1 Spri	18	.444		119	16.70		135.70	157
9600	Waterflow indicator, with recycling retard and									
9610	two single pole retard switches, 2" thru 6" pipe size	1 Spri	8	1	Ea.	109	37.50		146.50	177

13900 | Fire Suppression

		13960 | **CO2 Fire Extinguishing**	CREW	DAILY OUTPUT	LABOR-HOURS	UNIT	2003 BARE COSTS				TOTAL INCL O&P	
							MAT.	LABOR	EQUIP.	TOTAL		
200	0010	**AUTOMATIC FIRE SUPPRESSION SYSTEMS**										200
	0040	For detectors and control stations, see division 13850										
	0100	Control panel, single zone with batteries (2 zones det., 1 suppr.)	1 Elec	1	8	Ea.	1,275	300		1,575	1,850	
	0150	Multizone (4) with batteries (8 zones det., 4 suppr.)	"	.50	16		2,450	600		3,050	3,600	
	1000	Dispersion nozzle, CO2, 3" x 5"	1 Plum	18	.444		50	16.60		66.60	80	
	1100	FM200, 1-1/2"	"	14	.571		50	21.50		71.50	87	
	2000	Extinguisher, CO2 system, high pressure, 75 lb. cylinder	Q-1	6	2.667		950	89.50		1,039.50	1,175	
	2010	Duplex 75 lb. cylinders	"	3	5.333	▼	1,900	179		2,079	2,375	
	2080	1/2" rubber tubing	1 Plum	300	.027	L.F.	1.06	1		2.06	2.67	
	2100	100 lb. cylinder	Q-1	5	3.200	Ea.	1,025	108		1,133	1,300	
	2400	FM200 system, filled, with mounting bracket										
	2460	26 lb. container	Q-1	8	2	Ea.	1,800	67.50		1,867.50	2,075	
	2480	44 lb. container		7	2.286		2,400	77		2,477	2,775	
	2500	63 lb. container		6	2.667		2,800	89.50		2,889.50	3,200	
	2520	101 lb. container		5	3.200		3,750	108		3,858	4,300	
	2540	196 lb. container	▼	4	4		5,800	135		5,935	6,575	
	3000	Electro/mechanical release	L-1	4	4		125	150		275	365	
	3400	Manual pull station	1 Plum	6	1.333		45	50		95	125	
	4000	Pneumatic damper release	"	8	1	▼	175	37.50		212.50	250	
	6000	Average FM200 system, minimum				C.F.	1.25			1.25	1.38	
	6020	Maximum				"	2.50			2.50	2.75	

15800 | Air Distribution

15820 | Duct Accessories

			CREW	DAILY OUTPUT	LABOR-HOURS	UNIT	2003 BARE COSTS				TOTAL INCL O&P
							MAT.	LABOR	EQUIP.	TOTAL	
300	0010	**DUCT ACCESSORIES**									300
	8300	Relief damper, electronic bypass with tight seal									
	8310	8" x 6"	1 Shee	22	.364	Ea.	101	13.45		114.45	132
	8314	10" x 6"		22	.364		114	13.45		127.45	146
	8318	10" x 10"		21	.381		147	14.10		161.10	184
	8322	12" x 12"		20	.400		158	14.80		172.80	196
	8326	12" x 16"		19	.421		164	15.60		179.60	204
	8330	16" x 10"		20	.400		158	14.80		172.80	197
	8334	16" x 14"		18	.444		165	16.45		181.45	208
	8338	16" x 18"		17	.471		182	17.40		199.40	227
	8342	18" x 12"		18	.444		164	16.45		180.45	207
	8346	18" x 18"		15	.533		171	19.75		190.75	219
	8354	20" x 18"		13	.615		175	23		198	227
	8358	24" x 12"		13	.615		182	23		205	236
	8363	24" x 24"		10	.800		204	29.50		233.50	270
	8365	24" x 48"		6	1.333		264	49.50		313.50	365
	8378	30" x 18"		8	1		199	37		236	276
	8382	30" x 24"		6	1.333		197	49.50		246.50	293
	8390	46" x 36"		4	2		277	74		351	420
	8394	48" x 48"		3	2.667		320	98.50		418.50	500
	8396	54" x 36"		2	4		340	148		488	605

15860 | Air Cleaning Devices

			CREW	DAILY OUTPUT	LABOR-HOURS	UNIT	MAT.	LABOR	EQUIP.	TOTAL	TOTAL INCL O&P
100	0010	**AIR FILTERS**									100
	0050	Activated charcoal type, full flow				MCFM	600			600	660
	0060	Activated charcoal type, full flow, impregnated media 12" deep					175			175	193
	0070	Activated charcoal type, HEPA filter & frame for field erection					175			175	193
	0080	Activated charcoal type, HEPA filter-diffuser, ceiling install.					165			165	182
	0500	Chemical media filtration type									
	1100	Industrial air fume & odor scrubber unit w/pump & motor									
	1110	corrosion resistant PVC construction									
	1120	Single pack filter, horizontal type									
	1130	500 CFM	Q-9	14	1.143	Ea.	3,800	38		3,838	4,225
	1140	1000 CFM		11	1.455		4,450	48.50		4,498.50	4,975
	1150	2000 CFM		8	2		5,400	66.50		5,466.50	6,050
	1160	3000 CFM		7	2.286		6,250	76		6,326	7,025
	1170	5000 CFM		5	3.200		8,150	107		8,257	9,150
	1180	8000 CFM		4	4		11,400	133		11,533	12,700
	1190	12,000 CFM		3	5.333		15,100	178		15,278	16,900
	1200	16,000 CFM		2.50	6.400		18,700	213		18,913	20,800
	1210	20,000 CFM		2	8		23,400	266		23,666	26,200
	1220	26,000 CFM		1.50	10.667		27,000	355		27,355	30,300
	1230	30,000 CFM	Q-10	2	12		30,700	415		31,115	34,300
	1240	40,000 CFM	"	1.50	16		40,100	550		40,650	45,000
	1250	50,000 CFM	Q-11	2	16		48,800	565		49,365	54,500
	1260	55,000 CFM		1.80	17.778		53,500	625		54,125	59,500
	1270	60,000 CFM		1.50	21.333		57,500	755		58,255	64,000
	1300	Double pack filter, horizontal type									
	1310	500 CFM	Q-9	10	1.600	Ea.	4,950	53.50		5,003.50	5,525
	1320	1000 CFM		8	2		5,925	66.50		5,991.50	6,625
	1330	2000 CFM		6	2.667		7,150	89		7,239	7,975
	1340	3000 CFM		5	3.200		8,550	107		8,657	9,575
	1350	5000 CFM		4	4		10,900	133		11,033	12,100
	1360	8000 CFM		3	5.333		14,300	178		14,478	16,100
	1370	12,000 CFM		2.50	6.400		19,500	213		19,713	21,700

15800 | Air Distribution

			DAILY	LABOR-			2003 BARE COSTS				TOTAL	
15860	**Air Cleaning Devices**	CREW	OUTPUT	HOURS	UNIT	MAT.	LABOR	EQUIP.	TOTAL		INCL O&P	
100	1380	16,000 CFM	Q-9	2	8	Ea.	25,400	266		25,666	28,300	100
	1390	20,000 CFM		1.50	10.667		30,800	355		31,155	34,500	
	1400	26,000 CFM		1	16		35,700	535		36,235	40,000	
	1410	30,000 CFM	Q-10	1.50	16		41,800	550		42,350	46,900	
	1420	40,000 CFM	"	1.30	18.462		53,500	635		54,135	60,000	
	1430	50,000 CFM	Q-11	1.50	21.333		67,000	755		67,755	74,500	
	1440	55,000 CFM		1.30	24.615		73,000	870		73,870	82,000	
	1450	60,000 CFM		1	32		79,500	1,125		80,625	89,000	
	1500	Single pack filter, vertical type										
	1510	500 CFM	Q-9	24	.667	Ea.	3,625	22		3,647	4,025	
	1520	1000 CFM		18	.889		4,300	29.50		4,329.50	4,775	
	1530	2000 CFM		12	1.333		5,150	44.50		5,194.50	5,725	
	1540	3000 CFM		9	1.778		6,000	59		6,059	6,725	
	1550	5000 CFM		6	2.667		8,000	89		8,089	8,950	
	1560	8000 CFM		4	4		11,400	133		11,533	12,700	
	1570	12,000 CFM		3	5.333		15,500	178		15,678	17,400	
	1580	16,000 CFM		2	8		18,200	266		18,466	20,400	
	1590	20,000 CFM		1.80	8.889		22,900	296		23,196	25,700	
	1600	24,000 CFM		1.60	10		25,600	335		25,935	28,600	
	1650	Double pack filter, vertical type										
	1660	500 CFM	Q-9	22	.727	Ea.	4,700	24		4,724	5,225	
	1670	1000 CFM		16	1		5,625	33.50		5,658.50	6,225	
	1680	2000 CFM		10	1.600		6,750	53.50		6,803.50	7,500	
	1690	3000 CFM		7	2.286		7,925	76		8,001	8,850	
	1700	5000 CFM		5	3.200		10,400	107		10,507	11,600	
	1710	8000 CFM		3	5.333		14,200	178		14,378	15,900	
	1720	12,000 CFM		2.50	6.400		19,200	213		19,413	21,400	
	1730	16,000 CFM		2	8		24,100	266		24,366	27,000	
	1740	20,000 CFM		1.50	10.667		30,100	355		30,455	33,700	
	1750	24,000 CFM		1	16		33,600	535		34,135	37,800	
	1800	Inlet or outlet transition, horizontal										
	1810	Single pack to 12,000 CFM, add					4%					
	1820	Single pack to 30,000 CFM, add					6%					
	1830	Single pack to 60,000 CFM, add					8%					
	1840	Double pack to 12,000 CFM, add					3%					
	1850	Double pack to 30,000 CFM, add					5%					
	1860	Double pack to 60,000 CFM, add					6%					
	1870	Inlet or outlet transition, vertical										
	1880	Single pack to 5000 CFM, add					2%					
	1890	Single pack to 24,000 CFM, add					3%					
	1900	Double pack to 24,000 CFM, add					2%					
	2000	Electronic air cleaner, duct mounted										
	2150	400 - 1000 CFM	1 Shee	2.30	3.478	Ea.	660	129		789	925	
	2200	1000 - 1400 CFM		2.20	3.636		685	135		820	965	
	2250	1400 - 2000 CFM		2.10	3.810		760	141		901	1,050	
	2260	2000 - 2500 CFM		2	4		780	148		928	1,100	
	2950	Mechanical media filtration units										
	3000	High efficiency type, with frame, non-supported				MCFM	45			45	49.50	
	3100	Supported type					55			55	60.50	
	4000	Medium efficiency, extended surface					5			5	5.50	
	4500	Permanent washable					20			20	22	
	5000	Renewable disposable roll					120			120	132	
	5500	Throwaway glass or paper media type				Ea.	4.60			4.60	5.05	
	5505	Air filter, glass/paper media					4.60			4.60	5.05	
	5610	Filter for 37,570 CFM, .15 S.P. drop, w/detergent wash	Q-10	.40	60		1,025	2,075		3,100	4,325	
	5620	46,650 CFM, .15 S.P. drop, w/detergent wash	"	.40	60		1,250	2,075		3,325	4,575	

15860 | Air Cleaning Devices

		CREW	DAILY OUTPUT	LABOR-HOURS	UNIT	2003 BARE COSTS				TOTAL INCL O&P
						MAT.	LABOR	EQUIP.	TOTAL	
100	5800	Filter, bag type									100
	5810	90-95% efficiency									
	5820	24" x 12" x 29", .75-1.25 MCFM	1 Shee	1.90	4.211	Ea.	32.50	156		188.50	277
	5830	24" x 24" x 29", 1.5-2.5 MCFM	"	1.90	4.211	"	63	156		219	310
	5850	80-85% efficiency									
	5860	24" x 12" x 29", .75-1.25 MCFM	1 Shee	1.90	4.211	Ea.	29	156		185	273
	5870	24" x 24" x 29", 1.5-2.5 MCFM	"	1.90	4.211	"	51.50	156		207.50	298
	6000	HEPA filter complete w/particle board,									
	6010	kraft paper frame, separator material									
	6020	95% DOP efficiency									
	6030	12" x 12" x 6", 150 CFM	1 Shee	3.70	2.162	Ea.	29.50	80		109.50	157
	6034	24" x 12" x 6", 375 CFM		1.90	4.211		31.50	156		187.50	276
	6038	24" x 18" x 6", 450 CFM		1.90	4.211		40	156		196	285
	6042	24" x 24" x 6", 700 CFM		1.90	4.211		47	156		203	293
	6046	12" x 12" x 12", 250 CFM		3.70	2.162		40	80		120	168
	6050	24" x 12" x 12", 500 CFM		1.90	4.211		47	156		203	293
	6054	24" x 18" x 12", 875 CFM		1.90	4.211		63.50	156		219.50	310
	6058	24" x 24" x 12", 1000 CFM		1.90	4.211		66	156		222	315
	6100	99% DOP efficiency									
	6110	12" x 12" x 6", 150 CFM	1 Shee	3.70	2.162	Ea.	50	80		130	179
	6114	24" x 12" x 6", 325 CFM		1.90	4.211		55	156		211	300
	6118	24" x 18" x 6", 550 CFM		1.90	4.211		77	156		233	325
	6122	24" x 24" x 6", 775 CFM		1.90	4.211		79	156		235	330
	6126	12" x 12" x 12", 250 CFM		3.60	2.222		56.50	82		138.50	189
	6130	24" x 12" x 12", 500 CFM		1.90	4.211		68	156		224	315
	6134	24" x 18" x 12", 775 CFM		1.90	4.211		109	156		265	360
	6138	24" x 24" x 12", 1100 CFM		1.90	4.211		114	156		270	365
	6500	HEPA filter housing, 14 ga. galv. sheet metal									
	6510	12" x 12" x 6"	1 Shee	2.50	3.200	Ea.	450	118		568	680
	6514	24" x 12" x 6"		2	4		500	148		648	780
	6518	12" x 12" x 12"		2.40	3.333		450	123		573	685
	6522	14" x 12" x 12"		2.30	3.478		500	129		629	750
	6526	24" x 18" x 6"		1.90	4.211		585	156		741	880
	6530	24" x 24" x 6"		1.80	4.444		585	164		749	895
	6534	24" x 48" x 6"		1.70	4.706		780	174		954	1,125
	6538	24" x 72" x 6"		1.60	5		1,000	185		1,185	1,375
	6542	24" x 18" x 12"		1.80	4.444		585	164		749	895
	6546	24" x 24" x 12"		1.70	4.706		585	174		759	910
	6550	24" x 48" x 12"		1.60	5		780	185		965	1,150
	6554	24" x 72" x 12"		1.50	5.333		1,000	197		1,197	1,400
	6558	48" x 48" x 6"	Q-9	2.80	5.714		1,125	190		1,315	1,525
	6562	48" x 72" x 6"		2.60	6.154		1,400	205		1,605	1,875
	6566	48" x 96" x 6"		2.40	6.667		1,575	222		1,797	2,075
	6570	48" x 48" x 12"		2.70	5.926		1,125	197		1,322	1,525
	6574	48" x 72" x 12"		2.50	6.400		1,400	213		1,613	1,875
	6578	48" x 96" x 12"		2.30	6.957		1,575	232		1,807	2,075
	6582	114" x 72" x 12"		2	8		2,400	266		2,666	3,050
	8000	Portable, remove bioterrorist hazard w/HEPA filter, 110V, 700 CFM	2 Clab	12	1.333		5,000	33		5,033	5,550
	8010	110V, 1000 CFM		12	1.333		6,600	33		6,633	7,300
	8020	110V, 2000 CFM		12	1.333		8,000	33		8,033	8,850

MECHANICAL 15

16100 | Wiring Methods

		16139	Residential Wiring	CREW	DAILY OUTPUT	LABOR-HOURS	UNIT	2003 BARE COSTS				TOTAL INCL O&P	
								MAT.	LABOR	EQUIP.	TOTAL		
700	0010		**RESIDENTIAL WIRING**										700
	0020		20' avg. runs and #14/2 wiring incl. unless otherwise noted										
	1000		Service & panel, includes 24' SE-AL cable, service eye, meter,										
	1010		Socket, panel board, main bkr., ground rod, 15 or 20 amp										
	6410		Outdoor PAR floodlights, 1 lamp, 150 watt	1 Elec	20	.400	Ea.	20	15.05		35.05	44.50	
	6420		2 lamp, 150 watt each		20	.400		33.50	15.05		48.55	59.50	
	6430		For infrared security sensor, add	↓	32	.250	↓	87	9.40		96.40	110	

16200 | Electrical Power

		16221	Fuel Cells	CREW	DAILY OUTPUT	LABOR-HOURS	UNIT	2003 BARE COSTS				TOTAL INCL O&P	
								MAT.	LABOR	EQUIP.	TOTAL		
950	0010		**FUEL CELLS**				System	860,000			860,000	946,000	950
	2000		Large comm units, 200KW, 480/277V, burns natural gas, unit only									1,050,000	
	2001		Complete system, natural gas, installed, 200 kW									1,980,000	
	2002		400 kW									2,795,000	
	2003		600 kW									3,660,000	
	2004		800 kW									4,575,000	
	2005		1000 kW				↓						
	2010		Comm type, for battery charging, uses hydrogen, 100 watt, 12V				Ea.	2,175			2,175	2,400	
	2020		500 watt, 12V					4,450			4,450	4,900	
	2030		1000 watt, 48V				↓	7,250			7,250	7,975	

		16230	Generator Assemblies	CREW	DAILY OUTPUT	LABOR-HOURS	UNIT	2003 BARE COSTS				TOTAL INCL O&P	
								MAT.	LABOR	EQUIP.	TOTAL		
450	0010		**GENERATOR SET**										450
	0020		Gas or gasoline operated, includes battery,										
	0050		charger, muffler & transfer switch										
	0200		3 phase 4 wire, 277/480 volt, 7.5 kW	R-3	.83	24.096	Ea.	6,000	890	197	7,087	8,150	
	0300		11.5 kW		.71	28.169		8,500	1,050	230	9,780	11,200	
	0400		20 kW		.63	31.746		10,000	1,175	259	11,434	13,000	
	0500		35 kW		.55	36.364		12,000	1,350	297	13,647	15,600	
	0520		60 kW		.50	40		16,500	1,475	325	18,300	20,800	
	0600		80 kW		.40	50		20,500	1,850	410	22,760	25,800	
	0700		100 kW		.33	60.606		22,500	2,250	495	25,245	28,700	
	0800		125 kW		.28	71.429		46,000	2,650	585	49,235	55,000	
	0900		185 kW	↓	.25	80		61,000	2,950	655	64,605	72,000	
	0905		Generator set, gas/gasoline, 185kW					61,000			61,000	67,000	
	1000		Gas turbine, 2500 kW, 3125 kVA, 1800 rpm	R-13	.05	840						1,808,500	
	1005		Generator set, gas turbine, 2500kW									1,760,000	
	1100		9000 kW, 4812 KVA, 14500 rpm	R-13	.02	2,100	↓					1,882,000	
	2000		Diesel engine, including battery, charger,										
	2010		muffler, automatic transfer switch & day tank, 30 kW	R-3	.55	36.364	Ea.	16,000	1,350	297	17,647	20,000	
	2020		40 kW		.49	40.816		18,500	1,500	335	20,335	23,000	
	2100		50 kW		.42	47.619		19,700	1,775	390	21,865	24,800	
	2110		60 kW		.39	51.282		21,300	1,900	420	23,620	26,700	
	2200		75 kW		.35	57.143		25,700	2,125	465	28,290	32,000	
	2220		80 kW		.34	58.824		27,800	2,175	480	30,455	34,400	
	2300		100 kW		.31	64.516		28,500	2,400	525	31,425	35,600	
	2400		125 kW		.29	68.966		30,000	2,550	565	33,115	37,400	
	2500		150 kW	↓	.26	76.923	↓	34,400	2,850	630	37,880	42,800	

16200 | Electrical Power

16230 | Generator Assemblies

			CREW	DAILY OUTPUT	LABOR-HOURS	UNIT	2003 BARE COSTS				TOTAL INCL O&P
							MAT.	LABOR	EQUIP.	TOTAL	
450	2600	175 kW	R-3	.25	80	Ea.	37,500	2,950	655	41,105	46,400	450
	2700	200 kW		.24	83.333		38,700	3,075	680	42,455	48,000
	2800	250 kW		.23	86.957		45,600	3,225	710	49,535	55,500
	2850	275 kW		.22	90.909		45,600	3,375	740	49,715	56,000
	2900	300 kW		.22	90.909		49,300	3,375	740	53,415	60,000
	3000	350 kW		.20	100		55,500	3,700	815	60,015	68,000
	3100	400 kW		.19	105		69,000	3,900	860	73,760	82,500
	3200	500 kW		.18	111		86,500	4,125	905	91,530	102,000
	3220	600 kW		.17	117		113,500	4,350	960	118,810	132,500
	3225	Generator set, diesel, 600kW	▼				113,500			113,500	125,000
	3230	650 kW	R-13	.38	110		135,000	3,950	445	139,395	155,000
	3240	750 kW		.38	110		142,500	3,950	445	146,895	163,500
	3250	800 kW		.36	116		148,000	4,175	470	152,645	170,000
	3260	900 kW		.31	135		171,000	4,850	545	176,395	196,000
	3270	1000 kW	▼	.27	155	▼	176,000	5,550	625	182,175	203,000

16260 | Static Power Converters

			CREW	DAILY OUTPUT	LABOR-HOURS	UNIT	2003 BARE COSTS				TOTAL INCL O&P
							MAT.	LABOR	EQUIP.	TOTAL	
800	0010	**UNINTERRUPTIBLE POWER SUPPLY/CONDITIONER TRANSFORMERS**										800
	0100	Volt. regulating, isolating trans., w/invert. & 10 min. battery pack									
	0110	Single-phase, 120 V, 0.35 kVA	1 Elec	2.29	3.493	Ea.	900	131		1,031	1,175
	0120	0.5 kVA		2	4		945	150		1,095	1,275
	0130	For additional 55 min. battery, add to .35 kVA		2.29	3.493		530	131		661	780
	0140	Add to 0.5 kVA		1.14	7.018		560	264		824	1,000
	0150	Single-phase, 120 V, 0.75 kVA		.80	10		1,200	375		1,575	1,875
	0160	1.0 kVA	▼	.80	10		1,700	375		2,075	2,425
	0170	1.5 kVA	2 Elec	1.14	14.035		2,950	530		3,480	4,025
	0180	2 kVA	"	.89	17.978		3,200	675		3,875	4,500
	0190	3 kVA	R-3	.63	31.746		3,875	1,175	259	5,309	6,275
	0200	5 kVA		.42	47.619		5,600	1,775	390	7,765	9,250
	0210	7.5 kVA		.33	60.606		7,150	2,250	495	9,895	11,800
	0220	10 kVA		.28	71.429		7,600	2,650	585	10,835	12,900
	0230	15 kVA	▼	.22	90.909	▼	10,500	3,375	740	14,615	17,500
	0500	For options & accessories add to above, minimum									10%
	0520	Maximum									35%
	0600	For complex & special design systems to meet specific									
	0610	requirements, obtain quote from vendor									

16500 | Lighting

16510 | Interior Luminaires

			CREW	DAILY OUTPUT	LABOR-HOURS	UNIT	2003 BARE COSTS				TOTAL INCL O&P
							MAT.	LABOR	EQUIP.	TOTAL	
440	0010	**INTERIOR LIGHTING FIXTURES** Including lamps, mounting										440
	0030	hardware and connections									
	6850	Vandalproof, surface mounted, fluorescent, two 40 watt	1 Elec	3.20	2.500	Ea.	171	94		265	330
	6860	Incandescent, one 150 watt	"	8	1	"	53	37.50		90.50	114

16520 | Exterior Luminaires

			CREW	DAILY OUTPUT	LABOR-HOURS	UNIT	2003 BARE COSTS				TOTAL INCL O&P
							MAT.	LABOR	EQUIP.	TOTAL	
300	0010	**EXTERIOR FIXTURES** With lamps										300
	0200	Wall mounted, incandescent, 100 watt	1 Elec	8	1	Ea.	28	37.50		65.50	87

ELECTRICAL 16

259

16500 | Lighting

16520 | Exterior Luminaires

		CREW	DAILY OUTPUT	LABOR-HOURS	UNIT	2003 BARE COSTS				TOTAL INCL O&P
						MAT.	LABOR	EQUIP.	TOTAL	
300 0400	Quartz, 500 watt	1 Elec	5.30	1.509	Ea.	53.50	57		110.50	144 **300**
1100	Wall pack, low pressure sodium, 35 watt		4	2		208	75		283	340
1150	55 watt		4	2		280	75		355	420
1160	High pressure sodium, 70 watt		4	2		185	75		260	315
1170	150 watt		4	2		228	75		303	365
1180	Metal Halide, 175 watt		4	2		255	75		330	395
1190	250 watt	▼	4	2	▼	260	75		335	400
1200	Floodlights with ballast and lamp,									
1400	pole mounted, pole not included									
1500	Mercury vapor, 250 watt	1 Elec	2.40	3.333	Ea.	200	125		325	405
1600	400 watt	2 Elec	4.40	3.636		278	137		415	510
1950	Metal halide, 175 watt	1 Elec	2.70	2.963		300	111		411	495
2000	400 watt	2 Elec	4.40	3.636		350	137		487	590
2200	1000 watt		4	4		470	150		620	740
2210	1500 watt	▼	3.70	4.324		500	163		663	795
2250	Low pressure sodium, 55 watt	1 Elec	2.70	2.963		485	111		596	700
2270	90 watt		2	4		535	150		685	815
2290	180 watt		2	4		680	150		830	975
2340	High pressure sodium, 70 watt		2.70	2.963		193	111		304	380
2360	100 watt		2.70	2.963		198	111		309	385
2380	150 watt	▼	2.70	2.963		220	111		331	410
2400	400 watt	2 Elec	4.40	3.636		340	137		477	575
2600	1000 watt	"	4	4		500	150		650	775
2610	Incandescent, 300 watt	1 Elec	4	2		85	75		160	206
2620	500 watt	"	4	2		128	75		203	253
2630	1000 watt	2 Elec	6	2.667		138	100		238	300
2640	1500 watt	"	6	2.667		151	100		251	315
2650	Roadway area luminaire, low pressure sodium, 135 watt	1 Elec	2	4		535	150		685	815
2700	180 watt	"	2	4		565	150		715	845
2720	Mercury vapor, 400 watt	2 Elec	4.40	3.636		340	137		477	580
2730	1000 watt		4	4		425	150		575	695
2750	Metal halide, 400 watt		4.40	3.636		445	137		582	690
2760	1000 watt		4	4		530	150		680	805
2780	High pressure sodium, 400 watt		4.40	3.636		500	137		637	755
2790	1000 watt	▼	4	4	▼	555	150		705	835
2800	Light poles, anchor base									
2820	not including concrete bases									
2840	Aluminum pole, 8' high	1 Elec	4	2	Ea.	470	75		545	630
2850	10' high		4	2		495	75		570	650
2860	12' high		3.80	2.105		515	79		594	685
2870	14' high		3.40	2.353		535	88.50		623.50	720
2880	16' high	▼	3	2.667		590	100		690	795
3000	20' high	R-3	2.90	6.897		615	255	56.50	926.50	1,125
3200	30' high		2.60	7.692		1,200	285	63	1,548	1,825
3400	35' high		2.30	8.696		1,300	320	71	1,691	1,975
3600	40' high	▼	2	10		1,475	370	81.50	1,926.50	2,275
3800	Bracket arms, 1 arm	1 Elec	8	1		80.50	37.50		118	145
4000	2 arms		8	1		162	37.50		199.50	234
4200	3 arms		5.30	1.509		243	57		300	350
4400	4 arms		5.30	1.509		325	57		382	440
4500	Steel pole, galvanized, 8' high		3.80	2.105		420	79		499	580
4510	10' high		3.70	2.162		440	81.50		521.50	605
4520	12' high		3.40	2.353		475	88.50		563.50	655
4530	14' high		3.10	2.581		505	97		602	700
4540	16' high		2.90	2.759		535	104		639	745
4550	18' high	▼	2.70	2.963	▼	565	111		676	785

16500 | Lighting

16520 | Exterior Luminaires

		CREW	DAILY OUTPUT	LABOR-HOURS	UNIT	2003 BARE COSTS				TOTAL INCL O&P	
						MAT.	LABOR	EQUIP.	TOTAL		
300	4600	20' high	R-3	2.60	7.692	Ea.	745	285	63	1,093	1,325	300
	4800	30' high		2.30	8.696		875	320	71	1,266	1,525	
	5000	35' high		2.20	9.091		960	335	74	1,369	1,625	
	5200	40' high		1.70	11.765		1,175	435	96	1,706	2,050	
	5400	Bracket arms, 1 arm	1 Elec	8	1		122	37.50		159.50	190	
	5600	2 arms		8	1		189	37.50		226.50	264	
	5800	3 arms		5.30	1.509		205	57		262	310	
	6000	4 arms		5.30	1.509		285	57		342	400	

16530 | Emergency Lighting

		CREW	DAILY OUTPUT	LABOR-HOURS	UNIT	2003 BARE COSTS				TOTAL INCL O&P	
320	0010	**EXIT AND EMERGENCY LIGHTING**										320
	0080	Exit light ceiling or wall mount, incandescent, single face	1 Elec	8	1	Ea.	37.50	37.50		75	97.50	
	0084	Exit light w/armored cable	"	4	2		55.50	75		130.50	173	
	0085	Fixture, exit sign, single face					37.50			37.50	41.50	
	0100	Double face	1 Elec	6.70	1.194		44	45		89	116	
	0120	Explosion proof		3.80	2.105		370	79		449	525	
	0150	Fluorescent, single face		8	1		62	37.50		99.50	124	
	0160	Double face		6.70	1.194		65	45		110	139	
	0200	L.E.D. standard, single face		8	1		62	37.50		99.50	124	
	0220	Double face		6.70	1.194		65	45		110	139	
	0240	L.E.D. w/battery unit, single face		4.40	1.818		105	68.50		173.50	218	
	0260	Double face		4	2		107	75		182	230	
	0290	L.E.D. retrofit kits		60	.133		34	5		39	45	
	0300	Emergency light units, battery operated										
	0350	Twin sealed beam light, 25 watt, 6 volt each										
	0500	Lead battery operated	1 Elec	4	2	Ea.	110	75		185	233	
	0504	Emergency light w/armored cable		2.50	3.200		137	120		257	330	
	0700	Nickel cadmium battery operated		4	2		505	75		580	665	
	0705	Fixture, emerg light, ni-cad battery, 2 heads					505			505	555	
	0780	Additional remote mount, sealed beam, 25W 6V	1 Elec	26.70	.300		21	11.25		32.25	40	
	0783	Emergency remote lamp	"	27	.296		21	11.15		32.15	39.50	
	0785	Lamp, sealed beam, emergency light, 25W					21			21	23	
	0790	Twin sealed beam light, 25W 6V each	1 Elec	26.70	.300		40	11.25		51.25	61	
	0900	Self-contained fluorescent lamp pack	"	10	.800		121	30		151	178	

16800 | Sound & Video

16820 | Sound Reinforcement

		CREW	DAILY OUTPUT	LABOR-HOURS	UNIT	2003 BARE COSTS				TOTAL INCL O&P	
						MAT.	LABOR	EQUIP.	TOTAL		
840	0010	**SOUND SYSTEM** not including rough-in wires, cables & conduits										840
	0100	Components, outlet, projector	1 Elec	8	1	Ea.	44	37.50		81.50	105	
	0200	Microphone		4	2		49	75		124	166	
	0400	Speakers, ceiling or wall		8	1		85	37.50		122.50	150	
	0410	Speakers with call back		8	1		85	37.50		122.50	150	
	0600	Trumpets		4	2		154	75		229	281	

16850 | Television Equipment

		CREW	DAILY OUTPUT	LABOR-HOURS	UNIT	2003 BARE COSTS				TOTAL INCL O&P	
600	0010	**T.V. SYSTEMS** not including rough-in wires, cables & conduits										600
	2000	Closed circuit, surveillance, one station (camera & monitor)	2 Elec	2.60	6.154	Total	965	231		1,196	1,400	
	2200	For additional camera stations, add	1 Elec	2.70	2.963	Ea.	540	111		651	760	
	2400	Industrial quality, one station (camera & monitor)	2 Elec	2.60	6.154	Total	2,000	231		2,231	2,550	

16800 | Sound & Video

		16850	Television Equipment	CREW	DAILY OUTPUT	LABOR-HOURS	UNIT	2003 BARE COSTS				TOTAL INCL O&P	
								MAT.	LABOR	EQUIP.	TOTAL		
600	2600		For additional camera stations, add	1 Elec	2.70	2.963	Ea.	1,225	111		1,336	1,525	**600**
	2610		For low light, add		2.70	2.963		985	111		1,096	1,250	
	2620		For very low light, add		2.70	2.963		7,250	111		7,361	8,150	
	2800		For weatherproof camera station, add		1.30	6.154		755	231		986	1,175	
	3000		For pan and tilt, add		1.30	6.154		1,950	231		2,181	2,500	
	3200		For zoom lens - remote control, add, minimum		2	4		1,800	150		1,950	2,200	
	3400		Maximum		2	4		6,575	150		6,725	7,450	
	3410		For automatic iris for low light, add		2	4		1,575	150		1,725	1,950	

How to Use the Assemblies Cost Tables

The following is a detailed explanation of a sample Assemblies Cost Table. Most Assembly Tables are separated into three parts: 1) an illustration of the system to be estimated; 2) the components and related costs of a typical system; and 3) the costs for similar systems with dimensional and/or size variations. For costs of the components that comprise these systems or "assemblies" refer to the Unit Price Section. Next to each bold number below is the item being described with the appropriate component of the sample entry following in parenthesis. In most cases, if the work is to be subcontracted, the general contractor will need to add an additional markup (R.S. Means suggests using 10%) to the "Total" figures.

1 System/Line Numbers (D4010 425 0580)

Each Assemblies Cost Line has been assigned a unique identification number based on the UNIFORMAT II classification sytem.

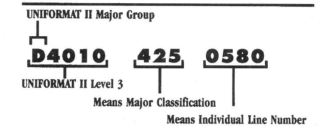

UNIFORMAT II Major Group

D4010 425 0580

UNIFORMAT II Level 3

Means Major Classification

Means Individual Line Number

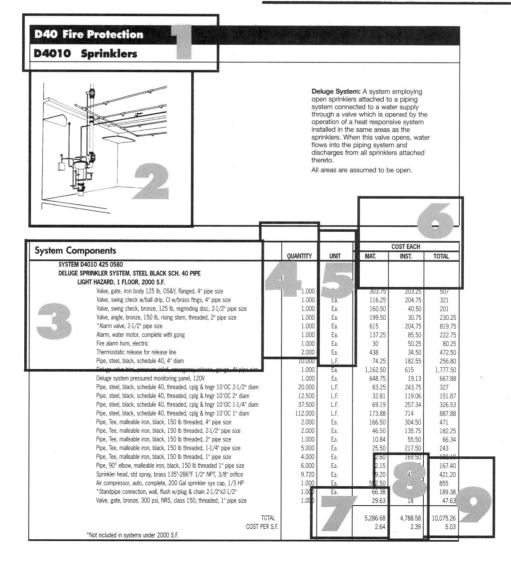

D40 Fire Protection

D4010 Sprinklers

Deluge System: A system employing open sprinklers attached to a piping system connected to a water supply through a valve which is opened by the operation of a heat responsive system installed in the same areas as the sprinklers. When this valve opens, water flows into the piping system and discharges from all sprinklers attached thereto.

All areas are assumed to be open.

System Components	QUANTITY	UNIT	COST EACH		
			MAT.	INST.	TOTAL
SYSTEM D4010 425 0580					
DELUGE SPRINKLER SYSTEM, STEEL BLACK SCH. 40 PIPE					
LIGHT HAZARD, 1 FLOOR, 2000 S.F.					
Valve, gate, iron body 125 lb, OS&Y, flanged, 4" pipe size	1.000		303.75	203.25	507
Valve, swing check w/ball drip, CI w/brass ftngs, 4" pipe size	1.000	Ea.	116.25	204.75	321
Valve, swing check, bronze, 125 lb, regrinding disc, 2-1/2" pipe size	1.000	Ea.	160.50	40.50	201
Valve, angle, bronze, 150 lb, rising stem, threaded, 2" pipe size	1.000	Ea.	199.50	30.75	230.25
*Alarm valve, 2-1/2" pipe size	1.000	Ea.	615	204.75	819.75
Alarm, water motor, complete with gong	1.000	Ea.	137.25	85.50	222.75
Fire alarm horn, electric	1.000	Ea.	30	50.25	80.25
Thermostatic release for release line	2.000	Ea.	438	34.50	472.50
Pipe, steel, black, schedule 40, 4" diam	10.000	L.F.	74.25	182.55	256.80
Deluge valve trim, pressure relief, emergency release, gauge, 4" pipe size	1.000	Ea.	1,162.50	615	1,777.50
Deluge system pressured monitoring panel, 120V	1.000	Ea.	648.75	19.13	667.88
Pipe, steel, black, schedule 40, threaded, cplg & hngr 10'OC 2-1/2" diam	20.000	L.F.	83.25	243.75	327
Pipe, steel, black, schedule 40, threaded, cplg & hngr 10'OC 2" diam	12.500	L.F.	32.81	119.06	151.87
Pipe, steel, black, schedule 40, threaded, cplg & hngr 10'OC 1-1/4" diam	37.500	L.F.	69.19	257.34	326.53
Pipe, steel, black, schedule 40, threaded, cplg & hngr 10'OC 1" diam	112.000	L.F.	173.88	714	887.88
Pipe, Tee, malleable iron, black, 150 lb threaded, 4" pipe size	2.000	Ea.	166.50	304.50	471
Pipe, Tee, malleable iron, black, 150 lb threaded, 2-1/2" pipe size	2.000	Ea.	46.50	135.75	182.25
Pipe, Tee, malleable iron, black, 150 lb threaded, 2" pipe size	1.000	Ea.	10.84	55.50	66.34
Pipe, Tee, malleable iron, black, 150 lb threaded, 1-1/4" pipe size	5.000	Ea.	25.50	217.50	243
Pipe, Tee, malleable iron, black, 150 lb threaded, 1" pipe size	4.000	Ea.	2.60	169.50	172.10
Pipe, 90° elbow, malleable iron, black, 150 lb threaded 1" pipe size	6.000	Ea.	2.15		167.40
Sprinkler head, std spray, brass 135°-286°F 1/2" NPT, 3/8" orifice	9.720	Ea.	9.20		421.20
Air compressor, auto, complete, 200 Gal sprinkler sys cap, 1/3 HP	1.000	Ea.	502.50		855
*Standpipe connection, wall, flush w/plug & chain 2-1/2"x2-1/2"	1.000	Ea.	66.38		189.38
Valve, gate, bronze, 300 psi, NRS, class 150, threaded, 1" pipe size	1.000		29.63	18	47.63
TOTAL			5,286.68	4,788.58	10,075.26
COST PER S.F.			2.64	2.39	5.03

*Not included in systems under 2000 S.F.

263

2 Illustration

At the top of most assembly pages is an illustration, a brief description, and the design criteria used to develop the cost.

3 System Components

The components of a typical system are listed separately to show what has been included in the development of the total system price. The table below contains prices for other similar systems with dimensional and/or size variations.

4 Quantity

This is the number of line item units required for one system unit.

5 Unit of Measure for Each Item

The abbreviated designation indicates the unit of measure, as defined by industry standards, upon which the price of the component is based. For example, baseboard radiation is priced by the linear foot.

6 Unit of Measure for Each System (Cost Each)

Costs shown in the three right hand columns have been adjusted by the component quantity and unit of measure for the entire system. In this example, "Cost Each" is the unit of measure for this system or "assembly."

7 Materials (5,286.68)

This column contains the Materials Cost of each component. These cost figures are bare costs plus 10% for profit.

8 Installation (4,788.58)

Installation includes labor and equipment plus the installing contractor's overhead and profit. Equipment costs are the bare rental costs plus 10% for profit. The labor overhead and profit is defined on the inside back cover of this book.

9 Total (10,075.26)

The figure in this column is the sum of the material and installation costs.

Material Cost	+	Installation Cost	=	Total
$5,286.68	+	$4,788.58	=	$10,075.26

B20 Exterior Enclosure

B2010   Exterior Walls

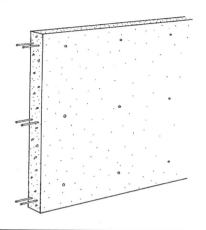

The table below describes a concrete wall system for exterior closure. There are several types of wall finishes priced from plain finish to a finish with 3/4" rustication strip.

Design Assumptions:
Conc. f'c = 3000 to 5000 psi
Reinf. fy = 60,000 psi

System Components			COST PER S.F.		
	QUANTITY	UNIT	MAT.	INST.	TOTAL
SYSTEM B2010 101 2100					
CONC. WALL, REINFORCED, 8' HIGH, 6" THICK, PLAIN FINISH, 3,000 PSI					
Forms in place, wall, job built plyform to 8' high, 4 uses	2.000	SFCA	1.52	10.60	12.12
Reinforcing in place, walls, #3 to #7	.752	Lb.	.24	.24	.48
Concrete ready mix, regular weight, 3000 psi	.018	C.Y.	1.39		1.39
Place and vibrate concrete, walls 6" thick, pump	.018	C.Y.		.64	.64
Finish wall, break ties, patch voids	2.000	S.F.	.06	1.32	1.38
TOTAL			3.21	12.80	16.01

B2010 101	Cast In Place Concrete	COST PER S.F.		
		MAT.	INST.	TOTAL
2100	Conc wall reinforced, 8' high, 6" thick, plain finish, 3000 PSI	3.21	12.80	16.01
2200	4000 PSI	3.32	12.80	16.12
2300	5000 PSI	3.37	12.80	16.17
2400	Rub concrete 1 side, 3000 PSI	3.24	14.85	18.09
2500	4000 PSI	3.35	14.85	18.20
2600	5000 PSI	3.40	14.85	18.25
2700	Aged wood liner, 3000 PSI	7.25	13.30	20.55
2800	4000 PSI	7.35	13.30	20.65
2900	5000 PSI	7.40	13.30	20.70
3000	Sand blast light 1 side, 3000 PSI	3.45	13.70	17.15
3100	4000 PSI	3.56	13.70	17.26
3300	5000 PSI	3.61	13.70	17.31
3400	Sand blast heavy 1 side, 3000 PSI	3.68	15.50	19.18
3500	4000 PSI	3.79	15.50	19.29
3600	5000 PSI	3.84	15.50	19.34
3700	3/4" bevel rustication strip, 3000 PSI	3.40	15.35	18.75
3800	4000 PSI	3.51	15.35	18.86
3900	5000 PSI	3.56	15.35	18.91
4000	8" thick, plain finish, 3000 PSI	3.77	13.10	16.87
4100	4000 PSI	3.92	13.10	17.02
4200	5000 PSI	3.98	13.10	17.08
4300	Rub concrete 1 side, 3000 PSI	3.80	15.15	18.95
4400	4000 PSI	3.95	15.15	19.10
4500	5000 PSI	4.01	15.15	19.16
4550	8" thick, aged wood liner, 3000 PSI	7.80	13.65	21.45
4600	4000 PSI	7.95	13.65	21.60

B20 Exterior Enclosure

B2010 Exterior Walls

B2010 101	Cast In Place Concrete	COST PER S.F.		
		MAT.	INST.	TOTAL
4700	5000 PSI	8	13.65	21.65
4750	Sand blast light 1 side, 3000 PSI	4.01	14.05	18.06
4800	4000 PSI	4.16	14.05	18.21
4900	5000 PSI	4.22	14.05	18.27
5000	Sand blast heavy 1 side, 3000 PSI	4.24	15.85	20.09
5100	4000 PSI	4.39	15.85	20.24
5200	5000 PSI	4.45	15.85	20.30
5300	3/4" bevel rustication strip, 3000 PSI	3.96	15.65	19.61
5400	4000 PSI	4.11	15.65	19.76
5500	5000 PSI	4.17	15.65	19.82
5600	10" thick, plain finish, 3000 PSI	4.32	13.40	17.72
5700	4000 PSI	4.52	13.40	17.92
5800	5000 PSI	4.59	13.40	17.99
5900	Rub concrete 1 side, 3000 PSI	4.35	15.45	19.80
6000	4000 PSI	4.55	15.45	20
6100	5000 PSI	4.62	15.45	20.07
6200	Aged wood liner, 3000 PSI	8.35	13.95	22.30
6300	4000 PSI	8.55	13.95	22.50
6400	5000 PSI	8.65	13.95	22.60
6500	Sand blast light 1 side, 3000 PSI	4.56	14.35	18.91
6600	4000 PSI	4.76	14.35	19.11
6700	5000 PSI	4.83	14.35	19.18
6800	Sand blast heavy 1 side, 3000 PSI	4.79	16.15	20.94
6900	4000 PSI	4.99	16.15	21.14
7000	5000 PSI	5.05	16.15	21.20
7100	3/4" bevel rustication strip, 3000 PSI	4.51	15.95	20.46
7200	4000 PSI	4.71	15.95	20.66
7300	5000 PSI	4.78	15.95	20.73
7400	12" thick, plain finish, 3000 PSI	4.96	13.80	18.76
7500	4000 PSI	5.20	13.80	19
7600	5000 PSI	5.30	13.80	19.10
7700	Rub concrete 1 side, 3000 PSI	4.99	15.85	20.84
7800	4000 PSI	5.25	15.85	21.10
7900	5000 PSI	5.30	15.85	21.15
8000	Aged wood liner, 3000 PSI	9	14.30	23.30
8100	4000 PSI	9.25	14.30	23.55
8200	5000 PSI	9.35	14.30	23.65
8300	Sand blast light 1 side, 3000 PSI	5.20	14.70	19.90
8400	4000 PSI	5.45	14.70	20.15
8500	5000 PSI	5.55	14.70	20.25
8600	Sand blast heavy 1 side, 3000 PSI	5.45	16.50	21.95
8700	4000 PSI	5.65	16.50	22.15
8800	5000 PSI	5.75	16.50	22.25
8900	3/4" bevel rustication strip, 3000 PSI	5.15	16.30	21.45
9000	4000 PSI	5.40	16.30	21.70
9500	5000 PSI	5.50	16.30	21.80

B2010   Exterior Walls

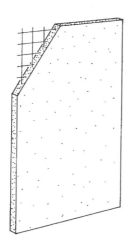

Precast concrete wall panels are either solid or insulated with plain, colored or textured finishes. Transportation is an important cost factor. Prices below are based on delivery within fifty miles of a plant. Engineering data is available from fabricators to assist with construction details. Usual minimum job size for economical use of panels is about 5000 S.F. Small jobs can double the prices below. For large, highly repetitive jobs, deduct up to 15% from the prices below.

B2010 103 — Flat Precast Concrete

	THICKNESS (IN.)	PANEL SIZE (FT.)	FINISHES	RIGID INSULATION (IN)	TYPE	COST PER S.F. MAT.	COST PER S.F. INST.	COST PER S.F. TOTAL
3000	4	5x18	smooth gray	none	low rise	5.20	5.85	11.05
3050		6x18				4.35	4.87	9.22
3100		8x20				6.70	1.83	8.53
3150		12x20				6.35	1.73	8.08
3200	6	5x18	smooth gray	2	low rise	6.05	6.20	12.25
3250		6x18				5.20	5.25	10.45
3300		8x20				7.70	2.29	9.99
3350		12x20				7	2.10	9.10
3400	8	5x18	smooth gray	2	low rise	9.80	2.86	12.66
3450		6x18				9.30	2.74	12.04
3500		8x20				8.55	2.52	11.07
3550		12x20				7.80	2.32	10.12
3600	4	4x8	white face	none	low rise	16.40	3.38	19.78
3650		8x8				12.30	2.53	14.83
3700		10x10				10.80	2.22	13.02
3750		20x10				9.80	2.01	11.81
3800	5	4x8	white face	none	low rise	16.75	3.45	20.20
3850		8x8				12.65	2.60	15.25
3900		10x10				11.20	2.30	13.50
3950		20x20				10.25	2.11	12.36
4000	6	4x8	white face	none	low rise	17.35	3.57	20.92
4050		8x8				13.20	2.71	15.91
4100		10x10				11.60	2.39	13.99
4150		20x10				10.65	2.19	12.84
4200	6	4x8	white face	2	low rise	18.25	4.01	22.26
4250		8x8				14.10	3.15	17.25
4300		10x10				12.50	2.83	15.33
4350		20x10				10.65	2.19	12.84
4400	7	4x8	white face	none	low rise	17.75	3.66	21.41
4450		8x8				13.65	2.81	16.46
4500		10x10				12.25	2.52	14.77
4550		20x10				11.20	2.30	13.50

B20 Exterior Enclosure

B2010 Exterior Walls

| B2010 103 | Flat Precast Concrete | | | | | | | |

	THICKNESS (IN.)	PANEL SIZE (FT.)	FINISHES	RIGID INSULATION (IN)	TYPE	COST PER S.F.		
						MAT.	INST.	TOTAL
4600	7	4x8	white face	2	low rise	18.65	4.10	22.75
4650		8x8				14.55	3.25	17.80
4700		10x10				13.15	2.96	16.11
4750		20x10				12.10	2.74	14.84
4800	8	4x8	white face	none	low rise	18.20	3.74	21.94
4850		8x8				14	2.88	16.88
4900		10x10				12.60	2.59	15.19
4950		20x10				11.60	2.38	13.98
5000	8	4x8	white face	2	low rise	19.05	4.18	23.23
5050		8x8				14.90	3.32	18.22
5100		10x10				13.50	3.03	16.53
5150		20x10				12.50	2.82	15.32

| B2010 103 | Fluted Window or Mullion Precast Concrete | | | | | | | |

	THICKNESS (IN.)	PANEL SIZE (FT.)	FINISHES	RIGID INSULATION (IN)	TYPE	COST PER S.F.		
						MAT.	INST.	TOTAL
5200	4	4x8	smooth gray	none	high rise	11.90	13.35	25.25
5250		8x8				8.50	9.55	18.05
5300		10x10				12.85	3.50	16.35
5350		20x10				11.25	3.06	14.31
5400	5	4x8	smooth gray	none	high rise	12.10	13.55	25.65
5450		8x8				8.80	9.90	18.70
5500		10x10				13.40	3.64	17.04
5550		20x10				11.85	3.22	15.07
5600	6	4x8	smooth gray	none	high rise	12.45	13.90	26.35
5650		8x8				9.10	10.20	19.30
5700		10x10				13.75	3.75	17.50
5750		20x10				12.25	3.33	15.58
5800	6	4x8	smooth gray	2	high rise	13.30	14.35	27.65
5850		8x8				10	10.65	20.65
5900		10x10				14.65	4.19	18.84
5950		20x10				13.10	3.77	16.87
6000	7	4x8	smooth gray	none	high rise	12.70	14.20	26.90
6050		8x8				9.35	10.45	19.80
6100		10x10				14.35	3.91	18.26
6150		20x10				12.60	3.43	16.03
6200	7	4x8	smooth gray	2	high rise	13.60	14.65	28.25
6250		8x8				10.25	10.90	21.15
6300		10x10				15.25	4.35	19.60
6350		20x10				13.50	3.87	17.37
6400	8	4x8	smooth gray	none	high rise	12.85	14.40	27.25
6450		8x8				9.60	10.75	20.35
6500		10x10				14.80	4.04	18.84
6550		20x10				13.25	3.60	16.85
6600	8	4x8	smooth gray	2	high rise	13.75	14.85	28.60
6650		8x8				10.50	11.20	21.70
6700		10x10				15.70	4.48	20.18
6750		20x10				14.10	4.04	18.14
6800	4	4x8	aggregate	none	high rise	13.15	13.30	26.45
6850		8x8				9.60	9.75	19.35
6900		10x10				14.15	3.53	17.68
6950		20x10				12.50	3.11	15.61

B20 Exterior Enclosure

B2010 Exterior Walls

B2010 103 — Fluted Window or Mullion Precast Concrete

	THICKNESS (IN.)	PANEL SIZE (FT.)	FINISHES	RIGID INSULATION (IN)	TYPE	COST PER S.F.		
						MAT.	INST.	TOTAL
7000	5	4x8	aggregate	none	high rise	13.40	13.55	26.95
7050		8x8				9.90	10.05	19.95
7100		10x10				14.70	3.67	18.37
7150		20x10				13.10	3.27	16.37
7200	6	4x8	aggregate	none	high rise	13.65	13.85	27.50
7250		8x8				10.15	10.30	20.45
7300		10x10				15.15	3.78	18.93
7350		20x10				13.60	3.39	16.99
7400	6	4x8	aggregate	2	high rise	14.55	14.30	28.85
7450		8x8				11.05	10.75	21.80
7500		10x10				16.05	4.22	20.27
7550		20x10				14.50	3.83	18.33
7600	7	4x8	aggregate	none	high rise	13.95	14.15	28.10
7650		8x8				10.40	10.55	20.95
7700		10x10				15.65	3.90	19.55
7750		20x10				14	3.49	17.49
7800	7	4x8	aggregate	2	high rise	14.85	14.60	29.45
7850		8x8				11.30	11	22.30
7900		10x10				16.55	4.34	20.89
7950		20x10				14.85	3.93	18.78
8000	8	4x8	aggregate	none	high rise	14.20	14.40	28.60
8050		8x8				10.70	10.85	21.55
8100		10x10				16.20	4.04	20.24
8150		20x10				14.60	3.64	18.24
8200	8	4x8	aggregate	2	high rise	15.10	14.85	29.95
8250		8x8				11.60	11.30	22.90
8300		10x10				17.05	4.48	21.53
8350		20x10				15.50	4.08	19.58

B2010 105 — Precast Concrete Specialties

	TYPE	SIZE				COST PER L.F.		
						MAT.	INST.	TOTAL
8400	Coping, precast	6" wide				19.15	9.35	28.50
8450	Stock units	10" wide				11.55	10	21.55
8460		12" wide				23	10.80	33.80
8480		14" wide				15.95	11.70	27.65
8500	Window sills	6" wide				10.65	10	20.65
8550	Precast	10" wide				14.65	11.70	26.35
8600		14" wide				14.85	14	28.85
8610								

B20 Exterior Enclosure

B2010 Exterior Walls

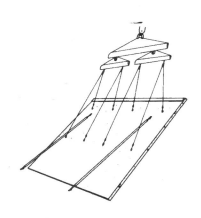

The advantage of tilt up construction is in the low cost of forms and placing of concrete and reinforcing. Tilt up has been used for several types of buildings, including warehouses, stores, offices, and schools. The panels are cast in forms on the ground, or floor slab. Most jobs use 5-1/2" thick solid reinforced concrete panels.

Design Assumptions:
Conc. f'c = 3000 psi
Reinf. fy = 60,000

System Components	QUANTITY	UNIT	COST PER S.F.		
			MAT.	INST.	TOTAL
SYSTEM B2010 106 3200					
TILT-UP PANELS, 20'X25', BROOM FINISH, 5-1/2" THICK, 3000 PSI					
Apply liquid bond breaker	500.000	S.F.	22.50	47.50	70
Edge forms in place for slab on grade	120.000	L.F.	52.80	298.80	351.60
Reinforcing in place	.350	Ton	204.75	290.50	495.25
Footings, form braces, steel	1.000	Set	382.20		382.20
Concrete ready mix, regular weight, 3000 psi	8.550	C.Y.	658.35		658.35
Place and vibrate concrete for slab on grade, 4" thick, direct chute	8.550	C.Y.		155.19	155.19
Finish floor, monolithic broom finish	500.000	S.F.		285	285
Cure with curing compound, sprayed	500.000	S.F.	27.50	32.50	60
Erection crew	.058	Day		475.60	475.60
TOTAL	500.000	S.F.	1,408.60	2,181.69	3,590.29
Cost per S.F.			2.82	4.36	7.18

B2010 106	Tilt-Up Concrete Panel	COST PER S.F.		
		MAT.	INST.	TOTAL
3200	Tilt up conc panels, broom finish, 5-1/2" thick, 3000 PSI	2.80	4.35	7.15
3250	5000 PSI	2.92	4.29	7.21
3300	6" thick, 3000 PSI	3.11	4.48	7.59
3350	5000 PSI	3.22	4.40	7.62
3400	7-1/2" thick, 3000 PSI	3.96	4.66	8.62
3450	5000 PSI	4.11	4.57	8.68
3500	8" thick, 3000 PSI	4.25	4.76	9.01
3550	5000 PSI	4.41	4.68	9.09
3700	Steel trowel finish, 5-1/2" thick, 3000 PSI	2.83	4.45	7.28
3750	5000 PSI	2.92	4.37	7.29
3800	6" thick, 3000 PSI	3.11	4.56	7.67
3850	5000 PSI	3.22	4.48	7.70
3900	7-1/2" thick, 3000 PSI	3.96	4.74	8.70
3950	5000 PSI	4.11	4.65	8.76
4000	8" thick, 3000 PSI	4.25	4.84	9.09
4050	5000 PSI	4.41	4.76	9.17
4200	Exp. aggregate finish, 5-1/2" thick, 3000 PSI	7.25	4.45	11.70
4250	5000 PSI	7.35	4.37	11.72
4300	6" thick, 3000 PSI	7.55	4.57	12.12
4350	5000 PSI	7.65	4.48	12.13
4400	7-1/2" thick, 3000 PSI	8.40	4.74	13.14
4450	5000 PSI	8.55	4.66	13.21

B2010 Exterior Walls

B2010 106	Tilt-Up Concrete Panel	COST PER S.F.		
		MAT.	INST.	TOTAL
4500	8" thick, 3000 PSI	8.65	4.84	13.49
4550	5000 PSI	8.85	4.76	13.61
4600	Exposed aggregate & vert. rustication 5-1/2" thick, 3000 PSI	8.70	7.30	16
4650	5000 PSI	8.80	7.25	16.05
4700	6" thick, 3000 PSI	9	7.45	16.45
4750	5000 PSI	9.10	7.35	16.45
4800	7-1/2" thick, 3000 PSI	9.85	7.60	17.45
4850	5000 PSI	10	7.50	17.50
4900	8" thick, 3000 PSI	10.10	7.70	17.80
4950	5000 PSI	10.30	7.60	17.90
5000	Vertical rib & light sandblast, 5-1/2" thick, 3000 PSI	7.65	5.30	12.95
5050	5000 PSI	7.75	5.20	12.95
5100	6" thick, 3000 PSI	7.95	5.40	13.35
5150	5000 PSI	8.05	5.30	13.35
5200	7-1/2" thick, 3000 PSI	8.80	5.55	14.35
5250	5000 PSI	8.95	5.50	14.45
5300	8" thick, 3000 PSI	9.10	5.65	14.75
5350	5000 PSI	9.25	5.60	14.85
6000	Broom finish w/2" polystyrene insulation, 6" thick, 3000 PSI	2.69	5.35	8.04
6050	5000 PSI	2.81	5.35	8.16
6100	Broom finish 2" fiberplank insulation, 6" thick, 3000 PSI	3.21	5.30	8.51
6150	5000 PSI	3.33	5.30	8.63
6200	Exposed aggregate w/2"polystyrene insulation, 6" thick, 3000 PSI	7.05	5.45	12.50
6250	5000 PSI	7.15	5.45	12.60
6300	Exposed aggregate 2" fiberplank insulation, 6" thick, 3000 PSI	7.55	5.40	12.95
6350	5000 PSI	7.70	5.40	13.10

B20 Exterior Enclosure

B2010 Exterior Walls

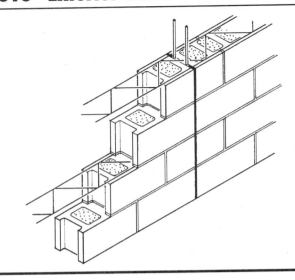

Exterior concrete block walls are defined in the following terms; structural reinforcement, weight, percent solid, size, strength and insulation. Within each of these categories, two to four variations are shown. No costs are included for brick shelf or relieving angles.

System Components	QUANTITY	UNIT	COST PER S.F.		
			MAT.	INST.	TOTAL
SYSTEM B2010 109 1400					
UNREINFORCED CONCRETE BLOCK WALL, 8″ X 8″ X 16″, PERLITE CORE FILL					
Concrete block wall, 8″ thick	1.000	S.F.	1.62	4.80	6.42
Perlite insulation	1.000	S.F.	.47	.29	.76
Horizontal joint reinforcing, alternate courses	.800	S.F.	.07	.13	.20
Control joint	.050	L.F.	.05	.05	.10
TOTAL			2.21	5.27	7.48

B2010 109		Concrete Block Wall - Regular Weight				COST PER S.F.		
	TYPE	SIZE (IN.)	STRENGTH (P.S.I.)	CORE FILL		MAT.	INST.	TOTAL
1200	Hollow	4x8x16	2,000	none		1.12	4.35	5.47
1250			4,500	none		1.02	4.35	5.37
1300		6x8x16	2,000	perlite		1.94	4.89	6.83
1310				styrofoam		2.56	4.66	7.22
1340				none		1.62	4.66	6.28
1350			4,500	perlite		1.64	4.89	6.53
1360				styrofoam		2.26	4.66	6.92
1390				none		1.32	4.66	5.98
1400		8x8x16	2,000	perlite		2.21	5.25	7.46
1410				styrofoam		2.68	4.98	7.66
1440				none		1.74	4.98	6.72
1450			4,500	perlite		2.01	5.25	7.26
1460				styrofoam		2.48	4.98	7.46
1490				none		1.54	4.98	6.52
1500		12x8x16	2,000	perlite		3.28	7	10.28
1510				styrofoam		3.67	6.40	10.07
1540				none		2.51	6.40	8.91
1550			4,500	perlite		2.89	7	9.89
1560				styrofoam		3.28	6.40	9.68
1590				none		2.12	6.40	8.52
2000	75% solid	4x8x16	2,000	none		1.10	4.40	5.50
2050			4,500	none		1.23	4.40	5.63

B2010 Exterior Walls

B2010 109 — Concrete Block Wall - Regular Weight

	TYPE	SIZE (IN.)	STRENGTH (P.S.I.)	CORE FILL		COST PER S.F. MAT.	INST.	TOTAL
2100	75% solid	6x8x16	2,000	perlite		1.63	4.84	6.47
2140				none		1.47	4.72	6.19
2150			4,500	perlite		2	4.84	6.84
2190				none		1.84	4.72	6.56
2200		8x8x16	2,000	perlite		2.44	5.20	7.64
2240				none		2.20	5.05	7.25
2250			4,500	perlite		2.73	5.20	7.93
2290				none		2.49	5.05	7.54
2300		12x8x16	2,000	perlite		3	6.80	9.80
2340				none		2.61	6.50	9.11
2350			4,500	perlite		4.04	6.80	10.84
2390				none		3.65	6.50	10.15
2500	Solid	4x8x16	2,000	none		1.51	4.50	6.01
2550			4,500	none		1.23	4.45	5.68
2600		6x8x16	2,000	none		1.78	4.84	6.62
2650			4,500	none		1.84	4.78	6.62
2700		8x8x16	2,000	none		2.59	5.20	7.79
2750			4,500	none		2.49	5.10	7.59
2800		12x8x16	2,000	none		3.85	6.65	10.50
2850			4,500	none		3.65	6.55	10.20

B2010 109 — Concrete Block Wall - Lightweight

	TYPE	SIZE (IN.)	WEIGHT (P.C.F.)	CORE FILL		COST PER S.F. MAT.	INST.	TOTAL
3100	Hollow	8x4x16	105	perlite		1.51	4.97	6.48
3110				styrofoam		1.98	4.68	6.66
3140				none		1.04	4.68	5.72
3150			85	perlite		3.53	4.86	8.39
3160				styrofoam		4	4.57	8.57
3190				none		3.06	4.57	7.63
3200		4x8x16	105	none		1.32	4.25	5.57
3250			85	none		1.33	4.16	5.49
3300		6x8x16	105	perlite		2.08	4.78	6.86
3310				styrofoam		2.70	4.55	7.25
3340				none		1.76	4.55	6.31
3350			85	perlite		2.04	4.68	6.72
3360				styrofoam		2.66	4.45	7.11
3390				none		1.72	4.45	6.17
3400		8x8x16	105	perlite		2.61	5.15	7.76
3410				styrofoam		3.08	4.86	7.94
3440				none		2.14	4.86	7
3450			85	perlite		2.34	5.05	7.39
3460				styrofoam		2.81	4.74	7.55
3490				none		1.87	4.74	6.61
3500		12x8x16	105	perlite		4.04	6.80	10.84
3510				styrofoam		4.43	6.20	10.63
3540				none		3.27	6.20	9.47
3550			85	perlite		3.33	6.65	9.98
3560				styrofoam		3.72	6.05	9.77
3590				none		2.56	6.05	8.61
3600		4x8x24	105	none		.97	4.73	5.70
3650			85	none		2.09	3.99	6.08
3690	For stacked bond add						.40	.40

B20 Exterior Enclosure

B2010 Exterior Walls

B2010 109 — Concrete Block Wall - Lightweight

	TYPE	SIZE (IN.)	WEIGHT (P.C.F.)	CORE FILL		MAT.	INST.	TOTAL
						COST PER S.F.		
3700	Hollow	6x8x24	105	perlite		1.60	5.15	6.75
3710				styrofoam		2.22	4.94	7.16
3740				none		1.28	4.94	6.22
3750			85	perlite		3.18	4.39	7.57
3760				styrofoam		3.80	4.16	7.96
3790				none		2.86	4.16	7.02
3800		8x8x24	105	perlite		2.03	5.50	7.53
3810				styrofoam		2.50	5.25	7.75
3840				none		1.56	5.25	6.81
3850			85	perlite		3.84	4.71	8.55
3860				styrofoam		4.31	4.42	8.73
3890				none		3.37	4.42	7.79
3900		12x8x24	105	perlite		3.12	6.55	9.67
3910				styrofoam		3.51	5.95	9.46
3940				none		2.35	5.95	8.30
3950			85	perlite		5.20	6.40	11.60
3960				styrofoam		5.60	5.80	11.40
3990				none		4.45	5.80	10.25
4000	75% solid	4x8x16	105	none		1.12	4.30	5.42
4050			85	none		2.29	4.21	6.50
4100		6x8x16	105	perlite		1.71	4.72	6.43
4140				none		1.55	4.60	6.15
4150			85	perlite		2.81	4.62	7.43
4190				none		2.65	4.50	7.15
4200		8x8x16	105	perlite		2.33	5.05	7.38
4240				none		2.09	4.92	7.01
4250			85	perlite		3.86	4.95	8.81
4290				none		3.62	4.80	8.42
4300		12x8x16	105	perlite		4.26	6.60	10.86
4340				none		3.87	6.30	10.17
4350			85	perlite		5.25	6.40	11.65
4390				none		4.87	6.10	10.97
4500	Solid	4x8x16	105	none		1.42	4.45	5.87
4550			85	none		1.83	4.25	6.08
4600		6x8x16	105	none		1.96	4.78	6.74
4650			85	none		2.87	4.55	7.42
4700		8x8x16	105	none		2.64	5.10	7.74
4750			85	none		3.85	4.86	8.71
4800		12x8x16	105	none		4.77	6.55	11.32
4850			85	none		5.90	6.20	12.10
4900	For stacked bond, add					.40	.40	

B2010 112 — Reinforced Concrete Block Wall - Regular Weight

	TYPE	SIZE (IN.)	STRENGTH (P.S.I.)	VERT. REINF & GROUT SPACING		MAT.	INST.	TOTAL
						COST PER S.F.		
5200	Hollow	4x8x16	2,000	#4 @ 48"		1.22	4.83	6.05
5250			4,500	#4 @ 48"		1.12	4.83	5.95
5300		6x8x16	2,000	#4 @ 48"		1.80	5.15	6.95
5330				#5 @ 32"		1.93	5.35	7.28
5340				#5 @ 16"		2.23	6.05	8.28
5350			4,500	#4 @ 28"		1.50	5.15	6.65
5380				#5 @ 32"		1.63	5.35	6.98
5390				#5 @ 16"		1.93	6.05	7.98

B2010 Exterior Walls

B2010 112		Reinforced Concrete Block Wall - Regular Weight						

	TYPE	SIZE (IN.)	STRENGTH (P.S.I.)	VERT. REINF & GROUT SPACING		COST PER S.F.		
						MAT.	INST.	TOTAL
5400	Hollow	8x8x16	2,000	#4 @ 48"		1.97	5.50	7.47
5430				#5 @ 32"		2.11	5.80	7.91
5440				#5 @ 16"		2.47	6.65	9.12
5450		8x8x16	4,500	#4 @ 48"		1.76	5.60	7.36
5480				#5 @ 32"		1.91	5.80	7.71
5490				#5 @ 16"		2.27	6.65	8.92
5500		12x8x16	2,000	#4 @ 48"		2.83	7.05	9.88
5530				#5 @ 32"		3.02	7.25	10.27
5540				#5 @ 16"		3.54	8.15	11.69
5550			4,500	#4 @ 48"		2.44	7.05	9.49
5580				#5 @ 32"		2.63	7.25	9.88
5590				#5 @ 16"		3.15	8.15	11.30
6100	75% solid	6x8x16	2,000	#4 @ 48"		1.56	5.15	6.71
6130				#5 @ 32"		1.65	5.30	6.95
6140				#5 @ 16"		1.82	5.85	7.67
6150			4,500	#4 @ 48"		1.93	5.15	7.08
6180				#5 @ 32"		2.02	5.30	7.32
6190				#5 @ 16"		2.19	5.85	8.04
6200		8x8x16	2,000	#4 @ 48"		2.30	5.55	7.85
6230				#5 @ 32"		2.39	5.70	8.09
6240				#5 @ 16"		2.58	6.40	8.98
6250			4,500	#4 @ 48"		2.59	5.55	8.14
6280				#5 @ 32"		2.68	5.70	8.38
6290				#5 @ 16"		2.87	6.40	9.27
6300		12x8x16	2,000	#4 @ 48"		2.79	7	9.79
6330				#5 @ 32"		2.92	7.20	10.12
6340				#5 @ 16"		3.22	7.90	11.12
6350			4,500	#4 @ 48"		3.83	7	10.83
6380				#4 @ 32"		3.96	7.20	11.16
6390				#5 @ 16"		4.26	7.90	12.16
6500	Solid-double Wythe	2-4x8x16	2,000	#4 @ 48" E.W.		3.66	10.20	13.86
6530				#5 @ 16" E.W.		4.08	10.80	14.88
6550			4,500	#4 @ 48" E.W.		3.10	10.10	13.20
6580				#5 @ 16" E.W.		3.52	10.70	14.22
6600		2-6x8x16	2,000	#4 @ 48" E.W.		4.19	10.90	15.09
6630				#5 @ 16" E.W.		4.61	11.50	16.11
6650			4,000	#4 @ 48" E.W.		4.31	10.75	15.06
6680				#5 @ 16" E.W.		4.73	11.40	16.13

B2010 112		Reinforced Concrete Block Wall - Lightweight						

	TYPE	SIZE (IN.)	WEIGHT (P.C.F.)	VERT REINF. & GROUT SPACING		COST PER S.F.		
						MAT.	INST.	TOTAL
7100	Hollow	8x4x16	105	#4 @ 48"		1.26	5.30	6.56
7130				#5 @ 32"		1.41	5.50	6.91
7140				#5 @ 16"		1.77	6.35	8.12
7150			85	#4 @ 48"		3.28	5.15	8.43
7180				#5 @ 32"		3.43	5.40	8.83
7190				#5 @ 16"		3.79	6.25	10.04
7200		4x8x16	105	#4 @ 48"		1.42	4.73	6.15
7250			85	#4 @ 48"		1.43	4.64	6.07

B20 Exterior Enclosure

B2010 Exterior Walls

B2010 112 — Reinforced Concrete Block Wall - Lightweight

	TYPE	SIZE (IN.)	WEIGHT (P.C.F.)	VERT REINF. & GROUT SPACING		COST PER S.F. MAT.	COST PER S.F. INST.	COST PER S.F. TOTAL
7300	Hollow	6x8x16	105	#4 @ 48"		1.94	5.05	6.99
7330				#5 @ 32"		2.07	5.25	7.32
7340				#5 @ 16"		2.37	5.95	8.32
7350			85	#4 @ 48"		1.90	4.94	6.84
7380				#5 @ 32"		2.03	5.15	7.18
7390				#5 @ 16"		2.33	5.85	8.18
7400		8x8x16	105	#4 @ 48"		2.36	5.45	7.81
7430				#5 @ 32"		2.51	5.70	8.21
7440				#5 @ 16"		2.87	6.55	9.42
7450		8x8x16	85	#4 @ 48"		2.09	5.35	7.44
7480				#5 @ 32"		2.24	5.55	7.79
7490				#5 @ 16"		2.60	6.45	9.05
7510		12x8x16	105	#4 @ 48"		3.59	6.85	10.44
7530				#5 @ 32"		3.78	7.05	10.83
7540				#5 @ 16"		4.30	7.95	12.25
7550			85	#4 @ 48"		2.88	6.70	9.58
7580				#5 @ 32"		3.07	6.90	9.97
7590				#5 @ 16"		3.59	7.80	11.39
7600		4x8x24	105	#4 @ 48"		1.07	5.20	6.27
7650			85	#4 @ 48"		2.19	4.47	6.66
7700		6x8x24	105	#4 @ 48"		1.46	5.45	6.91
7730				#5 @ 32"		1.59	5.65	7.24
7740				#5 @ 16"		1.89	6.30	8.19
7750			85	#4 @ 48"		3.04	4.65	7.69
7780				#5 @ 32"		3.17	4.85	8.02
7790				#5 @ 16"		3.47	5.55	9.02
7800		8x8x24	105	#4 @ 48"		1.78	5.85	7.63
7840				#5 @ 16"		2.29	6.90	9.19
7850			85	#4 @ 48"		3.59	5	8.59
7880				#5 @ 32"		3.74	5.25	8.99
7890				#5 @ 16"		4.10	6.10	10.20
7900		12x8x24	105	#4 @ 48"		2.67	6.60	9.27
7930				#5 @ 32"		2.86	6.80	9.66
7940				#5 @ 16"		3.38	7.70	11.08
7950			85	#4 @ 48"		4.77	6.45	11.22
7980				#5 @ 32"		4.96	6.65	11.61
7990				#5 @ 16"		5.50	7.55	13.05
8100	75% solid	6x8x16	105	#4 @ 48"		1.64	5	6.64
8130				#5 @ 32"		1.73	5.15	6.88
8140				#5 @ 16"		1.90	5.75	7.65
8150			85	#4 @ 48"		2.74	4.92	7.66
8180				#5 @ 32"		2.83	5.05	7.88
8190				#5 @ 16"		3	5.65	8.65
8200		8x8x16	105	#4 @ 48"		2.19	5.40	7.59
8230				#5 @ 32"		2.28	5.60	7.88
8240				#5 @ 16"		2.47	6.25	8.72
8250			85	#4 @ 48"		3.72	5.30	9.02
8280				#5 @ 32"		3.81	5.45	9.26
8290				#5 @ 16"		4	6.15	10.15

B2010 Exterior Walls

B2010 112	Reinforced Concrete Block Wall - Lightweight

	TYPE	SIZE (IN.)	WEIGHT (P.C.F.)	VERT REINF. & GROUT SPACING		COST PER S.F.		
						MAT.	INST.	TOTAL
8300	75% Solid	12x8x16	105	#4 @ 48"		4.05	6.80	10.85
8330				#5 @ 32"		4.18	7	11.18
8340				#5 @ 16"		4.48	7.70	12.18
8350			85	#4 @ 48"		5.05	6.60	11.65
8380				#5 @ 32"		5.20	6.80	12
8390				. #5 @ 16"		5.50	7.50	13
8500	Solid-double	2-4x8x16	105	#4 @ 48"		3.48	10.10	13.58
8530	Wythe		105	#5 @ 16"		3.90	10.70	14.60
8550			85	#4 @ 48"		4.30	9.70	14
8580				#5 @ 16"		4.72	10.30	15.02
8600		2-6x8x16	105	#4 @ 48"		4.55	10.75	15.30
8630				#5 @ 16"		4.97	11.40	16.37
8650			85	#4 @ 48"		6.35	10.30	16.65
8680				#5 @ 16"		6.80	10.95	17.75
8900	For stacked bond add						.40	.40
8910								

B20 Exterior Enclosure

B2010 Exterior Walls

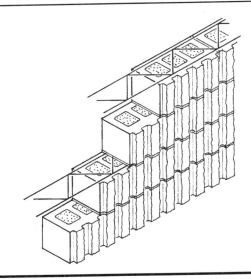

Exterior split ribbed block walls are defined in the following terms; structural reinforcement, weight, percent solid, size, number of ribs and insulation. Within each of these categories two to four variations are shown. No costs are included for brick shelf or relieving angles. Costs include control joints every 20′ and horizontal reinforcing.

System Components	QUANTITY	UNIT	COST PER S.F.		
			MAT.	INST.	TOTAL
SYSTEM B2010 113 1430					
UNREINFORCED SPLIT RIB BLOCK WALL, 8″X8″X16″, 8 RIBS(HEX), PERLITE FILL					
Split ribbed block wall, 8″ thick	1.000	S.F.	3.88	5.90	9.78
Perlite insulation	1.000	S.F.	.47	.29	.76
Horizontal joint reinforcing, alternate courses	.800	L.F.	.07	.13	.20
Control joint	.050	L.F.	.05	.05	.10
TOTAL			4.47	6.37	10.84

B2010 113		Split Ribbed Block Wall - Regular Weight					COST PER S.F.		
	TYPE	SIZE (IN.)	RIBS	CORE FILL			MAT.	INST.	TOTAL
1220	Hollow	4x8x16	4	none			2.20	5.35	7.55
1250			8	none			2.56	5.35	7.91
1280			16	none			2.09	5.45	7.54
1330		4x8x16	4	none			3.49	5.95	9.44
1340				styrofoam			4.11	5.70	9.81
1350				none			3.17	5.70	8.87
1360			16	perlite			3.09	6.05	9.14
1370				styrofoam			3.71	5.80	9.51
1380				none			2.77	5.80	8.57
1430		8x8x16	8	perlite			4.47	6.35	10.82
1440				styrofoam			4.94	6.10	11.04
1450				none			4	6.10	10.10
1460			16	perlite			3.70	6.45	10.15
1470				styrofoam			4.17	6.20	10.37
1480				none			3.23	6.20	9.43
1530		12x8x16	8	perlite			5.65	8.45	14.10
1540				styrofoam			6	7.85	13.85
1550				none			4.86	7.85	12.71
1560			16	perlite			4.74	8.60	13.34
1570				styrofoam			5.15	8	13.15
1580				none			3.97	8	11.97

B2010 Exterior Walls

| B2010 113 | Split Ribbed Block Wall - Regular Weight | | | | | | | |

	TYPE	SIZE (IN.)	RIBS	CORE FILL		COST PER S.F.		
						MAT.	INST.	TOTAL
2120	75% solid	4x8x16	4	none		2.76	5.45	8.21
2150			8	none		3.27	5.45	8.72
2180			16	none		2.65	5.50	8.15
2230	75% solid	6x8x16	8	perlite		4.23	5.95	10.18
2250				none		4.07	5.80	9.87
2260			16	perlite		3.70	6	9.70
2280				none		3.54	5.85	9.39
2330		8x8x16	8	perlite		5.35	6.35	11.70
2350				none		5.10	6.20	11.30
2360			16	perlite		4.33	6.45	10.78
2380				none		4.09	6.30	10.39
2430		12x8x16	8	perlite		6.50	8.30	14.80
2450				none		6.15	8	14.15
2460			16	perlite		5.45	8.45	13.90
2480				none		5.05	8.15	13.20
2520	Solid	4x8x16	4	none		3.37	5.50	8.87
2550			8	none		3.95	5.50	9.45
2580			16	none		3.18	5.60	8.78
2620		6x8x16	8	none		4.92	5.85	10.77
2650			16	none		4.27	5.95	10.22
2680		8x8x16	8	none		6.20	6.30	12.50
2720			16	none		4.94	6.40	11.34
2750		12x8x16	8	none		7.45	8.15	15.60
2780			16	none		6.10	8.30	14.40

| B2010 113 | Split Ribbed Block Wall - Lightweight | | | | | | | |

	TYPE	SIZE (IN.)	RIBS	CORE FILL		COST PER S.F.		
						MAT.	INST.	TOTAL
3250	Hollow	4x8x16	8	none		2.74	5.20	7.94
3280			16	none		2.28	5.30	7.58
3330		6x8x16	8	perlite		3.71	5.75	9.46
3340				styrofoam		4.33	5.50	9.83
3350				none		3.39	5.50	8.89
3360			16	perlite		3.32	5.85	9.17
3370				styrofoam		3.94	5.60	9.54
3380				none		3	5.60	8.60
3430		8x8x16	8	perlite		5.20	6.15	11.35
3440				styrofoam		5.65	5.90	11.55
3450				none		4.72	5.90	10.62
3460			16	perlite		3.96	6.25	10.21
3470				styrofoam		4.43	6	10.43
3480				none		3.49	6	9.49
3530		12x8x16	8	perlite		6.20	8.20	14.40
3540				styrofoam		6.60	7.60	14.20
3550				none		5.45	7.60	13.05
3560			16	perlite		5.05	8.30	13.35
3570				styrofoam		5.45	7.70	13.15
3580				none		4.28	7.70	11.98
4150	75% solid	4x8x16	8	none		3.53	5.30	8.83
4180			16	none		2.86	5.35	8.21

B20 Exterior Enclosure

B2010 Exterior Walls

B2010 113 — Split Ribbed Block Wall - Lightweight

	TYPE	SIZE (IN.)	RIBS	CORE FILL		COST PER S.F.		
						MAT.	INST.	TOTAL
4230	75% Solid	6x8x16	8	perlite		4.46	5.75	10.21
4250				none		4.30	5.60	9.90
4260			16	perlite		3.98	5.85	9.83
4280				none		3.82	5.70	9.52
4330		8x8x16	8	perlite		6.25	6.15	12.40
4350				none		6	6	12
4360			16	perlite		4.68	6.25	10.93
4380		8x8x16	16	none		4.44	6.10	10.54
4430		12x8x16	8	perlite		7.30	8	15.30
4450				none		6.95	7.70	14.65
4460			16	perlite		5.80	8.15	13.95
4480				none		5.45	7.85	13.30
4550	Solid	4x8x16	8	none		4.26	5.35	9.61
4580			16	none		3.48	5.45	8.93
4650		6x8x16	8	none		5.20	5.70	10.90
4680			16	none		4.62	5.80	10.42
4750		8x8x16	8	none		7.30	6.10	13.40
4780			16	none		5.35	6.20	11.55
4850		12x8x16	8	none		8.40	7.85	16.25
4880			16	none		6.60	8	14.60

B2010 113 — Reinforced Split Ribbed Block Wall - Regular Weight

	TYPE	SIZE (IN.)	RIBS	VERT. REINF. & GROUT SPACING		COST PER S.F.		
						MAT.	INST.	TOTAL
5200	Hollow	4x8x16	4	#4 @ 48"		2.30	5.85	8.15
5230			8	#4 @ 48"		2.66	5.85	8.51
5260			16	#4 @ 48"		2.19	5.95	8.14
5330		6x8x16	8	#4 @ 48"		3.35	6.20	9.55
5340				#5 @ 32"		3.48	6.40	9.88
5350				#5 @ 16"		3.78	7.10	10.88
5360			16	#4 @ 48"		2.95	6.30	9.25
5370				#5 @ 32"		3.08	6.50	9.58
5380				#5 @ 16"		3.38	7.20	10.58
5430		8x8x16	8	#4 @ 48"		4.22	6.70	10.92
5440				#5 @ 32"		4.37	6.90	11.27
5450				#5 @ 16"		4.73	7.75	12.48
5460			16	#4 @ 48"		3.45	6.80	10.25
5470				#5 @ 32"		3.60	7	10.60
5480				#5 @ 16"		3.96	7.85	11.81
5530		12x8x16	8	#4 @ 48"		5.20	8.50	13.70
5540				#5 @ 32"		5.35	8.70	14.05
5550				#5 @ 16"		5.90	9.60	15.50
5560			16	#4 @ 48"		4.29	8.65	12.94
5570				#5 @ 32"		4.48	8.85	13.33
5580				#5 @ 16"		5	9.75	14.75
6230	75% Solid	6x8x16	8	#4 @ 48"		4.16	6.25	10.41
6240				#5 @ 32"		4.25	6.40	10.65
6250				#5 @ 16"		4.42	6.95	11.37
6260			16	#4 @ 48"		3.63	6.30	9.93
6270				#5 @ 32"		3.72	6.45	10.17
6280				#5 @ 16"		3.89	7	10.89

B2010 Exterior Walls

B2010 113 — Reinforced Split Ribbed Block Wall - Regular Weight

	TYPE	SIZE (IN.)	RIBS	VERT. REINF. & GROUT SPACING		MAT.	INST.	TOTAL
6330	75% Solid	8x8x16	8	#4 @ 48"		5.20	6.65	11.85
6340				#5 @ 32"		5.30	6.85	12.15
6350				#5 @ 16"		5.50	7.50	13
6360			16	#4 @ 48"		4.19	6.75	10.94
6370				#5 @ 32"		4.28	6.95	11.23
6380				#5 @ 16"		4.47	7.60	12.07
6430		12x8x16	8	#4 @ 48"		6.30	8.50	14.80
6440				#5 @ 32"		6.45	8.70	15.15
6450				#5 @ 16"		6.75	9.40	16.15
6460			16	#4 @ 48"		5.20	8.65	13.85
6470				#5 @ 32"		5.35	8.85	14.20
6480				#5 @ 16"		5.65	9.55	15.20
6500	Solid-double Wythe	2-4x8x16	4	#4 @ 48"		4.07	6.65	10.72
6520				#5 @ 16"		4.27	6.95	11.22
6530			8	#4 @ 48"		4.65	6.65	11.30
6550				#5 @ 16"		4.85	6.95	11.80
6560			16	#4 @ 48"		3.88	6.75	10.63
6580				#5 @ 16"		4.08	7.05	11.13
6630		2-6x8x16	8	#4 @ 48"		5.60	7.05	12.65
6650				#5 @ 16"		5.80	7.35	13.15
6660			16	#4 @ 48"		4.97	7.15	12.12
6680				#5 @ 16"		5.15	7.45	12.60

B2010 113 — Reinforced Split Ribbed Block Wall - Lightweight

	TYPE	SIZE (IN.)	RIBS	VERT. REINF. & GROUT SPACING		MAT.	INST.	TOTAL
7230	Hollow	4x8x16	8	#4 @ 48"		2.84	5.70	8.54
7260			16	#4 @ 48"		2.38	5.80	8.18
7330		6x8x16	8	#4 @ 48"		3.57	6	9.57
7340				#5 @ 32"		3.70	6.20	9.90
7350				#5 @ 16"		4	6.90	10.90
7360			16	#4 @ 48"		3.18	6.10	9.28
7370				#5 @ 32"		3.31	6.30	9.61
7380				#5 @ 16"		3.61	7	10.61
7430		8x8x16	8	#4 @ 48"		4.94	6.50	11.44
7440				#5 @ 32"		5.10	6.70	11.80
7450				#5 @ 16"		5.45	7.55	13
7460			16	#4 @ 48"		3.71	6.60	10.31
7470				#5 @ 32"		3.86	6.80	10.66
7480				#5 @ 16"		4.22	7.65	11.87
7530		12x8x16	8	#4 @ 48"		5.75	8.25	14
7540				#5 @ 32"		5.95	8.45	14.40
7550				#5 @ 16"		6.45	9.35	15.80
7560			16	#4 @ 48"		4.60	8.35	12.95
7570				#5 @ 32"		4.79	8.55	13.34
7580				#5 @ 16"		5.30	9.45	14.75
8230	75% Solid	6x8x16	8	#4 @ 48"		4.39	6.05	10.44
8240				#5 @ 32"		4.48	6.20	10.68
8250				#5 @ 16"		4.65	6.75	11.40
8260			16	#4 @ 48"		3.91	6.15	10.06
8270				#5 @ 32"		4	6.30	10.30
8280				#5 @ 16"		4.17	6.85	11.02

B20 Exterior Enclosure

B2010 Exterior Walls

B2010 113		Reinforced Split Ribbed Block Wall - Lightweight						
	TYPE	SIZE (IN.)	RIBS	VERT. REINF. & GROUT SPACING		COST PER S.F.		
						MAT.	INST.	TOTAL
8330	75% Solid	8x8x16	8	#4 @ 48"		6.10	6.45	12.55
8340				#5 @ 32"		6.20	6.65	12.85
8350				#5 @ 16"		6.40	7.30	13.70
8360			16	#4 @ 48"		4.54	6.55	11.09
8370				#5 @ 32"		4.63	6.75	11.38
8380				#5 @ 16"		4.82	7.40	12.22
8430		12x8x16	8	#4 @ 48"		7.10	8.20	15.30
8440				#5 @ 32"		7.25	8.40	15.65
8450				#5 @ 16"		7.55	9.10	16.65
8460			16	#4 @ 48"		5.60	8.35	13.95
8470				#5 @ 32"		5.75	8.55	14.30
8480				#5 @ 16"		6.05	9.25	15.30
8530	Solid double Wythe	2-4x8x16	8	#4 @ 48" E.W		5	6.70	11.70
8550				#5 @ 16" E.W.		5.45	7.35	12.80
8560			16	#4 @ 48" E.W.		4.23	6.80	11.03
8580				#5 @ 16" E.W.		4.65	7.45	12.10
8630	Solid double Wythe	2-6x8x16	8	#4 @ 48" E.W.		5.95	7.10	13.05
8650				#5 @ 16" E.W.		6.40	7.70	14.10
8660			16	#4 @ 48" E.W.		5.35	7.20	12.55
8680				#5 @ 16" E.W.		5.80	7.80	13.60
8900	For stacked bond, add						.40	.40

B2010 Exterior Walls

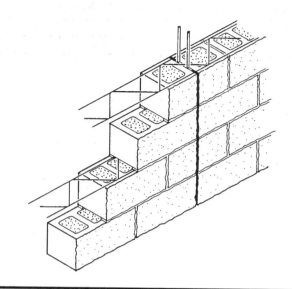

Exterior split face block walls are defined in the following terms; structural reinforcement, weight, percent solid, size, scores and insulation. Within each of these categories two to four variations are shown. No costs are included for brick shelf or relieving angles. Costs include control joints every 20' and horizontal reinforcing.

System Components		QUANTITY	UNIT	COST PER S.F.		
				MAT.	INST.	TOTAL
SYSTEM B2010 115 1600						
UNREINFORCED SPLIT FACE BLOCK WALL, 8"X8"X16", O SCORES, PERLITE FILL						
Split face block wall, 8" thick		1.000	S.F.	3.27	6.10	9.37
Perlite insulation		1.000	S.F.	.47	.29	.76
Horizontal joint reinforcing, alternate course		.800	L.F.	.07	.13	.20
Control joint		.050	L.F.	.05	.05	.10
	TOTAL			3.86	6.57	10.43

B2010 115		Split Face Block Wall - Regular Weight						
	TYPE	SIZE (IN.)	SCORES	CORE FILL		COST PER S.F.		
						MAT.	INST.	TOTAL
1200	Hollow	8x4x16	0	perlite		6.55	7	13.55
1210				styrofoam		7	6.75	13.75
1240				none		6.05	6.75	12.80
1250			1	perlite		7	7	14
1260				styrofoam		7.45	6.75	14.20
1290				none		6.50	6.75	13.25
1300		12x4x16	0	perlite		8.55	8	16.55
1310				styrofoam		8.95	7.40	16.35
1340				none		7.80	7.40	15.20
1350			1	perlite		9	8	17
1360				styrofoam		9.40	7.40	16.80
1390				none		8.25	7.40	15.65
1400		4x8x16	0	none		2.20	5.30	7.50
1450			1	none		2.48	5.35	7.83
1500		6x8x16	0	perlite		3.18	6.10	9.28
1510				styrofoam		3.80	5.85	9.65
1540				none		2.86	5.85	8.71
1550			1	perlite		3.47	6.20	9.67
1560				styrofoam		4.09	5.95	10.04
1590				none		3.15	5.95	9.10

B20 Exterior Enclosure

B2010 Exterior Walls

B2010 115 — Split Face Block Wall - Regular Weight

	TYPE	SIZE (IN.)	SCORES	CORE FILL		MAT.	INST.	TOTAL
						\<COST PER S.F.\>		
1600	Hollow	8x8x16	0	perlite		3.86	6.55	10.41
1610				styrofoam		4.33	6.30	10.63
1640				none		3.39	6.30	9.69
1650		8x8x16	1	perlite		4.09	6.65	10.74
1660				styrofoam		4.56	6.40	10.96
1690				none		3.62	6.40	10.02
1700		12x8x16	0	perlite		4.97	8.60	13.57
1710				styrofoam		5.35	8	13.35
1740				none		4.20	8	12.20
1750			1	perlite		5.20	8.75	13.95
1760				styrofoam		5.60	8.15	13.75
1790				none		4.44	8.15	12.59
1800	75% Solid	8x4x16	0	perlite		7.90	7	14.90
1840				none		7.65	6.85	14.50
1850			1	perlite		8.40	7	15.40
1890				none		8.15	6.85	15
1900		12x4x16	0	perlite		10.25	7.85	18.10
1940				none		9.90	7.55	17.45
1950			1	perlite		10.65	7.85	18.50
1990				none		10.30	7.55	17.85
2000		4x8x16	0	none		2.76	5.35	8.11
2050			1	none		3	5.45	8.45
2100		6x8x16	0	perlite		3.84	7.10	10.94
2140				none		3.68	6.95	10.63
2150			1	perlite		4.08	6.20	10.28
2190				none		3.92	6.05	9.97
2200		8x8x16	0	perlite		4.53	6.55	11.08
2240				none		4.29	6.40	10.69
2250			1	perlite		4.76	6.65	11.41
2290				none		4.52	6.50	11.02
2300		12x8x16	0	perlite		5.70	8.45	14.15
2340				none		5.35	8.15	13.50
2350			1	perlite		5.90	8.60	14.50
2390				none		5.55	8.30	13.85
2400	Solid	8x4x16	0	none		9.35	7	16.35
2450			1	none		9.85	7	16.85
2500		12x4x16	0	none		11.90	7.70	19.60
2550			1	none		12.40	8.95	21.35
2600		4x8x16	0	none		3.37	5.45	8.82
2650			1	none		3.60	5.50	9.10
2700		6x8x16	0	none		4.49	6.05	10.54
2750			1	none		4.72	6.15	10.87
2800		8x8x16	0	none		5.15	6.50	11.65
2850			1	none		5.40	6.65	12.05
2900		12x8x16	0	none		6.45	8.30	14.75
2950			1	none		6.65	8.45	15.10

B2010 115 — Split Face Block Wall - Lightweight

	TYPE	SIZE (IN.)	SCORES	CORE FILL		MAT.	INST.	TOTAL
						\<COST PER S.F.\>		
3200	Hollow	8x4x16	0	perlite		6.75	7.85	14.60
3210				styrofoam		7.20	7.60	14.80
3240				none		6.25	7.60	13.85

284

B2010 Exterior Walls

B2010 115	Split Face Block Wall - Lightweight

	TYPE	SIZE (IN.)	SCORES	CORE FILL		COST PER S.F.		
						MAT.	INST.	TOTAL
3250	Hollow		1	perlite		7.25	6.75	14
3260				styrofoam		7.70	6.50	14.20
3290				none		6.75	6.50	13.25
3300		12x4x16	0	perlite		8.90	7.70	16.60
3310				styrofoam		9.30	7.10	16.40
3340				none		8.15	7.10	15.25
3350		12x4x16	1	perlite		9.35	8.90	18.25
3360				styrofoam		9.75	8.30	18.05
3390				none		8.60	8.30	16.90
3400		4x8x16	0	none		2.39	5.15	7.54
3450			1	none		2.60	5.20	7.80
3500		6x8x16	0	perlite		3.53	5.95	9.48
3510				styrofoam		4.15	5.70	9.85
3540				none		3.21	5.70	8.91
3550			1	perlite		3.75	6.05	9.80
3560				styrofoam		4.37	5.80	10.17
3590				none		3.43	5.80	9.23
3600		8x8x16	0	perlite		4.15	6.35	10.50
3610				styrofoam		4.62	6.10	10.72
3640				none		3.68	6.10	9.78
3650			1	perlite		4.39	6.45	10.84
3660				styrofoam		4.86	6.20	11.06
3690				none		3.92	6.20	10.12
3700		12x8x16	0	perlite		5.25	8.30	13.55
3710				styrofoam		5.65	7.70	13.35
3740				none		4.50	7.70	12.20
3750			1	perlite		5.50	8.45	13.95
3760				styrofoam		5.90	7.85	13.75
3790				none		4.73	7.85	12.58
3800	75% solid	8x4x16	0	perlite		8.40	7	15.40
3840				none		8.15	6.85	15
3850			1	perlite		8.75	6.80	15.55
3890				none		8.50	6.65	15.15
3900		12x4x16	0	perlite		10.65	7.85	18.50
3940				none		10.30	7.55	17.85
3950			1	perlite		11.15	8.75	19.90
3990				none		10.80	8.45	19.25
4000		4x8x16	0	none		3.01	5.20	8.21
4050			1	none		3.26	5.30	8.56
4100		6x8x16	0	perlite		4.22	5.95	10.17
4140				none		4.06	5.80	9.86
4150			1	perlite		4.46	6	10.46
4190				none		4.30	5.85	10.15
4200		8x8x16	0	perlite		4.94	6.35	11.29
4240				none		4.70	6.20	10.90
4250			1	perlite		5.15	6.45	11.60
4290				none		4.91	6.30	11.21
4300		12x8x16	0	perlite		6.05	8.15	14.20
4340				none		5.70	7.85	13.55
4350			1	perlite		6.30	8.30	14.60
4390				none		5.95	8	13.95

B20 Exterior Enclosure

B2010 Exterior Walls

B2010 115 — Split Face Block Wall - Lightweight

	TYPE	SIZE (IN.)	SCORES	CORE FILL		MAT.	INST.	TOTAL
						COST PER S.F.		
4400	Solid	8x4x16	0	none		9.70	6.75	16.45
4450			1	none		10.15	6.75	16.90
4500		12x4x16	0	none		12.50	7.40	19.90
4550			1	none		13	8.60	21.60
4600		4x8x16	0	none		3.65	5.30	8.95
4650			1	none		3.89	5.35	9.24
4700		6x8x16	0	none		4.93	5.85	10.78
4750			1	none		5.15	5.95	11.10
4800		8x8x16	0	none		5.65	6.30	11.95
4850			1	none		5.90	6.40	12.30
4900		12x8x16	0	none		6.85	8	14.85
4950			1	none		7.10	8.15	15.25

B2010 115 — Reinforced Split Face Block Wall - Regular Weight

	TYPE	SIZE (IN.)	SCORES	VERT. REINF. & GROUT SPACING		MAT.	INST.	TOTAL
						COST PER S.F.		
5200	Hollow	8x4x16	0	#4 @ 48"		6.30	7.35	13.65
5210				#5 @ 32"		6.45	7.55	14
5240				#5 @ 16"		6.80	8.40	15.20
5250			1	#4 @ 48"		6.75	7.35	14.10
5260				#5 @ 32"		6.90	7.55	14.45
5290				#5 @ 16"		7.25	8.40	15.65
5300		12x4x16	0	#4 @ 48"		8.10	8.05	16.15
5310				#5 @ 32"		8.30	8.25	16.55
5340				#5 @ 16"		8.80	9.15	17.95
5350			1	#4 @ 48"		8.55	8.05	16.60
5360				#5 @ 32"		8.75	8.25	17
5390				#5 @ 16"		9.25	9.15	18.40
5400		4x8x16	0	#4 @ 48"		2.30	5.80	8.10
5450			1	#4 @ 48"		2.58	5.85	8.43
5500		6x8x16	0	#4 @ 48"		3.04	6.35	9.39
5510				#5 @ 32"		3.17	6.55	9.72
5540				#5 @ 16"		3.47	7.25	10.72
5550			1	#4 @ 48"		3.33	6.45	9.78
5560				#5 @ 32"		3.46	6.65	10.11
5590				#5 @ 16"		3.76	7.35	11.11
5600		8x8x16	0	#4 @ 48"		3.61	6.90	10.51
5610				#5 @ 32"		3.76	7.10	10.86
5640				#5 @ 16"		3.92	7.55	11.47
5650			1	#4 @ 48"		5.30	9.50	14.80
5660				#5 @ 32"		3.99	7.20	11.19
5690				#5 @ 16"		4.35	8.05	12.40
5700		12x8x16	0	#4 @ 48"		4.52	8.65	13.17
5710				#5 @ 32"		4.71	8.85	13.56
5740				#5 @ 16"		5.25	9.75	15
5750			1	#4 @ 48"		4.76	8.80	13.56
5760				#5 @ 32"		4.95	9	13.95
5790				#5 @ 16"		5.45	9.90	15.35

B2010 Exterior Walls

B2010 115 — Reinforced Split Face Block Wall - Regular Weight

	TYPE	SIZE (IN.)	SCORES	VERT. REINF. & GROUT SPACING		COST PER S.F.		
						MAT.	INST.	TOTAL
6000	75% solid	8x4x16	0	#4 @ 48"		7.75	7.30	15.05
6010				#5 @ 32"		7.85	7.50	15.35
6040				#5 @ 16"		8.05	8.15	16.20
6050			1	#4 @ 48"		8.25	7.30	15.55
6060				#5 @ 32"		8.35	7.50	15.85
6090				#5 @ 16"		8.55	8.15	16.70
6100		12x4x16	0	#4 @ 48"		10.05	8.05	18.10
6110				#5 @ 32"		10.20	8.25	18.45
6140				#5 @ 16"		10.45	8.85	19.30
6150			1	#4 @ 48"		10.45	8.05	18.50
6160				#5 @ 32"		10.60	8.25	18.85
6190				#5 @ 16"		10.90	8.95	19.85
6200		6x8x16	0	#4 @ 48"		3.77	7.40	11.17
6210				#5 @ 32"		3.86	7.55	11.41
6240				#5 @ 16"		4.03	8.10	12.13
6250			1	#4 @ 48"		4.01	6.50	10.51
6260				#5 @ 32"		4.10	6.65	10.75
6290				#5 @ 16"		4.27	7.20	11.47
6300		8x8x16	0	#4 @ 48"		4.39	6.85	11.24
6310				#5 @ 32"		4.48	7.05	11.53
6340				#5 @ 16"		4.67	7.70	12.37
6350			1	#4 @ 48"		4.62	6.95	11.57
6360				#5 @ 32"		4.71	7.15	11.86
6390				#5 @ 16"		4.90	7.80	12.70
6400	75% solid	12x8x16	0	#4 @ 48"		5.50	8.65	14.15
6410				#5 @ 32"		5.65	8.85	14.50
6440				#5 @ 16"		5.95	9.55	15.50
6450			1	#4 @ 48"		5.70	8.80	14.50
6460				#5 @ 32"		5.85	9	14.85
6490				#5 @ 16"		6.15	9.70	15.85
6700	Solid-double Wythe	2-4x8x16	0	#4 @ 48" E.W.		7.40	12.10	19.50
6710				#5 @ 32" E.W.		7.55	12.20	19.75
6740				#5 @ 16" E.W.		7.80	12.75	20.55
6750			1	#4 @ 48" E.W.		7.85	12.20	20.05
6760				#5 @ 32" E.W.		8	12.30	20.30
6790				#5 @ 16" E.W.		8.25	12.85	21.10
6800		2-6x8x16	0	#4 @ 48" E.W.		9.60	13.35	22.95
6810				#5 @ 32" E.W.		9.75	13.45	23.20
6840				#5 @ 16" E.W.		10.05	13.95	24
6850			1	#4 @ 48" E.W.		10.05	13.55	23.60
6860				#5 @ 32" E.W.		10.20	13.65	23.85
6890				#5 @ 16" E.W.		10.50	14.15	24.65

B2010 115 — Reinforced Split Face Block Wall - Lightweight

	TYPE	SIZE (IN.)	SCORES	VERT. REINF. & GROUT SPACING		COST PER S.F.		
						MAT.	INST.	TOTAL
7200	Hollow	8x4x16	0	#4 @ 48"		6.50	8.20	14.70
7210				#5 @ 32"		6.65	8.40	15.05
7240				#5 @ 16"		7	9.25	16.25
7250			1	#4 @ 48"		7	7.10	14.10
7260				#5 @ 32"		7.15	7.30	14.45
7290				#5 @ 16"		7.50	8.15	15.65

B20 Exterior Enclosure

B2010 Exterior Walls

B2010 115 — Reinforced Split Face Block Wall - Lightweight

	TYPE	SIZE (IN.)	SCORES	VERT. REINF. & GROUT SPACING		COST PER S.F. MAT.	INST.	TOTAL
7300	Hollow	12x4x16	0	#4 @ 48"		8.45	7.75	16.20
7310				#5 @ 32"		8.65	7.95	16.60
7340				#5 @ 16"		9.15	8.85	18
7350			1	#4 @ 48"		8.90	8.95	17.85
7360				#5 @ 32"		9.10	9.15	18.25
7390				#5 @ 16"		9.60	10.05	19.65
7400		4x8x16	0	#4 @ 48"		2.49	5.65	8.14
7450			1	#4 @ 48"		2.70	5.70	8.40
7500		6x8x16	0	#4 @ 48"		3.39	6.20	9.59
7510				#5 @ 32"		3.52	6.40	9.92
7540				#5 @ 16"		3.82	7.10	10.92
7550			1	#4 @ 48"		3.61	6.30	9.91
7560				#5 @ 32"		3.74	6.50	10.24
7590				#5 @ 16"		4.04	7.20	11.24
7600		8x8x16	0	#4 @ 48"		3.90	6.70	10.60
7610				#5 @ 32"		4.05	6.90	10.95
7640				#5 @ 16"		4.41	7.75	12.16
7650			1	#4 @ 48"		4.14	6.80	10.94
7660				#5 @ 32"		4.29	7	11.29
7690				#5 @ 16"		4.65	7.85	12.50
7700		12x8x16	0	#4 @ 48"		4.82	8.35	13.17
7710				#5 @ 32"		5	8.55	13.55
7740		12x8x16	0	#5 @ 16"		5.55	9.45	15
7750			1	#4 @ 48"		5.05	8.50	13.55
7760				#5 @ 16"		5.25	8.70	13.95
7790				#5 @ 16"		5.75	9.60	15.35
8000	75% solid	8x4x16	0	#4 @ 48"		8.25	7.30	15.55
8010				#5 @ 32"		8.35	7.50	15.85
8040				#5 @ 16"		8.55	8.15	16.70
8050			1	#4 @ 48"		8.60	7.10	15.70
8060				#5 @ 32"		8.70	7.30	16
8090				#5 @ 16"		8.90	7.95	16.85
8100		12x4x16	0	#4 @ 48"		10.45	8.05	18.50
8110				#5 @ 32"		10.60	8.25	18.85
8140				#5 @ 16"		10.90	8.95	19.85
8150			1	#4 @ 48"		10.95	8.95	19.90
8160				#5 @ 32"		11.10	9.15	20.25
8190				#5 @ 16"		11.40	9.85	21.25
8200		6x8x16	0	#4 @ 48"		4.15	6.25	10.40
8210				#5 @ 32"		4.24	6.40	10.64
8240				#5 @ 16"		4.41	6.95	11.36
8250			1	#4 @ 48"		4.39	6.30	10.69
8260				#5 @ 32"		4.48	6.45	10.93
8290				#5 @ 16"		4.65	7	11.65
8300		8x8x16	0	#4 @ 48"		4.80	6.65	11.45
8310				#5 @ 32"		4.89	6.85	11.74
8340				#5 @ 16"		5.10	7.50	12.60
8350			1	#4 @ 48"		5	6.75	11.75
8360				#5 @ 32"		5.10	6.95	12.05
8390				#5 @ 16"		5.30	7.60	12.90

B2010 Exterior Walls

B2010 115			**Reinforced Split Face Block Wall - Lightweight**				

	TYPE	SIZE (IN.)	SCORES	VERT. REINF. & GROUT SPACING		COST PER S.F.		
						MAT.	INST.	TOTAL
8400	75% Solid	12x8x16	0	#4 @ 48"		5.85	8.35	14.20
8410				#5 @ 32"		6	8.55	14.55
8440				#5 @ 16"		6.30	9.25	15.55
8450			1	#4 @ 48"		6.10	8.50	14.60
8460				#5 @ 32"		6.25	8.70	14.95
8490				#5 @ 16"		6.55	9.40	15.95
8700	Solid-double	2-4x8x16	0	#4 @ 48" E.W.		7.95	11.80	19.75
8710	Wythe			#5 @ 32" E.W.		8.10	11.90	20
8740				#5 @ 16" E.W.		8.35	12.45	20.80
8750			1	#4 @ 48" E.W.		8.40	11.90	20.30
8760				#5 @ 32" E.W.		8.55	12	20.55
8790				#5 @ 16" E.W.		8.85	12.55	21.40
8800		2-6x8x16	0	#4 @ 48" E.W.		10.50	12.95	23.45
8810				#5 @ 32" E.W.		10.65	13.05	23.70
8840				#5 @ 16" E.W.		10.90	13.55	24.45
8850			1	#4 @ 48" E.W.		10.95	13.15	24.10
8860				#5 @ 32" E.W.		11.10	13.25	24.35
8890				#5 @ 16" E.W.		11.40	13.75	25.15

B20 Exterior Enclosure

B2010 Exterior Walls

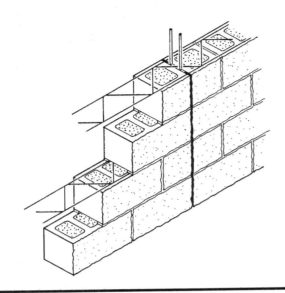

Exterior ground face block walls are defined in the following terms; structural reinforcement, weight, percent solid, size, scores and insulation. Within each of these categories two to four variations are shown. No costs are included for brick shelf or relieving angles. Costs include control joints every 20' and horizontal reinforcing.

System Components	QUANTITY	UNIT	COST PER S.F.		
			MAT.	INST.	TOTAL
SYSTEM B2010 117 1600					
UNREINF. GROUND FACE BLOCK WALL, 8"X8"X16", 0 SCORES, PERLITE FILL					
Ground face block wall, 8" thick	1.000	S.F.	5.60	6.20	11.80
Perlite insulation	1.000	S.F.	.47	.29	.76
Horizontal joint reinforcing, alternate course	.800	L.F.	.07	.13	.20
Control joint	.050	L.F.	.05	.05	.10
TOTAL			6.19	6.67	12.86

B2010 117		Ground Face Block Wall			COST PER S.F.		
	TYPE	SIZE (IN.)	SCORES	CORE FILL	MAT.	INST.	TOTAL
1200	Hollow	4x8x16	0	none	3.96	5.35	9.31
1250			1	none	4.03	5.45	9.48
1300			2 to 5	none	4.14	5.50	9.64
1400		6x8x16	0	perlite	5.15	6.20	11.35
1410				styrofoam	5.80	5.95	11.75
1440				none	4.84	5.95	10.79
1450			1	perlite	5.25	6.30	11.55
1460				styrofoam	5.85	6.05	11.90
1490				none	4.91	6.05	10.96
1500			2 to 5	perlite	5.35	6.40	11.75
1510				styrofoam	5.95	6.15	12.10
1540				none	5	6.15	11.15
1600		8x8x16	0	perlite	6.20	6.65	12.85
1610				styrofoam	6.65	6.40	13.05
1640				none	5.70	6.40	12.10
1650			1	perlite	6.30	6.75	13.05
1660				styrofoam	6.75	6.50	13.25
1690				none	5.80	6.50	12.30
1700			2 to 5	perlite	6.40	6.90	13.30
1710				styrofoam	6.85	6.65	13.50
1740				none	5.90	6.65	12.55

B2010 Exterior Walls

B2010 117 — Ground Face Block Wall

	TYPE	SIZE (IN.)	SCORES	CORE FILL		COST PER S.F. MAT.	INST.	TOTAL
1800	Hollow	12x8x16	0	perlite		8.20	8.75	16.95
1810				styrofoam		8.60	8.15	16.75
1840				none		7.45	8.15	15.60
1850			1	perlite		8.25	8.90	17.15
1860				styrofoam		8.65	8.30	16.95
1890				none		7.50	8.30	15.80
1900		12x8x16	2 to 5	perlite		8.35	9.05	17.40
1910				styrofoam		8.75	8.45	17.20
1940				none		7.60	8.45	16.05
2200	75% solid	4x8x16	0	none		5.10	5.45	10.55
2250			1	none		5.15	5.50	10.65
2300			2 to 5	none		5.20	5.60	10.80
2400		6x8x16	0	perlite		6.40	6.20	12.60
2440				none		6.20	6.05	12.25
2450			1	perlite		6.45	6.30	12.75
2490				none		6.25	6.15	12.40
2500			2 to 5	perlite		6.55	6.40	12.95
2540				none		6.35	6.25	12.60
2600		8x8x16	0	perlite		7.60	6.65	14.25
2640				none		7.35	6.50	13.85
2650			1	perlite		7.65	6.80	14.45
2690				none		7.40	6.65	14.05
2700			2 to 5	perlite		7.70	6.90	14.60
2740				none		7.45	6.75	14.20
2800		12x8x16	0	perlite		9.90	8.60	18.50
2840				none		9.55	8.30	17.85
2850			1	perlite		9.95	8.75	18.70
2890				none		9.60	8.45	18.05
2900			2 to 5	perlite		10.05	8.90	18.95
2940				none		9.70	8.60	18.30
3200	Solid	4x8x16	0	none		6.20	5.50	11.70
3250			1	none		6.25	5.60	11.85
3300			2 to 5	none		6.35	5.70	12.05
3400		6x8x16	0	none		7.55	6.15	13.70
3450			1	none		7.60	6.25	13.85
3500			2 to 5	none		7.65	6.35	14
3600		8x8x16	0	none		8.95	6.65	15.60
3650			1	none		9	6.75	15.75
3700			2 to 5	none		9.10	6.85	15.95
3800		12x8x16	0	none		11.60	8.45	20.05
3850			1	none		11.70	8.60	20.30
3900			2 to 5	none		11.75	8.80	20.55

B2010 117 — Reinforced Ground Face Block Wall

	TYPE	SIZE (IN.)	SCORES	VERT. REINF. & GROUT SPACING		COST PER S.F. MAT.	INST.	TOTAL
5200	Hollow	4x8x16	0	#4 @ 48"		4.06	5.85	9.91
5250			1	#4 @ 48"		4.13	5.95	10.08
5300			2 to 5	#4 @ 48"		4.24	6	10.24
5400		6x8x16	0	#4 @ 48"		5	6.45	11.45
5420				#5 @ 32"		5.15	6.65	11.80
5430				#5 @ 16"		5.45	7.35	12.80

B20 Exterior Enclosure

B2010 Exterior Walls

B2010 117		Reinforced Ground Face Block Wall					

	TYPE	SIZE (IN.)	SCORES	VERT. REINF. & GROUT SPACING		COST PER S.F.		
						MAT.	INST.	TOTAL
5450	Hollow		1	#4 @ 48"		5.10	6.55	11.65
5470				#5 @ 32"		5.20	6.75	11.95
5480				#5 @ 16"		5.50	7.45	12.95
5500			2 to 5	#4 @ 48"		5.20	6.65	11.85
5520				#5 @ 32"		5.35	6.85	12.20
5530				#5 @ 16"		5.65	7.55	13.20
5600		8x8x16	0	#4 @ 48"		5.95	7	12.95
5620				#5 @ 32"		6.10	7.20	13.30
5630				#5 @ 16"		6.45	8.05	14.50
5650			1	#4 @ 48"		6.05	7.10	13.15
5670				#5 @ 32"		6.20	7.30	13.50
5680				#5 @ 16"		6.55	8.15	14.70
5700			2 to 5	#4 @ 48"		6.15	7.25	13.40
5720				#5 @ 32"		6.30	7.45	13.75
5730				#5 @ 16"		6.65	8.30	14.95
5800		12x8x16	0	#4 @ 48"		7.75	8.80	16.55
5820				#5 @ 32"		7.95	9	16.95
5830				#5 @ 16"		8.45	9.90	18.35
5850			1	#4 @ 48"		7.80	8.95	16.75
5870				#5 @ 32"		8	9.15	17.15
5880				#5 @ 16"		8.50	10.05	18.55
5900			2 to 5	#4 @ 48"		7.90	9.10	17
5920				#5 @ 32"		8.10	9.30	17.40
5930				#5 @ 16"		8.60	10.20	18.80
6200	75% solid	6x8x16	0	#4 @ 48"		6.35	6.40	12.75
6220				#5 @ 32"		6.45	6.50	12.95
6230				#5 @ 16"		6.65	7	13.65
6250			1	#4 @ 48"		6.40	6.50	12.90
6270				#5 @ 32"		6.50	6.60	13.10
6280				#5 @ 16"		6.70	7.10	13.80
6300			2 to 5	#4 @ 48"		6.50	6.60	13.10
6330				#5 @ 16"		6.80	7.20	14
6400		8x8x16	0	#4 @ 48"		7.50	6.85	14.35
6420				#5 @ 32"		7.60	7.05	14.65
6430				#5 @ 16"		7.85	7.55	15.40
6450			1	#4 @ 48"		7.55	7	14.55
6470				#5 @ 32"		7.65	7.20	14.85
6480				#5 @ 16"		7.90	7.70	15.60
6500			2 to 5	#4 @ 48"		7.60	7.10	14.70
6520				#5 @ 32"		7.70	7.30	15
6530				#5 @ 16"		7.95	7.80	15.75
6600		12x8x16	0	#4 @ 48"		9.70	8.70	18.40
6620				#5 @ 32"		9.85	8.90	18.75
6630				#5 @ 16"		10.15	9.40	19.55
6650			1	#4 @ 48"		9.75	8.85	18.60
6670				#5 @ 32"		9.90	9.05	18.95
6680				#5 @ 16"		10.20	9.55	19.75
6700			2 to 5	#4 @ 48"		9.85	9	18.85
6720				#5 @ 32"		10	9.20	19.20
6730				#5 @ 16"		10.30	9.70	20

B2010 Exterior Walls

B2010 117	Reinforced Ground Face Block Wall

	TYPE	SIZE (IN.)	SCORES	VERT. REINF. & GROUT SPACING		COST PER S.F.		
						MAT.	INST.	TOTAL
6800	Solid-double Wythe	2-4x8x16	0	#4 @ 48" E.W.		13.05	12.10	25.15
6830				#5 @ 16" E.W.		13.40	12.60	26
6850			1	#4 @ 48" E.W.		13.15	12.30	25.45
6880				#5 @ 16" E.W.		13.50	12.80	26.30
6900			2 to 5	#4 @ 48" E.W.		13.35	12.50	25.85
6930				#5 @ 16" E.W.		13.70	13	26.70
7000		2-6x8x16	0	#4 @ 48" E.W.		15.75	13.40	29.15
7030				#5 @ 16" E.W.		16.10	13.90	30
7050			1	#4 @ 48" E.W.		15.85	13.60	29.45
7080				#5 @ 16" E.W.		16.20	14.10	30.30
7100			2 to 5	#4 @ 48" E.W.		15.95	13.80	29.75
7130				#5 @ 16" E.W.		16.30	14.30	30.60

B20 Exterior Enclosure

B2010 Exterior Walls

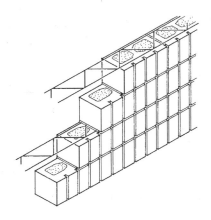

Exterior miscellaneous block walls are defined in the following terms: structural reinforcement, finish texture, percent solid, size, weight and insulation. Within each of these categories two to four variations are shown. No costs are included for brick shelf or relieving angles. Costs include control joints every 20' and horizontal reinforcing.

System Components	QUANTITY	UNIT	COST PER S.F.		
			MAT.	INST.	TOTAL
SYSTEM B2010 118 2700 **UNREINFORCED HEXAGONAL BLOCK WALL, 8"X8"X16", 125PCF, PERLITE FILL**					
Hexagonal block partition, 8" thick	1.000	S.F.	3.44	6.20	9.64
Perlite insulation	1.000	S.F.	.47	.29	.76
Horizontal joint reinf., alternate courses	.800	L.F.	.07	.13	.20
Control joint	.050	L.F.	.05	.05	.10
TOTAL			4.03	6.67	10.70

B2010 118		Miscellaneous Block Wall					COST PER S.F.		
	TYPE	SIZE (IN.)	WEIGHT (P.C.F.)	CORE FILL			MAT.	INST.	TOTAL
1100	Deep groove-hollow	4x8x16	125	none			2.64	5.35	7.99
1150			105	none			2.76	5.20	7.96
1200		6x8x16	125	perlite			3.71	5.95	9.66
1210				styrofoam			4.33	5.70	10.03
1240				none			3.39	5.70	9.09
1250			105	perlite			3.86	5.45	9.31
1260				styrofoam			4.48	5.20	9.68
1290				none			3.54	5.20	8.74
1300		8x8x16	125	perlite			4.81	6.45	11.26
1310				styrofoam			5.30	6.20	11.50
1340				none			4.34	6.20	10.54
1350			105	perlite			5.25	6.25	11.50
1360				styrofoam			5.70	6	11.70
1390				none			4.78	6	10.78
1400	Deep groove-75% solid	4x8x16	125	none			3.38	5.45	8.83
1450			105	none			3.53	5.30	8.83
1500		6x8x16	125	perlite			4.46	5.95	10.41
1540				none			4.30	5.80	10.10
1550			105	perlite			4.67	5.75	10.42
1590				none			4.51	5.60	10.11

B2010 Exterior Walls

| B2010 118 | | Miscellaneous Block Wall | | | | | |

	TYPE	SIZE (IN.)	WEIGHT (P.C.F.)	CORE FILL		COST PER S.F.		
						MAT.	INST.	TOTAL
1600	Deep groove-75% solid	8x8x16	125	perlite		5.75	6.45	12.20
1640				none		5.50	6.30	11.80
1650			105	perlite		6.35	6.25	12.60
1690				none		6.10	6.10	12.20
1700	Deep groove-solid	4x8x16	125	none		4.08	5.50	9.58
1750			105	none		4.29	5.35	9.64
1800		6x8x16	125	none		5.20	5.85	11.05
1850			105	none		5.50	5.70	11.20
1900		8x8x16	125	none		6.75	6.40	13.15
1950			105	none		7.40	6.20	13.60
2100	Fluted	4x8x16	125	none		2.65	5.35	8
2150			105	none		2.73	5.20	7.93
2200		6x8x16	125	perlite		3.56	5.95	9.51
2210				styrofoam		4.18	5.70	9.88
2240				none		3.24	5.70	8.94
2300		8x8x16	125	perlite		4.35	6.45	10.80
2310				styrofoam		4.82	6.20	11.02
2340				none		3.88	6.20	10.08
2500	Hex-hollow	4x8x16	125	none		1.91	5.35	7.26
2550			105	none		2.04	5.20	7.24
2600		6x8x16	125	perlite		2.99	6.20	9.19
2610				styrofoam		3.61	5.95	9.56
2640				none		2.67	5.95	8.62
2650			105	perlite		3.21	6.05	9.26
2660				styrofoam		3.83	5.80	9.63
2690				none		2.89	5.80	8.69
2700		8x8x16	125	perlite		4.03	6.65	10.68
2710				styrofoam		4.50	6.40	10.90
2740				none		3.56	6.40	9.96
2750			105	perlite		4.29	6.45	10.74
2760				styrofoam		4.76	6.20	10.96
2790				none		3.82	6.20	10.02
2800	Hex-solid	4x8x16	125	none		2.59	5.50	8.09
2850			105	none		2.81	5.35	8.16
3100	Slump block	4x4x16	125	none		3.18	4.41	7.59
3200		6x4x16	125	perlite		4.85	4.77	9.62
3210				styrofoam		5.45	4.54	9.99
3240				none		4.53	4.54	9.07
3300		8x4x16	125	perlite		5.50	4.99	10.49
3310				styrofoam		5.95	4.70	10.65
3340				none		5	4.70	9.70
3400		12x4x16	125	perlite		10.30	6.20	16.50
3410				styrofoam		10.65	5.60	16.25
3440				none		9.55	5.60	15.15
3600		6x6x16	125	perlite		4.52	4.91	9.43
3610				styrofoam		5.15	4.68	9.83
3640				none		4.20	4.68	8.88
3700		8x6x16	125	perlite		5.95	5.15	11.10
3710				styrofoam		6.40	4.85	11.25
3740				none		5.45	4.85	10.30
3800		12x6x16	125	perlite		9.40	6.65	16.05
3810				styrofoam		9.75	6.05	15.80
3840				none		8.65	6.05	14.70

B20 Exterior Enclosure

B2010 Exterior Walls

| B2010 118 | Reinforced Misc. Block Walls |

	TYPE	SIZE (IN.)	WEIGHT (P.C.F.)	VERT. REINF. & GROUT SPACING		MAT.	INST.	TOTAL
5100	Deep groove-hollow	4x8x16	125	#4 @ 48"		2.74	5.85	8.59
5150			105	#4 @ 48"		2.86	5.70	8.56
5200		6x8x16	125	#4 @ 48"		3.57	6.20	9.77
5220				#5 @ 32"		3.70	6.40	10.10
5230				#5 @ 16"		4	7.10	11.10
5250			105	#4 @ 48"		3.72	5.70	9.42
5270				#5 @ 32"		3.85	5.90	9.75
5280				#5 @ 16"		4.15	6.60	10.75
5300		8x8x16	125	#4 @ 48"		4.56	6.80	11.36
5320				#5 @ 32"		4.71	7	11.71
5330				#5 @ 16"		5.05	7.85	12.90
5350			105	#4 @ 48"		5	6.60	11.60
5370				#5 @ 32"		5.15	6.80	11.95
5380				#5 @ 16"		5.50	7.65	13.15
5500	Deep groove-75% solid	6x8x16	125	#4 @ 48"		4.42	6.15	10.57
5520				#5 @ 32"		4.52	6.25	10.77
5530				#5 @ 16"		4.74	6.75	11.49
5550			105	#4 @ 48"		4.63	5.95	10.58
5570				#5 @ 32"		4.76	6.15	10.91
5580				#5 @ 16"		4.95	6.55	11.50
5600		8x8x16	125	#4 @ 48"		5.65	6.65	12.30
5620				#5 @ 32"		5.75	6.85	12.60
5630				#5 @ 16"		6	7.35	13.35
5650			105	#4 @ 48"		6.25	6.45	12.70
5670				#5 @ 32"		6.35	6.65	13
5680				#5 @ 16"		6.60	7.15	13.75
5700	Deep groove-solid	2-4x8x16	125	#4 @ 48" E.W.		8.75	12.10	20.85
5730	Double wythe			#5 @ 16" E.W.		9.15	12.65	21.80
5750			105	#4 @ 48" E.W.		9.20	11.80	21
5780				#5 @ 16" E.W.		9.60	12.35	21.95
5800		2-6x8x16	125	#4 @ 48" E.W.		11.05	12.80	23.85
5830				#5 @ 16" E.W.		11.45	13.35	24.80
5850			105	#4 @ 48" E.W.		11.65	12.50	24.15
5880				#5 @ 16" E.W.		12.05	13.05	25.10
6100	Fluted	4x8x16	125	#4 @ 48"		2.75	5.85	8.60
6150			105	#4 @ 48"		2.83	5.70	8.53
6200		6x8x16	125	#4 @ 48"		3.42	6.20	9.62
6220				#5 @ 32"		3.55	6.40	9.95
6230				#5 @ 16"		3.85	7.10	10.95
6300		8x8x16	125	#4 @ 48"		4.10	6.80	10.90
6320				#5 @ 32"		4.25	7	11.25
6330				#5 @ 16"		4.61	7.85	12.46
6500	Hex-hollow	4x8x16	125	#4 @ 48"		2.01	5.85	7.86
6550			105	#4 @ 48"		2.14	5.70	7.84
6620				#5 @ 32"		2.98	6.65	9.63
6630				#5 @ 16"		3.28	7.35	10.63
6650		6x8x16	105	#4 @ 48"		3.07	6.30	9.37
6670				#5 @ 32"		3.20	6.50	9.70
6680				#5 @ 16"		3.50	7.20	10.70
6700		8x8x16	125	#4 @ 48"		3.78	7	10.78
6720				#5 @ 32"		3.93	7.20	11.13
6730				#5 @ 16"		4.29	8.05	12.34

COST PER S.F.

B2010 Exterior Walls

| B2010 118 | | Reinforced Misc. Block Walls | | | | | |

	TYPE	SIZE (IN.)	WEIGHT (P.C.F.)	VERT. REINF. & GROUT SPACING		COST PER S.F.		
						MAT.	INST.	TOTAL
6750	Hex-Hollow		105	#4 @ 48"		4.04	6.80	10.84
6770				#5 @ 32"		4.19	7	11.19
6800	Hex-solid	2-4x8x16	125	#4 @ 48" E.W.		5.75	12.05	17.80
6830	Double wythes			#5 @ 16" E.W.		6.20	12.65	18.85
6850			105	#4 @ 48" E.W.		6.20	11.75	17.95
6880				#5 @ 16" E.W.		6.65	12.35	19
7100	Slump block	4x4x16	125	#4 @ 48"		3.28	4.89	8.17
7200		6x4x16	125	#4 @ 48"		4.71	5.05	9.76
7220				#5 @ 32"		4.84	5.45	10.29
7230				#5 @ 16"		5.15	5.90	11.05
7300		8x4x16	125	#4 @ 48"		5.25	5.30	10.55
7320				#5 @ 32"		5.40	5.50	10.90
7330				#5 @ 16"		5.75	6.40	12.15
7400		12x4x16	125	#4 @ 48"		9.85	6.25	16.10
7420				#5 @ 32"		10.05	6.45	16.50
7430				#5 @ 16"		10.55	7.35	17.90
7600		6x6x16	125	#4 @ 48"		4.38	5.20	9.58
7620				#5 @ 32"		4.51	5.35	9.86
7630				#5 @ 16"		4.81	6.05	10.86
7700		8x6x16	125	#4 @ 48"		5.70	5.45	11.15
7720				#5 @ 32"		5.85	5.65	11.50
7730				#5 @ 16"		6.20	6.55	12.75
7800		12x6x16	125	#4 @ 48"		8.95	6.70	15.65
7820				#5 @ 32"		9.15	6.90	16.05
7830				#5 @ 16"		9.65	7.80	17.45

C10 Interior Construction

C1010 Partitions

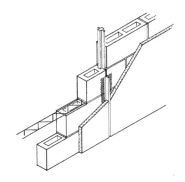

The Concrete Block Partition Systems are defined by weight and type of block, thickness, type of finish and number of sides finished. System components include joint reinforcing on alternate courses and vertical control joints.

System Components	QUANTITY	UNIT	COST PER S.F.		
			MAT.	INST.	TOTAL
SYSTEM C1010 102 1020					
CONC. BLOCK PARTITION, 8″ X 16″, 4″ TK., 2 CT. GYP. PLASTER 2 SIDES					
Conc. block partition, 4″ thick	1.000	S.F.	1.01	4.19	5.20
Control joint	.050	L.F.	.06	.11	.17
Horizontal joint reinforcing	.800	L.F.	.05	.05	.10
Gypsum plaster, 2 coat, on masonry	2.000	S.F.	.69	3.95	4.64
TOTAL			1.81	8.30	10.11

C1010 102		Concrete Block Partitions - Regular Weight					
	TYPE	THICKNESS (IN.)	TYPE FINISH	SIDES FINISHED		COST PER S.F.	
					MAT.	INST.	TOTAL
1000	Hollow	4	none	0	1.12	4.35	5.47
1010			gyp. plaster 2 coat	1	1.46	6.30	7.76
1020				2	1.81	8.30	10.11
1100			lime plaster - 2 coat	1	1.33	6.30	7.63
1150			lime portland - 2 coat	1	1.34	6.30	7.64
1200			portland - 3 coat	1	1.36	6.60	7.96
1400			5/8″ drywall	1	1.49	5.75	7.24
1410				2	1.86	7.15	9.01
1500		6	none	0	1.62	4.66	6.28
1510			gyp. plaster 2 coat	1	1.96	6.60	8.56
1520				2	2.31	8.60	10.91
1600			lime plaster - 2 coat	1	1.83	6.60	8.43
1650			lime portland - 2 coat	1	1.84	6.60	8.44
1700			portland - 3 coat	1	1.86	6.90	8.76
1900			5/8″ drywall	1	1.99	6.05	8.04
1910				2	2.36	7.45	9.81
2000		8	none	0	1.74	4.98	6.72
2010			gyp. plaster 2 coat	1	2.08	6.95	9.03
2020			gyp. plaster 2 coat	2	2.43	8.90	11.33
2100		8	lime plaster - 2 coat	1	1.95	6.95	8.90
2150			lime portland - 2 coat	1	1.96	6.95	8.91
2200			portland - 3 coat	1	1.98	7.20	9.18
2400			5/8″ drywall	1	2.11	6.40	8.51
2410				2	2.48	7.80	10.28

C1010 Partitions

C1010 102 — Concrete Block Partitions - Regular Weight

	TYPE	THICKNESS (IN.)	TYPE FINISH	SIDES FINISHED	MAT.	INST.	TOTAL
2500	Hollow	10	none	0	2.43	5.20	7.63
2510			gyp. plaster 2 coat	1	2.77	7.15	9.92
2520				2	3.12	9.15	12.27
2600			lime plaster - 2 coat	1	2.64	7.15	9.79
2650		10	lime portland - 2 coat	1	2.65	7.15	9.80
2700			portland - 3 coat	1	2.67	7.45	10.12
2900			5/8" drywall	1	2.80	6.60	9.40
2910				2	3.17	8	11.17
3000	Solid	2	none	0	.98	4.30	5.28
3010			gyp. plaster	1	1.32	6.25	7.57
3020				2	1.67	8.25	9.92
3100			lime plaster - 2 coat	1	1.19	6.25	7.44
3150			lime portland - 2 coat	1	1.20	6.25	7.45
3200			portland - 3 coat	1	1.22	6.55	7.77
3400			5/8" drywall	1	1.35	5.70	7.05
3410				2	1.72	7.10	8.82
3500		4	none	0	1.51	4.50	6.01
3510			gyp. plaster	1	1.92	6.50	8.42
3520				2	2.20	8.45	10.65
3600			lime plaster - 2 coat	1	1.72	6.45	8.17
3650			lime portland - 2 coat	1	1.73	6.45	8.18
3700			portland - 3 coat	1	1.75	6.75	8.50
3900			5/8" drywall	1	1.88	5.90	7.78
3910				2	2.25	7.30	9.55
4000		6	none	0	1.78	4.84	6.62
4010			gyp. plaster	1	2.12	6.80	8.92
4020				2	2.47	8.75	11.22
4100			lime plaster - 2 coat	1	1.99	6.80	8.79
4150			lime portland - 2 coat	1	2	6.80	8.80
4200			portland - 3 coat	1	2.02	7.10	9.12
4400			5/8" drywall	1	2.15	6.25	8.40
4410				2	2.52	7.65	10.17

C1010 102 — Concrete Block Partitions - Lightweight

	TYPE	THICKNESS (IN.)	TYPE FINISH	SIDES FINISHED	MAT.	INST.	TOTAL
5000	Hollow	4	none	0	1.32	4.25	5.57
5010			gyp. plaster	1	1.66	6.20	7.86
5020				2	2.01	8.20	10.21
5100			lime plaster - 2 coat	1	1.53	6.20	7.73
5150			lime portland - 2 coat	1	1.54	6.20	7.74
5200			portland - 3 coat	1	1.56	6.50	8.06
5400			5/8" drywall	1	1.69	5.65	7.34
5410				2	2.06	7.05	9.11
5500		6	none	0	1.76	4.55	6.31
5520			gyp. plaster	2	2.45	8.50	10.95
5600			lime plaster - 2 coat	1	1.97	6.50	8.47
5650			lime portland - 2 coat	1	1.98	6.50	8.48
5700			portland - 3 coat	1	2	6.80	8.80
5900			5/8" drywall	1	2.13	5.95	8.08
5910				2	2.50	7.35	9.85
6000		8	none	0	2.14	4.86	7

C10 Interior Construction

C1010 Partitions

| C1010 102 | Concrete Block Partitions - Lightweight |

	TYPE	THICKNESS (IN.)	TYPE FINISH	SIDES FINISHED		COST PER S.F.		
						MAT.	INST.	TOTAL
6010	Hollow		gyp. plaster	1		2.48	6.80	9.28
6020				2		2.83	8.80	11.63
6100			lime plaster - 2 coat	1		2.35	6.80	9.15
6150			lime portland - 2 coat	1		2.36	6.80	9.16
6200			portland - 3 coat	1		2.38	7.10	9.48
6400		8	5/8" drywall	1		2.51	6.25	8.76
6410				2		2.88	7.65	10.53
6500		10	none	0		2.79	5.10	7.89
6510			gyp. plaster	1		3.13	7.05	10.18
6520				2		3.48	9	12.48
6600			lime plaster - 2 coat	1		3	7.05	10.05
6650			lime portland - 2 coat	1		3.01	7.05	10.06
6700			portland - 3 coat	1		3.03	7.30	10.33
6900			5/8" drywall	1		3.16	6.50	9.66
6910				2		3.53	7.90	11.43
7000	Solid	4	none	0		1.42	4.45	5.87
7010			gyp. plaster	1		1.76	6.40	8.16
7020				2		2.11	8.40	10.51
7100			lime plaster - 2 coat	1		1.63	6.40	8.03
7150			lime portland - 2 coat	1		1.64	6.40	8.04
7200			portland - 3 coat	1		1.66	6.70	8.36
7400			5/8" drywall	1		1.79	5.85	7.64
7410				2		2.16	7.25	9.41
7500		6	none	0		1.96	4.78	6.74
7510			gyp. plaster	1		2.36	6.80	9.16
7520				2		2.65	8.70	11.35
7600			lime plaster - 2 coat	1		2.17	6.75	8.92
7650			lime portland - 2 coat	1		2.18	6.75	8.93
7700			portland - 3 coat	1		2.20	7	9.20
7900			5/8" drywall	1		2.33	6.20	8.53
7910				2		2.70	7.60	10.30
8000		8	none	0		2.64	5.10	7.74
8010			gyp. plaster	1		2.98	7.05	10.03
8020				2		3.33	9.05	12.38
8100			lime plaster - 2 coat	1		2.85	7.05	9.90
8150			lime portland - 2 coat	1		2.86	7.05	9.91
8200			portland - 3 coat	1		2.88	7.35	10.23
8400			5/8" drywall	1		3.01	6.50	9.51
8410				2		3.38	7.90	11.28

C1010 Partitions

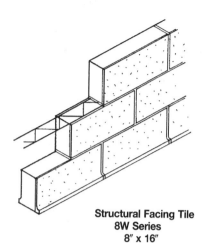

Structural Facing Tile
8W Series
8" x 16"

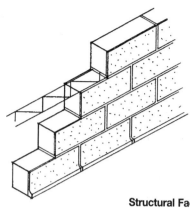

Structural Facing Tile
6T Series
5-1/3" x 12"

C1010 120	Tile Partitions	COST PER S.F.		
		MAT.	INST.	TOTAL
1000	8W series 8"x16", 4" thick wall, reinf every 2 courses, glazed 1 side	8.05	5.20	13.25
1100	Glazed 2 sides	10.20	5.55	15.75
1200	Glazed 2 sides, using 2 wythes of 2" thick tile	14.10	10	24.10
1300	6" thick wall, horizontal reinf every 2 courses, glazed 1 side	11.35	5.45	16.80
1400	Glazed 2 sides, each face different color, 2" and 4" tile	15.10	10.20	25.30
1500	8" thick wall, glazed 2 sides using 2 wythes of 4" thick tile	16.10	10.40	26.50
1600	10" thick wall, glazed 2 sides using 1 wythe of 4" tile & 1 wythe of 6" tile	19.40	10.65	30.05
1700	Glazed 2 sides cavity wall, using 2 wythes of 4" thick tile	16.10	10.40	26.50
1800	12" thick wall, glazed 2 sides using 2 wythes of 6" thick tile	22.50	10.90	33.40
1900	Glazed 2 sides cavity wall, using 2 wythes of 4" thick tile	16.10	10.40	26.50
2100	6T series 5-1/3"x12" tile, 4" thick, non load bearing glazed one side,	7.45	8.20	15.65
2200	Glazed two sides	12.55	9.25	21.80
2300	Glazed two sides, using two wythes of 2" thick tile	12.80	16	28.80
2400	6" thick, glazed one side	11.55	8.55	20.10
2500	Glazed two sides	14.40	9.75	24.15
2600	Glazed two sides using 2" thick tile and 4" thick tile	13.85	16.20	30.05
2700	8" thick, glazed one side	14.45	10	24.45
2800	Glazed two sides using two wythes of 4" thick tile	14.90	16.40	31.30
2900	Glazed two sides using 6" thick tile and 2" thick tile	17.95	16.55	34.50
3000	10" thick cavity wall, glazed two sides using two wythes of 4" tile	14.90	16.40	31.30
3100	12" thick, glazed two sides using 4" thick tile and 8" thick tile	22	18.20	40.20
3200	2" thick facing tile, glazed one side, on 6" concrete block	8.55	9.50	18.05
3300	On 8" concrete block	8.65	9.80	18.45
3400	On 10" concrete block	9.35	10	19.35

D40 Fire Protection

D4010 Sprinklers

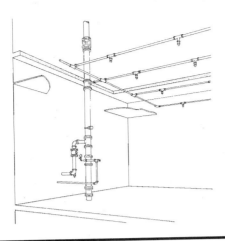

Wet Pipe System. A system employing automatic sprinklers attached to a piping system containing water and connected to a water supply so that water discharges immediately from sprinklers opened by heat from a fire.

All areas are assumed to be open.

System Components	QUANTITY	UNIT	COST EACH MAT.	COST EACH INST.	COST EACH TOTAL
SYSTEM D4010 305 0580					
WET PIPE SPRINKLER, STEEL, BLACK, SCH. 40 PIPE					
LIGHT HAZARD, ONE FLOOR, 2000 S.F.					
Valve, gate, iron body, 125 lb, OS&Y, flanged, 4″ diam	1.000	Ea.	303.75	203.25	507
Valve, swing check, bronze, 125 lb, regrinding disc, 2-1/2″ pipe size	1.000	Ea.	160.50	40.50	201
Valve, angle, bronze, 150 lb, rising stem, threaded, 2″ diam	1.000	Ea.	199.50	30.75	230.25
*Alarm valve, 2-1/2″ pipe size	1.000	Ea.	615	204.75	819.75
Alarm, water motor, complete with gong	1.000	Ea.	137.25	85.50	222.75
Valve, swing check, w/balldrip CI with brass trim 4″ pipe size	1.000	Ea.	116.25	204.75	321
Pipe, steel, black, schedule 40, 4″ diam	10.000	L.F.	74.25	182.55	256.80
*Flow control valve, trim & gauges, 4″ pipe size	1.000	Set	1,237.50	465	1,702.50
Fire alarm horn, electric	1.000	Ea.	30	50.25	80.25
Pipe, steel, black, schedule 40, threaded, cplg & hngr 10′OC, 2-1/2″ diam	20.000	L.F.	83.25	243.75	327
Pipe, steel, black, schedule 40, threaded, cplg & hngr 10′OC, 2″ diam	12.500	L.F.	32.81	119.06	151.87
Pipe, steel, black, schedule 40, threaded, cplg & hngr 10′OC, 1-1/4″ diam	37.500	L.F.	69.19	257.34	326.53
Pipe steel, black, schedule 40, threaded cplg & hngr 10′OC, 1″ diam	112.000	L.F.	173.88	714	887.88
Pipe Tee, malleable iron black, 150 lb threaded, 4″ pipe size	2.000	Ea.	166.50	304.50	471
Pipe Tee, malleable iron black, 150 lb threaded, 2-1/2″ pipe size	2.000	Ea.	46.50	135.75	182.25
Pipe Tee, malleable iron black, 150 lb threaded, 2″ pipe size	1.000	Ea.	10.84	55.50	66.34
Pipe Tee, malleable iron black, 150 lb threaded, 1-1/4″ pipe size	5.000	Ea.	25.50	217.50	243
Pipe Tee, malleable iron black, 150 lb threaded, 1″ pipe size	4.000	Ea.	12.60	169.50	182.10
Pipe 90° elbow, malleable iron black, 150 lb threaded, 1″ pipe size	6.000	Ea.	12.15	155.25	167.40
Sprinkler head, standard spray, brass 135°-286°F 1/2″ NPT, 3/8″ orifice	12.000	Ea.	79.20	342	421.20
Valve, gate, bronze, NRS, class 150, threaded, 1″ pipe size	1.000	Ea.	29.63	18	47.63
*Standpipe connection, wall, single, flush w/plug & chain 2-1/2″x2-1/2″	1.000	Ea.	66.38	123	189.38
TOTAL			3,682.43	4,322.45	8,004.88
COST PER S.F.			1.84	2.16	4

*Not included in systems under 2000 S.F.

D4010 305	Wet Pipe Sprinkler Systems	COST PER S.F. MAT.	COST PER S.F. INST.	COST PER S.F. TOTAL
0520	Wet pipe sprinkler systems, steel, black, sch. 40 pipe			
0530	Light hazard, one floor, 500 S.F.	1.11	2.07	3.18
0560	1000 S.F.	1.77	2.15	3.92
0580	2000 S.F.	1.84	2.16	4
0600	5000 S.F.	.87	1.50	2.37
0620	10,000 S.F.	.57	1.29	1.86

D40 Fire Protection

D4010 Sprinklers

D4010 305	Wet Pipe Sprinkler Systems	COST PER S.F.		
		MAT.	INST.	TOTAL
0640	50,000 S.F.	.37	1.16	1.53
0660	Each additional floor, 500 S.F.	.51	1.75	2.26
0680	1000 S.F.	.55	1.63	2.18
0700	2000 S.F.	.49	1.48	1.97
0720	5000 S.F.	.34	1.24	1.58
0740	10,000 S.F.	.33	1.17	1.50
0760	50,000 S.F.	.26	.91	1.17
1000	Ordinary hazard, one floor, 500 S.F.	1.21	2.22	3.43
1020	1000 S.F.	1.73	2.11	3.84
1040	2000 S.F.	1.91	2.27	4.18
1060	5000 S.F.	.99	1.62	2.61
1080	10,000 S.F.	.69	1.68	2.37
1100	50,000 S.F.	.63	1.67	2.30
1140	Each additional floor, 500 S.F.	.62	1.98	2.60
1160	1000 S.F.	.51	1.61	2.12
1180	2000 S.F.	.57	1.63	2.20
1200	5000 S.F.	.58	1.54	2.12
1220	10,000 S.F.	.45	1.57	2.02
1240	50,000 S.F.	.48	1.49	1.97
1500	Extra hazard, one floor, 500 S.F.	3.31	3.43	6.74
1520	1000 S.F.	2.14	2.99	5.13
1540	2000 S.F.	2.02	3.05	5.07
1560	5000 S.F.	1.26	2.65	3.91
1580	10,000 S.F.	1.18	2.54	3.72
1600	50,000 S.F.	1.25	2.45	3.70
1660	Each additional floor, 500 S.F.	.88	2.45	3.33
1680	1000 S.F.	.85	2.34	3.19
1700	2000 S.F.	.76	2.34	3.10
1720	5000 S.F.	.62	2.06	2.68
1740	10,000 S.F.	.75	1.93	2.68
1760	50,000 S.F.	.74	1.83	2.57
2020	Grooved steel, black sch. 40 pipe, light hazard, one floor, 2000 S.F.	1.86	1.84	3.70
2060	10,000 S.F.	.72	1.13	1.85
2100	Each additional floor, 2000 S.F.	.52	1.20	1.72
2150	10,000 S.F.	.35	.97	1.32
2200	Ordinary hazard, one floor, 2000 S.F.	1.88	1.96	3.84
2250	10,000 S.F.	.68	1.39	2.07
2300	Each additional floor, 2000 S.F.	.54	1.32	1.86
2350	10,000 S.F.	.44	1.28	1.72
2400	Extra hazard, one floor, 2000 S.F.	2.03	2.50	4.53
2450	10,000 S.F.	.94	1.83	2.77
2500	Each additional floor, 2000 S.F.	.79	1.92	2.71
2550	10,000 S.F.	.65	1.63	2.28
3050	Grooved steel black sch. 10 pipe, light hazard, one floor, 2000 S.F.	1.83	1.82	3.65
3100	10,000 S.F.	.57	1.07	1.64
3150	Each additional floor, 2000 S.F.	.49	1.18	1.67
3200	10,000 S.F.	.33	.95	1.28
3250	Ordinary hazard, one floor, 2000 S.F.	1.86	1.93	3.79
3300	10,000 S.F.	.66	1.36	2.02
3350	Each additional floor, 2000 S.F.	.52	1.29	1.81
3400	10,000 S.F.	.42	1.25	1.67
3450	Extra hazard, one floor, 2000 S.F.	2.01	2.48	4.49
3500	10,000 S.F.	.90	1.79	2.69
3550	Each additional floor, 2000 S.F.	.77	1.90	2.67
3600	10,000 S.F.	.64	1.60	2.24
4050	Copper tubing, type M, light hazard, one floor, 2000 S.F.	1.90	1.79	3.69
4100	10,000 S.F.	.67	1.10	1.77
4150	Each additional floor, 2000 S.F.	.57	1.18	1.75

D40 Fire Protection

D4010 Sprinklers

D4010 305	Wet Pipe Sprinkler Systems	COST PER S.F.		
		MAT.	INST.	TOTAL
4200	10,000 S.F.	.43	.99	1.42
4250	Ordinary hazard, one floor, 2000 S.F.	1.96	2.01	3.97
4300	10,000 S.F.	.75	1.30	2.05
4350	Each additional floor, 2000 S.F.	.64	1.30	1.94
4400	10,000 S.F.	.48	1.16	1.64
4450	Extra hazard, one floor, 2000 S.F.	2.14	2.52	4.66
4500	10,000 S.F.	1.50	1.96	3.46
4550	Each additional floor, 2000 S.F.	.90	1.94	2.84
4600	10,000 S.F.	1.01	1.74	2.75
5050	Copper tubing, type M, T-drill system, light hazard, one floor			
5060	2000 S.F.	1.89	1.66	3.55
5100	10,000 S.F.	.60	.90	1.50
5150	Each additional floor, 2000 S.F.	.56	1.05	1.61
5200	10,000 S.F.	.36	.79	1.15
5250	Ordinary hazard, one floor, 2000 S.F.	1.88	1.71	3.59
5300	10,000 S.F.	.70	1.15	1.85
5350	Each additional floor, 2000 S.F.	.54	1.07	1.61
5400	10,000 S.F.	.46	1.04	1.50
5450	Extra hazard, one floor, 2000 S.F.	1.95	2.06	4.01
5500	10,000 S.F.	1.14	1.42	2.56
5550	Each additional floor, 2000 S.F.	.76	1.51	2.27
5600	10,000 S.F.	.65	1.20	1.85

D4010 Sprinklers

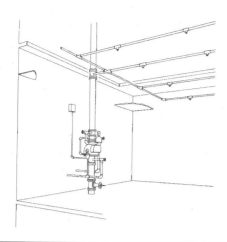

Dry Pipe System: A system employing automatic sprinklers attached to a piping system containing air under pressure, the release of which as from the opening of sprinklers permits the water pressure to open a valve known as a "dry pipe valve". The water then flows into the piping system and out the opened sprinklers.

All areas are assumed to be open.

System Components	QUANTITY	UNIT	COST EACH		
			MAT.	INST.	TOTAL
SYSTEM D4010 400 0580					
DRY PIPE SPRINKLER, STEEL BLACK, SCH. 40 PIPE					
LIGHT HAZARD, ONE FLOOR, 2000 S.F.					
Valve, gate, iron body 125 lb, OS&Y, flanged, 4" pipe size	1.000	Ea.	303.75	203.25	507
Valve, swing check, bronze, 125 lb, regrinding disc, 2-1/2" pipe size	1.000	Ea.	160.50	40.50	201
Valve, angle, bronze, 150 lb, rising stem, threaded, 2" pipe size	1.000	Ea.	199.50	30.75	230.25
*Alarm valve, 2-1/2" pipe size	1.000	Ea.	615	204.75	819.75
Alarm, water motor, complete with gong,	1.000	Ea.	137.25	85.50	222.75
Fire alarm horn, electric	1.000	Ea.	30	50.25	80.25
Valve swing check w/balldrip CI with brass trim, 4" pipe size	1.000	Ea.	116.25	204.75	321
Pipe, steel, black, schedule 40, 4" diam	10.000	L.F.	74.25	182.55	256.80
Dry pipe valve, trim & gauges, 4" pipe size	1.000	Ea.	975	615	1,590
Pipe, steel, black, schedule 40, threaded, cplg & hngr 10'OC 2-1/2" diam	20.000	L.F.	83.25	243.75	327
Pipe, steel, black, schedule 40, threaded, cplg & hngr 10'OC 2" diam	12.500	L.F.	32.81	119.06	151.87
Pipe, steel, black, schedule 40, threaded, cplg & hngr 10'OC 1-1/4" diam	37.500	L.F.	69.19	257.34	326.53
Pipe, steel, black, schedule 40, threaded, cplg & hngr 10'OC 1" diam	112.000	L.F.	173.88	714	887.88
Pipe Tee, malleable iron black, 150 lb threaded, 4" pipe size	2.000	Ea.	166.50	304.50	471
Pipe Tee, malleable iron black, 150 lb threaded, 2-1/2" pipe size	2.000	Ea.	46.50	135.75	182.25
Pipe Tee, malleable iron black, 150 lb threaded, 2" pipe size	1.000	Ea.	10.84	55.50	66.34
Pipe Tee, malleable iron black, 150 lb threaded, 1-1/4" pipe size	5.000	Ea.	25.50	217.50	243
Pipe Tee, malleable iron black, 150 lb threaded, 1" pipe size	4.000	Ea.	12.60	169.50	182.10
Pipe 90° elbow malleable iron black, 150 lb threaded, 1" pipe size	6.000	Ea.	12.15	155.25	167.40
Sprinkler head dry 1/2" orifice 1" NPT, 3" to 4-3/4" length	12.000	Ea.	456	390	846
Air compressor, 200 Gal sprinkler system capacity, 1/3 HP	1.000	Ea.	592.50	262.50	855
*Standpipe connection, wall, flush, brs w/plug & chain 2-1/2"x2-1/2"	1.000	Ea.	66.38	123	189.38
Valve gate bronze, 300 psi, NRS, class 150, threaded, 1" pipe size	1.000	Ea.	29.63	18	47.63
TOTAL			4,389.23	4,782.95	9,172.18
COST PER S.F.			2.19	2.39	4.58

*Not included in systems under 2000 S.F.

D4010 400	Dry Pipe Sprinkler Systems	COST PER S.F.		
		MAT.	INST.	TOTAL
0520	Dry pipe sprinkler systems, steel, black, sch. 40 pipe			
0530	Light hazard, one floor, 500 S.F.	4.49	4.07	8.56
0560	1000 S.F.	2.47	2.37	4.84
0580	2000 S.F.	2.20	2.40	4.60
0600	5000 S.F.	1.08	1.60	2.68
0620	10,000 S.F.	.74	1.35	2.09

D40 Fire Protection

D4010 Sprinklers

D4010 400	Dry Pipe Sprinkler Systems	COST PER S.F.		
		MAT.	INST.	TOTAL
0640	50,000 S.F.	.50	1.19	1.69
0660	Each additional floor, 500 S.F.	.75	1.96	2.71
0680	1000 S.F.	.68	1.61	2.29
0700	2000 S.F.	.63	1.50	2.13
0720	5000 S.F.	.49	1.26	1.75
0740	10,000 S.F.	.46	1.19	1.65
0760	50,000 S.F.	.40	1.05	1.45
1000	Ordinary hazard, one floor, 500 S.F.	4.55	4.11	8.66
1020	1000 S.F.	2.49	2.40	4.89
1040	2000 S.F.	2.27	2.50	4.77
1060	5000 S.F.	1.24	1.72	2.96
1080	10,000 S.F.	.92	1.75	2.67
1100	50,000 S.F.	.84	1.73	2.57
1140	Each additional floor, 500 S.F.	.81	2	2.81
1160	1000 S.F.	.75	1.81	2.56
1180	2000 S.F.	.76	1.65	2.41
1200	5000 S.F.	.69	1.41	2.10
1220	10,000 S.F.	.58	1.38	1.96
1240	50,000 S.F.	.61	1.29	1.90
1500	Extra hazard, one floor, 500 S.F.	6.20	5.10	11.30
1520	1000 S.F.	3.56	3.69	7.25
1540	2000 S.F.	2.46	3.20	5.66
1560	5000 S.F.	1.41	2.40	3.81
1580	10,000 S.F.	1.42	2.32	3.74
1600	50,000 S.F.	1.50	2.24	3.74
1660	Each additional floor, 500 S.F.	1.16	2.48	3.64
1680	1000 S.F.	1.13	2.37	3.50
1700	2000 S.F.	1.04	2.37	3.41
1720	5000 S.F.	.87	2.06	2.93
1740	10,000 S.F.	1.02	1.92	2.94
1760	50,000 S.F.	1.03	1.84	2.87
2020	Grooved steel, black, sch. 40 pipe, light hazard, one floor, 2000 S.F.	2.17	2.07	4.24
2060	10,000 S.F.	.76	1.15	1.91
2100	Each additional floor, 2000 S.F.	.66	1.22	1.88
2150	10,000 S.F.	.48	.99	1.47
2200	Ordinary hazard, one floor, 2000 S.F.	2.24	2.19	4.43
2250	10,000 S.F.	.91	1.46	2.37
2300	Each additional floor, 2000 S.F.	.73	1.34	2.07
2350	10,000 S.F.	.63	1.31	1.94
2400	Extra hazard, one floor, 2000 S.F.	2.48	2.74	5.22
2450	10,000 S.F.	1.26	1.90	3.16
2500	Each additional floor, 2000 S.F.	1.07	1.95	3.02
2550	10,000 S.F.	.93	1.66	2.59
3050	Grooved steel black sch. 10 pipe, light hazard, one floor, 2000 S.F.	2.14	2.05	4.19
3100	10,000 S.F.	.74	1.13	1.87
3150	Each additional floor, 2000 S.F.	.63	1.20	1.83
3200	10,000 S.F.	.46	.97	1.43
3250	Ordinary hazard, one floor, 2000 S.F.	2.22	2.16	4.38
3300	10,000 S.F.	.89	1.43	2.32
3350	Each additional floor, 2000 S.F.	.71	1.31	2.02
3400	10,000 S.F.	.61	1.28	1.89
3450	Extra hazard, one floor, 2000 S.F.	2.46	2.72	5.18
3500	10,000 S.F.	1.22	1.86	3.08
3550	Each additional floor, 2000 S.F.	1.05	1.93	2.98
3600	10,000 S.F.	.92	1.63	2.55
4050	Copper tubing, type M, light hazard, one floor, 2000 S.F.	2.21	2.02	4.23
4100	10,000 S.F.	.84	1.16	2
4150	Each additional floor, 2000 S.F.	.71	1.20	1.91

D4010 Sprinklers

D4010 400	Dry Pipe Sprinkler Systems	COST PER S.F.		
		MAT.	INST.	TOTAL
4200	10,000 S.F.	.56	1.01	1.57
4250	Ordinary hazard, one floor, 2000 S.F.	2.32	2.24	4.56
4300	10,000 S.F.	.98	1.37	2.35
4350	Each additional floor, 2000 S.F.	.91	1.37	2.28
4400	10,000 S.F.	.67	1.19	1.86
4450	Extra hazard, one floor, 2000 S.F.	2.59	2.76	5.35
4500	10,000 S.F.	1.83	2.04	3.87
4550	Each additional floor, 2000 S.F.	1.18	1.97	3.15
4600	10,000 S.F.	1.29	1.77	3.06
5050	Copper tubing, type M, T-drill system, light hazard, one floor			
5060	2000 S.F.	2.20	1.89	4.09
5100	10,000 S.F.	.77	.96	1.73
5150	Each additional floor, 2000 S.F.	.70	1.07	1.77
5200	10,000 S.F.	.49	.81	1.30
5250	Ordinary hazard, one floor, 2000 S.F.	2.24	1.94	4.18
5300	10,000 S.F.	.93	1.22	2.15
5350	Each additional floor, 2000 S.F.	.73	1.09	1.82
5400	10,000 S.F.	.63	1.01	1.64
5450	Extra hazard, one floor, 2000 S.F.	2.40	2.30	4.70
5500	10,000 S.F.	1.47	1.50	2.97
5550	Each additional floor, 2000 S.F.	.99	1.51	2.50
5600	10,000 S.F.	.93	1.23	2.16

D40 Fire Protection

D4010 Sprinklers

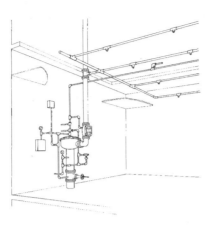

Pre-Action System: A system employing automatic sprinklers attached to a piping system containing air that may or may not be under pressure, with a supplemental heat responsive system of generally more sensitive characteristics than the automatic sprinklers themselves, installed in the same areas as the sprinklers. Actuation of the heat responsive system, as from a fire, opens a valve which permits water to flow into the sprinkler piping system and to be discharged from those sprinklers which were opened by heat from the fire.

All areas are assumed to be open.

System Components	QUANTITY	UNIT	COST EACH		
			MAT.	INST.	TOTAL
SYSTEM D4010 415 0580					
PREACTION SPRINKLER SYSTEM, STEEL BLACK SCH. 40 PIPE					
LIGHT HAZARD, 1 FLOOR, 2000 S.F.					
Valve, gate, iron body 125 lb, OS&Y, flanged, 4″ pipe size	1.000	Ea.	303.75	203.25	507
*Valve, swing check w/ball drip CI with brass trim 4″ pipe size	1.000	Ea.	116.25	204.75	321
Valve, swing check, bronze, 125 lb, regrinding disc, 2-1/2″ pipe size	1.000	Ea.	160.50	40.50	201
Valve, angle, bronze, 150 lb, rising stem, threaded, 2″ pipe size	1.000	Ea.	199.50	30.75	230.25
*Alarm valve, 2-1/2″ pipe size	1.000	Ea.	615	204.75	819.75
Alarm, water motor, complete with gong	1.000	Ea.	137.25	85.50	222.75
Fire alarm horn, electric	1.000	Ea.	30	50.25	80.25
Thermostatic release for release line	2.000	Ea.	438	34.50	472.50
Pipe, steel, black, schedule 40, 4″ diam	10.000	L.F.	74.25	182.55	256.80
Dry pipe valve, trim & gauges, 4″ pipe size	1.000	Ea.	975	615	1,590
Pipe, steel, black, schedule 40, threaded, cplg & hngr 10'OC 2-1/2″ diam	20.000	L.F.	83.25	243.75	327
Pipe steel black, schedule 40, threaded, cplg & hngr 10'OC 2″ diam	12.500	L.F.	32.81	119.06	151.87
Pipe, steel, black, schedule 40, threaded, cplg & hngr 10'OC 1-1/4″ diam	37.500	L.F.	69.19	257.34	326.53
Pipe, steel, black, schedule 40, threaded, cplg & hngr 10'OC 1″ diam	112.000	L.F.	173.88	714	887.88
Pipe, Tee, malleable iron, black, 150 lb threaded, 4″ diam	2.000	Ea.	166.50	304.50	471
Pipe, Tee, malleable iron, black, 150 lb threaded, 2-1/2″ pipe size	2.000	Ea.	46.50	135.75	182.25
Pipe, Tee, malleable iron, black, 150 lb threaded, 2″ pipe size	1.000	Ea.	10.84	55.50	66.34
Pipe, Tee, malleable iron, black, 150 lb threaded, 1-1/4″ pipe size	5.000	Ea.	25.50	217.50	243
Pipe, Tee, malleable iron, black, 150 lb threaded, 1″ pipe size	4.000	Ea.	12.60	169.50	182.10
Pipe, 90° elbow, malleable iron, blk, 150 lb threaded, 1″ pipe size	6.000	Ea.	12.15	155.25	167.40
Sprinkler head, std spray, brass 135°-286°F 1/2″ NPT, 3/8″ orifice	12.000	Ea.	79.20	342	421.20
Air compressor auto complete 200 Gal sprinkler sys cap, 1/3 HP	1.000	Ea.	592.50	262.50	855
*Standpipe conn.,wall,flush,brass w/plug & chain 2-1/2″ x 2-1/2″	1.000	Ea.	66.38	123	189.38
Valve, gate, bronze, 300 psi, NRS, class 150, threaded, 1″ pipe size	1.000	Ea.	29.63	18	47.63
TOTAL			4,450.43	4,769.45	9,219.88
COST PER S.F.			2.23	2.38	4.61

*Not included in systems under 2000 S.F.

D4010 415	Preaction Sprinkler Systems	COST PER S.F.		
		MAT.	INST.	TOTAL
0520	Preaction sprinkler systems, steel, black, sch. 40 pipe			
0530	Light hazard, one floor, 500 S.F.	4.45	3.23	7.68
0560	1000 S.F.	2.56	2.43	4.99
0580	2000 S.F.	2.23	2.39	4.62

D4010 Sprinklers

D4010 415	Preaction Sprinkler Systems	COST PER S.F.		
		MAT.	INST.	TOTAL
0600	5000 S.F.	1.11	1.59	2.70
0620	10,000 S.F.	.76	1.34	2.10
0640	50,000 S.F.	.52	1.18	1.70
0660	Each additional floor, 500 S.F.	.94	1.74	2.68
0680	1000 S.F.	.76	1.61	2.37
0700	2000 S.F.	.71	1.50	2.21
0720	5000 S.F.	.52	1.25	1.77
0740	10,000 S.F.	.48	1.18	1.66
0760	50,000 S.F.	.46	1.09	1.55
1000	Ordinary hazard, one floor, 500 S.F.	1.67	2.37	4.04
1020	1000 S.F.	2.52	2.39	4.91
1040	2000 S.F.	2.41	2.51	4.92
1060	5000 S.F.	1.23	1.71	2.94
1080	10,000 S.F.	.88	1.73	2.61
1100	50,000 S.F.	.79	1.71	2.50
1140	Each additional floor, 500 S.F.	1.06	2.01	3.07
1160	1000 S.F.	.73	1.63	2.36
1180	2000 S.F.	.68	1.64	2.32
1200	5000 S.F.	.74	1.53	2.27
1220	10,000 S.F.	.60	1.58	2.18
1240	50,000 S.F.	.62	1.50	2.12
1500	Extra hazard, one floor, 500 S.F.	6.15	4.49	10.64
1520	1000 S.F.	3.38	3.37	6.75
1540	2000 S.F.	2.40	3.19	5.59
1560	5000 S.F.	1.43	2.59	4.02
1580	10,000 S.F.	1.36	2.57	3.93
1600	50,000 S.F.	1.41	2.48	3.89
1660	Each additional floor, 500 S.F.	1.32	2.48	3.80
1680	1000 S.F.	1.07	2.36	3.43
1700	2000 S.F.	.98	2.36	3.34
1720	5000 S.F.	.80	2.07	2.87
1740	10,000 S.F.	.90	1.94	2.84
1760	50,000 S.F.	.87	1.81	2.68
2020	Grooved steel, black, sch. 40 pipe, light hazard, one floor, 2000 S.F.	2.25	2.07	4.32
2060	10,000 S.F.	.78	1.14	1.92
2100	Each additional floor of 2000 S.F.	.74	1.22	1.96
2150	10,000 S.F.	.50	.98	1.48
2200	Ordinary hazard, one floor, 2000 S.F.	2.27	2.19	4.46
2250	10,000 S.F.	.87	1.44	2.31
2300	Each additional floor, 2000 S.F.	.76	1.34	2.10
2350	10,000 S.F.	.59	1.29	1.88
2400	Extra hazard, one floor, 2000 S.F.	2.42	2.73	5.15
2450	10,000 S.F.	1.14	1.89	3.03
2500	Each additional floor, 2000 S.F.	1.01	1.94	2.95
2550	10,000 S.F.	.80	1.64	2.44
3050	Grooved steel, black, sch. 10 pipe light hazard, one floor, 2000 S.F.	2.22	2.05	4.27
3100	10,000 S.F.	.76	1.12	1.88
3150	Each additional floor, 2000 S.F.	.71	1.20	1.91
3200	10,000 S.F.	.48	.96	1.44
3250	Ordinary hazard, one floor, 2000 S.F.	2.22	2.02	4.24
3300	10,000 S.F.	.74	1.40	2.14
3350	Each additional floor, 2000 S.F.	.74	1.31	2.05
3400	10,000 S.F.	.57	1.26	1.83
3450	Extra hazard, one floor, 2000 S.F.	2.40	2.71	5.11
3500	10,000 S.F.	1.09	1.84	2.93
3550	Each additional floor, 2000 S.F.	.99	1.92	2.91
3600	10,000 S.F.	.79	1.61	2.40
4050	Copper tubing, type M, light hazard, one floor, 2000 S.F.	2.29	2.02	4.31

D40 Fire Protection

D4010 Sprinklers

D4010 415	Preaction Sprinkler Systems	COST PER S.F.		
		MAT.	INST.	TOTAL
4100	10,000 S.F.	.86	1.15	2.01
4150	Each additional floor, 2000 S.F.	.79	1.20	1.99
4200	10,000 S.F.	.47	.99	1.46
4250	Ordinary hazard, one floor, 2000 S.F.	2.35	2.24	4.59
4300	10,000 S.F.	.94	1.35	2.29
4350	Each additional floor, 2000 S.F.	.79	1.22	2.01
4400	10,000 S.F.	.59	1.08	1.67
4450	Extra hazard, one floor, 2000 S.F.	2.53	2.75	5.28
4500	10,000 S.F.	1.69	2.01	3.70
4550	Each additional floor, 2000 S.F.	1.12	1.96	3.08
4600	10,000 S.F.	1.16	1.75	2.91
5050	Copper tubing, type M, T-drill system, light hazard, one floor			
5060	2000 S.F.	2.28	1.89	4.17
5100	10,000 S.F.	.79	.95	1.74
5150	Each additional floor, 2000 S.F.	.78	1.07	1.85
5200	10,000 S.F.	.51	.80	1.31
5250	Ordinary hazard, one floor, 2000 S.F.	2.27	1.94	4.21
5300	10,000 S.F.	.89	1.20	2.09
5350	Each additional floor, 2000 S.F.	.76	1.10	1.86
5400	10,000 S.F.	.61	1.05	1.66
5450	Extra hazard, one floor, 2000 S.F.	2.34	2.29	4.63
5500	10,000 S.F.	1.33	1.47	2.80
5550	Each additional floor, 2000 S.F.	.93	1.50	2.43
5600	10,000 S.F.	.80	1.21	2.01

D4010 Sprinklers

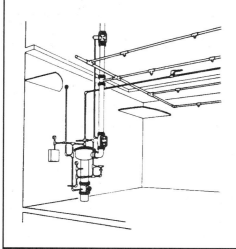

Deluge System: A system employing open sprinklers attached to a piping system connected to a water supply through a valve which is opened by the operation of a heat responsive system installed in the same areas as the sprinklers. When this valve opens, water flows into the piping system and discharges from all sprinklers attached thereto.

All areas are assumed to be open.

System Components	QUANTITY	UNIT	COST EACH MAT.	COST EACH INST.	COST EACH TOTAL
SYSTEM D4010 425 0580					
DELUGE SPRINKLER SYSTEM, STEEL BLACK SCH. 40 PIPE					
LIGHT HAZARD, 1 FLOOR, 2000 S.F.					
Valve, gate, iron body 125 lb, OS&Y, flanged, 4″ pipe size	1.000	Ea.	303.75	203.25	507
Valve, swing check w/ball drip, Cl w/brass ftngs, 4″ pipe size	1.000	Ea.	116.25	204.75	321
Valve, swing check, bronze, 125 lb, regrinding disc, 2-1/2″ pipe size	1.000	Ea.	160.50	40.50	201
Valve, angle, bronze, 150 lb, rising stem, threaded, 2″ pipe size	1.000	Ea.	199.50	30.75	230.25
*Alarm valve, 2-1/2″ pipe size	1.000	Ea.	615	204.75	819.75
Alarm, water motor, complete with gong	1.000	Ea.	137.25	85.50	222.75
Fire alarm horn, electric	1.000	Ea.	30	50.25	80.25
Thermostatic release for release line	2.000	Ea.	438	34.50	472.50
Pipe, steel, black, schedule 40, 4″ diam	10.000	L.F.	74.25	182.55	256.80
Deluge valve trim, pressure relief, emergency release, gauge, 4″ pipe size	1.000	Ea.	1,162.50	615	1,777.50
Deluge system pressured monitoring panel, 120V	1.000	Ea.	648.75	19.13	667.88
Pipe, steel, black, schedule 40, threaded, cplg & hngr 10′OC 2-1/2″ diam	20.000	L.F.	83.25	243.75	327
Pipe, steel, black, schedule 40, threaded, cplg & hngr 10′OC 2″ diam	12.500	L.F.	32.81	119.06	151.87
Pipe, steel, black, schedule 40, threaded, cplg & hngr 10′OC 1-1/4″ diam	37.500	L.F.	69.19	257.34	326.53
Pipe, steel, black, schedule 40, threaded, cplg & hngr 10′OC 1″ diam	112.000	L.F.	173.88	714	887.88
Pipe, Tee, malleable iron, black, 150 lb threaded, 4″ pipe size	2.000	Ea.	166.50	304.50	471
Pipe, Tee, malleable iron, black, 150 lb threaded, 2-1/2″ pipe size	2.000	Ea.	46.50	135.75	182.25
Pipe, Tee, malleable iron, black, 150 lb threaded, 2″ pipe size	1.000	Ea.	10.84	55.50	66.34
Pipe, Tee, malleable iron, black, 150 lb threaded, 1-1/4″ pipe size	5.000	Ea.	25.50	217.50	243
Pipe, Tee, malleable iron, black, 150 lb threaded, 1″ pipe size	4.000	Ea.	12.60	169.50	182.10
Pipe, 90° elbow, malleable iron, black, 150 lb threaded 1″ pipe size	6.000	Ea.	12.15	155.25	167.40
Sprinkler head, std spray, brass 135°-286°F 1/2″ NPT, 3/8″ orifice	9.720	Ea.	79.20	342	421.20
Air compressor, auto, complete, 200 Gal sprinkler sys cap, 1/3 HP	1.000	Ea.	592.50	262.50	855
*Standpipe connection, wall, flush w/plug & chain 2-1/2″x2-1/2″	1.000	Ea.	66.38	123	189.38
Valve, gate, bronze, 300 psi, NRS, class 150, threaded, 1″ pipe size	1.000	Ea.	29.63	18	47.63
TOTAL			5,286.68	4,788.58	10,075.26
COST PER S.F.			2.64	2.39	5.03

*Not included in systems under 2000 S.F.

D40 Fire Protection

D4010 Sprinklers

D4010 425	Deluge Sprinkler Systems	COST PER S.F.		
		MAT.	INST.	TOTAL
0520	Deluge sprinkler systems, steel, black, sch. 40 pipe			
0530	Light hazard, one floor, 500 S.F.	5.70	3.27	8.97
0560	1000 S.F.	3.16	2.34	5.50
0580	2000 S.F.	2.64	2.40	5.04
0600	5000 S.F.	1.28	1.59	2.87
0620	10,000 S.F.	.84	1.34	2.18
0640	50,000 S.F.	.53	1.18	1.71
0660	Each additional floor, 500 S.F.	.94	1.74	2.68
0680	1000 S.F.	.76	1.61	2.37
0700	2000 S.F.	.71	1.50	2.21
0720	5000 S.F.	.52	1.25	1.77
0740	10,000 S.F.	.48	1.18	1.66
0760	50,000 S.F.	.46	1.09	1.55
1000	Ordinary hazard, one floor, 500 S.F.	6.10	3.75	9.85
1020	1000 S.F.	3.14	2.41	5.55
1040	2000 S.F.	2.82	2.52	5.34
1060	5000 S.F.	1.40	1.71	3.11
1080	10,000 S.F.	.96	1.73	2.69
1100	50,000 S.F.	.84	1.74	2.58
1140	Each additional floor, 500 S.F.	1.06	2.01	3.07
1160	1000 S.F.	.73	1.63	2.36
1180	2000 S.F.	.68	1.64	2.32
1200	5000 S.F.	.68	1.40	2.08
1220	10,000 S.F.	.59	1.39	1.98
1240	50,000 S.F.	.59	1.38	1.97
1500	Extra hazard, one floor, 500 S.F.	7.35	4.53	11.88
1520	1000 S.F.	4.20	3.50	7.70
1540	2000 S.F.	2.81	3.20	6.01
1560	5000 S.F.	1.50	2.38	3.88
1580	10,000 S.F.	1.39	2.34	3.73
1600	50,000 S.F.	1.44	2.29	3.73
1660	Each additional floor, 500 S.F.	1.32	2.48	3.80
1680	1000 S.F.	1.07	2.36	3.43
1700	2000 S.F.	.98	2.36	3.34
1720	5000 S.F.	.80	2.07	2.87
1740	10,000 S.F.	.92	2.01	2.93
1760	50,000 S.F.	.92	1.93	2.85
2000	Grooved steel, black, sch. 40 pipe, light hazard, one floor			
2150	10,000 S.F.	.50	.98	1.48
2200	Ordinary hazard, one floor, 2000 S.F.	2.27	2.19	4.46
2250	10,000 S.F.	.95	1.44	2.39
2300	Each additional floor, 2000 S.F.	.76	1.34	2.10
2350	10,000 S.F.	.59	1.29	1.88
2400	Extra hazard, one floor, 2000 S.F.	2.83	2.74	5.57
3100	10,000 S.F.	.84	1.12	1.96
3150	Each additional floor, 2000 S.F.	.71	1.20	1.91
3200	10,000 S.F.	.48	.96	1.44
3250	Ordinary hazard, one floor, 2000 S.F.	2.66	2.17	4.83
3300	10,000 S.F.	.82	1.40	2.22
3350	Each additional floor, 2000 S.F.	.74	1.31	2.05
3500	10,000 S.F.	1.17	1.84	3.01
3550	Each additional floor, 2000 S.F.	.99	1.92	2.91
3600	10,000 S.F.	.79	1.61	2.40
4000	Copper tubing, type M, light hazard, one floor			
4050	2000 S.F.	2.70	2.03	4.73
4100	10,000 S.F.	.94	1.15	2.09
4150	Each additional floor, 2000 S.F.	.79	1.20	1.99
4200	10,000 S.F.	.47	.99	1.46

D40 Fire Protection

D4010 Sprinklers

D4010 425	Deluge Sprinkler Systems	COST PER S.F.		
		MAT.	INST.	TOTAL
4250	Ordinary hazard, one floor, 2000 S.F.	2.76	2.25	5.01
4300	10,000 S.F.	1.02	1.35	2.37
4350	Each additional floor, 2000 S.F.	.79	1.22	2.01
4400	10,000 S.F.	.59	1.08	1.67
4450	Extra hazard, one floor, 2000 S.F.	2.94	2.76	5.70
4500	10,000 S.F.	1.79	2.02	3.81
4550	Each additional floor, 2000 S.F.	1.12	1.96	3.08
4600	10,000 S.F.	1.16	1.75	2.91
5000	Copper tubing, type M, T-drill system, light hazard, one floor			
5050	2000 S.F.	2.69	1.90	4.59
5100	10,000 S.F.	.87	.95	1.82
5150	Each additional floor, 2000 S.F.	.79	1.09	1.88
5200	10,000 S.F.	.51	.80	1.31
5250	Ordinary hazard, one floor, 2000 S.F.	2.68	1.95	4.63
5300	10,000 S.F.	.97	1.20	2.17
5350	Each additional floor, 2000 S.F.	.76	1.09	1.85
5400	10,000 S.F.	.61	1.05	1.66
5450	Extra hazard, one floor, 2000 S.F.	2.75	2.30	5.05
5500	10,000 S.F.	1.41	1.47	2.88
5550	Each additional floor, 2000 S.F.	.93	1.50	2.43
5600	10,000 S.F.	.80	1.21	2.01

D40 Fire Protection

D4010 Sprinklers

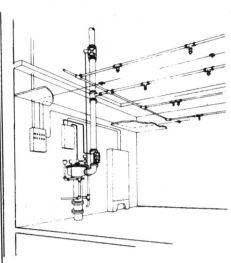

Firecycle is a fixed fire protection sprinkler system utilizing water as its extinguishing agent. It is a time delayed, recycling, preaction type which automatically shuts the water off when heat is reduced below the detector operating temperature and turns the water back on when that temperature is exceeded.

The system senses a fire condition through a closed circuit electrical detector system which controls water flow to the fire automatically. Batteries supply up to 90 hour emergency power supply for system operation. The piping system is dry (until water is required) and is monitored with pressurized air. Should

any leak in the system piping occur, an alarm will sound, but water will not enter the system until heat is sensed by a Firecycle detector.

All areas are assumed to be open.

System Components	QUANTITY	UNIT	COST EACH		
			MAT.	INST.	TOTAL
SYSTEM D4010 435 0580					
FIRECYCLE SPRINKLER SYSTEM, STEEL BLACK SCH. 40 PIPE					
LIGHT HAZARD, ONE FLOOR, 2000 S.F.	1.000	Ea.	303.75	203.25	507
Valve, gate, iron body 125 lb, OS&Y, flanged, 4″ pipe size	1.000	Ea.	199.50	30.75	230.25
Valve, angle, bronze, 150 lb, rising stem, threaded, 2″ pipe size	1.000	Ea.	160.50	40.50	201
Valve, swing check, bronze, 125 lb, regrinding disc, 2-1/2″ pipe size	1.000	Ea.	615	204.75	819.75
*Alarm valve, 2-1/2″ pipe size	1.000	Ea.	137.25	85.50	222.75
Alarm, water motor, complete with gong	10.000	L.F.	74.25	182.55	256.80
Pipe, steel, black, schedule 40, 4″ diam	1.000	Ea.	30	50.25	80.25
Fire alarm, horn, electric	20.000	L.F.	83.25	243.75	327
Pipe, steel, black, schedule 40, threaded, cplg & hngr 10′OC 2-1/2″ diam	12.500	L.F.	32.81	119.06	151.87
Pipe, steel, black, schedule 40, threaded, cplg & hngr 10′OC 2″ diam	37.500	L.F.	69.19	257.34	326.53
Pipe, steel, black, schedule 40, threaded, cplg & hngr 10′OC 1-1/4″ diam	112.000	L.F.	173.88	714	887.88
Pipe, steel, black, schedule 40, threaded, cplg & hngr 10′OC 1″ diam	2.000	Ea.	166.50	304.50	471
Pipe, Tee, malleable iron, black, 150 lb threaded, 4″ pipe size	2.000	Ea.	46.50	135.75	182.25
Pipe, Tee, malleable iron, black, 150 lb threaded, 2-1/2″ pipe size	1.000	Ea.	10.84	55.50	66.34
Pipe, Tee, malleable iron, black, 150 lb threaded, 2″ pipe size	5.000	Ea.	25.50	217.50	243
Pipe, Tee, malleable iron, black, 150 lb threaded, 1-1/4″ pipe size	4.000	Ea.	12.60	169.50	182.10
Pipe, Tee, malleable iron, black, 150 lb threaded, 1″ pipe size	6.000	Ea.	12.15	155.25	167.40
Pipe, 90° elbow, malleable iron, black, 150 lb threaded, 1″ pipe size	12.000	Ea.	79.20	342	421.20
Sprinkler head std spray, brass 135°-286°F 1/2″ NPT, 3/8″ orifice	1.000	Ea.	6,412.50	1,312.50	7,725
Firecycle controls, incls panel, battery, solenoid valves, press switches	2.000	Ea.	472.50	42.75	515.25
Detector, firecycle system	1.000	Ea.	1,743.75	615	2,358.75
Firecycle pkg, swing check & flow control valves w/trim 4″ pipe size	1.000	Ea.	592.50	262.50	855
Air compressor, auto, complete, 200 Gal sprinkler sys cap, 1/3 HP	1.000	Ea.	66.38	123	189.38
*Standpipe connection, wall, flush, brass w/plug & chain 2-1/2″x2-1/2″	1.000	Ea.	29.63	18	47.63
Valve, gate, bronze, 300 psi, NRS, class 150, threaded, 1″ diam					
TOTAL			11,549.93	5,885.45	17,435.38
COST PER S.F.			5.77	2.94	8.71

*Not included in systems under 2000 S.F.

D40 Fire Protection

D4010 Sprinklers

D4010 435	Firecycle Sprinkler Systems	COST PER S.F.		
		MAT.	INST.	TOTAL
0520	Firecycle sprinkler systems, steel black sch. 40 pipe			
0530	Light hazard, one floor, 500 S.F.	18.95	6.45	25.40
0560	1000 S.F.	9.75	4.02	13.77
0580	2000 S.F.	5.75	2.95	8.70
0600	5000 S.F.	2.54	1.82	4.36
0620	10,000 S.F.	1.50	1.46	2.96
0640	50,000 S.F.	.69	1.21	1.90
0660	Each additional floor of 500 S.F.	.97	1.75	2.72
0680	1000 S.F.	.78	1.61	2.39
0700	2000 S.F.	.61	1.49	2.10
0720	5000 S.F.	.53	1.26	1.79
0740	10,000 S.F.	.52	1.19	1.71
0760	50,000 S.F.	.48	1.10	1.58
1000	Ordinary hazard, one floor, 500 S.F.	19.05	6.70	25.75
1020	1000 S.F.	9.75	3.98	13.73
1040	2000 S.F.	5.85	3.06	8.91
1060	5000 S.F.	2.66	1.94	4.60
1080	10,000 S.F.	1.62	1.85	3.47
1100	50,000 S.F.	1.08	1.95	3.03
1140	Each additional floor, 500 S.F.	1.09	2.02	3.11
1160	1000 S.F.	.75	1.63	2.38
1180	2000 S.F.	.78	1.51	2.29
1200	5000 S.F.	.69	1.41	2.10
1220	10,000 S.F.	.58	1.37	1.95
1240	50,000 S.F.	.60	1.32	1.92
1500	Extra hazard, one floor, 500 S.F.	20.50	7.70	28.20
1520	1000 S.F.	10.55	4.95	15.50
1540	2000 S.F.	5.95	3.75	9.70
1560	5000 S.F.	2.76	2.61	5.37
1580	10,000 S.F.	2.08	2.67	4.75
1600	50,000 S.F.	1.72	2.94	4.66
1660	Each additional floor, 500 S.F.	1.35	2.49	3.84
1680	1000 S.F.	1.09	2.36	3.45
1700	2000 S.F.	1	2.36	3.36
1720	5000 S.F.	.81	2.08	2.89
1740	10,000 S.F.	.94	1.95	2.89
1760	50,000 S.F.	.93	1.87	2.80
2020	Grooved steel, black, sch. 40 pipe, light hazard, one floor			
2030	2000 S.F.	5.80	2.63	8.43
2060	10,000 S.F.	1.64	1.76	3.40
2100	Each additional floor, 2000 S.F.	.76	1.22	1.98
2150	10,000 S.F.	.54	.99	1.53
2200	Ordinary hazard, one floor, 2000 S.F.	5.80	2.75	8.55
2250	10,000 S.F.	1.71	1.65	3.36
2300	Each additional floor, 2000 S.F.	.78	1.34	2.12
2350	10,000 S.F.	.63	1.30	1.93
2400	Extra hazard, one floor, 2000 S.F.	5.95	3.29	9.24
2450	10,000 S.F.	1.86	1.99	3.85
2500	Each additional floor, 2000 S.F.	1.03	1.94	2.97
2550	10,000 S.F.	.84	1.65	2.49
3050	Grooved steel, black, sch. 10 pipe light hazard, one floor,			
3060	2000 S.F.	5.75	2.61	8.36
3100	10,000 S.F.	1.50	1.24	2.74
3150	Each additional floor, 2000 S.F.	.73	1.20	1.93
3200	10,000 S.F.	.52	.97	1.49
3250	Ordinary hazard, one floor, 2000 S.F.	5.80	2.72	8.52

D40 Fire Protection

D4010 Sprinklers

D4010 435	Firecycle Sprinkler Systems	COST PER S.F.		
		MAT.	INST.	TOTAL
		1.59	1.53	3.12
3300	10,000 S.F.	.76	1.31	2.07
3350	Each additional floor, 2000 S.F.	.61	1.27	1.88
3400	10,000 S.F.	5.95	3.27	9.22
3450	Extra hazard, one floor, 2000 S.F.	1.82	1.95	3.77
3500	10,000 S.F.	1.01	1.92	2.93
3550	Each additional floor, 2000 S.F.	.83	1.62	2.45
3600	10,000 S.F.	5.85	2.58	8.43
4060	Copper tubing, type M, light hazard, one floor, 2000 S.F.	1.60	1.27	2.87
4100	10,000 S.F.	.81	1.20	2.01
4150	Each additional floor, 2000 S.F.	.62	1.01	1.63
4200	10,000 S.F.	5.90	2.80	8.70
4250	Ordinary hazard, one floor, 2000 S.F.	1.68	1.47	3.15
4300	10,000 S.F.	.81	1.22	2.03
4350	Each additional floor, 2000 S.F.	.62	1.07	1.69
4400	10,000 S.F.	6.10	3.31	9.41
4450	Extra hazard, one floor, 2000 S.F.	2.49	2.15	4.64
4500	10,000 S.F.	1.14	1.96	3.10
4550	Each additional floor, 2000 S.F.	1.20	1.76	2.96
4600	10,000 S.F.	5.85	2.45	8.30
5060	Copper tubing, type M, T-drill system, light hazard, one floor 2000 S.F.	1.53	1.07	2.60
5100	10,000 S.F.	.90	1.13	2.03
5150	Each additional floor, 2000 S.F.	.55	.81	1.36
5200	10,000 S.F.	5.80	2.50	8.30
5250	Ordinary hazard, one floor, 2000 S.F.	1.63	1.32	2.95
5300	10,000 S.F.	.78	1.09	1.87
5350	Each additional floor, 2000 S.F.	.65	1.06	1.71
5400	10,000 S.F.	5.90	2.85	8.75
5450	Extra hazard, one floor, 2000 S.F.	2.06	1.58	3.64
5500	10,000 S.F.	.95	1.50	2.45
5550	Each additional floor, 2000 S.F.	.84	1.22	2.06
5600	10,000 S.F.			

D4090 Other Fire Protection Systems

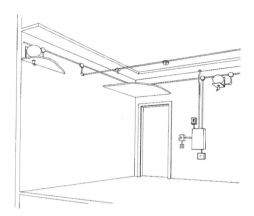

General: Automatic fire protection (suppression) systems other than water sprinklers may be desired for special environments, high risk areas, isolated locations or unusual hazards. Some typical applications would include:

Paint dip tanks
Securities vaults
Electronic data processing
Tape and data storage
Transformer rooms
Spray booths
Petroleum storage
High rack storage

Piping and wiring costs are dependent on the individual application and must be added to the component costs shown below.

All areas are assumed to be open.

D4090 410	Unit Components	COST EACH		
		MAT.	INST.	TOTAL
0020	Detectors with brackets			
0040	Fixed temperature heat detector	31	56	87
0060	Rate of temperature rise detector	37	56	93
0080	Ion detector (smoke) detector	82.50	72.50	155
0200	Extinguisher agent			
0240	200 lb FM200, container	6,375	203	6,578
0280	75 lb carbon dioxide cylinder	1,050	135	1,185
0320	Dispersion nozzle			
0340	FM200 1-1/2" dispersion nozzle	55	32	87
0380	Carbon dioxide 3" x 5" dispersion nozzle	55	25	80
0420	Control station			
0440	Single zone control station with batteries	1,400	450	1,850
0470	Multizone (4) control station with batteries	2,700	900	3,600
0490				
0500	Electric mechanical release	138	225	363
0520				
0550	Manual pull station	49.50	75	124.50
0570				
0640	Battery standby power 10" x 10" x 17"	760	112	872
0700				
0740	Bell signalling device	54.50	56	110.50

D4090 410	FM200 Systems	COST PER C.F.		
		MAT.	INST.	TOTAL
0820	Average FM200 system, minimum			1.38
0840	Maximum			2.75

D50 Electrical

D5030 Communications and Security

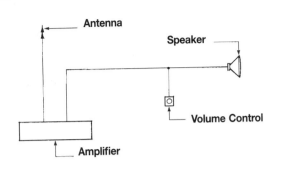

Antenna

Speaker

Volume Control

Amplifier

Sound System Includes AM–FM antenna, outlets, rigid conduit, and copper wire.
Fire Detection System Includes pull stations, signals, smoke and heat detectors, rigid conduit, and copper wire.
Intercom System Includes master and remote stations, rigid conduit, and copper wire.
Master Clock System Includes clocks, bells, rigid conduit, and copper wire.
Master TV Antenna Includes antenna, VHF–UHF reception and distribution, rigid conduit, and copper wire.

System Components	QUANTITY	UNIT	COST EACH		
			MAT.	INST.	TOTAL
SYSTEM D5030 810 0220					
SOUND SYSTEM, INCLUDES OUTLETS, BOXES, CONDUIT & WIRE					
Steel intermediate conduit, (IMC) 1/2″ diam	1200.000	L.F.	1,728	5,388	7,116
Wire sound shielded w/drain, #22-2 conductor	15.500	C.L.F.	244.13	868	1,112.13
Sound system speakers ceiling or wall	12.000	Ea.	1,122	672	1,794
Sound system volume control	12.000	Ea.	810	672	1,482
Sound system amplifier, 250 Watts	1.000	Ea.	1,350	450	1,800
Sound system antenna, AM FM	1.000	Ea.	169	112	281
Sound system monitor panel	1.000	Ea.	305	112	417
Sound system cabinet	1.000	Ea.	660	450	1,110
Steel outlet box 4″ square	12.000	Ea.	27.72	270	297.72
Steel outlet box 4″ plaster rings	12.000	Ea.	15	84	99
TOTAL			6,430.85	9,078	15,508.85

D5030 810	Communication & Alarm Systems	COST EACH		
		MAT.	INST.	TOTAL
0200	Communication & alarm systems, includes outlets, boxes, conduit & wire	4,625	5,675	10,300
0210	Sound system, 6 outlets	6,425	9,075	15,500
0220	12 outlets	11,100	17,200	28,300
0240	30 outlets	33,500	57,500	91,000
0280	100 outlets	2,250	4,700	6,950
0320	Fire detection systems, 12 detectors	3,950	7,975	11,925
0360	25 detectors	7,600	15,600	23,200
0400	50 detectors	13,800	28,100	41,900
0440	100 detectors	2,525	3,875	6,400
0480	Intercom systems, 6 stations	5,150	7,725	12,875
0520	12 stations	8,750	14,900	23,650
0560	25 stations	16,900	28,000	44,900
0600	50 stations	33,500	54,500	88,000
0640	100 stations	3,825	6,325	10,150
0680	Master clock systems, 6 rooms	5,700	10,800	16,500
0720	12 rooms	7,600	15,300	22,900
0760	20 rooms	12,300	28,100	40,400
0800	30 rooms	19,600	47,500	67,100
0840	50 rooms	37,500	94,000	131,500
0880	100 rooms	2,200	4,000	6,200
0920	Master TV antenna systems, 6 outlets	4,100	7,475	11,575
0960	12 outlets	8,200	17,300	25,500
1000	30 outlets	27,100	56,500	83,600
1040	100 outlets			

D5090 Other Electrical Systems

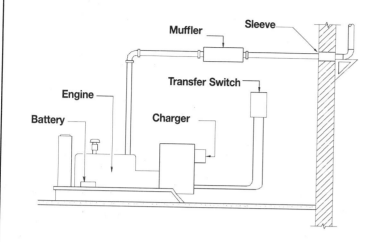

Description: System below tabulates the installed cost for generators by KW. Included in costs are battery, charger, muffler, and transfer switch.

No conduit, wire, or terminations included.

System Components	QUANTITY	UNIT	COST PER kW		
			MAT.	INST.	TOTAL
SYSTEM D5090 210 0200 **GENERATOR SET, INCL. BATTERY, CHARGER, MUFFLER & TRANSFER SWITCH** **GAS/GASOLINE OPER., 3 PHASE, 4 WIRE, 277/480V, 7.5 kW** Generator set, gas, 3 phase, 4 wire, 277/480V, 7.5 kW	.133	Ea.	880	205.47	1,085.47
TOTAL			880	205.47	1,085.47

D5090 210	Generators (by kW)	COST PER kW		
		MAT.	INST.	TOTAL
0190	Generator sets, include battery, charger, muffler & transfer switch			
0200	Gas/gasoline operated, 3 phase, 4 wire, 277/480 volt, 7.5 kW	880	206	1,086
0240	11.5 kW	815	157	972
0280	20 kW	550	102	652
0320	35 kW	375	67.50	442.50
0360	80 kW	283	40	323
0400	100 kW	248	39	287
0440	125 kW	405	36.50	441.50
0480	185 kW	360	28	388
0560	Diesel engine with fuel tank, 30 kW	585	78.50	663.50
0600	50 kW	435	61.50	496.50
0640	75 kW	375	49.50	424.50
0680	100 kW	315	42	357
0720	125 kW	264	35.50	299.50
0760	150 kW	252	33	285
0800	175 kW	236	29.50	265.50
0840	200 kW	213	27	240
0880	250 kW	200	22.50	222.50
0920	300 kW	180	19.55	199.55
0960	350 kW	176	18.40	194.40
1000	400 kW	189	16.90	205.90
1040	500 kW	190	14.30	204.30

E10 Equipment

E1010 Commercial Equipment

E1010 110	Security/Vault, EACH	COST EACH		
		MAT.	INST.	TOTAL
0100	Bank equipment, drive up window, drawer & mike, no glazing, economy	4,025	1,025	5,050
0110	Deluxe	7,925	2,075	10,000
0120	Night depository, economy	5,875	1,025	6,900
0130	Deluxe	8,475	2,075	10,550
0140	Pneumatic tube systems, 2 station, standard	21,200	3,400	24,600
0150	Teller, automated, 24 hour, single unit	39,200	3,400	42,600
0160	Teller window, bullet proof glazing, 44" x 60"	2,850	625	3,475
0170	Pass through, painted steel, 72" x 40"	3,050	1,300	4,350
0300	Safe, office type, 1 hr. rating, 34" x 20" x 20"	1,650		1,650
0310	4 hr. rating, 62" x 33" x 20"	6,975		6,975
0320	Data storage, 4 hr. rating, 63" x 44" x 16"	9,375		9,375
0330	Jewelers, 63" x 44" x 16"	16,000		16,000
0340	Money, "B" label, 9" x 14" x 14"	495		495
0350	Tool and torch resistive, 24" x 24" x 20"	7,050	154	7,204
0500	Security gates-scissors type, painted steel, single, 6' high, 5-1/2' wide	136	259	395
0510	Double gate, 7-1/2' high, 14' wide	410	520	930
0110	Parking equipment, automatic gates, 8 ft. arm, one way	3,425	815	4,240
0120	Traffic detectors, single treadle	2,275	375	2,650
0130	Booth for attendant, economy	5,375		5,375
0140	Deluxe	24,000		24,000
0150	Ticket printer/dispenser, rate computing	7,625	640	8,265
0160	Key station on pedestal	695	219	914

G4020 Site Lighting

The Site Lighting System includes the complete unit from foundation to electrical fixtures. Each system includes: excavation; concrete base; backfill by hand; compaction with a plate compacter; pole of specified material; all fixtures; and lamps.

The Expanded System Listing shows Site Lighting Systems that use one of three types of lamps: high pressure sodium; mercury vapor; and metal halide. Systems are listed for 400-watt and 1000-watt lamps. Pole height varies from 20' to 40'. There are four types of poles listed: aluminum, fiberglass, steel and wood.

G4020 110	Site Lighting	COST EACH		
		MAT.	INST.	TOTAL
2320	Site lighting, high pressure sodium, 400 watt, aluminum pole, 20' high	1,275	970	2,245
2360	40' high	2,250	1,525	3,775
2920	Wood pole, 20' high	865	945	1,810
2960	40' high	1,125	1,425	2,550
3120	1000 watt, aluminum pole, 20' high	1,350	990	2,340
3160	40' high	2,325	1,550	3,875
3520	Wood pole, 20' high	925	965	1,890
3560	40' high	1,175	1,450	2,625
5820	Metal halide, 400 watt, aluminum pole, 20' high	1,225	970	2,195
5860	40' high	2,200	1,525	3,725
7620	1000 watt, aluminum pole, 20' high	1,300	990	2,290
7661	40' high	2,300	1,550	3,850

Crews

Crew No.	Bare Costs Hr.	Bare Costs Daily	Incl. Subs O & P Hr.	Incl. Subs O & P Daily	Cost Per Labor-Hour Bare Costs	Cost Per Labor-Hour Incl. O&P
Crew A-2					Bare Costs	Incl. O&P
2 Laborers	$24.65	$394.40	$38.50	$616.00	$24.73	$38.33
1 Truck Driver (light)	24.90	199.20	38.00	304.00		
1 Light Truck, 1.5 Ton		120.20		132.20	5.01	5.51
24 L.H., Daily Totals		$713.80		$1052.20	$29.74	$43.84
Crew B-1	Hr.	Daily	Hr.	Daily	Bare Costs	Incl. O&P
1 Labor Foreman (outside)	$26.65	$213.20	$41.65	$333.20	$25.32	$39.55
2 Laborers	24.65	394.40	38.50	616.00		
24 L.H., Daily Totals		$607.60		$949.20	$25.32	$39.55
Crew B-2	Hr.	Daily	Hr.	Daily	Bare Costs	Incl. O&P
1 Labor Foreman (outside)	$26.65	$213.20	$41.65	$333.20	$25.05	$39.13
4 Laborers	24.65	788.80	38.50	1232.00		
40 L.H., Daily Totals		$1002.00		$1565.20	$25.05	$39.13
Crew B-3	Hr.	Daily	Hr.	Daily	Bare Costs	Incl. O&P
1 Labor Foreman (outside)	$26.65	$213.20	$41.65	$333.20	$26.64	$41.05
2 Laborers	24.65	394.40	38.50	616.00		
1 Equip. Oper. (med.)	32.60	260.80	49.35	394.80		
2 Truck Drivers (heavy)	25.65	410.40	39.15	626.40		
1 F.E. Loader, T.M., 2.5 C.Y.		778.40		856.25		
2 Dump Trucks, 16 Ton		899.20		989.10	34.95	38.45
48 L.H., Daily Totals		$2956.40		$3815.75	$61.59	$79.50
Crew B-6	Hr.	Daily	Hr.	Daily	Bare Costs	Incl. O&P
2 Laborers	$24.65	$394.40	$38.50	$616.00	$26.80	$41.37
1 Equip. Oper. (light)	31.10	248.80	47.10	376.80		
1 Backhoe Loader, 48 H.P.		218.80		240.70	9.12	10.03
24 L.H., Daily Totals		$862.00		$1233.50	$35.92	$51.40
Crew B-16	Hr.	Daily	Hr.	Daily	Bare Costs	Incl. O&P
1 Labor Foreman (outside)	$26.65	$213.20	$41.65	$333.20	$25.40	$39.45
2 Laborers	24.65	394.40	38.50	616.00		
1 Truck Driver (heavy)	25.65	205.20	39.15	313.20		
1 Dump Truck, 16 Ton		449.60		494.55	14.05	15.46
32 L.H., Daily Totals		$1262.40		$1756.95	$39.45	$54.91
Crew B-17	Hr.	Daily	Hr.	Daily	Bare Costs	Incl. O&P
2 Laborers	$24.65	$394.40	$38.50	$616.00	$26.51	$40.81
1 Equip. Oper. (light)	31.10	248.80	47.10	376.80		
1 Truck Driver (heavy)	25.65	205.20	39.15	313.20		
1 Backhoe Loader, 48 H.P.		218.80		240.70		
1 Dump Truck, 12 Ton		306.00		336.60	16.40	18.04
32 L.H., Daily Totals		$1373.20		$1883.30	$42.91	$58.85
Crew B-22	Hr.	Daily	Hr.	Daily	Bare Costs	Incl. O&P
1 Labor Foreman (out)	$26.65	$213.20	$41.65	$333.20	$29.02	$45.04
1 Skilled Worker	32.25	258.00	50.50	404.00		
1 Laborer	24.65	197.20	38.50	308.00		
.75 Equip. Oper. (crane)	33.70	202.20	51.00	306.00		
.75 S.P. Crane, 5 Ton		244.80		269.30	8.16	8.98
30 L.H., Daily Totals		$1115.40		$1620.50	$37.18	$54.02
Crew B-29	Hr.	Daily	Hr.	Daily	Bare Costs	Incl. O&P
1 Labor Foreman (outside)	$26.65	$213.20	$41.65	$333.20	$26.75	$41.36
4 Laborers	24.65	788.80	38.50	1232.00		
1 Equip. Oper. (crane)	33.70	269.60	51.00	408.00		
1 Equip. Oper. Oiler	28.30	226.40	42.85	342.80		
1 Gradall, 3 Ton, 1/2 C.Y.		846.40		931.05	15.11	16.63
56 L.H., Daily Totals		$2344.40		$3247.05	$41.86	$57.99

Crew No.	Bare Costs Hr.	Bare Costs Daily	Incl. Subs O & P Hr.	Incl. Subs O & P Daily	Cost Per Labor-Hour Bare Costs	Cost Per Labor-Hour Incl. O&P
Crew B-30	Hr.	Daily	Hr.	Daily	Bare Costs	Incl. O&P
1 Equip. Oper. (med.)	$32.60	$260.80	$49.35	$394.80	$27.97	$42.55
2 Truck Drivers (heavy)	25.65	410.40	39.15	626.40		
1 Hyd. Excavator, 1.5 C.Y.		728.80		801.70		
2 Dump Trucks, 16 Ton		899.20		989.10	67.83	74.62
24 L.H., Daily Totals		$2299.20		$2812.00	$95.80	$117.17
Crew B-34B	Hr.	Daily	Hr.	Daily	Bare Costs	Incl. O&P
1 Truck Driver (heavy)	$25.65	$205.20	$39.15	$313.20	$25.65	$39.15
1 Dump Truck, 16 Ton		449.60		494.55	56.20	61.82
8 L.H., Daily Totals		$654.80		$807.75	$81.85	$100.97
Crew B-80	Hr.	Daily	Hr.	Daily	Bare Costs	Incl. O&P
1 Labor Foreman	$26.65	$213.20	$41.65	$333.20	$25.83	$41.31
1 Laborer	24.65	197.20	38.50	308.00		
1 Truck Driver (light)	24.90	199.20	38.00	304.00		
1 Equip. Oper. (light)	31.10	248.80	47.10	376.80		
1 Flatbed Truck, 3 Ton		138.00		151.80		
1 Fence Post Auger, T.M.		361.20		397.30	15.60	17.16
32 L.H., Daily Totals		$1357.60		$1871.10	$42.43	$58.47
Crew B-80A	Hr.	Daily	Hr.	Daily	Bare Costs	Incl. O&P
3 Laborers	$24.65	$591.60	$38.50	$924.00	$24.65	$38.50
1 Flatbed Truck, 3 Ton		138.00		151.80	5.75	6.33
24 L.H., Daily Totals		$729.60		$1075.80	$30.40	$44.83
Crew B-80B	Hr.	Daily	Hr.	Daily	Bare Costs	Incl. O&P
3 Laborers	$24.65	$591.60	$38.50	$924.00	$26.26	$40.65
1 Equip. Oper. (light)	31.10	248.80	47.10	376.80		
1 Crane, Flatbed Mnt.		203.80		224.20	6.37	7.01
32 L.H., Daily Totals		$1044.20		$1525.00	$32.63	$47.66
Crew D-1	Hr.	Daily	Hr.	Daily	Bare Costs	Incl. O&P
1 Bricklayer	$32.40	$259.20	$49.80	$398.40	$28.50	$43.80
1 Bricklayer Helper	24.60	196.80	37.80	302.40		
16 L.H., Daily Totals		$456.00		$700.80	$28.50	$43.80
Crew D-8	Hr.	Daily	Hr.	Daily	Bare Costs	Incl. O&P
3 Bricklayers	$32.40	$777.60	$49.80	$1195.20	$29.28	$45.00
2 Bricklayer Helpers	24.60	393.60	37.80	604.80		
40 L.H., Daily Totals		$1171.20		$1800.00	$29.28	$45.00
Crew E-4	Hr.	Daily	Hr.	Daily	Bare Costs	Incl. O&P
1 Struc. Steel Foreman	$37.65	$301.20	$68.35	$546.80	$36.15	$65.65
3 Struc. Steel Workers	35.65	855.60	64.75	1554.00		
1 Gas Welding Machine		78.80		86.70	2.46	2.71
32 L.H., Daily Totals		$1235.60		$2187.50	$38.61	$68.36
Crew E-24	Hr.	Daily	Hr.	Daily	Bare Costs	Incl. O&P
3 Structural Steel Worker	$35.65	$855.60	$64.75	$1554.00	$34.89	$60.90
1 Equipment Operator (medium)	32.60	260.80	49.35	394.80		
1-25 Ton Crane		654.60		720.05	20.46	22.50
32 L.H., Daily Totals		$1771.00		$2668.85	$55.35	$83.40
Crew G-2	Hr.	Daily	Hr.	Daily	Bare Costs	Incl. O&P
1 Plasterer	$29.00	$232.00	$44.55	$356.40	$26.17	$40.40
1 Plasterer Helper	24.85	198.80	38.15	305.20		
1 Building Laborer	24.65	197.20	38.50	308.00		
1 Grouting Equipment		120.15		132.15	5.01	5.51
24 L.H., Daily Totals		$748.15		$1101.75	$31.18	$45.91

Crew No.	Bare Costs		Incl. Subs O & P		Cost Per Labor-Hour	
Crew J-4	Hr.	Daily	Hr.	Daily	Bare Costs	Incl. O&P
1 Tile Layer	$30.40	$243.20	$44.85	$358.80	$27.15	$40.05
1 Tile Layer Helper	23.90	191.20	35.25	282.00		
16 L.H., Daily Totals		$434.40		$640.80	$27.15	$40.05
Crew L-1	Hr.	Daily	Hr.	Daily	Bare Costs	Incl. O&P
1 Electrician	$37.60	$300.80	$56.15	$449.20	$37.47	$56.28
1 Plumber	37.35	298.80	56.40	451.20		
16 L.H., Daily Totals		$599.60		$900.40	$37.47	$56.28
Crew L-3	Hr.	Daily	Hr.	Daily	Bare Costs	Incl. O&P
1 Carpenter	$31.55	$252.40	$49.30	$394.40	$34.42	$52.98
.5 Electrician	37.60	150.40	56.15	224.60		
.5 Sheet Metal Worker	37.00	148.00	57.15	228.60		
16 L.H., Daily Totals		$550.80		$847.60	$34.42	$52.98
Crew Q-1	Hr.	Daily	Hr.	Daily	Bare Costs	Incl. O&P
1 Plumber	$37.35	$298.80	$56.40	$451.20	$33.63	$50.78
1 Plumber Apprentice	29.90	239.20	45.15	361.20		
16 L.H., Daily Totals		$538.00		$812.40	$33.63	$50.78
Crew Q-9	Hr.	Daily	Hr.	Daily	Bare Costs	Incl. O&P
1 Sheet Metal Worker	$37.00	$296.00	$57.15	$457.20	$33.30	$51.43
1 Sheet Metal Apprentice	29.60	236.80	45.70	365.60		
16 L.H., Daily Totals		$532.80		$822.80	$33.30	$51.43
Crew Q-10	Hr.	Daily	Hr.	Daily	Bare Costs	Incl. O&P
2 Sheet Metal Workers	$37.00	$592.00	$57.15	$914.40	$34.53	$53.33
1 Sheet Metal Apprentice	29.60	236.80	45.70	365.60		
24 L.H., Daily Totals		$828.80		$1280.00	$34.53	$53.33
Crew Q-11	Hr.	Daily	Hr.	Daily	Bare Costs	Incl. O&P
1 Sheet Metal Foreman (inside)	$37.50	$300.00	$57.90	$463.20	$35.28	$54.48
2 Sheet Metal Workers	37.00	592.00	57.15	914.40		
1 Sheet Metal Apprentice	29.60	236.80	45.70	365.60		
32 L.H., Daily Totals		$1128.80		$1743.20	$35.28	$54.48
Crew Q-12	Hr.	Daily	Hr.	Daily	Bare Costs	Incl. O&P
1 Sprinkler Installer	$37.55	$300.40	$56.95	$455.60	$33.80	$51.28
1 Sprinkler Apprentice	30.05	240.40	45.60	364.80		
16 L.H., Daily Totals		$540.80		$820.40	$33.80	$51.28
Crew Q-13	Hr.	Daily	Hr.	Daily	Bare Costs	Incl. O&P
1 Sprinkler Foreman (inside)	$38.05	$304.40	$57.70	$461.60	$35.80	$54.30
2 Sprinkler Installers	37.55	600.80	56.95	911.20		
1 Sprinkler Apprentice	30.05	240.40	45.60	364.80		
32 L.H., Daily Totals		$1145.60		$1737.60	$35.80	$54.30
Crew R-3	Hr.	Daily	Hr.	Daily	Bare Costs	Incl. O&P
1 Electrician Foreman	$38.10	$304.80	$56.90	$455.20	$37.02	$55.42
1 Electrician	37.60	300.80	56.15	449.20		
.5 Equip. Oper. (crane)	33.70	134.80	51.00	204.00		
.5 S.P. Crane, 5 Ton		163.20		179.50	8.16	8.98
20 L.H., Daily Totals		$903.60		$1287.90	$45.18	$64.40

Crew No.	Bare Costs		Incl. Subs O & P		Cost Per Labor-Hour	
Crew R-13	Hr.	Daily	Hr.	Daily	Bare Costs	Incl. O&P
1 Electrician Foreman	$38.10	$304.80	$56.90	$455.20	$35.74	$53.51
3 Electricians	37.60	902.40	56.15	1347.60		
.25 Equip. Oper. (crane)	33.70	67.40	51.00	102.00		
1 Equipment Oiler	28.30	226.40	42.85	342.80		
.25-1 Hyd. Crane, 33 Ton		168.95		185.85	4.02	4.42
42 L.H., Daily Totals		$1669.95		$2433.45	$39.76	$57.93
Crew R-19	Hr.	Daily	Hr.	Daily	Bare Costs	Incl. O&P
.5 Electrician Foreman	$38.10	$152.40	$56.90	$227.60	$37.70	$56.30
2 Electricians	37.60	601.60	56.15	898.40		
20 L.H., Daily Totals		$754.00		$1126.00	$37.70	$56.30
Crew R-30	Hr.	Daily	Hr.	Daily	Bare Costs	Incl. O&P
.25 Electricians	$39.60	$79.20	$59.10	$118.20	$29.78	$45.52
1 Electricians	37.60	300.80	56.15	449.20		
2 Laborers, (Semi-Skilled)	24.65	394.40	38.50	616.00		
26 L.H., Daily Totals		$774.40		$1183.40	$29.78	$45.52

323

Location Factors

Costs shown in *Means cost data publications* are based on National Averages for materials and installation. To adjust these costs to a specific location, simply multiply the base cost by the factor for that city. The data is arranged alphabetically by state and postal zip code numbers. For a city not listed, use the factor for a nearby city with similar economic characteristics.

STATE/ZIP	CITY	Residential	Commercial
ALABAMA			
350-352	Birmingham	.87	.88
354	Tuscaloosa	.80	.78
355	Jasper	.76	.77
356	Decatur	.78	.79
357-358	Huntsville	.85	.86
359	Gadsden	.79	.80
360-361	Montgomery	.82	.80
362	Anniston	.72	.73
363	Dothan	.77	.76
364	Evergreen	.78	.76
365-366	Mobile	.80	.81
367	Selma	.78	.76
368	Phenix City	.81	.79
369	Butler	.77	.75
ALASKA			
995-996	Anchorage	1.27	1.26
997	Fairbanks	1.26	1.25
998	Juneau	1.26	1.25
999	Ketchikan	1.33	1.32
ARIZONA			
850,853	Phoenix	.91	.88
852	Mesa/Tempe	.89	.86
855	Globe	.87	.84
856-857	Tucson	.89	.86
859	Show Low	.88	.84
860	Flagstaff	.91	.87
863	Prescott	.88	.84
864	Kingman	.88	.84
865	Chambers	.86	.83
ARKANSAS			
716	Pine Bluff	.80	.80
717	Camden	.69	.69
718	Texarkana	.73	.72
719	Hot Springs	.68	.68
720-722	Little Rock	.82	.82
723	West Memphis	.77	.77
724	Jonesboro	.77	.77
725	Batesville	.74	.74
726	Harrison	.75	.75
727	Fayetteville	.68	.65
728	Russellville	.76	.73
729	Fort Smith	.82	.79
CALIFORNIA			
900-902	Los Angeles	1.07	1.07
903-905	Inglewood	1.04	1.04
906-908	Long Beach	1.05	1.05
910-912	Pasadena	1.05	1.05
913-916	Van Nuys	1.07	1.07
917-918	Alhambra	1.07	1.07
919-921	San Diego	1.09	1.05
922	Palm Springs	1.08	1.04
923-924	San Bernardino	1.07	1.03
925	Riverside	1.11	1.07
926-927	Santa Ana	1.08	1.05
928	Anaheim	1.10	1.08
930	Oxnard	1.12	1.07
931	Santa Barbara	1.10	1.07
932-933	Bakersfield	1.11	1.06
934	San Luis Obispo	1.12	1.07
935	Mojave	1.08	1.04
936-938	Fresno	1.12	1.08
939	Salinas	1.11	1.11
940-941	San Francisco	1.21	1.24
942,956-958	Sacramento	1.12	1.11
943	Palo Alto	1.14	1.17
944	San Mateo	1.15	1.18
945	Vallejo	1.10	1.13
946	Oakland	1.15	1.18
947	Berkeley	1.15	1.18
948	Richmond	1.14	1.17
949	San Rafael	1.25	1.19
950	Santa Cruz	1.15	1.13
951	San Jose	1.22	1.20
952	Stockton	1.12	1.08
953	Modesto	1.12	1.08

STATE/ZIP	CITY	Residential	Commercial
CALIFORNIA (CONT'D)			
954	Santa Rosa	1.13	1.16
955	Eureka	1.08	1.07
959	Marysville	1.09	1.08
960	Redding	1.11	1.10
961	Susanville	1.11	1.10
COLORADO			
800-802	Denver	1.00	.96
803	Boulder	.88	.85
804	Golden	.99	.95
805	Fort Collins	.97	.91
806	Greeley	.90	.85
807	Fort Morgan	.97	.91
808-809	Colorado Springs	.95	.93
810	Pueblo	.94	.92
811	Alamosa	.89	.87
812	Salida	.89	.87
813	Durango	.89	.87
814	Montrose	.86	.85
815	Grand Junction	.89	.85
816	Glenwood Springs	.98	.93
CONNECTICUT			
060	New Britain	1.05	1.06
061	Hartford	1.04	1.05
062	Willimantic	1.04	1.05
063	New London	1.05	1.04
064	Meriden	1.05	1.06
065	New Haven	1.06	1.07
066	Bridgeport	1.03	1.06
067	Waterbury	1.06	1.06
068	Norwalk	1.03	1.07
069	Stamford	1.05	1.09
D.C.			
200-205	Washington	.94	.96
DELAWARE			
197	Newark	1.01	1.02
198	Wilmington	1.01	1.02
199	Dover	1.01	1.02
FLORIDA			
320,322	Jacksonville	.83	.82
321	Daytona Beach	.86	.85
323	Tallahassee	.74	.76
324	Panama City	.69	.71
325	Pensacola	.83	.81
326,344	Gainesville	.83	.80
327-328,347	Orlando	.85	.83
329	Melbourne	.89	.88
330-332,340	Miami	.83	.85
333	Fort Lauderdale	.82	.84
334,349	West Palm Beach	.85	.82
335-336,346	Tampa	.78	.80
337	St. Petersburg	.79	.81
338	Lakeland	.78	.80
339,341	Fort Myers	.78	.78
342	Sarasota	.77	.79
GEORGIA			
300-303,399	Atlanta	.85	.90
304	Statesboro	.71	.73
305	Gainesville	.74	.79
306	Athens	.76	.81
307	Dalton	.67	.66
308-309	Augusta	.75	.76
310-312	Macon	.80	.80
313-314	Savannah	.79	.80
315	Waycross	.73	.73
316	Valdosta	.75	.75
317	Albany	.76	.78
318-319	Columbus	.77	.77
HAWAII			
967	Hilo	1.26	1.22
968	Honolulu	1.27	1.23

STATE/ZIP	CITY	Residential	Commercial
STATES & POSS.			
969	Guam	1.34	1.30
IDAHO			
832	Pocatello	.93	.92
833	Twin Falls	.78	.77
834	Idaho Falls	.82	.81
835	Lewiston	1.08	1.00
836-837	Boise	.94	.93
838	Coeur d'Alene	.94	.87
ILLINOIS			
600-603	North Suburban	1.11	1.10
604	Joliet	1.11	1.10
605	South Suburban	1.11	1.10
606	Chicago	1.15	1.14
609	Kankakee	1.03	1.03
610-611	Rockford	1.06	1.05
612	Rock Island	1.07	.98
613	La Salle	1.08	1.01
614	Galesburg	1.08	1.01
615-616	Peoria	1.09	1.02
617	Bloomington	1.05	1.01
618-619	Champaign	1.05	1.02
620-622	East St. Louis	1.00	1.00
623	Quincy	1.00	.98
624	Effingham	1.02	.99
625	Decatur	1.01	.98
626-627	Springfield	1.03	.99
628	Centralia	.98	.98
629	Carbondale	.97	.97
INDIANA			
460	Anderson	.94	.92
461-462	Indianapolis	.97	.95
463-464	Gary	1.04	1.02
465-466	South Bend	.94	.92
467-468	Fort Wayne	.91	.92
469	Kokomo	.92	.91
470	Lawrenceburg	.92	.89
471	New Albany	.92	.88
472	Columbus	.94	.91
473	Muncie	.92	.91
474	Bloomington	.95	.93
475	Washington	.92	.92
476-477	Evansville	.93	.93
478	Terre Haute	.95	.94
479	Lafayette	.91	.91
IOWA			
500-503,509	Des Moines	.96	.92
504	Mason City	.88	.82
505	Fort Dodge	.86	.80
506-507	Waterloo	.87	.82
508	Creston	.88	.83
510-511	Sioux City	.94	.88
512	Sibley	.79	.77
513	Spencer	.79	.77
514	Carroll	.83	.78
515	Council Bluffs	.95	.89
516	Shenandoah	.81	.76
520	Dubuque	1.00	.89
521	Decorah	.87	.78
522-524	Cedar Rapids	1.00	.92
525	Ottumwa	.94	.86
526	Burlington	.92	.86
527-528	Davenport	.99	.97
KANSAS			
660-662	Kansas City	.99	.97
664-666	Topeka	.85	.84
667	Fort Scott	.86	.84
668	Emporia	.82	.81
669	Belleville	.85	.79
670-672	Wichita	.89	.86
673	Independence	.81	.78
674	Salina	.84	.80
675	Hutchinson	.78	.75
676	Hays	.83	.79
677	Colby	.83	.79
678	Dodge City	.83	.80
679	Liberal	.77	.74
KENTUCKY			
400-402	Louisville	.94	.91
403-405	Lexington	.86	.83

STATE/ZIP	CITY	Residential	Commercial
KENTUCKY (CONT'D)			
406	Frankfort	.90	.84
407-409	Corbin	.76	.71
410	Covington	.98	.95
411-412	Ashland	.96	.97
413-414	Campton	.75	.72
415-416	Pikeville	.81	.82
417-418	Hazard	.75	.72
420	Paducah	.96	.92
421-422	Bowling Green	.94	.90
423	Owensboro	.89	.87
424	Henderson	.94	.92
425-426	Somerset	.75	.71
427	Elizabethtown	.93	.89
LOUISIANA			
700-701	New Orleans	.88	.87
703	Thibodaux	.85	.85
704	Hammond	.83	.82
705	Lafayette	.83	.80
706	Lake Charles	.82	.82
707-708	Baton Rouge	.81	.80
710-711	Shreveport	.80	.80
712	Monroe	.78	.78
713-714	Alexandria	.77	.77
MAINE			
039	Kittery	.84	.86
040-041	Portland	.89	.91
042	Lewiston	.90	.91
043	Augusta	.86	.86
044	Bangor	.91	.91
045	Bath	.87	.87
046	Machias	.85	.85
047	Houlton	.87	.87
048	Rockland	.84	.84
049	Waterville	.84	.83
MARYLAND			
206	Waldorf	.87	.87
207-208	College Park	.90	.90
209	Silver Spring	.89	.89
210-212	Baltimore	.91	.91
214	Annapolis	.88	.89
215	Cumberland	.86	.87
216	Easton	.72	.72
217	Hagerstown	.89	.88
218	Salisbury	.75	.76
219	Elkton	.81	.82
MASSACHUSETTS			
010-011	Springfield	1.02	1.01
012	Pittsfield	.98	.98
013	Greenfield	1.00	.98
014	Fitchburg	1.06	1.02
015-016	Worcester	1.10	1.06
017	Framingham	1.04	1.05
018	Lowell	1.07	1.07
019	Lawrence	1.07	1.07
020-022, 024	Boston	1.14	1.15
023	Brockton	1.04	1.06
025	Buzzards Bay	1.01	1.03
026	Hyannis	1.03	1.04
027	New Bedford	1.05	1.06
MICHIGAN			
480,483	Royal Oak	1.03	1.02
481	Ann Arbor	1.04	1.03
482	Detroit	1.09	1.08
484-485	Flint	.98	.99
486	Saginaw	.96	.97
487	Bay City	.96	.97
488-489	Lansing	1.02	.99
490	Battle Creek	1.01	.95
491	Kalamazoo	1.00	.93
492	Jackson	.99	.96
493,495	Grand Rapids	.89	.86
494	Muskegon	.95	.92
496	Traverse City	.90	.86
497	Gaylord	.88	.89
498-499	Iron Mountain	.98	.95
MINNESOTA			
550-551	Saint Paul	1.14	1.12
553-555	Minneapolis	1.17	1.13

Location Factors

STATE/ZIP	CITY	Residential	Commercial
556-558	Duluth	1.02	1.03
559	Rochester	1.05	1.02
560	Mankato	1.00	.99
561	Windom	.91	.90
562	Willmar	.94	.93
563	St. Cloud	1.13	1.05
564	Brainerd	1.07	.99
565	Detroit Lakes	.91	.98
566	Bemidji	.92	.99
567	Thief River Falls	.87	.94
MISSISSIPPI			
386	Clarksdale	.68	.65
387	Greenville	.79	.75
388	Tupelo	.69	.70
389	Greenwood	.70	.67
390-392	Jackson	.79	.75
393	Meridian	.75	.74
394	Laurel	.71	.67
395	Biloxi	.83	.79
396	McComb	.79	.77
397	Columbus	.69	.70
MISSOURI			
630-631	St. Louis	.99	1.02
633	Bowling Green	.92	.94
634	Hannibal	.98	.92
635	Kirksville	.85	.89
636	Flat River	.94	.96
637	Cape Girardeau	.92	.95
638	Sikeston	.90	.92
639	Poplar Bluff	.90	.92
640-641	Kansas City	1.05	1.02
644-645	St. Joseph	.92	.96
646	Chillicothe	.81	.85
647	Harrisonville	1.01	.99
648	Joplin	.83	.85
650-651	Jefferson City	.97	.91
652	Columbia	.99	.93
653	Sedalia	.99	.92
654-655	Rolla	.94	.88
656-658	Springfield	.86	.88
MONTANA			
590-591	Billings	.92	.90
592	Wolf Point	.90	.88
593	Miles City	.90	.88
594	Great Falls	.91	.90
595	Havre	.89	.88
596	Helena	.90	.89
597	Butte	.90	.89
598	Missoula	.88	.87
599	Kalispell	.87	.86
NEBRASKA			
680-681	Omaha	.92	.91
683-685	Lincoln	.90	.85
686	Columbus	.77	.76
687	Norfolk	.84	.83
688	Grand Island	.88	.84
689	Hastings	.84	.80
690	Mccook	.78	.74
691	North Platte	.85	.81
692	Valentine	.76	.72
693	Alliance	.73	.70
NEVADA			
889-891	Las Vegas	1.05	1.04
893	Ely	.93	.94
894-895	Reno	.94	.99
897	Carson City	.96	.99
898	Elko	.91	.93
NEW HAMPSHIRE			
030	Nashua	.92	.93
031	Manchester	.92	.93
032-033	Concord	.91	.92
034	Keene	.76	.77
035	Littleton	.80	.81
036	Charleston	.75	.75
037	Claremont	.74	.75
038	Portsmouth	.90	.89

STATE/ZIP	CITY	Residential	Commercial
NEW JERSEY			
070-071	Newark	1.11	1.10
072	Elizabeth	1.08	1.06
073	Jersey City	1.10	1.09
074-075	Paterson	1.09	1.09
076	Hackensack	1.08	1.08
077	Long Branch	1.08	1.06
078	Dover	1.10	1.08
079	Summit	1.07	1.05
080,083	Vineland	1.09	1.06
081	Camden	1.09	1.06
082,084	Atlantic City	1.09	1.06
085-086	Trenton	1.09	1.08
087	Point Pleasant	1.08	1.06
088-089	New Brunswick	1.10	1.08
NEW MEXICO			
870-872	Albuquerque	.88	.90
873	Gallup	.88	.90
874	Farmington	.88	.90
875	Santa Fe	.87	.89
877	Las Vegas	.87	.89
878	Socorro	.87	.89
879	Truth/Consequences	.86	.86
880	Las Cruces	.84	.84
881	Clovis	.89	.89
882	Roswell	.90	.90
883	Carrizozo	.90	.90
884	Tucumcari	.89	.89
NEW YORK			
100-102	New York	1.33	1.33
103	Staten Island	1.30	1.30
104	Bronx	1.28	1.28
105	Mount Vernon	1.19	1.19
106	White Plains	1.19	1.19
107	Yonkers	1.21	1.21
108	New Rochelle	1.19	1.19
109	Suffern	1.14	1.14
110	Queens	1.29	1.29
111	Long Island City	1.30	1.30
112	Brooklyn	1.30	1.30
113	Flushing	1.31	1.31
114	Jamaica	1.29	1.29
115,117,118	Hicksville	1.24	1.24
116	Far Rockaway	1.31	1.31
119	Riverhead	1.26	1.26
120-122	Albany	.96	.96
123	Schenectady	.96	.96
124	Kingston	1.11	1.09
125-126	Poughkeepsie	1.13	1.11
127	Monticello	1.10	1.08
128	Glens Falls	.93	.91
129	Plattsburgh	.94	.92
130-132	Syracuse	.97	.95
133-135	Utica	.89	.92
136	Watertown	.90	.93
137-139	Binghamton	.93	.93
140-142	Buffalo	1.06	1.02
143	Niagara Falls	1.06	1.02
144-146	Rochester	.98	.99
147	Jamestown	.97	.93
148-149	Elmira	.94	.92
NORTH CAROLINA			
270,272-274	Greensboro	.75	.76
271	Winston-Salem	.74	.75
275-276	Raleigh	.76	.76
277	Durham	.75	.76
278	Rocky Mount	.68	.68
279	Elizabeth City	.69	.69
280	Gastonia	.73	.74
281-282	Charlotte	.73	.74
283	Fayetteville	.75	.75
284	Wilmington	.73	.74
285	Kinston	.67	.67
286	Hickory	.65	.66
287-288	Asheville	.72	.74
289	Murphy	.66	.67
NORTH DAKOTA			
580-581	Fargo	.80	.85
582	Grand Forks	.76	.81
583	Devils Lake	.78	.83
584	Jamestown	.75	.80
585	Bismarck	.81	.85

Location Factors

STATE/ZIP	CITY	Residential	Commercial
NORTH DAKOTA (CONT'D)			
586	Dickinson	.81	.84
587	Minot	.83	.87
588	Williston	.79	.83
OHIO			
430-432	Columbus	.98	.96
433	Marion	.93	.94
434-436	Toledo	1.02	1.01
437-438	Zanesville	.93	.92
439	Steubenville	.97	.97
440	Lorain	1.03	.97
441	Cleveland	1.09	1.03
442-443	Akron	1.00	.99
444-445	Youngstown	1.00	.97
446-447	Canton	.96	.95
448-449	Mansfield	.96	.94
450	Hamilton	1.00	.94
451-452	Cincinnati	1.00	.94
453-454	Dayton	.93	.92
455	Springfield	.95	.93
456	Chillicothe	1.02	.96
457	Athens	.91	.90
458	Lima	.95	.94
OKLAHOMA			
730-731	Oklahoma City	.81	.83
734	Ardmore	.82	.81
735	Lawton	.84	.83
736	Clinton	.79	.81
737	Enid	.82	.81
738	Woodward	.81	.81
739	Guymon	.68	.67
740-741	Tulsa	.84	.81
743	Miami	.85	.82
744	Muskogee	.74	.72
745	Mcalester	.75	.76
746	Ponca City	.81	.80
747	Durant	.78	.80
748	Shawnee	.78	.80
749	Poteau	.84	.80
OREGON			
970-972	Portland	1.07	1.05
973	Salem	1.05	1.04
974	Eugene	1.05	1.04
975	Medford	1.05	1.04
976	Klamath Falls	1.05	1.04
977	Bend	1.05	1.04
978	Pendleton	1.02	1.00
979	Vale	.98	.96
PENNSYLVANIA			
150-152	Pittsburgh	1.02	1.00
153	Washington	1.00	.98
154	Uniontown	.99	.97
155	Bedford	1.01	.94
156	Greensburg	1.00	.98
157	Indiana	1.03	.96
158	Dubois	1.02	.95
159	Johnstown	1.03	.96
160	Butler	1.00	.97
161	New Castle	1.00	.97
162	Kittanning	1.01	.98
163	Oil City	.89	.94
164-165	Erie	.97	.96
166	Altoona	1.03	.95
167	Bradford	.97	.96
168	State College	.95	.95
169	Wellsboro	.92	.93
170-171	Harrisburg	.96	.95
172	Chambersburg	.94	.93
173-174	York	.96	.94
175-176	Lancaster	.94	.92
177	Williamsport	.89	.88
178	Sunbury	.94	.93
179	Pottsville	.93	.92
180	Lehigh Valley	1.02	1.01
181	Allentown	1.02	1.01
182	Hazleton	.96	.96
183	Stroudsburg	.99	.98
184-185	Scranton	.94	.97
186-187	Wilkes-Barre	.92	.95
188	Montrose	.92	.95
189	Doylestown	.94	1.05

STATE/ZIP	CITY	Residential	Commercial
PENNSYLVANIA (CONT'D)			
190-191	Philadelphia	1.13	1.11
193	Westchester	1.07	1.06
194	Norristown	1.09	1.07
195-196	Reading	.95	.96
PUERTO RICO			
009	San Juan	.85	.85
RHODE ISLAND			
028	Newport	1.00	1.02
029	Providence	1.00	1.02
SOUTH CAROLINA			
290-292	Columbia	.71	.74
293	Spartanburg	.70	.72
294	Charleston	.72	.74
295	Florence	.70	.72
296	Greenville	.69	.72
297	Rock Hill	.63	.66
298	Aiken	.81	.85
299	Beaufort	.67	.69
SOUTH DAKOTA			
570-571	Sioux Falls	.87	.81
572	Watertown	.83	.78
573	Mitchell	.83	.77
574	Aberdeen	.86	.80
575	Pierre	.85	.79
576	Mobridge	.84	.77
577	Rapid City	.84	.78
TENNESSEE			
370-372	Nashville	.86	.86
373-374	Chattanooga	.81	.80
375,380-381	Memphis	.86	.86
376	Johnson City	.81	.80
377-379	Knoxville	.79	.79
382	Mckenzie	.76	.76
383	Jackson	.71	.78
384	Columbia	.78	.78
385	Cookeville	.76	.76
TEXAS			
750	Mckinney	.87	.80
751	Waxahackie	.81	.81
752-753	Dallas	.89	.85
754	Greenville	.77	.72
755	Texarkana	.86	.76
756	Longview	.83	.73
757	Tyler	.90	.79
758	Palestine	.71	.71
759	Lufkin	.74	.74
760-761	Fort Worth	.83	.82
762	Denton	.86	.77
763	Wichita Falls	.79	.79
764	Eastland	.72	.71
765	Temple	.76	.75
766-767	Waco	.80	.79
768	Brownwood	.71	.70
769	San Angelo	.78	.74
770-772	Houston	.87	.88
773	Huntsville	.72	.72
774	Wharton	.74	.75
775	Galveston	.85	.86
776-777	Beaumont	.80	.82
778	Bryan	.80	.81
779	Victoria	.76	.76
780	Laredo	.75	.76
781-782	San Antonio	.80	.81
783-784	Corpus Christi	.78	.77
785	Mc Allen	.76	.74
786-787	Austin	.77	.80
788	Del Rio	.66	.66
789	Giddings	.71	.70
790-791	Amarillo	.80	.80
792	Childress	.74	.77
793-794	Lubbock	.77	.78
795-796	Abilene	.78	.78
797	Midland	.76	.77
798-799,885	El Paso	.78	.77
UTAH			
840-841	Salt Lake City	.91	.90
842,844	Ogden	.90	.88

Location Factors

STATE/ZIP	CITY	Residential	Commercial
UTAH (CONT'D)			
843	Logan	.91	.89
845	Price	.80	.79
846-847	Provo	.90	.89
VERMONT			
050	White River Jct.	.77	.76
051	Bellows Falls	.77	.76
052	Bennington	.77	.76
053	Brattleboro	.77	.77
054	Burlington	.85	.86
056	Montpelier	.83	.84
057	Rutland	.86	.85
058	St. Johnsbury	.74	.75
059	Guildhall	.73	.74
VIRGINIA			
220-221	Fairfax	.89	.90
222	Arlington	.89	.90
223	Alexandria	.91	.92
224-225	Fredericksburg	.83	.83
226	Winchester	.77	.78
227	Culpeper	.78	.79
228	Harrisonburg	.74	.75
229	Charlottesville	.83	.81
230-232	Richmond	.86	.84
233-235	Norfolk	.82	.82
236	Newport News	.82	.81
237	Portsmouth	.81	.81
238	Petersburg	.86	.84
239	Farmville	.73	.72
240-241	Roanoke	.76	.75
242	Bristol	.79	.74
243	Pulaski	.72	.71
244	Staunton	.75	.74
245	Lynchburg	.80	.76
246	Grundy	.71	.71
WASHINGTON			
980-981,987	Seattle	.98	1.03
982	Everett	.95	1.01
983-984	Tacoma	1.04	1.02
985	Olympia	1.04	1.02
986	Vancouver	1.09	1.03
988	Wenatchee	.92	.96
989	Yakima	1.00	.98
990-992	Spokane	.98	.97
993	Richland	.99	.98
994	Clarkston	.97	.96
WEST VIRGINIA			
247-248	Bluefield	.89	.89
249	Lewisburg	.91	.91
250-253	Charleston	.95	.95
254	Martinsburg	.83	.83
255-257	Huntington	.93	.95
258-259	Beckley	.93	.93
260	Wheeling	.93	.95
261	Parkersburg	.92	.94
262	Buckhannon	.97	.94
263-264	Clarksburg	.97	.94
265	Morgantown	.97	.94
266	Gassaway	.94	.94
267	Romney	.91	.91
268	Petersburg	.94	.92
WISCONSIN			
530,532	Milwaukee	1.02	1.01
531	Kenosha	1.01	1.00
534	Racine	1.05	1.00
535	Beloit	1.01	.98
537	Madison	1.00	.98
538	Lancaster	.96	.94
539	Portage	.98	.96
540	New Richmond	1.04	.96
541-543	Green Bay	1.00	.97
544	Wausau	.99	.94
545	Rhinelander	1.00	.96
546	La Crosse	.98	.95
547	Eau Claire	1.04	.96
548	Superior	1.04	.98
549	Oshkosh	.98	.95

STATE/ZIP	CITY	Residential	Commercial
WYOMING			
820	Cheyenne	.84	.80
821	Yellowstone Nat. Pk.	.79	.76
822	Wheatland	.81	.77
823	Rawlins	.80	.76
824	Worland	.77	.75
825	Riverton	.80	.77
826	Casper	.85	.81
827	Newcastle	.78	.74
828	Sheridan	.82	.79
829-831	Rock Springs	.82	.77
CANADIAN FACTORS (reflect Canadian currency)			
ALBERTA			
	Calgary	1.00	.97
	Edmonton	1.00	.97
	Fort McMurray	.99	.96
	Lethbridge	.99	.96
	Lloydminster	.99	.96
	Medicine Hat	.99	.96
	Red Deer	.99	.96
BRITISH COLUMBIA			
	Kamloops	1.02	1.03
	Prince George	1.03	1.04
	Vancouver	1.05	1.06
	Victoria	1.04	1.05
MANITOBA			
	Brandon	.97	.96
	Portage la Prairie	.96	.96
	Winnipeg	.97	.96
NEW BRUNSWICK			
	Bathurst	.93	.91
	Dalhousie	.93	.91
	Fredericton	.96	.94
	Moncton	.93	.91
	Newcastle	.93	.91
	Saint John	.96	.94
NEWFOUNDLAND			
	Corner Brook	.95	.94
	St. John's	.95	.94
NORTHWEST TERRITORIES			
	Yellowknife	.92	.91
NOVA SCOTIA			
	Dartmouth	.96	.95
	Halifax	.96	.95
	New Glasgow	.96	.95
	Sydney	.94	.93
	Yarmouth	.96	.95
ONTARIO			
	Barrie	1.08	1.06
	Brantford	1.09	1.07
	Cornwall	1.07	1.05
	Hamilton	1.11	1.07
	Kingston	1.08	1.06
	Kitchener	1.04	1.03
	London	1.08	1.06
	North Bay	1.07	1.05
	Oshawa	1.08	1.06
	Ottawa	1.08	1.06
	Owen Sound	1.08	1.06
	Peterborough	1.07	1.05
	Sarnia	1.10	1.08
	St. Catharines	1.04	1.02
	Sudbury	1.04	1.02
	Thunder Bay	1.04	1.03
	Toronto	1.11	1.10
	Windsor	1.05	1.03
PRINCE EDWARD ISLAND			
	Charlottetown	.92	.90
	Summerside	.92	.90

STATE/ZIP	CITY	Residential	Commercial
QUEBEC			
	Cap-de-la-Madeleine	1.02	1.01
	Charlesbourg	1.02	1.01
	Chicoutimi	1.01	1.00
	Gatineau	1.01	1.00
	Laval	1.02	1.01
	Montreal	1.07	1.01
	Quebec	1.09	1.02
	Sherbrooke	1.02	1.01
	Trois Rivieres	1.02	1.01
SASKATCHEWAN			
	Moose Jaw	.91	.91
	Prince Albert	.91	.91
	Regina	.92	.92
	Saskatoon	.91	.91
YUKON			
	Whitehorse	.92	.91

Installing Contractor's Overhead & Profit

Below are the **average** installing contractor's percentage mark-ups applied to base labor rates to arrive at typical billing rates.

Column A: Labor rates are based on union wages averaged for 30 major U.S. cities. Base rates including fringe benefits are listed hourly and daily. These figures are the sum of the wage rate and employer-paid fringe benefits such as vacation pay, employer-paid health and welfare costs, pension costs, plus appropriate training and industry advancement funds costs.

Column B: Workers' Compensation rates are the national average of state rates established for each trade.

Column C: Column C lists average fixed overhead figures for all trades. Included are Federal and State Unemployment costs set at 6.5%; Social Security Taxes (FICA) set at 7.65%; Builder's Risk Insurance costs set at 0.44%; and Public Liability costs set at 2.02%. All the percentages except those for Social Security Taxes vary from state to state as well as from company to company.

Columns D and E: Percentages in Columns D and E are based on the presumption that the installing contractor has annual billing of $4,000,000 and up. Overhead percentages may increase with smaller annual billing. The overhead percentages for any given contractor may vary greatly and depend on a number of factors, such as the contractor's annual volume, engineering and logistical support costs, and staff requirements. The figures for overhead and profit will also vary depending on the type of job, the job location, and the prevailing economic conditions. All factors should be examined very carefully for each job.

Column F: Column F lists the total of Columns B, C, D, and E.

Column G: Column G is Column A (hourly base labor rate) multiplied by the percentage in Column F (O&P percentage).

Column H: Column H is the total of Column A (hourly base labor rate) plus Column G (Total O&P).

Column I: Column I is Column H multiplied by eight hours.

		A		B	C	D	E	F	G	H	I
		Base Rate Incl. Fringes		Workers' Comp. Ins.	Average Fixed Over-head	Over-head	Profit	Total Overhead & Profit		Rate with O & P	
Abbr.	Trade	Hourly	Daily					%	Amount	Hourly	Daily
Skwk	Skilled Workers Average (35 trades)	$32.25	$258.00	17.0%	16.6%	13.0%	10%	56.6%	$18.25	$50.50	$404.00
	Helpers Average (5 trades)	23.70	189.60	18.7		11.0		56.3	13.35	37.05	296.40
	Foreman Average, Inside ($.50 over trade)	32.75	262.00	17.0		13.0		56.6	18.55	51.30	410.40
	Foreman Average, Outside ($2.00 over trade)	34.25	274.00	17.0		13.0		56.6	19.40	53.65	429.20
Clab	Common Building Laborers	24.65	197.20	18.6		11.0		56.2	13.85	38.50	308.00
Asbe	Asbestos/Insulation Workers/Pipe Coverers	34.70	277.60	16.5		16.0		59.1	20.50	55.20	441.60
Boil	Boilermakers	38.70	309.60	14.5		16.0		57.1	22.10	60.80	486.40
Bric	Bricklayers	32.40	259.20	16.1		11.0		53.7	17.40	49.80	398.40
Brhe	Bricklayer Helpers	24.60	196.80	16.1		11.0		53.7	13.20	37.80	302.40
Carp	Carpenters	31.55	252.40	18.6		11.0		56.2	17.75	49.30	394.40
Cefi	Cement Finishers	30.20	241.60	10.6		11.0		48.2	14.55	44.75	358.00
Elec	Electricians	37.60	300.80	6.7		16.0		49.3	18.55	56.15	449.20
Elev	Elevator Constructors	38.75	310.00	7.7		16.0		50.3	19.50	58.25	466.00
Eqhv	Equipment Operators, Crane or Shovel	33.70	269.60	10.8		14.0		51.4	17.30	51.00	408.00
Eqmd	Equipment Operators, Medium Equipment	32.60	260.80	10.8		14.0		51.4	16.75	49.35	394.80
Eqlt	Equipment Operators, Light Equipment	31.10	248.80	10.8		14.0		51.4	16.00	47.10	376.80
Eqol	Equipment Operators, Oilers	28.30	226.40	10.8		14.0		51.4	14.55	42.85	342.80
Eqmm	Equipment Operators, Master Mechanics	34.20	273.60	10.8		14.0		51.4	17.60	51.80	414.40
Glaz	Glaziers	30.95	247.60	14.2		11.0		51.8	16.05	47.00	376.00
Lath	Lathers	29.65	237.20	11.5		11.0		49.1	14.55	44.20	353.60
Marb	Marble Setters	31.05	248.40	16.1		11.0		53.7	16.65	47.70	381.60
Mill	Millwrights	32.95	263.60	10.7		11.0		48.3	15.90	48.85	390.80
Mstz	Mosaic & Terrazzo Workers	30.40	243.20	9.9		11.0		47.5	14.45	44.85	358.80
Pord	Painters, Ordinary	28.05	224.40	13.7		11.0		51.3	14.40	42.45	339.60
Psst	Painters, Structural Steel	28.90	231.20	50.2		11.0		87.8	25.35	54.25	434.00
Pape	Paper Hangers	28.20	225.60	13.7		11.0		51.3	14.45	42.65	341.20
Pile	Pile Drivers	30.90	247.20	25.2		16.0		67.8	20.95	51.85	414.80
Plas	Plasterers	29.00	232.00	16.0		11.0		53.6	15.55	44.55	356.40
Plah	Plasterer Helpers	24.85	198.80	16.0		11.0		53.6	13.30	38.15	305.20
Plum	Plumbers	37.35	298.80	8.4		16.0		51.0	19.05	56.40	451.20
Rodm	Rodmen (Reinforcing)	35.55	284.40	27.4		14.0		68.0	24.15	59.70	477.60
Rofc	Roofers, Composition	27.65	221.20	33.1		11.0		70.7	19.55	47.20	377.60
Rots	Roofers, Tile & Slate	27.95	223.60	33.1		11.0		70.7	19.75	47.70	381.60
Rohe	Roofers, Helpers (Composition)	20.55	164.40	33.1		11.0		70.7	14.55	35.10	280.80
Shee	Sheet Metal Workers	37.00	296.00	11.8		16.0		54.4	20.15	57.15	457.20
Spri	Sprinkler Installers	37.55	300.40	9.1		16.0		51.7	19.40	56.95	455.60
Stpi	Steamfitters or Pipefitters	37.60	300.80	8.4		16.0		51.0	19.20	56.80	454.40
Ston	Stone Masons	32.30	258.40	16.1		11.0		53.7	17.35	49.65	397.20
Sswk	Structural Steel Workers	35.65	285.20	41.0		14.0		81.6	29.10	64.75	518.00
Tilf	Tile Layers	30.40	243.20	9.9		11.0		47.5	14.45	44.85	358.80
Tilh	Tile Layers Helpers	23.90	191.20	9.9		11.0		47.5	11.35	35.25	282.00
Trlt	Truck Drivers, Light	24.90	199.20	15.1		11.0		52.7	13.10	38.00	304.00
Trhv	Truck Drivers, Heavy	25.65	205.20	15.1		11.0		52.7	13.50	39.15	313.20
Sswl	Welders, Structural Steel	35.65	285.20	41.0		14.0		81.6	29.10	64.75	518.00
Wrck	*Wrecking	24.65	197.20	41.4		11.0		79.0	19.45	44.10	352.80

*Not included in averages

Part Three
Appendix, Resources, Glossary & Index

Appendix: Audit Checklists

The security standards presented in the following two audit checklists were developed by the U.S. Department of Justice in response to the bombing of the Alfred P. Murrah Federal Building in Oklahoma City. Typically applied to federal facilities to determine their vulnerability to acts of terrorism and other forms of violence, these checklists can be applied to other facilities as well. In the "Standard" column are facilities or security devices to be reviewed. The "Type" column lists DOJ guidelines for what level of performance is desired. The "Status" column is an opportunity for the facility to indicate its compliance with the standards.

The Level I checklist can be applied to facilities that have:

- 10 employees or fewer
- 2,500 S.F. of office space or less
- A low volume of public contact

The Level II checklist can be applied to facilities that have:

- 11-150 employees
- 2,500-80,000 S.F.
- A moderate volume of public contact
- Activities that are routine in nature, similar to commercial activities.

In addition to these checklists, another useful guide for security planning and design is the *Facilities Standards for the Public Buildings Service*, published by the U.S. General Services Administration (PBS-P100), and available on-line at the following Web site address: http://hydra.gsa.gov/pbs/pc/facilitiesstandards/

Chapter 8 of this document covers security planning and cost, and security concerns for architecture and interior design; new and existing construction; historic buildings; structural, mechanical, electrical, and fire protection engineering; electronic security, and parking.

FACILITY SECURITY CERTIFICATION FORM
DOJ SECURITY LEVEL I

AGENCY:
FACILITY:
ADDRESS:
LEASED/OWNED:
UPGRADE COSTS:
REVIEW TEAM:
REVIEW DATE:
FACILITY POC:
CERTIFIED Y/N:

I. PERIMETER SECURITY

A. PARKING

STANDARD	TYPE	STATUS
Control of Facility Parking	Desirable	
Control of Adjacent Parking	Desirable	
Avoid leases where parking cannot be controlled	Desirable	
Leases should provide security control for adjacent parking	Desirable	
Post signs and arrange for towing of unauthorized vehicles	Based on facility evaluation	
ID system and procedures for unauthorized parking (placard, decal, card key, etc.)	Desirable	
Adequate lighting for parking areas	Desirable	

B. CLOSED CIRCUIT TELEVISION (CCTV) MONITORING

STANDARD	TYPE	STATUS
CCTV with time lapse video recording	Desirable	
Post signs advising of 24 hour video surveillance	Desirable	

(Courtesy of the U.S. Department of Justice)

C. LIGHTING

STANDARD	TYPE	STATUS
Lighting with emergency power backup	MINIMUM	

D. PHYSICAL BARRIERS

STANDARD	TYPE	STATUS
Extend physical perimeter with barriers (concrete and/or steel composition)	Not applicable	
Parking barriers	Not applicable	

II. ENTRY SECURITY

A. RECEIVING AND SHIPPING

STANDARD	TYPE	STATUS
Review receiving/shipping procedures (current)	MINIMUM	
Implement modified procedures	Desirable	

B. ACCESS CONTROL

STANDARD	TYPE	STATUS
Evaluate facility for security guard requirements	Desirable	
Security guard patrol	Desirable	
IDS with CMS capability	Desirable	
Upgrade to current life safety standards (fire detection, fire suppression systems, etc.)	MINIMUM	

C. ENTRANCES/EXITS

STANDARD	TYPE	STATUS
X-ray & magnetometer at public entrances	N/A	
Require x-ray screening of all mail/packages	N/A	
Peep holes	Based on facility evaluation	
Intercom	Based on facility evaluation	
Entry control w/CCTV and door strikes	Desirable	
High security locks	MINIMUM	

III. INTERIOR SECURITY

A. EMPLOYEE/VISITOR IDENTIFICATION

STANDARD	TYPE	STATUS
Agency photo ID for all personnel displayed at all times	N/A	
Visitor control/screening system	Desirable	
Visitor identification accountability system	N/A	
Establish ID issuing authority	Based on facility evaluation	

B. UTILITIES

STANDARD	TYPE	STATUS
Prevent unauthorized access to utility areas	Based on facility evaluation	
Provide emergency power to critical systems (alarm, radio communications, computer facilities)	MINIMUM	

C. OCCUPANT EMERGENCY PLANS

STANDARD	TYPE	STATUS
Examine OEP and contingency procedures based on threat	MINIMUM	
OEPs in place, updated annually, periodic testing exercise	MINIMUM	
Assign & train OEP officials (assignment based on largest tenant in facility)	MINIMUM	
Annual tenant	MINIMUM	

D. DAY CARE

STANDARD	TYPE	STATUS
Evaluate whether to locate daycare facilities in buildings with high threat activities	N/A	
Compare feasibility of locating daycare in facilities outside locations	N/A	

IV. SECURITY PLANNING

A. INTELLIGENCE SHARING

STANDARD	TYPE	STATUS
Establish law enforcement agency/security liaisons	MINIMUM	
Review/establish procedure for intelligence receipt/dissemination	MINIMUM	
Establish uniform security/threat nomenclature	MINIMUM	

B. TRAINING

STANDARD	TYPE	STATUS
Conduct annual security awareness training	MINIMUM	
Establish standardized unarmed guard qualifications/training requirements	MINIMUM	
Established standardized armed guard qualifications/training requirements	MINIMUM	

C. TENANT ASSIGNMENT

STANDARD	TYPE	STATUS
Co-locate agencies with similar security needs	Desirable	
Do not co-locate high/low risk agencies	Desirable	

D. ADMINISTRATIVE PROCEDURES

STANDARD	TYPE	STATUS
Establish flexible work scheduled in high threat/high risk areas to minimize employee vulnerability to criminal activity	Based on facility evaluation	
Arrange for employee parking in/near building after normal work hours	Based on facility evaluation	
Conduct background security checks and/or establish security control procedures for service contract personnel	MINIMUM	

E. CONSTRUCTION/RENOVATION

STANDARD	TYPE	STATUS
Install mylar film on all exterior windows (shatter protection)	Desirable	
Review current projects for blast standards	MINIMUM	
Review/establish uniform standards for construction	MINIMUM	
Review/establish new design standard for blast resistance	Based on facility evaluation	
Establish street set-back for new construction	Desirable	

FACILITY SECURITY CERTIFICATION FORM
DOJ SECURITY LEVEL II

AGENCY:
FACILITY:
ADDRESS:
LEASED/OWNED:
UPGRADE COSTS:
REVIEW TEAM:
REVIEW DATE:
FACILITY POC:
CERTIFIED Y/N:

I. PERIMETER SECURITY

A. PARKING

STANDARD	TYPE	STATUS
Control of Facility Parking	Desirable	
Control of Adjacent Parking	Desirable	
Avoid leases where parking cannot be controlled	Desirable	
Leases should provide security control for adjacent parking	Desirable	
Post signs and arrange for towing of unauthorized vehicles	Based on facility evaluation	
ID system and procedures for unauthorized parking (placard, decal, card key, etc.)	Desirable	
Adequate lighting for parking areas	Desirable	

B. CLOSED CIRCUIT TELEVISION (CCTV) MONITORING

STANDARD	TYPE	STATUS
CCTV with time lapse video recording	Based on facility evaluation	
Post signs advising of 24 hour video surveillance	Based on facility evaluation	

(Courtesy of the U.S. Department of Justice)

C. LIGHTING

STANDARD	TYPE	STATUS
Lighting with emergency power backup	MINIMUM	

D. PHYSICAL BARRIERS

STANDARD	TYPE	STATUS
Extend physical perimeter with barriers (concrete and/or steel composition)	Not applicable	
Parking barriers	Not applicable	

II. ENTRY SECURITY

A. RECEIVING AND SHIPPING

STANDARD	TYPE	STATUS
Review receiving/shipping procedures (current)	MINIMUM	
Implement modified procedures	Based on facility evaluation	

B. ACCESS CONTROL

STANDARD	TYPE	STATUS
Evaluate facility for security guard requirements	Based on facility evaluation	
Security guard patrol	Desirable	
IDS with CMS capability	Based on facility evaluation	
Upgrade to current life safety standards (fire detection, fire suppression systems, etc.)	MINIMUM	

C. ENTRANCES/EXITS

STANDARD	TYPE	STATUS
X-ray & magnetometer at public entrances	Desirable	
Require x-ray screening of all mail/packages	Desirable	
Peep holes	Based on facility evaluation	
Intercom	Based on facility evaluation	
Entry control w/CCTV and door strikes	Based on facility evaluation	
High security locks	MINIMUM	

III. INTERIOR SECURITY

A. EMPLOYEE/VISITOR IDENTIFICATION

STANDARD	TYPE	STATUS
Agency photo ID for all personnel displayed at all times	Desirable	
Visitor control/screening system	MINIMUM	
Visitor identification accountability system	Desirable	
Establish ID issuing authority	Based on facility evaluation	

B. UTILITIES

STANDARD	TYPE	STATUS
Prevent unauthorized access to utility areas	Based on facility evaluation	
Provide emergency power to critical systems (alarm, radio communications, computer facilities)	MINIMUM	

C. OCCUPANT EMERGENCY PLANS

STANDARD	TYPE	STATUS
Examine OEP and contingency procedures based on threat	MINIMUM	
OEPs in place, updated annually, periodic testing exercise	MINIMUM	
Assign & train OEP officials (assignment based on largest tenant in facility)	MINIMUM	
Annual tenant	MINIMUM	

D. DAY CARE

STANDARD	TYPE	STATUS
Evaluate whether to locate daycare facilities in buildings with high threat activities	MINIMUM	
Compare feasibility of locating daycare in facilities outside locations	MINIMUM	

IV. SECURITY PLANNING

A. INTELLIGENCE SHARING

STANDARD	TYPE	STATUS
Establish law enforcement agency/security liaisons	MINIMUM	
Review/establish procedure for intelligence receipt/dissemination	MINIMUM	
Establish uniform security/threat nomenclature	MINIMUM	

B. TRAINING

STANDARD	TYPE	STATUS
Conduct annual security awareness training	MINIMUM	
Establish standardized unarmed guard qualifications/training requirements	MINIMUM	
Established standardized armed guard qualifications/training requirements	MINIMUM	

C. TENANT ASSIGNMENT

STANDARD	TYPE	STATUS
Co-locate agencies with similar security needs	Desirable	
Do not co-locate high/low risk agencies	Desirable	

D. ADMINISTRATIVE PROCEDURES

STANDARD	TYPE	STATUS
Establish flexible work scheduled in high threat/high risk areas to minimize employee vulnerability to criminal activity	Based on facility evaluation	
Arrange for employee parking in/near building after normal work hours	Based on facility evaluation	
Conduct background security checks and/or establish security control procedures for service contract personnel	MINIMUM	

E. CONSTRUCTION/RENOVATION

STANDARD	TYPE	STATUS
Install mylar film on all exterior windows (shatter protection)	Desirable	
Review current projects for blast standards	MINIMUM	
Review/establish uniform standards for construction	MINIMUM	
Review/establish new design standard for blast resistance	Based on facility evaluation	
Establish street set-back for new construction	Desirable	

Resources

The following is a list of organizations, associations, services, and product manufacturers that can be contacted for additional information regarding security-related topics.

Professional & Government Organizations

Agency for Toxic Substances and Disease Registry (ATSDR)
1600 Clifton Road
Atlanta, GA 30333
888-42-ATSDR
http://www.atsdr.cdc.gov:8080/query-phs.html

American Association of Poison Control Centers
3201 New Mexico Avenue
Suite 330
Washington, DC 20016
202-362-7217
http://www.aapcc.org

American Chemistry Council (ACC)
1300 Wilson Boulevard
Arlington, VA 22209
703-741-5000
http://www.americanchemistry.com

American Psychological Association
750 First Street, NE
Washington, DC 20002-4242
800-374-2721
http://helping.apa.org/daily/terrorism.html
On-line guide about coping with terrorist attacks, disaster, trauma, and bioterrorism.

American Society for Industrial Security (ASIS)
1625 Prince Street
Alexandria, VA 22314
703-522-5800
http://www.asisonline.org
On-line buyer's guide:
http://www.sibgonline.com/public/index2.asp

American Society of Safety Engineers
1800 E Oakton Street
Des Plaines, IL 60018
847-699-2929
http://www.asse.org

The Associated Locksmiths of America, Inc.
3003 Live Oak Street
Dallas, TX 75204
214-827-1701
http://www.aloa.org

Building Owners and Managers Association (BOMA) International
1201 New York Avenue, NW
Suite 300
Washington, DC 20005
202-408-2662
http://www.boma.org/emergency

Buildings.com
Stamats Buildings Media, Inc.
615 5th Street, SE
Cedar Rapids, IA 52401
*On-line magazine that includes security articles and a
buyer's guide.*

Center for Civilian Biodefense Strategies
Johns Hopkins University
410-223-1667
http://www.hopkins-biodefense.org/index.html

Center for Disease Control (CDC)
SafeUSA Federal Safety hotline
888-252-7751
http://www.cdc.gov
*Develops disease prevention and control, environmental health, and
health promotion. Part of the Web site focuses on Terrorism and Public
Health:* http://www.bt.cdc.gov

Chemical & Biological Defense Information Analysis Center (CBIAC)
Aberdeen Proving Ground–Edgewood Area
P.O. Box 196
Gunpowder, MD 21010-0196
410-676-9030
http://www.cbiac.apgea.army.mil

CHEMDEX
http://www.chemdex.org
A comprehensive on-line directory of chemistry.

Emergency Planning for Chemicals
http://www.chemicalspill.org

Federal Emergency Management Association
500 C Street, SW
Washington, DC 20472
202-566-1600
http://www.fema.gov

Preparation and Prevention
http://www.fema.gov/library/prepandprev.shtm

Terrorism Incident
http://www.au.af.mil/au/awc/awcgate/frp/frpterr.htm

Terrorist Incident Planning Guidelines
http://www.fema.gov/rrr/pte052101.shtm

Terrorism Site
http://www.rris.fema.gov

Henry L. Stimson Center
11 Dupont Circle
Suite 900
Washington, DC 20036
202-223-5956
http://www.stimson.org
A nonprofit institution that aims to enhance international peace and security through analysis and outreach.

The Infrastructure Security Partnership (TISP)
1801 Alexander Bell Drive
Reston, VA 20191
703-295-6234
http://www.tisp.org
An association consisting of organizations and agencies that collaborate on security issues pertaining to the U.S.'s built environment.

International Association of Professional Security Consultants (IAPSC)
1444 I Street
Suite 700
Washington, DC 20005-2210
202-712-9043
http://www.iapsc.org

International Labour Organization
4, route des Morillons
CH-1211 Geneva 22
Switzerland
http://www.oit.org
Web site includes area "Safe Work" that focuses on workplace safety and health:
http://www.oit.org/public/english/protection/safework/index.htm

International Security Management Association
P.O. Box 623
Buffalo, IA 52728
800-368-1894
http://www.ismanet.com

The International Society for Infectious Diseases
181 Longwood Avenue
Boston, MA 02115
617-277-0551
http://www.promedmail.org/pls/askus/f?p=2400:1000
Web site for reporting of outbreaks of infectious diseases and toxin-related illnesses.

KI4U, Inc.
212 Oil Patch Lane
Gonzales, TX 78629
830-672-8734
http://www.ki4u.com
Web site about potassium iodide.

Material Safety Data Sheets (MSDS) online
888-255-6737
http://www.msdssolutions.com/en

National Burglar & Fire Alarm Association (NBFAA)
8300 Colesville Road
Suite 750
Silver Spring, MD 20910
301-585-1855
http://www.alarm.org

National Council on Radiation Protection and Measurements
7910 Woodmont Avenue
Suite 400
Bethesda, MD 20814-3095
301-657-2652
http://www.ncrp.com

National Crime Prevention Council
1700 K Street, NW
Second Floor
Washington, DC 20006-3817
202-466-6272
http://www.ncpc.org

National Domestic Preparedness Office (NDPO)
202-324-8186
http://fas.org/irp/agency/doj/fbi/ndpo

National Fire Protection Association
1 Batterymarch Park
P.O. Box 9101
Quincy, MA 02269-9101
617-770-3000
http://www.nfpa.org

National Institute for Occupational Safety and Health (NIOSH)
200 Independence Avenue, SW
Washington, DC 20201
800-35-NIOSH
http://www.cdc.gov/niosh/homepage.html

National Institute of Justice
Center for Civil Force Protection
Sandia National Laboratories
P.O. Box 5800 MS 0763
Albuquerque, NM 87185-0763
888-577-4849
http://www.nlectc.org/ccfp

National Mental Health Association
2001 N. Beauregard Street
12th Floor
Alexandria, VA 22311
703-684-7722
www.nmha.org/reassurance/waitingForWar.cfm
On-line guide to coping with long-term stress such as war or terrorist attacks.

National Research Council
National Academy of Sciences
500 Fifth Street, NW
Washington, DC 20001
http://www.nas.edu/nrc

National Response Team
NRT c/o U.S. EPA
Mail Code 5104A
1200 Pennsylvania Avenue, NW
Washington, DC 20460
http://www.nrt.org

National Safety Information Exchange (NSIE)
P.O. Box 1256
Port Richey, FL 34673-1256
727-844-5999
http://www.nsie.org

National Security Institute (NSI)
116 Main Street
Suite 200
Medway, MA 02053
508-533-9099
http://www.nsi.org
Extensive information on workplace violence and security.

Nuclear, Biological, and Chemical (NBC) Protect
GEOMET Technologies, Inc.
20251 Century Boulevard
Germantown, MD 20874
301-428-9898
http://www.nbcprotect.com

The Office of Justice Programs
Office for Domestic Preparedness
810 Seventh Street, NW
Washington, DC 20531
800-368-6498
http://www.ojp.usdoj.gov/odp
Aims to mitigate the consequences of domestic terrorism, and provides training and technical assistance.

Partnership for Community Safety: Strengthening America's Readiness
http://www.hospitalconnect.com/DesktopServlet
Aims to promote readiness for biological, chemical, and nuclear terrorism and other disasters.

Rand Corporation
1700 Main Street
P.O. Box 2138
Santa Monica, CA 90407-2138
310-393-0411
http://www.RAND.org
A nonprofit institution that seeks to improve policy and decision-making through research and analysis.

Red Cross
431 18th Street, NW
Washington, DC 20006
202-639-3520
http://redcross.org
Brochures include: "Emergency Management Guide for Business and Industry," "Terrorism: Preparing for the Unexpected," and "Preparing Your Business for the Unthinkable."

Sandia National Laboratories
U.S. Department of Energy
P.O. Box 5800
Albuquerque, NM 87185
http://www.sandia.gov/about/index.html
A government-owned/contractor operated facility that develops science-based technologies that support national security.

Security Industry Association (SIA)
635 Slaters Lane, Suite 110
Alexandria, VA 22314
703-683-2075
http://www.siaonline.org/c.html
An international trade organization representing companies in the electronic and life safety industry.

Security Links
http://www.securitylinks.org
On-line links to information about retail loss prevention, private security, law enforcement, and other aspects of the security industry.

Security Magazine Online
http://www.secmag.com
Security *Magazine's Web site contains useful information on a variety of security topics.*

Security Management Online Magazine
1625 Prince Street
Alexandria, VA 22314
http://www.securitymanagement.com

Security Products
5151 Beltline Road
10th Floor
Dallas, Texas 75254
972-687-6700
http://www.secprodonline.com

Security Professional's Site
http://www.securityprofessionalssite.com
On-line resources for security professionals.

Tactical VR
888-752-4205
http://www.tacticalvr.com/contact.html
An emergency response planning company that uses state-of-the-art digital imaging to produce virtual reality "floor plans" for facilities.

The Terrorism Research Center (TRC)
http://www.homelandsecurity.com

U.S. Army Center for Health Promotion and Preventive Medicine
http://chppm-www.apgea.army.mil/ento

U.S. Army Medical Research and Material Command
http://mrmc-www.army.mil

U.S. Army Soldier & Biological Chemical Command (SBCCOM)
5183 Blackhawk Road
Bldg. E5101, Rm. 225
Aberdeen Proving Ground, MD 21010-5424
http://www.sbccom.army.mil

U.S. Department of Defense
http://www.defenselink.mil
Provides official, timely, and accurate information about defense policies, organizations, functions, and operations.

U.S. Department of Energy
1000 Independence Avenue, SW
Washington, DC 20585
800-dial-DOE
http://www.energy.gov
Aims to enhance national security and includes national defense programs that help ensure nuclear weapon safety.

U.S. Department of Health Services
200 Independence Avenue, SW
Washington, DC 20201
877-696-6775
http://www.hhs.gov
The U.S. government's principal agency for protecting the health of Americans, including preventing outbreak of infectious diseases and ensuring food and drug safety. Its Office of Emergency Preparedness coordinates health and medical social services and recovery from major emergencies and federal disasters:

Office of Emergency Preparedness
National Disaster Medical System
12300 Twinbrook Parkway
Suite 360
Rockville, MD 20857
301-443-1167
http://ndms.dhhs.gov

U.S. Department of Homeland Security
Nebraska Avenue Complex
Washington, DC 20393
http://www.dhs.gov/dhspublic
http://ready.gov

U.S. Department of Labor
Occupational Safety & Health Administration (OSHA)
200 Constitution Avenue, NW
Washington, DC 20210
800-321-OSHA
http://www.osha.gov

U.S. Environmental Protection Agency
Chemical Emergency Preparedness and Prevention Office
Ariel Rios Federal Building
1200 Pennsylvania Avenue, NW
Washington, DC 20460
800-424-9346
http://www.epa.gov/swercepp/cntr-ter.html
Aims to protect the environment and human health from the effects of chemical, biological, and nuclear materials.

U.S. Postal Service
http://www.usps.com/news/2001/press/pr01_1010tips.htm
On-line guide about handling suspicious mail that may contain biological agents.

World Health Organization
Avenue Appia 20
1211 Geneva 27
Switzerland
http://www.who.int/en

School & University Security Resources

International Association of Campus Law Enforcement Administrators
638 Prospect Avenue
Hartford, CT 06105-4298
860-586-7517
http://www.iaclea.org

National Alliance for Safe Schools
Ice Mountain
P.O. Box 290
Slanesville, WV 25444-0290
304-496-8100
http://www.safeschools.org

National School Safety Center
141 Duesenberg Drive
Suite 11
Westlake Village, CA 91362
805-373-9977
http://www.nssc1.org

Security on Campus, Inc.
601 South Henderson Road
Suite 205
King of Prussia, PA 19406-3596
888-251-7959
http://www.securityoncampus.org/aboutsoc/contact.html

U.S. Department of Education
600 Independence Avenue, SW
Washington, DC 20202-0498
800-USA-LEARN
http://www.ed.gov

Healthcare Facility Security Resources

ComCARE Alliance
888 17th Street, NW
12th Floor
Washington, DC 20006
202-429-0574
http://www.comcare.org
Encourages the development and deployment of life saving communications technologies to strengthen emergency response capabilities.

International Association for Healthcare Security & Safety (IAHHS)
P.O. Box 637
Lombard, IL 60148
888-353-0990
http://www.iahss.org

Patient Safety Institute
555 Republic Drive
Suite 200
Plano, TX 75074
972-444-9800
http://www.ptsafety.org

Products & Services

The following list of product manufacturers and services is not intended as an endorsement by the author, editors, or publisher. There are many additional sources of quality products. This list is provided as a starting point in a search for security equipment, devices, and services.

3M
3M Product Information Center
3M Center, Building 0304-01-01
St. Paul, MN 55144-1000
888-3M HELPS
http://www.3M.com
Safety and Security Systems Division includes retroreflective materials, theft protection systems, and security laminate and label systems.

Aiphone
1700 130th Avenue, NE
Bellevue, WA 98005
800-692-0200
http://www.aiphone.com/home.htm
Security and communications systems.

Anderson Detector Sales/Security Metal Detectors
2375 Mosby Avenue
Lynchburg, VA 24501-4341
800-528-3117
http://www.securitydetectors.com

Armorcore Bullet-Resistant Panels
Waco Composites I, Ltd.
P.O. Box 21223
Waco, TX 76702-1223
254-776-8880
http://www.armorcore.com

Armor Holdings, Inc.
BlastShield®
800-347-1200
http://www.armorholdings.com/mainframe.htm
Mitigation fixed shades to protect occupants from debris and glass from bombings and explosions.

ARMR Services Corporation
8301 Arlington Boulevard
Suite 206
Fairfax, VA 22031
703-876-9844
http://www.armrservices.com
High-security crash barriers, parking control equipment.

Barco Products
11 N Batavia Avenue
Batavia, IL 60510
630-879-0084
http://www.barcoproducts.com
Security barriers.

Bogen® Communications, Inc.
50 Spring Street
Ramsey, NJ 07446
201-934-8500
http://www.bogen.com
Sound systems and telephone peripherals.

Clarity Systems, Inc.
2203 Timberloch Place
Suite 100
The Woodlands, TX 77380
281-296-5818
http://www.clarity.com
Telecommunications Operational Support System (OSS).

Delta Scientific Corporation
24901 West Avenue, Stanford
Valencia, CA 91355
661-257-1800
http://www.deltascientific.com
Vehicle barriers.

Doty & Sons
Concrete Products, Inc.
1275 East State Street
Sycamore, IL 60178
800-233-3907
http://www.dotyconcrete.com
Concrete bollard and planter barriers.

DuPont Teijin Films U.S. Limited Partnership
Barley Mill Plaza, Bldg. 27
Lancaster Pike & Route 141
P.O. Box 80027
Wilmington, DE 19880-0027
800-635-4639
http://www.dupontteijinfilms.com

Durastone
1 Wallace Avenue
South Portland, ME 04106
800-439-7837
http://www.durastone.com
Architectural precast panel, cast stone, and GFRC.

FailSafe Air Safety Systems Corporation
79 Fillmore Avenue
Tonawanda, NY 14150
716-694-6390
http://www.hivroom.com/document_1.html
Air safety systems.

Fiber SenSys, Inc.
9640 SW Sunshine Court
Suite 400
Beaverton, OR 97005
503-641-8150
http://www.fibersensys.com
Perimeter security, intrusion detection.

GE Plastics, Lexan®
800-PLASTIC
http://www.gelexan.com/gelexan
Engineering thermoplastic used in bullet-resistant glass.

Glass Lock Designed Protection
320-C Turtle Creek Court
San Jose, CA 95125
408-999-0979
http://www.glasslock.com/main.htm
Glass retrofit protection.

Gunnebo Control
http://www.gunnebo-omega.com
Wide range of security products and systems.

HighCom Security, Inc.
27 Maiden Lane, Suite 590
San Francisco, CA 94108
800-987-9098
Metal detectors, x-ray machines, and digital recorders.

Hy-Security Gate Operators
1200 W Nickerson
Seattle, WA 98119
800-321-9947
http://www.hy-security.com

K-Tech International, Inc.
56 Ella Grasso Avenue
P.O. Box 1025
Torrington, CT 06790
800-993-9399
http://www.ktechonline.com
Safety barriers and ADA emergency telephones.

Line-X Industrial Coatings
800-831-3232
http://www.line-xicd.com
Coatings protecting against corrosion, abrasion, sliding, and impact.

Metorex Security Products, Inc.
250 Philips Boulevard
Ewing, NJ 08618
609-406-9000
http://www.metorexsecurity.com
Walk-through metal detectors.

Motorola Inc.
1303 E. Algonquin Road
Schaumburg, IL 60196
847-576-2469

Nasatka Barrier, Inc.
7702-B Old Alexandria Ferry Road
Clinton, MD 20735
301-868-0301
http://www.nasatka.com
Security and anti-terrorism vehicle barriers.

NextgenID
San Antonio, TX 78258
210-494-5399
http://www.nextgenid.com
Access control/biometrics.

Paxcon
http://www.paxcon.com
Anti-terrorism bomb blast protection.

Recognition Systems, Inc.
1520 Dell Avenue
Campbell, CA 95008
408-341-4100
http://www.handreader.com
Access control/biometrics.

Recognition Source, LLC
3820 Stern Avenue
St. Charles, IL 60174
630-762-4450
http://www.recognition-source.com
Wireless access control and security.

Safesec Corporation
450 N Sequoia Avenue
Ontario, CA 91761
909-605-0300
http://www.safesec.com
Building entrance security products.

SAFETYDRAPE™
800-638-8974
http://www.safetydrape.com
Drapery system to protect against bomb blast debris.

Sako & Associates, Inc.
3721 North Ventura Drive
Suite 100
Arlington Heights, IL 60004
847-392-8000
http://www.rjagroup.com
A security and communications consulting firm that specializes in security, bomb defense, and fire protection engineering.

Scanna MSC LTD
104 New Bond Street
London W1S 1SU, UK
(44) (0) 20 7355 3555
http://www.scanna-msc.com
Screening equipment.

Science & Engineering Associates, Inc.
SEA Corporate Headquarters
SEA Plaza
6100 Uptown Boulevard, NE
Suite 700
Albuquerque, NM 87110
505-884-2300
http://www.seabase.com
A nationally recognized company that offers engineering, scientific, and information technology expertise and provides cost-effective solutions for commercial and government clients.

Securitron Magnalock Corporation
550 Vista Boulevard
Sparks, NV 89434
775-355-5625
http://www.securitron.com
Locking systems.

Security Products
5151 Beltline Road
10th Floor
Dallas, TX 75254
972-687-6700
http://www.secprodonline.com

Surround Air Ionizers
Division of Indoor Purification Systems, Inc.
887 N. McCormick Way, # 3
Layton, UT 84041
888-812-1516
http://www.surroundair.com

Talk-A-Phone Company
5013 N Kedzie Avenue
Chicago, IL 60625-4988
773-539-1100
http://www.talkaphone.com
Rescue and emergency phone systems.

Urbitran
71 West 23rd Street
11th Floor
New York, NY 10010
http://www.urbitran.com
Vehicle barriers.

UTD Incorporated
8350 Alban Road
Suite 700
Springfield, VA 22150
703-440-8834
http://www.utdinc.com
An engineering firm that conducts field investigations and assessments for government and commercial clients, including facility condition, operations, security, and risk mitigation.

Valcom
5614 Hollins Road
Roanoke, VA 24019
540-563-2000
http://www.valcom.com
Loudspeaker paging and telecommunication systems.

VFA
266 Summer Street
Boston, MA 02210
800-693-3132
http://www.vfa.com
A company of architects, engineers, and software developers that determines facility conditions and integrates technology solutions for strategic capital planning.

Videx, Inc.
1105 NE Circle Boulevard
Corvallis, OR 97330
541-758-0521
http://www.videx.com
Data collection and access control systems.

Additional Resources

The following are additional security-related resources and their Web sites, recommended by the Federal Emergency Management Agency (FEMA) from Publication 426, "Reference Manual to Mitigate Potential Terrorist Attacks in High Occupancy Buildings," 50% draft, the most recent version available at the time of this publication. Reprinted with permission.

Alliance for Fire & Smoke Containment & Control
http://www.afscconline.org

American Lifelines Alliance
http://www.americanlifelinesalliance.org

Anser Institute for Homeland Security (ANSER)
http://www.homelandsecurity.org

Association of State Dam Safety Officials
http://www.damsafety.org

Battelle Memorial Institute, National Security Program
http://www.battelle.org/natsecurity/default.stm

Building Futures Council
http://www.thebfc.com

Center for Strategic and International Studies (CSIS)
http://www.csis.org

Central Intelligence Agency (CIA)
http://www.cia.gov

Council on Tall Buildings and Urban Habitat (CTBUH)
http://www.ctbuh.org

Defense Threat Reduction Agency (DTRA)
http://www.dtra.mil

Drexel (University) Intelligent Infrastructure & Transportation Safety Institute
http://www.di3.drexel.edu

Electronic Warfare Associates (EWA)
http://www.ewa.com

Federal Bureau of Investigation: Terrorism in the United States reports
http://www.fbi.gov/publications/terror/terroris.htm

Federal Emergency Management Agency (FEMA)
http://www.fema.gov

Building Performance Assessment Team
http://www.fema.gov/mit/bpat

Mitigation Planning
http://www.fema.gov/fima/planning.shtm

Human Caused Hazards
http://www.fema.gov/hazards

George Washington University, Institute for Crisis, Disaster, and Risk Management
http://www.cee.seas.gwu.edu
http://www.seas.gwu.edu/~icdm

Healthy Buildings International, Inc.
http://www.healthybuildings.com

Homeland Protection Institute, Ltd.
http://www.hpi-tech.org

Information Technology Association of America (ITAA)
http://www.itaa.org

International Code Council (ICC)
http://www.intlcode.org

International Crime Prevention Through Environmental Design Association (CPTED) (ICA)
http://new.cpted.net/home.amt

Lawrence Berkeley National Laboratory (LBNL)
http://securebuildings.lbl.gov

Multidisciplinary Center for Earthquake Engineering Research
http://mceer.buffalo.edu

National Academy of Sciences
http://www4.nationalacademies.org/nas/nashome.nsf

Federal Facilities Council (FFC) Standing Committee on Physical Security and Hazard Mitigation
http://www7.nationalacademies.org/ffc/Physical_Security_Hazard_Mitigation.html

National Research Council
http:www.nationalacademies.org/nrc

National Crime Prevention Institute
http://www.louisville.edu/a-s/ja/ncpi/courses.htm

National Cyber Security Alliance
http://www.staysafeonline.info

National Defense Industrial Association (NDIA)
http://www.ndia.org

National Emergency Managers Association (NEMA)
http://www.nemaweb.org

Naval Facilities Engineering Service Center (NFESC), Security Engineering Center of Expertise ESC66
http://atfp.nfesc.navy.mil

National Infrastructure Protection Center (NIPC)
http://www.nipc.gov

National Institute of Standards and Technology (NIST), Building and Fire Research Laboratory
http://www.bfrl.nist.gov

North American Electric Reliability Council (NERC)
http://www.nerc.com

Protective Glazing Council
http://www.protectiveglazing.org

Protective Technology Center at Penn State University
http://www.ptc.psu.edu

Public Entity Risk Institute
http://www.riskinstitute.org

SANS Institute (SysAdmin, Audit, Network, Security)
http://www.sans.org

SAVE International
http://www.value-eng.org

Security Design Coalition
http://www.designingforsecurity.org

Security Industry Association (SIA)
http://www.siaonline.org/

Society of Fire Protection Engineers
http://www.sfpe.org

Technical Support Working Group (Departments of Defense and State)
http://www.tswg.gov

U.S. Army Corps of Engineers
http://www.usace.army.mil

Blast Mitigation Action Group, U.S. Army Corps of Engineers Center of Expertise for Protective Design
http://bmag.nwo.usace.army.mil

U.S. Army Corps of Engineers, Electronic Security Center
http://www.hnd.usace.army.mil/esc

U.S. Army Corps of Engineers, Protective Design Center
http://pdc.nwo.usace.army.mil

U.S. Department of Energy
http://www.energy.gov

Architectural Surety Program
http://www.sandia.gov/archsur

Critical Infrastructure Protection Initiative
http://www.sandia.gov/LabNews/LN02-11-00/steam_story.html

U.S. General Services Administration (GSA)
http://www.gsa.gov

Office of Federal Protective Service (FPS) of GSA
http://www.gsa.gov/Portal/content/orgs_content.jsp?
contentOID=117945&contentType=1005&P=1&S=1

Office of Public Building Service (PBS) of GSA
http://www.gsa.gov/Portal/content/orgs_content.jsp?content
OID=22883&contentType=1005&PPzz=1&S=1

University of Missouri, Department of Civil & Environmental Engineering, National Center for Explosion Resistant Design
http://www.engineering.missouri.edu/explosion.htm

Glossary

Absorption
A security-conscious approach to design intended to protect a building's structural system and vital vertical systems from fatal damage, while at the same time permitting violent impacts or explosions to expend themselves on more absorbent and flexible materials. Examples include blast-resistant glass and coatings.

Access control mechanism
Security systems that detect and prevent unauthorized access to building components, such as areas of a building or information technology.

Acoustical security
Protection of a space from eavesdropping by means of soundproofing materials, appropriately configured HVAC ducting and openings, and possibly by the use of acoustical control devices, including sound control or "white noise" generators.

Alert systems
Devices used to alert building occupants to an emergency event and appropriate actions. Types of alert systems that could potentially be used include public address (PA) systems, zone paging systems, chain or telephone tree calling, and e-mail.

Anthrax
A potentially fatal disease caused by inhaling or handling products infected with bacteria known as Bacillus anthracis, which occurs in nature, in soil, and infects herbivores. Anthrax is many times more lethal than the most toxic chemical warfare agents.

Biological agent
A microorganism that causes disease in humans, animals, and plants, or deterioration of material.

Biological attack
The purposeful release of germs and/or biological substances, intended to cause harm or death in humans and other living creatures.

Biological defense
Procedures to establish and execute defensive measures against attacks using biological agents.

Biometrics
Electronic methods of identifying and authenticating a person's identity through the confirmation of his/her physiological or sometimes behavioral characteristics. Techniques include fingerprint matching, iris and retinal scanning, facial recognition, hand geometry matching, voice recognition, and vein matching.

Blood agent
A chemical compound that affects bodily function by preventing oxygen from the blood to transfer to the body tissue. Also called *cyanogen agent*.

Bollard
A barrier made up of a steel cylinder, often filled with concrete, that prevent vehicles from passing.

Bubonic plague
A disease caused by bacteria that initially manifests itself in the form of buboes, or swelling of the lymph glands, and can be transmitted through the respiratory system. The bubonic plague has been the cause of millions of deaths throughout history.

Catastrophe
A tragic event causing misfortune, loss, or devastation.

Chemical agent
A chemical substance intended for military use to incapacitate humans through its toxic physiological effects.

Chemical attack
The purposeful release of toxic material that is poisonous to humans and other species.

Chemical, biological, and radiological agents (CBR)
Toxic material used as a weapon that can be dispersed in the air or by physical contact.

Chemical weapons agents (CWAs)
Chemical weapons that are categorized into four basic types: blistering agents, blood agents, nerve agents, and incapacitating agents.

Close circuit television (CCTV)
A video recording system used as a surveillance device within a building. Output is recorded onto videotape for review.

Compartmentation
A security-conscious design approach that places certain areas (e.g., offices occupied by senior personnel) in spaces accessible only through a series of security points, or the provision of transaction counters at a 48" height to provide receptionists and others in open areas with some visual security.

Contingency
A possible event or condition, such as an emergency that may occur.

Crisis management
Measures taken to resolve a crisis situation.

Crisis management plan
The preparation and documentation of methods to respond to events that could disrupt a business or mission. The purpose of a crisis management plan is to prepare individuals within an organization to cope with a calamitous event. Also referred to as *Contingency Response Plan* or *Emergency Response Plan*.

Crisis management team
A permanent, small, core group that includes representatives from senior management, human resources, corporate services, real estate and/or facilities services, Datacom and Telecom, a public relations advisor, and possibly a contingency planning person, who may be the organization's or facility's Chief Security Officer. The crisis management team plays a major role in development of the crisis management plan.

Crisis recovery plan
A documented plan based on information on potential threats and the organization's mission, critical assets, vulnerabilities, and interdependencies of systems, as well as infrastructure. The crisis recovery plan should focus on reducing risks by minimizing vulnerabilities and ensuring continuity of operations.

Critical infrastructure
Principal systems of the infrastructure, including utilities and telecommunications, necessary to a facility's operation.

Cyanide
A toxic compound that can prevent the cells of the human body from absorbing oxygen from the blood. Burning silk, rubber, plastic, some paper, and cigarettes can generate cyanide, and it is commonly used in electroplating, photography, and the manufacturing of some plastics.

Departmental recovery groups
Ad hoc groups that are assembled to address a crisis, and who have broad departmental knowledge and skills, as well as an understanding of the organization's core objectives.

Desktop or tabletop practices
Rehearsals of procedures that should be carried out in the event of various types of emergencies, usually conducted in a meeting room. Desktop practice sessions may, in some cases, be accompanied by drills overseen by floor or area wardens or the departmental planning group members.

"Dirty bomb"
A device consisting of a conventional explosive material, such as dynamite, used to disperse radioactive material over a targeted area.

Disaster
A sudden catastrophic event that results in extensive damage or loss.

Diversion or deflection
A security-conscious design approach that involves impeding or deflecting an explosion or impacting force to a new or different, less harmful direction. Examples include a winding drive or roadway, ponds or pools, anticlines, and walls. These devices can serve as controlling elements for both pedestrians and vehicles.

Emergency response plan
See *Crisis management plan*.

EMS
Emergency power supply.

Evacuation
The process of exiting a potentially dangerous area in an organized way.

Evacuation plans
Documents including evacuation procedures and checklists that are prepared during response planning. These plans should include evacuation procedures and checklists, and may also include floor plans, lists of employees, and

other information.

Facial recognition
An identification method that recognizes the features of a human face.

Floor maps
Illustrations showing offices, rooms, workstations, furniture, and exit paths, used for drills and evacuations.

HEPA (High Efficiency Particulate Air) filter
A filtration system that removes at least 99.97% of all airborne bacteria and contaminants.

Intellectual property (IP)
Property or assets, often in the form of computer or hard copy files and documents, that include information on how an organization conducts business and transmits and stores confidential information, as well as current and future products.

Internal security
Awareness and control of the movement of personnel and visitors through a facility in order to prevent unauthorized individuals from achieving access to critical areas, such as LAN rooms, IDF rooms, and mechanical/electrical rooms.

Minimum safe distance (MSD)
The minimum distance away from a security crisis in order to be protected.

Monitor
In security, this can have a number of different meanings, including the VDT (CRT or plasma screen) used with computers, or the person stationed at the VDT, viewing CCTV pictures, data transmissions from

terminal points, and instructions. It can also refer to a terminal device, such as a CCTV camera or an infrared or motion detector, more properly termed "detecting devices," as well as automatic "monitoring" of the health or other conditions. A "monitoring station" refers to workstations, owner- or user-operated or outsourced to contract monitoring companies.

Natural hazard
A natural event, such as an earthquake, flood, or tornado, that damages humans and/or property.

Nerve agents
Lethal chemicals that work against the human respiratory, nervous, musculoskeletal, and cardiovascular systems. There are five basic nerve agents, the best known of which are tabun, sarin, and VX. Of these, VX is the most dangerous, as it can be absorbed through the skin and clothing.

Nuclear blast
An atomic explosion that results in dispersing radioactive materials that can contaminate the environment.

Obstruction
A security-conscious design approach that protects a building or site by using methods such as barriers, boulders, or concrete vehicle barriers; or strengthening of the structure's columns or berms.

Pathological behavior
Abnormal or dysfunctional human behavior that is often destructive, and can result in a related act of violence.

Perimeter security
Control and observation of areas of ingress and egress to a building and parking structure, including main lobby doors, rear plaza doors, truck docks, fire exits, and other points of access.

Personal protective equipment
Clothing and equipment that guards personnel from chemical, physical, and biological hazards.

Potassium iodide (KI)
An FDA-approved, nonprescription drug for use as a blocking agent to prevent the thyroid gland from absorbing radioactive iodine.

Proprietary system
A system that is exclusively monitored and maintained on-site.

Proximity (prox) cards
An identification card, which, when brought in close proximity to an RFID reader, is matched with the holder's ID within a database.

Contact-less prox cards are technically referred to as the "ISO II (1386) (International Organization for Standardization) card."

Radiation
Atomic emissions in the form of waves or particles.

Radiation threat
Using common explosives to disperse radioactive material over a targeted area. Also known as a "dirty bomb."

Radio frequency identification (RFID)
A form of identification that employs radio waves as a means of communication between it and a card reader. RFIDs identify a cardholder via the card reader, which matches the holder's ID with a database to permit access.

Risk analysis
An assessment of an organization's vulnerabilities in terms of resources, personnel, and internal risks, as well as its image, political/religious enemies, and neighbors (e.g., crime neighborhood or terrorist target next door).

Risk assessment team
An internal work group, possibly headed by a consultant with expertise in safety, security, and emergency response planning. The Assessment Team defines the risks to an organization or entity in order to develop a plan that will safeguard facility occupants and the organization's critical assets.

Security-conscious design
Design of a building that considers and anticipates security issues, such as allowing for added surveillance through placement of building elements or controlling access through placement of exits.

Significant threat
Advance confirmation of an explosive device or weapon of mass destruction that could result in a significant destructive event.

Smallpox virus
A contagious and sometimes fatal, infectious disease characterized by skin eruptions. Non-treatable, but preventable by vaccination.

Terrorism
The systematic use of violence or force by an individual or organized group to coerce or threaten others, such as societies or governments. Terrorist groups often possess convictions that their ideological or political beliefs are acceptable.

Terrorist incident
A violent, threatening act that breaches the criminal laws of a host country and is aimed at coercing a society or government.

UPS
Uninterruptible power supply.

Voice recognition
An identification method that recognizes the human voice.

Weapons of mass destruction (WMDs)
Devices intended to cause death or bodily injury to a group of people by releasing toxic, poisonous chemicals, diseases, or radiation.

Work groups
A collection of individuals who provide consultation and advice during the security planning process.

Work teams
Teams involved in the security planning and recovery processes. Members have clearly defined roles, such as investigating, considering, reporting, and rendering decisions, and executing team plans. They respond immediately to a security or crisis event.

Zone paging system
Software and a phone system that allow telephones to be used as a voice input station or PA system. All phones must be equipped with speaker capability.

FEMA Glossary

The following are additional security-related terms, recommended by the Federal Emergency Management Agency (FEMA) from Publication 426, "Reference Manual to Mitigate Potential Terrorist Attacks in High Occupancy Buildings," 50% draft, the most recent version available at the time of this publication. Reprinted with permission.

Alarm assessment
Verification and evaluation of an alarm alert through the use of closed circuit television or human observation. Systems used for alarm assessment are designed to respond rapidly, automatically, and predictably to the receipt of alarms at the security center.

Annunciation
A visual, audible, or other indication by a security system of a condition.

Assessment
The evaluation and interpretation of measurements and other information to provide a basis for decision-making.

Assessment system elements
Detection measures used to assist guards in visual verification of intrusion detection system alarms and access control system functions and to assist in visual detection by guards. Assessment system elements include closed-circuit television and protective lighting.

Asset
A resource of value requiring protection. An asset can be tangible such as people, buildings, facilities, equipment, activities, operations, and information; or intangible, such as processes or a company's information and reputation.

Asset criticality
The degree of debilitating impact that would be caused by the incapacity or destruction of an asset.

Blast curtains
Heavy curtains made of blast resistant materials that could protect the occupants of a room from flying debris.

Blast-resistant glazing
Window opening glazing that is resistant to blast effects because of the interrelated function of the frame and glazing material properties frequently dependent upon tempered glass, polycarbonate, or laminated glazing.

Business continuity program
An ongoing process supported by senior management and funded to ensure that the necessary steps are taken to identify the impact of potential losses, maintain viable recovery strategies and recovery plans, and ensure continuity services through personnel training, plan testing and maintenance.

Cable barrier
Cable or wire rope anchored to and suspended off the ground or attached to chain link fence to act as a barrier to moving vehicles.

Capacitance sensor
A device that detects an intruder approaching or touching a metal object by sensing a change in capacitance between the object and the ground.

Card reader
A device that gathers or reads information when a card is presented as an identification method.

Clear zone
An area that is clear of visual obstructions and landscape materials that could conceal a threat or perpetrator.

Continuity of services and operations
Controls to ensure that, when unexpected events occur, departmental/agency minimum essential infrastructure services and operations, including computer operations, continue without interruption or are promptly resumed and critical and sensitive data are protected through adequate contingency and business recovery plans and exercises.

Control center
A centrally located room or facility staffed by personnel charged with the oversight of specific situations and/or equipment.

Controlled area
An area into which access is controlled or limited. It is that portion of a restricted area usually near or surrounding a limited or exclusion area. Correlates with exclusion zone.

Conventional construction
Building construction that is not specifically designed to resist weapons, explosives, or chemical, biological, and radiological effects. Conventional construction is designed only to resist common loadings and environmental effects such as wind, seismic, and snow loads.

Damage assessment
The process used to appraise or determine the number of injuries and deaths, damage to public and private property, and the status of key facilities and services such as hospitals and other health care facilities, fire and police stations, communications networks, water and sanitation systems, utilities, and transportation networks resulting from a man-made or natural disaster.

Data transmission equipment
A path for transmitting data between two or more components (such as a sensor and alarm reporting system, a card reader and controller, a CCTV camera and monitor, or a transmitter and receiver).

Defense layer
Building design or exterior perimeter barriers intended to delay attempted forced entry.

Defensive measures
Protective measures which delay or prevent attack on an asset or which shield the asset from weapons, explosives, and CBR effects. Defensive measures include site work and building design.

Delay rating
A measure of the effectiveness of penetration protection of a defense layer.

Detection measures
Protective measures which detect intruders, weapons, or explosives; assist in assessing the validity of detection; control access to protected areas; and communicate the appropriate information to the response force. Detection measures include detection system, assessment system, and access control system elements.

Detection system elements
Detection measures which detect the presence of intruders, weapons, or explosives. Detection system elements include intrusion detection systems, weapons and explosives detectors, and guards.

Duress alarm devices
Also known as panic buttons, these devices are designated specifically to initiate a panic alarm.

Electromagnetic pulse (EMP)
A sharp pulse of energy radiated instantaneously by a nuclear detonation which may affect or damage electronic components and equipment. EMP can also be generated in lesser intensity by non-nuclear means in specific frequency ranges to perform the same disruptive function.

Electronic-emanations eavesdropping
Use of electronic-emanation surveillance equipment from outside a facility or its restricted area to monitor electronic emanations from computers, communications, and related equipment.

Electronic entry control systems
Electronic devices which automatically verify authorization for a person to enter or exit a controlled area.

Electronic security system
An integrated system which encompasses interior and exterior sensors, closed-circuit television systems for assessment of alarm conditions, electronic entry control systems, data transmission media, and alarm reporting systems for monitoring, control, and display of various alarm and system information.

Fence sensors
Exterior intrusion detection sensors which detect aggressors as they attempt to climb over, cut through, or otherwise disturb a fence.

First responder
Local police, fire, and emergency medical personnel who first arrive on the scene of an incident and take action to save lives, protect property, and meet basic human needs.

Fragment retention film
A thin, optically clear film applied to glass to minimize the spread of glass fragments when the glass is shattered.

Frangible construction
Building components which are designed to fail to vent blast pressures from an enclosure in a controlled manner and direction.

Glare security-lighting
Illumination projected from a secure perimeter into the surrounding area making it possible to see potential intruders at a considerable distance while making it difficult to observe activities within the secure perimeter.

Glass-break detector
Intrusion detection sensors that are designed to detect breaking glass either through vibration or acoustics.

Glazing
A material installed in a sash, ventilator, or panes such as glass, plastic, etc., including material such as thin granite installed in a curtain wall.

Hazard
A source of potential danger or adverse condition.

Hazardous material
Any substance or material that when involved in an accident and released in sufficient quantities, poses a risk to people's health, safety, and/or property. These substances and materials include explosives, radioactive materials, flammable liquids or solids, combustible liquids or solids, poisons, oxidizers, toxins, and corrosive materials.

High-hazard areas
Geographic locations that for planning purposes have been determined through historical experience and vulnerability analysis to be likely to experience the effects of a specific hazard (e.g., hurricane, earthquake, hazardous materials accident, etc.) resulting in vast property damage and loss of life.

High-risk target
Any material resource or facility that, because of mission sensitivity, ease of access, isolation, and symbolic value, may be an especially attractive or accessible terrorist target.

Human-caused hazard
Human caused hazards are *technological hazards* and *terrorism*. These are distinct from natural hazards primarily in that they originate from human activity. Within the military services, the term *threat* is typically used for human-caused hazard. See definitions of *technological hazards* and *terrorism* for further information.

Impact analysis
A management level analysis which identifies the impacts of losing the entity's resources. The analysis measures the effect of resource loss and escalating losses over time in order to provide the entity with reliable data upon which to base decisions on hazard mitigation and continuity planning.

Intrusion detection system
The combination of components, including sensors, control units, transmission lines, and monitor units, integrated to operate in a specified manner.

Jersey barrier
A protective concrete barrier initially and still used as a highway divider and now functions as an expedient method for traffic speed control at entrance gates and to keep vehicles away from buildings.

Layers of protection
A traditional approach in security engineering using concentric circles extending out from an area to be protected as demarcation points for different security strategies.

Magnetic lock
An electromagnetic lock that unlocks a door when power is removed.

Mass notification
Capability to provide real-time information to all building occupants or personnel in the immediate vicinity of a building during emergency situations.

Minimum measures
Protective measures that can be applied to all buildings regardless of the identified threat. These measures offer defense or detection opportunities for minimal cost, facilitate future upgrades, and may deter acts of aggression.

Protective barriers
Natural protective barriers are mountains and deserts, cliffs and ditches, water obstacles, or other terrain features that are difficult to traverse.

Non-persistent agent
An agent that, upon release, loses its ability to cause casualties after 10 to 15 minutes. It has a high evaporation rate, is lighter than air, and will disperse rapidly. It is considered to be a short-term hazard; however, in small, unventilated areas, the agent will be more persistent.

Open systems architecture
A term borrowed from the IT industry to claim that systems are capable of interfacing with other systems from any vendor, which also uses open system architecture. The opposite would be a proprietary system.

Passive infrared motion sensors
Devices that detect a change in the thermal energy pattern caused by a moving intruder and initiate an alarm when the change in energy satisfies the detector's alarm-criteria.

Passive vehicle barrier
A vehicle barrier which is permanently deployed and does not require response to be effective.

Perimeter barrier
A fence, wall, vehicle barrier, landform, or line of vegetation applied along an exterior perimeter used to obscure vision, hinder personnel access, or hinder or prevent vehicle access.

Persistent agent
An agent that, upon release, retains its casualty-producing effects for an extended period of time, usually anywhere from 30 minutes to several days. A persistent agent usually has a low evaporation rate and its vapor is heavier than air; therefore, its vapor cloud tends to hug the ground. It is considered to be a long-term hazard. Although inhalation hazards are still a concern, extreme caution should be taken to avoid skin contact as well.

Physical security
The part of security concerned with measures/concepts designed to safeguard personnel; to prevent unauthorized access to equipment, installations, material, and documents; and to safeguard them against espionage, sabotage, damage, and theft.

Planter barrier
A passive vehicle barrier, usually constructed of concrete and filled with dirt (and flowers for aesthetics). Planters, along with bollards, are the usual street furniture used to keep vehicles away from existing buildings. Overall size and the depth of installation below grade determine the vehicle stopping capability of the individual planter.

Pressure mat
A mat that generates an alarm when pressure is applied to any part of the mat's surface, as when someone steps on the mat. Pressure mats can be used to detect an intruder approaching a protected object, or they can be placed by doors and windows to detect entry.

Primary gathering building
Inhabited buildings routinely occupied by 50 or more personnel. This designation applies to the entire portion of a building that meets the population density requirements for an inhabited building.

Probability of detection
A measure of an intrusion detection sensor's performance in detecting an intruder within its detection zone.

Probability of intercept
The probability that an act of aggression will be detected and that a response force will intercept the aggressor before the asset can be compromised.

Progressive collapse
A chain reaction failure of building members to an extent disproportionate to the original localized damage. Such damage may result in upper floors of a building collapsing onto lower floors.

Protective barriers
Define the physical limits of a site, activity, or area by restricting, channeling, or impeding access and forming a continuous obstacle around the object.

Protective measures
Elements of a protective system which protect an asset against a threat. Protective measures are divided into defensive and detection measures.

Recovery
The long-term activities beyond the initial crisis period and emergency response phase of disaster operations that focus on returning all systems in the community to a normal status or to reconstitute these systems to a new condition that is less vulnerable.

Request-to-exit device
Passive infrared motion sensors or push buttons that are used to signal an electronic entry system that egress is imminent or to unlock a door.

Response force
The people who respond to an act of aggression. Depending on the nature of the threat, the response force could consist of guards, special reaction teams, military or civilian police, an explosives ordnance disposal team, or a fire department.

Response time
The length of time from the instant an attack is detected to the instant a security force arrives onsite.

Restricted area
Any area with access controls that is subject to these special restrictions or controls for security reasons. See also controlled area, limited area, exclusion area, and exclusion zone.

Retinal pattern
A biometric technology that is based on features of the human eye.

Risk
The potential for loss of, or damage to, an asset. It is measured based upon the value of the asset in relation to the threats and vulnerabilities associated with it.

Rotating drum or rotating plate vehicle barrier
An active vehicle barrier used at vehicle entrances to controlled areas based on a drum or plate rotating into the path of the vehicle when signaled.

Routinely occupied
For the purposes of these standards, an established or predictable pattern of activity within a building that terrorists could recognize and exploit.

Sacrificial roof or wall
Walls or roofs that can be lost in a blast without damage to the primary asset.

Safe haven
Secure areas within the interior of the facility. A safe haven should be designed such that it requires more time to penetrate by aggressors than it takes for the response force to reach the protected area to rescue the occupants. It may be a haven from a physical attack or air-isolated haven from CBR contamination.

Scramble keypad
A keypad that uses keys on which the numbers change pattern with each use to enhance security by preventing eavesdropping observation of the entered numbers.

Secondary hazard
A threat whose potential would be realized as the result of a triggering event that of itself would constitute an emergency. For example, dam failure might be a secondary hazard associated with earthquakes.

Security analysis
The method of studying the nature of and the relationship between assets, threats, and vulnerabilities.

Security engineering design process
The process through which assets requiring protection are identified, the threat to and vulnerability of those assets is determined, and a protective system is designed to protect the assets.

Security management system database
In a Security Management System, a database that is transferred to various nodes or panels throughout the system for faster data processing and protection against communication link downtime.

Segregation of duties
Policies, procedures, and an organizational structure established so that one individual cannot control key aspects of physical and/or computer-related operations and thereby conduct unauthorized actions or gain unauthorized access to minimum essential infrastructure resource elements.

Shielded wire
Wire with a conductive wrap used to mitigate electromagnetic emanations.

Situational crime prevention
A crime prevention strategy based on reducing the opportunities for crime by increasing the effort required to commit a crime, increasing the risks associated with committing the crime, and reducing the target appeal or vulnerability (whether property or person). This opportunity reduction is achieved by management and use policies such as procedures and training, as well as physical approaches such as alteration of the built environment.

Smart card
A newer card technology that allows data to be written, stored, and read on a card typically used for identification and/or access.

Software level integration
An integration strategy that uses software to interface systems. An example of this would be digital video displayed in the same computer application window and linked to events of a security management system.

Standoff distance
A distance maintained between a building or portion thereof and the potential location for an explosive detonation or other threat.

Strain-sensitive cable
Strain-sensitive cables are transducers that are uniformly sensitive along their entire length and generate an analog voltage when subject to mechanical distortions or stress resulting from fence motion. They are typically attached to a chain-link fence about halfway between the bottom and top of the fence fabric with plastic ties.

Structural protective barriers
Man-made devices (such as fences, walls, floors, roofs, grills, bars, roadblocks, signs, or other construction) used to restrict, channel, or impede access.

Tamper switch
Intrusion detection sensor that monitors an equipment enclosure for breach.

Tangle-foot wire
Barbed wire or tape suspended on short metal or wooden pickets outside a perimeter fence to create an obstacle to approach.

Taut-wire sensor
An intrusion detection sensor utilizing a column of uniformly spaced horizontal wires, securely anchored at each end and stretched taut. Each wire is attached to a sensor to indicate movement of the wire.

Threat
Any indication, circumstance, or event with the potential to cause loss of, or damage to an asset.

Threat analysis
A continual process of compiling and examining all available information concerning potential threats and human-caused hazards. A common method to evaluate terrorist groups is to review the factors of existence, capability, intentions, history, and targeting.

Tsunami
Sea waves produced by an undersea earthquake. Such sea waves can reach a height of 80 feet and can devastate coastal cities and low-lying coastal areas.

Twisted pair wire
Wire that uses pairs of wires twisted together to mitigate electromagnetic interference.

Two-person rule
A security strategy that requires two people to be present in or gain access to a secured area to prevent unobserved access by any individual.

Unobstructed space
Space around an inhabited building without obstruction large enough to conceal explosive devices 150 mm (6 inches) or greater in height.

Unshielded wire
Wire that does not have a conductive wrap.

Vault
A reinforced room for securing items.

Vertical rod
Typical door hardware often used with a crash bar to lock a door by inserting rods vertically from the door into the doorframe.

Vibration sensors
Intrusion detection sensors that change state when vibration is present.

Video intercom system
An intercom system that also incorporates a small CCTV system for verification.

Video motion detection
Motion detection technology that looks for changes in the pixels of a video image.

Visual surveillance
The aggressor uses ocular and photographic devices (such as binoculars and cameras with telephoto lenses) to monitor facility or installation operations or to see assets.

Volumetric motion sensors
Interior intrusion detection sensors which are designed to sense aggressor motion within a protected space.

Vulnerability
Any weakness in an asset or mitigation measure than can be exploited by an aggressor (potential threat element), adversary or competitor. It refers to the organization's susceptibility to injury.

Index

Assessing facilities by type, 33-34
Assessment teams and groups, 23-26
Assessment, of facility, 27-29
Assets,
   establishing a secure environment for, 52
   protection of, 52
ASTM, 140
Atomic bomb, 118
Atoms, and radiation, 116
Atropine, 115
Authority Having Jurisdiction (AHJ), 188
Automatic sprinkler system, 94

B

Background checking, 148-149
Backup Power Systems (BPS), 83
Bank equipment, cost data for, 239-240
Barricades, to separate private areas from public, 84
Barriers, 80, 136-139, 199
   acoustical, cost data for, 235
   cost data for, 206
   to separate private areas from public, 84, 86
Beams, protecting from fire, 81
Becquerels, 116
Benches, concrete, 80
Beta particles, 117
Biological agents, 108, 110-114
Biological attack, 129
Biometric readers, 169
Biometrics, 147-152, 199
Bio-terrorist, 114
Blackout drapes, 107
Blast curtain, 143-144
Blistering agents, 114
Blood agents, 114-115
Boilers, 6
Bollards, 80, 137, 199, 200
Bomb threat, 122
   drill, 9

Bomb wardens, 9, 50
Bomb-threat, 30
Brick walls, 199
Brick, 82
BSA 7799, 27
Bubonic plague, 111, 113
Budgeting, for security system, 91
Building codes, 20, 81
   requirements for exits, 92
   requirements for windows, 142
Building Management Systems, 189
Building plan, security-conscious, 85-86
Bullet, 81
Bulletproof materials, 11
Bullet-resistant glass, 141
Bullet-resistant protection, cost data for, 243
Bullet-resistant wallboard, 199
Bureau of Justice National Crime Victimization, 4
Bureau of Labor Statistics, 4
Bus depots, 5

C

C4, 82
Cameras, 186
   infrared television, 93
Campuses, 6, 27, 173
Carbon-12, 116
Cash flow, 57
Catastrophe, definition of, 41
Cellular phones, 7, 173
CFR, 140
Chain calling, 124, 125
Charcoal filtering system, 144, 146
Chemical agents, 108, 114-115
Chemical and biological detection systems, 199
Chemical, biological, and radiological agents (CBR), 108, 109-119
Chemical contaminants, 128-129
Chemical exposure, 30
Chemical plants, 4, 17